Lecture Notes in Computer Science   6539

Commenced Publication in 1973
Founding and Former Series Editors:
Gerhard Goos, Juris Hartmanis, and Jan van Leeuwen

Ricardo Rocha   John Launchbury (Eds.)

Practical Aspects of Declarative Languages

13th International Symposium, PADL 2011
Austin, TX, USA, January 24-25, 2011
Proceedings

 Springer

Volume Editors

Ricardo Rocha
University of Porto, CRACS & INESC-Porto LA, Faculty of Sciences
Rua do Campo Alegre, 1021, 4169-007 Porto, Portugal
E-mail: ricroc@dcc.fc.up.pt

John Launchbury
Galois, 421 SW 6th Ave. Suite 300, Portland, OR 97204, USA
E-mail: john@galois.com

ISSN 0302-9743   e-ISSN 1611-3349
ISBN 978-3-642-18377-5   e-ISBN 978-3-642-18378-2
DOI 10.1007/978-3-642-18378-2
Springer Heidelberg Dordrecht London New York

Library of Congress Control Number: 2010942579

CR Subject Classification (1998): D.3, D.1, F.3, D.2, I.2

LNCS Sublibrary: SL 2 – Programming and Software Engineering

Typesetting: Camera-ready by author, data conversion by Scientific Publishing Services, Chennai, India

Printed on acid-free paper

Springer is part of Springer Science+Business Media (www.springer.com)

Preface

This volume contains the proceedings of the 13th International Symposium on Practical Aspects of Declarative Languages (PADL 2011), held in Austin, Texas, during January 24–25, 2011. PADL is a yearly forum where researchers and practitioners present original work emphasizing new ideas and approaches pertaining to applications and implementation techniques of declarative languages.

This year, PADL accepted both full technical papers and shorter application papers. In both categories, 40 papers were submitted (35 technical papers and 5 application papers) and each submission was reviewed by at least 3 Program Committee members. At the end, the Program Committee decided to accept 18 papers, 1 of them being an application paper.

The set of accepted papers present a variety of contributions ranging from message-passing and mobile networks, concurrent and parallel programming, event processing and reactive programming, profiling and portability in Prolog, constraint programming, grammar combinators, belief set merging and work on new language extensions and tools. The conference program also included two invited talks, "Intel Core i7 Processor Execution Engine Validation in a Functional Language Based Formal Framework" by Roope Kaivola and "Learning Language from Its Perceptual Context" by Raymond J. Mooney.

As traditionally, the PADL symposium was co-located with the ACM Symposium on Principles of Programming Languages (POPL 2011). We thank ACM, the POPL organizers and the University of Texas at Dallas for their support, as well as the EasyChair conference management system for making the life of the Program Committee Chairs easier. Thanks should go also to the authors of all submitted papers for their contribution to making PADL alive and to the participants for making the event a meeting point for a fruitful exchange of ideas and feedback on recent developments. Finally, we want to express our gratitude to the Program Committee members and external reviewers, as the symposium would not have been possible without their dedicated and outstanding work. This gratitude is extended to Gopal Gupta for his advice and guidance in making the symposium a successful event.

November 2010

Ricardo Rocha
John Launchbury

Organization

Program Chairs

John Launchbury   Galois, USA
Ricardo Rocha   University of Porto, Portugal

Program Committee

Salvador Abreu   University of Évora, Portugal
Byron Cook   Microsoft Research, UK
Maria Garcia de la Banda   Monash University, Australia
Agostino Dovier   University of Udine, Italy
Martin Erwig   Oregon State University, USA
Neal Glew   Intel Corporation, USA
Xavier Leroy   INRIA, France
Yitzhak Mandelbaum   AT&T Labs Research, USA
Bryan O'Sullivan   Serpentine Green Design, USA
Germán Puebla   Technical University of Madrid, Spain
C.R. Ramakrishnan   SUNY Stony Brook, USA
Sukyoung Ryu   Advanced Institute of Science and Technology,
                              Korea
Konstantinos Sagonas   National Technical University of Athens,
                              Greece
André Santos   Federal University of Pernambuco, Brazil
Tom Schrijvers   Katholieke Universiteit Leuven, Belgium
Neng-Fa Zhou   CUNY Brooklyn College, USA

External Reviewers

Jesus M.   Hai-Feng Guo   Leaf Petersen
  Almendros-Jimenez   Steffen Jost   Carla Piazza
Tim Bauer   Hai Liu   Nicolas Pouillard
Clara Benac Earle   Matthieu Martel   André Rauber du Bois
Sheng Chen   Chris Mears   Gianfranco Rossi
Maria Christakis   Marino Miculan   Pedro Salgueiro
Raffaele Cipriano   José F. Morales   Vítor Santos Costa
João Costa Seco   Yang Ni   Joachim Schimpf
Giovanna D'Agostino   Henrik Nilsson   Josep Silva
Carlos Damásio   Vítor Nogueira   Guido Tack
Conal Elliott   Dominic Orchard   Eric Walkingshaw
Andrea Formisano   Nikolaos Papaspyrou   Mark Wallace
Massimo Franceschet   Jorge A. Perez   Michael Wybrow

Table of Contents

Language Extensions and Tools

Concurrent and Parallel Programming

Event Processing and Reactive Programming

Intel® Core™ i7 Processor Execution Engine Validation in a Functional Language Based Formal Framework

Roope Kaivola

Intel Corporation, JF4-451, 2111 NE 25th Avenue, Hillsboro, OR 97124, USA

Abstract. Formal verification of microprocessor components has been pursued in Intel processor development projects in various forms for over a decade. Usually formal verification has been used to supplement more traditional coverage oriented testing activities. For the Intel® Core™ i7 design we took a step further and used formal verification as the primary validation vehicle for the core execution cluster, the component responsible for the functional behaviour of all microinstructions. We applied symbolic simulation based formal verification techniques for full datapath, control and state validation for the cluster, and dropped coverage driven testing entirely [2]. The project, involving some twenty person years of verification work, is one of the most ambitious formal verification efforts in the hardware industry to date, and shows that under the right circumstances, full formal verification of a major design component is a feasible, industrially viable and competitive validation approach.

Technically the verification work was carried out in the Forte verification framework, originally built on top of the Voss system [1]. It is based on a strongly typed ML-like [4] lazy functional programming language *reFLect*. Most of the verification code is written in reFLect: specifications, whether they are functional specifications or relational constraints, verification facilities, analysis routines etc. The execution of an individual verification task in the framework amounts to the evaluation of a reFLect program, and the entire verification initiative involves significant software engineering aspects [3]. In the reFLect language binary decision diagrams are first-class objects: the type Bool includes not just the constants T and F, but arbitrary BDD's. For verification purposes, a very important feature of the language is that it allows *symbolic evaluation* of objects containing BDD's and symbolic circuit simulation using BDD's. Similar facilities exist for non-canonical graph representations of Booleans, used for interfacing with satisfiability solvers.

References

1. Hazelhurst, S., Seger, C.-J.H.: Symbolic trajectory evaluation. In: Kropf, T. (ed.) Formal Hardware Verification. LNCS, vol. 1287, pp. 3–78. Springer, Heidelberg (1997)
2. Kaivola, R., et al.: Replacing testing with formal verification in Intel Core i7 processor execution engine validation. In: Bouajjani, A., Maler, O. (eds.) CAV 2009. LNCS, vol. 5643, pp. 414–429. Springer, Heidelberg (2009)
3. Kaivola, R., Kohatsu, K.: Proof engineering in the large: formal verification of Pentium® 4 floating-point divider. Int'l J. on Software Tools for Technology Transfer 4, 323–334 (2003)
4. Paulson, L.: ML for the Working Programmer. Cambridge University Press, Cambridge (1996)

R. Rocha and J. Launchbury (Eds.): PADL 2011, LNCS 6539, p. 1, 2011.
© Springer-Verlag Berlin Heidelberg 2011

Learning Language from Its Perceptual Context

Raymond J. Mooney

Department of Computer Science, The University of Texas at Austin
1616 Guadalupe, Suite 2.408, Austin, TX 78701
mooney@cs.utexas.edu

Abstract. Current systems that learn to process natural language require laboriously constructed human-annotated training data. Ideally, a computer would be able to acquire language like a child by being exposed to linguistic input in the context of a relevant but ambiguous perceptual environment. As a step in this direction, we present a system that learns to sportscast simulated robot soccer games by example. The training data consists of textual human commentaries on Robocup simulation games. A set of possible alternative meanings for each comment is automatically constructed from game event traces. Our previously developed systems for learning to parse and generate natural language (KRISP and WASP) were augmented to learn from this data and then commentate novel games. Using this approach, the system has learned to sportscast in both English and Korean. The system has been evaluated based on its ability to properly match sentences to the events being described, parse sentences into correct meanings, and generate accurate linguistic descriptions of events. Human evaluation was also conducted on the overall quality of the generated sportscasts and compared to human-generated commentaries, demonstrating that its sportscasts are on par with those generated by humans.

Developing systems that can communicate in natural human language is a long standing goal of computer science and artificial intelligence that has proven incredibly challenging due to the complexity and ambiguity of human languages. Compared to manual programming, machine learning has proven to be a significantly more effective approach to constructing accurate and robust *natural language processing* (NLP) systems [2,8]. Therefore, most current NLP systems are built using statistical learning algorithms trained on large annotated corpora. However, annotating sentences with the requisite parse trees [9], word senses [5] and semantic roles [7] is a difficult and expensive undertaking. By contrast, children acquire language through exposure to linguistic input in the context of a rich, relevant, perceptual environment. Also, by connecting words and phrases to objects and events in the world, the semantics of language is grounded in perceptual experience [4]. Ideally, a machine learning system would be able to acquire language in a similar manner without explicit human supervision. As a step in this direction, we present a system that can describe events in a simulated soccer game by learning only from sample language commentaries paired with traces of simulated activity without any language-specific prior knowledge. A screenshot of our system with generated commentary is shown in Figure 1.

R. Rocha and J. Launchbury (Eds.): PADL 2011, LNCS 6539, pp. 2–4, 2011.

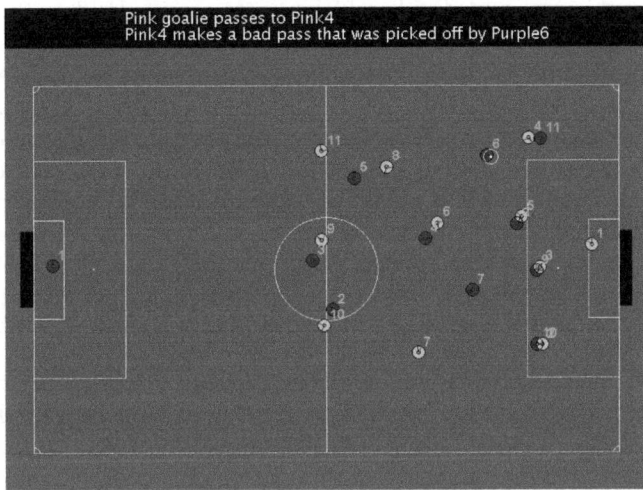

Fig. 1. Screenshot of our commentator system

We study the problem of perceptually-grounded language learning in a simulated environment that retains many of the important properties of a dynamic world with multiple agents and actions while avoiding many of the complexities of robotics and computer vision. Specifically, we use the RoboCup simulator which provides a fairly detailed physical simulation of robot soccer. While several groups have constructed RoboCup commentator systems [1] that provide a textual natural-language transcript of the simulated game, their systems use manually-developed templates and are not based on learning.

Our commentator system learns to semantically interpret and generate language in the RoboCup soccer domain by observing an on-going commentary of the game paired with the evolving simulator state. By exploiting existing techniques for abstracting a symbolic description of the activity on the field from the detailed states of the physical simulator [1], we obtain a pairing of natural language with a symbolic description of the perceptual context in which it was uttered. However, such training data is highly ambiguous because each comment usually co-occurs with several events in the game. We have integrated and enhanced our existing methods for learning semantic parsers and natural-language generators [6,10] in order to learn to understand and generate language from such ambiguous training data. We have also developed a system that, from the same ambiguous training data, learns which events are worth describing, so that it can also perform *strategic generation*, that is, deciding *what* to say as well as how to say it (*tactical generation*).

We have evaluated our system and demonstrated its language-independence by training it to generate soccer commentaries in both English and Korean. Experiments on test data (annotated for evaluation purposes only) have demonstrated that the system learns to accurately semantically parse sentences into formal logical representations, generate natural-language sentences from such logical representations, and decide which events are worth describing. Finally, subjective human evaluation of commentated game clips demonstrate that the system generates sportscasts that are generally similar in quality to those produced by humans. In particular, for English commentaries, human judges recruited using Amazon's Mechanical Turk could not reliably distinguish human from machine generated sportscasts. A full description of the system and detailed experimental evaluation results are presented in a recent article in the *Journal of Artificial Intelligence Research* [3].

Acknowledgements

I would like to thank David Chen, Joohyun Kim, and Rohit Kate for their significant contributions to this work. This research was supported by the National Science Foundation uner grants IIS-0712097 and IIS-1016312. All opinions expressed are solely those of the author.

References

1. André, E., Binsted, K., Tanaka-Ishii, K., Luke, S., Herzog, G., Rist, T.: Three RoboCup simulation league commentator systems. AI Magazine 21(1), 57–66 (2000)
2. Brill, E., Mooney, R.J.: An overview of empirical natural language processing. AI Magazine 18(4), 13–24 (1997)
3. Chen, D.L., Kim, J.H., Mooney, R.J.: Training a multilingual sportscaster: Using perceptual context to learn language. Journal of Artificial Intelligence Research 37, 397–435 (2010)
4. Harnad, S.: The symbol grounding problem. Physica D 42, 335–346 (1990)
5. Ide, N.A., Jéronis, J.: Introduction to the special issue on word sense disambiguation: The state of the art. Computational Linguistics 24(1), 1–40 (1998)
6. Kate, R.J., Mooney, R.J.: Learning language semantics from ambiguous supervision. In: Proceedings of the Twenty-Second Conference on Artificial Intelligence (AAAI 2007), Vancouver, Canada, pp. 895–900 (July 2007)
7. Kingsbury, P., Palmer, M., Marcus, M.: Adding semantic annotation to the Penn treebank. In: Proceedings of the Human Language Technology Conference, San Diego, CA (2002)
8. Manning, C.D., Schütze, H.: Foundations of Statistical Natural Language Processing. MIT Press, Cambridge (1999)
9. Marcus, M., Santorini, B., Marcinkiewicz, M.A.: Building a large annotated corpus of English: The Penn treebank. Computational Linguistics 19(2), 313–330 (1993)
10. Wong, Y.W., Mooney, R.J.: Generation by inverting a semantic parser that uses statistical machine translation. In: Proceedings of Human Language Technologies: The Conference of the North American Chapter of the Association for Computational Linguistics (NAACL-HLT 2007), Rochester, NY, pp. 172–179 (2007)

Detection of Asynchronous Message Passing
Errors Using Static Analysis

Maria Christakis[1] and Konstantinos Sagonas[1,2]

[1] School of Electrical and Computer Engineering,
National Technical University of Athens, Greece
[2] Department of Information Technology, Uppsala University, Sweden
{mchrista,kostis}@softlab.ntua.gr

Abstract. Concurrent programming is hard and prone to subtle errors.
In this paper we present a static analysis that is able to detect some
commonly occurring kinds of message passing errors in languages with
dynamic process creation and communication based on asynchronous
message passing. Our analysis is completely automatic, fast, and strikes
a proper balance between soundness and completeness: it is effective in
detecting errors and avoids false alarms by computing a close approximation of the interprocess communication topology of programs. We
have integrated our analysis in dialyzer, a widely used tool for detecting
software defects in Erlang programs, and demonstrate its effectiveness
on libraries and applications of considerable size. Despite the fact that
these applications have been developed over a long period of time and are
reasonably well-tested, our analysis has managed to detect a significant
number of previously unknown message passing errors in their code.

1 Introduction

Concurrent execution of programs is more or less a necessity these days. To
cater for this need, most programming languages come with built-in support
for creating processes or threads. Depending on the concurrency model of the
language, interprocess communication takes place through synchronized shared
structures (as in C/Pthreads, Java and Haskell), synchronous message passing
on typed channels (as in Concurrent ML), or asynchronous message passing (as
in Erlang). Even though certain problems associated with concurrent execution
of programs are completely avoided in some of these models, each of them comes
with its own set of gotchas and possibilities for programming errors. Independently of the concurrency model which is employed by the language, concurrent
programming is fundamentally more difficult than its sequential counterpart.

Tools that detect software errors early in the development cycle can help in
making concurrent programming more robust and easier for programmers. In
particular, tools based on static analysis seem promising as they are completely
automatic and in principle scale better than, for example, those based on model
checking. Unfortunately, designing and implementing an effective static analysis
for a concurrent language which has not been designed with analysis in mind is a

R. Rocha and J. Launchbury (Eds.): PADL 2011, LNCS 6539, pp. 5–18, 2011.

challenging task. For example, in a language based on processes communicating using asynchronous message passing such as Erlang, it is possible to create an unbounded number of processes, send any term as a message, communicate with processes located on any machine, local or remote, selectively retrieve messages from a process' mailbox using pattern matching, monitor other processes and register to receive their messages when they die, etc. On top of all that, the language is dynamically typed and higher-order, which makes the task of computing precise type and control-flow information very difficult, if not impossible.

In the context of such a real-world language, we aim to statically detect errors that arise from the use of asynchronous message passing. To do so, we have designed an effective analysis that determines the interprocess communication topology of Erlang programs, discovers which occurrences of the sending primitives match which occurrences of the receiving primitives, and emits warnings accordingly. Besides tailoring the analysis to the characteristics of the language, the main challenges for our work have been to develop an analysis that: 1) is completely automatic and requires no guidance from its user; 2) strikes a proper balance between soundness and completeness in order to be: 3) fast and scalable. As we will soon see, we have achieved these goals.

The contributions of our work are as follows:

- we document some of the most important kinds of errors associated with concurrency via asynchronous message passing;
- we present an effective and scalable analysis that detects these errors, and
- we demonstrate the effectiveness of our analysis on a set of widely used and reasonably well-tested libraries and open source applications by reporting a number of previously unknown message passing errors in their code bases.

The next section overviews the Erlang language and the defect detection tool which is the implementation platform for our work. Sect. 3 describes commonly occurring kinds of message passing errors in Erlang programs, followed by Sect. 4 which presents in detail the analysis we use to detect them. The effectiveness and performance of our analysis is evaluated in Sect. 5 and the paper ends with a review of related work (Sect. 6) and some final remarks.

2   Erlang and Dialyzer

Erlang [1] is a strict, dynamically typed functional programming language with support for concurrency, communication, distribution, fault-tolerance, on-the-fly code reloading, automatic memory management and support for multiple platforms. Erlang's primary application area has been in large-scale embedded control systems developed by the telecom industry. The main implementation of the language, the Erlang/OTP (Open Telecom Platform) system from Ericsson, has been open source since 1998 and has been used quite successfully both by Ericsson and by other companies around the world to develop software for large commercial applications. Nowadays, applications written in the language are significant, both in number and in code size, making Erlang one of the most industrially relevant declarative languages.

Erlang's main strength is that it has been built from the ground up to support concurrency. Its concurrency model differs from most other programming languages out there as it is not based on shared memory but on asynchronous message passing between extremely light-weight processes (lighter than OS threads). Erlang comes with a `spawn` family of primitives to create new processes, and with ! (send) and `receive` primitives for interprocess communication via message passing. Any data can be sent as a message and processes may be located on any machine. Each process has a *mailbox*, essentially a message queue, where each message sent to the process will arrive. Message selection from the mailbox occurs through pattern matching. To support robust systems, a process can register to receive a message if another one terminates. Erlang provides mechanisms for allowing a process to timeout while waiting for messages, a `try`/`catch`-style exception mechanism for error handling, and ways to organize processes in supervision hierarchies to restart or take over the duties of dead or unresponsive processes when things go wrong.

Since 2007, the Erlang/OTP distribution includes a static analysis tool, called dialyzer [2,3], for finding software defects (such as type errors, exception-raising code, code which has become unreachable due to some logical error, etc.) in single Erlang modules or entire applications. Nowadays, dialyzer is used extensively in the Erlang programming community and is often integrated in the build environment of many applications. The tool is totally automatic, easy to use and supports various modes of operation: command-line vs. GUI, starting the analysis from source vs. byte code, focussing on some kind of defects only, etc. In sequential programs notable characteristics of dialyzer's core analysis are that it is *sound for defect detection* (i.e., it produces no false alarms), *fast* and *scalable*. Its core analyses that detect defects are supported by various components for creating and manipulating function call graphs for a higher-order language, control-flow analyses, efficient representations of sets of values, data structures optimized for computing fixpoints, etc. Since November 2009, dialyzer's analysis has been enhanced with a component that automatically detects *data races* in Erlang programs [4]. Before we describe how we extended dialyzer's analyses to also detect message passing errors, let us first see how concurrency with asynchronous message passing works and the kinds of related defects that may exist in Erlang programs.

3   Message Passing in Erlang

As described in Sect. 2, Erlang's concurrency primitives `spawn`, ! (send) and `receive` allow a process to spawn new processes and communicate with others through asynchronous message passing. Let's see these primitives in detail:

Spawn. The `spawn` primitive creates a process and returns a *process identifier* (pid) for addressing the newly spawned process. The new process executes the code of the function denoted in the arguments of the `spawn`. In the example program shown in Fig. 1, a process is spawned that will execute the code of the function closure `Fun`.

```
-export([hello_world/0]).

hello_world() ->
  Fun = fun() -> world(self()) end,
  Pid = spawn(Fun),
  register(world, Pid),
  world ! hello.

world(Parent) ->
  receive
    hello -> Parent ! hi
  end.
```

Fig. 1. Simple example program

Send. The expression `Pid ! Msg` sends the message `Msg`, that may refer to any valid Erlang term, to the process with pid `Pid` in a non-blocking operation. Besides addressing a process by using its pid, there is also a mechanism, called the *process registry*, which acts as a node-local name server, for registering a process under a certain name so that messages can be sent to the process using that name. Names of processes are currently restricted to atoms. In our example program, the spawned process is registered under the name `world` which is then used to send the message `hello` to the process.

Receive. Messages are received with the `receive` construct. Each process has its own input queue for messages it receives. Any new messages are placed at the end of the queue. When a process executes a `receive`, the first message in the queue is matched against the patterns of the `receive` in sequential order. If the message matches some pattern, it is removed from the queue and the actions corresponding to the matching pattern are executed. However, if it does not match, the message is kept in the queue and the next message is tried instead. If this matches any pattern, it is removed from the queue while keeping the previous and any other message in the queue. In case the end of the queue is reached and no messages have been matched, the process blocks (i.e., stops execution) and waits to be rescheduled to repeat this procedure.

Misuse of these concurrency and communication primitives may lead to the following kinds of message passing errors in Erlang programs:

Receive with no messages (RN). A `receive` statement in the code executed by some process whose mailbox will be empty. This defect could reveal the occurrence of possible deadlocks in the patterns of interprocess communication — processes mutually waiting for messages from other processes.

Receive of the wrong kind (RW). A `receive` statement in the code of some process whose mailbox will contain messages of different kinds than the ones expected by the `receive`. Currently, such a defect can have devastating effects on a running system, overflowing the mailbox of some process and bringing the node down. To avoid being bitten by this, many Erlang programs adopt a defensive programming style and include a catch-all clause in `receive`s whose only purpose is to consume any unwanted messages.

This practice is not ideal because it might hide real communication problems. Additionally, it makes this kind of message passing errors hard to find.

Receive with unnecessary patterns (RU). A receive with clauses containing patterns that will never match messages sent to the process executing that code. This problem may be harmless (i.e., just some unreachable code in the receive) or, in conjunction with the existence of a catch-all pattern which consumes all messages as the last clause of the statement, may hide a serious functionality error.

Send nowhere received (SR). A send operation to a process whose code does not contain any (matching) receives. This defect can also result in the overflow of some mailbox and bring a node down.

Being able to statically detect such types of concurrency defects is crucial in safety-critical systems such as those developed in the telecommunications sector.

4   The Analysis

In a higher-order language with unlimited dynamic process creation, the kinds of message passing errors we described in the previous section are not simple to detect. In order to detect which message emissions match which receptions, it is necessary to determine the communication topology of processes, which will then be used as a basis for detecting these errors. We have designed and implemented such an analysis and describe it in this section.

Conceptually, our analysis has three distinct phases: an initial phase that scans the code to collect information needed by the subsequent phases, a phase where a *communication graph* is constructed, and a phase where message passing errors are detected. For efficiency reasons, the actual implementation blurs the lines separating these phases and employs some optimizations. False alarms are avoided by taking language characteristics and messages generated by the runtime system into account. Let's see all these in detail.

4.1   Collecting Information

We have integrated our analysis in dialyzer because many of the components that it relies upon were already available or could be easily extended to provide the information that the analysis needs. The analysis starts with the user specifying a set of directories/files to be analyzed. Rather than operating directly on Erlang source, all of dialyzer's passes operate at the level of Core Erlang [5], the language used internally by the Erlang compiler. Core Erlang significantly eases the analysis of Erlang programs by removing syntactic sugar and by introducing a let construct which makes the binding occurrence and scope of all variables explicit.

As the source code is translated to Core Erlang, dialyzer constructs the *control-flow graph* (CFG) of each function and function closure and then uses the escape analysis of Carlsson et al. [6] to determine values, in particular closures, that escape their defining function. For example, for the code of Fig. 1 the escape

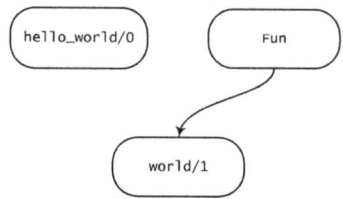

Fig. 2. Call graph of example program

analysis will determine that function hello_world defines a function closure that escapes from this function as it is passed as argument to a spawn. Given this information, dialyzer also constructs the *inter-modular call graph* of all functions and closures, so that subsequent analyses can use this information to speed up their fixpoint computations. For the example in the same figure, the call graph will contain three nodes for functions whose definitions appear in the code (functions hello_world, world, and the closure) and an edge from the node of the function closure to that of world, as shown in Fig. 2.

Besides control-flow, the analysis also needs data-flow information and more specifically it needs information on whether variables can possibly refer to the same data item or not. This information is computed and explicitly maintained by the *sharing/alias analysis* component in dialyzer's race analysis [4]. In addition, our analysis exploits the fact that dialyzer computes type information at a very fine-grained level. For example, different atoms $a_1, \ldots, a_n$ are represented as different *singleton types* in the type domain and their union $a_1 | \ldots | a_n$ is mapped to the supertype $atom()$ only when the size of the union exceeds a relatively high limit [7]. We will see how this information is used by the message analysis in Sect. 4.2 and 4.3.

4.2   Constructing the Communication Graph

The second phase of the analysis determines the interprocess communication topology in the form of a graph.

Each vertex of the graph represents an escaping function whose code may be run by a separate process at runtime. This information is computed by a pre-processing step during the construction of the call and control-flow graphs. The code of any function that is either a root node in the call graph or an argument to a spawn is assumed to be executed by a separate process. For our example program, the communication graph will contain two nodes, one for function hello_world and one for the closure.

Every edge of the communication graph is directed and corresponds to a communication channel between two processes. Naturally, its direction of communication is from the source to the target process, meaning that messages are sent in that direction. Each edge is annotated with the type information of the messages that are sent through the channel.

In order to determine the graph edges, we need to inspect every possible execution path of the program for messages that are passed between processes.

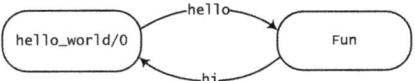

Fig. 3. Communication graph of example program

To this end, we start by traversing the CFGs of the functions corresponding to the vertices in the communication graph using depth-first search. The depth-first search starts by identifying program points containing a call to a pid-yielding primitive (i.e., the `self` primitive, that returns the pid of the calling process, and the `spawn` family of primitives), and then tries to find program points "deeper" in the graph containing send operations to the process with this pid. In case the search encounters either a call to or a `spawn` of some other statically known function, the traversal continues by examining its CFG, otherwise it is ignored. Built-ins for registering a pid under a certain name require special attention since the registered name may then be used to send a message to the process. A pre-processing step associates names with their registered pids so that the analysis can use this information to replace all name occurrences. Finally, if the traversal finds a send operation to some pid, the analysis takes variable sharing into account to determine whether this pid refers to the same process as the pid yielded by the primitive that initially triggered the depth-first search. If this is the case, an edge is added to the communication graph emanating from the vertex of the process whose CFG is traversed and incident on the vertex of the process identified by the pid, otherwise nothing is done. An annotation is added to the new edge indicating the type information of the message. If such an edge already exists in the graph, then the analysis simply updates its annotation to also include the type information of the new message. In the end, this traversal creates the complete set of edges in the communication graph.

For the code of Fig. 1, the communication graph will have two edges, one from vertex `hello_world` to the closure and one from the closure to `hello_world`. The annotations for these edges will be `hello` and `hi`, respectively. The communication graph for the example program is illustrated in Fig. 3.

4.3   Detecting Message Passing Errors

At this stage of the analysis, the CFG of each function that corresponds to a vertex in the communication graph is traversed anew to detect any message passing errors.

Each vertex in the communication graph has an in-degree that is either equal to or greater than zero. A vertex with in-degree equal to zero indicates that no messages are sent to the process it represents. Hence, the traversal of the CFG emits a warning for each `receive` construct it encounters. A vertex with in-degree greater than zero indicates that messages are sent to the process and the analysis determines whether these messages will be received. In case the process does not expect any messages (i.e., there are no `receives` in the CFG), a warning is emitted for each sent message. In case the process expects to receive messages, the analysis takes into account the type information of the messages and the `receive` patterns in order to decide whether they match. A message S matches a `receive` pattern R if the *infimum* (i.e., the greatest lower bound) of their type information is a non-empty subtype of R. Note that S is the annotation of the edge in the communication graph, while R is found in the CFG. As an example consider a sent tuple message with type $S :: \{gazonk, integer()\}$ and a `receive` pattern with type $R :: \{atom(), 42\}$. The analysis computes the infimum of these types, $\{gazonk, 42\}$, which is a subtype of R in this case. Actually, this message will only be received if the second element of the tuple is 42, but the analysis, aiming at being sound for defect detection, will flag this as an error only if it can statically determine that the second element of the message is a term other than the integer 42. In short, at the end of the CFG traversal, warnings are emitted for `receive` patterns or entire constructs that do not match any messages and for messages that do not match any `receive` patterns.

Loops in the communication graph indicate that messages are sent and received by the same process and require special treatment. If no messages sent by other processes match a `receive` pattern or construct, then messages sent to the process by itself at program points "higher" in the CFG should match, otherwise a warning is emitted.

Note that the traversal that searches for `receives`, unlike the traversal that searches for send operations described in the previous section, ignores any `spawns` of statically known functions since spawned processes cannot receive messages in place of the process being analyzed, although they may send messages to it.

For the example program, the analysis inspects the CFG of the `hello_world` vertex, which has in-degree one, and finds that there is no `receive` in the code executed by the process. Consequently, it emits a warning with the filename and line number of the send operation of the `hi` message reporting that this message will be nowhere received.

4.4   Some Optimizations

Although we have described the second and third phases of the analysis as being distinct, our implementation blurs this distinction, thereby avoiding redundant searches and speeding up the analysis. In addition, we also employ the following optimizations:

Control-flow graph minimization. The CFGs that dialyzer constructs by default contain the complete Core Erlang code of functions. This makes sense as most of its analyses, including the type and sharing analyses, need this information. However, note that the path traversal procedure of Sect. 4.2 and 4.3 requires only part of this information. For example, in the program illustrated on the left box of Fig. 4, the `io:format` call is irrelevant both for determining the complete set of edges in the communication graph and for detecting any message passing errors. Our analysis takes advantage of this by a pre-processing step that removes all this code from the CFGs and by recursively removing CFGs of *leaf* functions that do not contain any concurrency primitives either directly or indirectly.

Avoiding repeated traversals. After the CFGs are minimized as described above, the depth-first traversal starts from some vertex in the communication graph. The traversal of all paths from this vertex often encounters a split in the CFG (e.g., a point where a `case` statement begins) which is followed by a CFG join (the point where the `case` statement ends). All the straight-line code which lies between the join point and the next split, including any straight-line code in the CFGs of functions called there, does not need to be repeatedly traversed if it is found to contain no concurrency primitives during the traversal of its first depth-first search path. This optimization effectively prunes common sub-paths by condensing them to a single program point.

Avoiding redundant traversals. Another optimization is to collect, during the construction of the CFGs of functions, a set of program points containing send operations and another set of program points containing `receive` constructs. The first set is used in the construction of the communication graph to determine whether the CFG of a statically known function that is either called or spawned needs to be inspected. If no program point in the set is reachable from the function directly or indirectly (i.e., via some call or `spawn`), then the CFG is not traversed. The elements of the second set act like pointers and replace the vertices of the communication graph in the error detection phase of the analysis, thereby avoiding unnecessary traversals of the control flow graphs.

4.5   False Alarms and Their Avoidance

The analysis we have described so far may produce false alarms in case the available static information is too limited to construct the exact interprocess communication graph. To this effect, we employ techniques for completely avoiding false alarms, thus making the analysis sound for defect detection.

A factor that could limit the precision of our analysis is lack of precise knowledge about the behaviour of built-in functions (BIFs). For example, Erlang/OTP comes with BIFs, implemented in C, that create messages inside the VM and send them to processes in a non-transparent way. The left box of Fig. 4 shows a function from the code of the ibrowse application (file `ibrowse_test.erl`). On this code, a naïve implementation of the analysis would warn that the {`'DOWN'`, ...} pattern of the `receive` statement is unused because no such messages are ever constructed in the entire application, let alone in this module (whose code is only partly shown in the figure). However, such messages are created by the `spawn_monitor` BIF inside the VM and are placed in the message queue of the monitoring process when the spawned process dies. We have taken special care to provide our analysis with precise information about such BIFs and their behaviour. This information is fairly complete at this point so we entirely avoid this kind of false alarms. For similar reasons, the analysis can either have *a priori* knowledge about the behaviour of heavily used Erlang/OTP libraries, or pre-compute this information so as to avoid having to re-analyze these libraries in each run.

Another limiting factor is dialyzer's sharing/alias analysis component. Since the computation of variables referring to the same data is static, it may not

```
unit_tests(Opts) ->
  Opts1 = Options ++ [{connect_timeout, 5000}],
  {Pid, Ref} = spawn_monitor(?MODULE, ut1, [self(), Opts1]),
  receive
    {done, Pid} -> ok;
    {'DOWN', Ref, _, _, Info} ->
      io:format("Crashed: ~p~n", [Info])
  after 60000 ->
    ...
  end.

ut1(Parent, Opts) ->
  lists:foreach(...),
  Parent ! {done, self()}.  % the only send operation
```

```
-export([start/0]).

start() ->
  Pid = spawn(fun pong/0),
  ping(Pid).

ping(Pid) ->
  Pid ! {self(), ping},
  receive pong -> pang end.

pong() ->
  receive
    {Pid, ping} -> Pid ! pong
  end.
```

Fig. 4. Programs susceptible to false alarms

always be possible to find the complete sets of these variables. The right box of Fig. 4 shows a made up example of Erlang code for which the first implementations of our analysis incorrectly warned that the `receive` statement in the `ping` function would block. This false alarm was emitted because the sharing/alias analysis is unable to statically determine whether the {`self()`, `ping`} message will actually be received by the `pong` process. The analysis was therefore unable to conclude that the `Pid` variable in the received message is the pid of the `start` process. This was also the case when the analysis lost track of terms because data was stored in data structures (usually records, lists or ETS tables) and then retrieved from them. Again, we have taken special care to avoid these false alarms by acknowledging that the sharing/alias component has lost the data item — specifically the pid — assigned to a variable and thereby suppressing any warnings that would be emitted as a result of this inaccuracy.

Clearly, the optimization ideas and the techniques to avoid false alarms have a heavy impact on the effectiveness, performance and precision of our method. Let us therefore evaluate it on a suite of large, widely used Erlang applications.

5   Experimental Evaluation

The analysis we described in the previous section has been fully implemented and incorporated in the development version of dialyzer. We have paid special attention to integrate it smoothly with the existing analyses, reuse as much of the underlying infrastructure as possible, and fine-tune the analysis so that it incurs relatively little additional overhead to dialyzer's default mode of use. The core of the message analysis is about 2,000 lines of Erlang code and the user can turn it on either via a GUI button or a command-line option.

We have measured the effectiveness and performance of the analysis by applying it on a corpus of Erlang code bases of significant size; in total more than a million lines of code.[1] As these code bases have been developed and tested over a long period of time, it is perhaps not surprising that our analysis did not

---

[1] The source of Erlang/OTP distribution alone is about 800k lines of code.

Table 1. Applications for which the analysis detected message passing errors

Application libraries from the Erlang/OTP R14A distribution	
inets	A set of Internet clients and servers
observer	Tools for tracing and investigating distributed systems

Open source Erlang applications	
disco	A map/reduce framework for distributed computing
dynomite	A Dynamo clone
effigy	A mocking library for testing
eldap	An LDAP API
enet	A network stack
erlang_js	A driver for SpiderMonkey (the Mozilla JavaScript engine)
etap	A TAP (Test Anything Protocol) client library
iserve	An HTTP server
log_roller	A distributed logging system
natter	An XMPP client
pgsql	A PostgreSQL driver
stoplight	A mutex server based on the SIGMA algorithm
ubf	Universal binary format

find errors in most of them. Still, there are Erlang/OTP libraries and applications for which the analysis has detected concurrency errors in their code. The rest of this section focusses on these code bases. A short description of them appears in Table 1; most are heavily used and reasonably well-tested. For open source applications, we used the code from their public repositories at the end of October 2010.

The left part of Table 2 shows the lines of code (LOC) for each application and the number of message passing problems identified by the analysis. These are shown categorized as in Sect. 3: namely, as related to a `receive` that will block either because no messages are sent to the process (RN) or because the messages sent there are of the wrong kind (RW), as related to a `receive` with unnecessary patterns (RU), or related to a send operation to a process without a `receive` (SR). The right part of the table shows the elapsed wall clock time (in seconds), and memory requirements (in MB) for running dialyzer without and with the analysis component that detects message passing errors in these programs.[2] The evaluation was conducted on a machine with an Intel Core2 Quad CPU @ 2.66GHz with 3GB of RAM, running Linux. (But currently the analysis utilizes only one core.)

As can be seen in the table, the analysis detects a number of message passing problems, some of which can be detrimental to the functionality and

---

[2] The relatively high memory requirements of the enet application are due to an (automatically generated?) file containing just two functions of about 10,000 LOC each. When excluding this file, dialyzer needs 2.0 secs and 74MB in its default mode and 2.4 secs and 75MB with the analysis that detects message passing errors.

Table 2. Effectiveness and performance of the message analysis

Application	LOC	RN	RW	RU	SR	Time (secs) w/o msg	w msg	Space (MB) w/o msg	w msg
inets	29,389	-	-	2	-	26.1	60.1	89	119
observer	6,644	-	-	1	-	23.6	35.1	78	88
disco	11,846	-	-	2	-	17.3	20.8	85	126
dynomite	19,384	1	-	-	-	7.2	7.9	72	74
effigy	568	1	-	-	-	0.8	0.9	21	21
eldap	5,148	-	-	1	-	9.9	11.5	110	112
enet	23,028	-	-	1	-	15.0	15.8	765	766
erlang_js	1,720	-	-	1	-	11.0	12.2	73	80
etap	665	-	-	-	1	0.4	0.4	17	19
iserve	788	-	-	2	2	1.3	1.4	30	30
log_roller	2,539	-	1	-	-	3.1	3.5	33	46
natter	1,494	-	-	2	-	1.7	1.9	30	32
pgsql	1,253	-	-	1	-	1.6	3.0	31	41
stoplight	1,462	1	-	-	-	1.6	1.6	39	40
ubf	7,052	-	-	1	-	18.7	23.7	70	81

robustness of these applications. We have manually examined the source code of these applications and all these problems are genuine bugs.

Regarding performance, in most cases, the additional time and memory overhead of the message passing error detection component of the analysis is too small to care about. The only exception is inets on which the analysis takes about twice as much time to complete. Still the analysis times are reasonable. Given that the analysis is totally automatic and smoothly integrated in a defect detection tool which is widely used by the community, we see very little reason not to use it regularly when developing Erlang programs.

6   Related Work

Static analysis [8] is a fundamental and well studied technique for discovering program properties and reasoning about program behaviour, independently of language. Besides being the basis for most compiler optimizations, in recent years static analysis has been extensively used to detect software errors in programs, both sequential and concurrent.

In the context of higher-order functional languages, and starting with the work of Shivers [9], control-flow analyses aim to approximate which functions may be applied at runtime as a result of some computation. When concurrency comes into the picture, processes are dynamically created and functions are passed between processes and executed by any receiving process, the task becomes more complicated as a piece of code in the source program may be executed by any process and the control-flow analysis may need to be infinitary [10].

Some researchers have proposed using *effect-based type systems* to analyze the communication behaviour of message passing programs; an early such work is the analysis by Nielson and Nielson for detecting when programs written in CML have finite topology [11]. There has also been a number of *abstract interpretation based* analyses that are closer in spirit to the analysis we employ. Mercouroff designed and implemented an analysis for CSP programs with a static structure based on an approximation of the number of messages sent between processes [12] and Martel and Gengler an analysis that statically determines an approximation of the communication topology of a CML program [13]. The abstract interpretation based whole program analysis of Colby uses control paths to identify threads [14]. Unlike earlier work which collapsed multiple threads created at the same spawn point to a single approximate thread, control paths are able to distinguish multiple threads created at the same spawn point and thus compute a more precise interprocess communication topology of a program. Still, the precision problem was not completely solved.

A more precise, but also more complex and less scalable, control-flow analysis was proposed by Martel and Gengler [13]. Contrary to what we do, in their work the accuracy of the analysis is enhanced by building finite automata. More specifically, the analysis orders the synchronization primitives of any sequential processes in the system by building an automaton for each process. It then approximates how the different processes may interact with each other by building a reduced product automaton from the process automata. As a result, the analysis eliminates some impossible communication channels, computes the possibly matching emissions for each reception, and thus the possibly received values. An interesting future direction for our analysis is to see how we can use some of these ideas to enhance the precision of our analysis without sacrificing its soundness for defect detection (i.e., its "no false alarms" property) or its scalability.

7   Concluding Remarks and Future Work

We have presented a new analysis for identifying some commonly occurring kinds of concurrency errors that arise from the use of asynchronous message passing in a higher-order language with unlimited process creation, message queues and selective message reception based on pattern matching. By computing a close approximation of the interprocess communication topology of programs and by effectively matching occurrences of send with `receive` primitives, our analysis manages to achieve a good balance between precision and scalability. As shown in the experimental evaluation section of the paper, the analysis has managed to detect a significant number of message passing errors in widely used and reasonably well-tested applications written in Erlang.

The implementation of our analysis is fast and robust; we expect that it will be included in some upcoming release of Erlang/OTP. Still, there are some engineering issues to address. Among them, the most challenging one is to design and implement a framework for the explanation of message passing errors, perhaps by maintaining more information in the analysis and designing a component to visualize the communication topology of an application. But this is a general problem for static analyses that detect program errors: the more sophisticated the errors that an analysis detects are, the more difficult it is for programmers to trust the analysis results and, more importantly, to reason about the program change that will correct the error. Tools that help them in this task are needed.

References

1. Armstrong, J.: Programming Erlang: Software for a Concurrent World. The Pragmatic Bookshelf, Raleigh (2007)
2. Lindahl, T., Sagonas, K.: Detecting software defects in telecom applications through lightweight static analysis: A war story. In: Chin, W.-N. (ed.) APLAS 2004. LNCS, vol. 3302, pp. 91–106. Springer, Heidelberg (2004)
3. Sagonas, K.: Experience from developing the Dialyzer: A static analysis tool detecting defects in Erlang applications. In: Proceedings of the ACM SIGPLAN Workshop on the Evaluation of Software Defect Detection Tools (2005)
4. Christakis, M., Sagonas, K.: Static detection of race conditions in Erlang. In: Carro, M., Peña, R. (eds.) PADL 2010. LNCS, vol. 5937, pp. 119–133. Springer, Heidelberg (2010)
5. Carlsson, R.: An introduction to Core Erlang. In: Proceedings of the PLI 2001 Workshop on Erlang (2001)
6. Carlsson, R., Sagonas, K., Wilhelmsson, J.: Message analysis for concurrent programs using message passing. ACM Transactions on Programming Languages and Systems 28(4), 715–746 (2006)
7. Lindahl, T., Sagonas, K.: Practical type inference based on success typings. In: Proceedings of the 8th ACM SIGPLAN International Conference on Principles and Practice of Declarative Programming, pp. 167–178. ACM, New York (2006)
8. Nielson, F., Nielson, H.R., Hankin, C.: Principles of Program Analysis. Springer-Verlag New York, Inc., Secaucus (1999)
9. Shivers, O.: Control Flow Analysis in Scheme. In: Proceedings of the ACM SIGPLAN Conference on Programming Language Design and Implementation, pp. 164–174. ACM, New York (1988)
10. Nielson, F., Nielson, H.R.: Infinitary Control Flow Analysis: a Collecting Semantics for Closure Analysis. In: Proceedings of the 24th ACM SIGPLAN-SIGACT Symposium on Principles of Programming Languages, pp. 332–345. ACM, New York (1997)
11. Nielson, F., Nielson, H.R.: Higher-Order Concurrent Programs with Finite Communication Topology. In: Proceedings of the ACM-SIGPLAN Symposium on Principles of Programming Languages, pp. 84–97. ACM, New York (1994)
12. Mercouroff, N.: An Algorithm for Analyzing Communicating Processes. In: Schmidt, D., Main, M.G., Melton, A.C., Mislove, M.W., Brookes, S.D. (eds.) MFPS 1991. LNCS, vol. 598, pp. 312–325. Springer, Heidelberg (1992)
13. Martel, M., Gengler, M.: Communication Topology Analysis for Concurrent Programs. In: Havelund, K., Penix, J., Visser, W. (eds.) SPIN 2000. LNCS, vol. 1885, pp. 265–286. Springer, Heidelberg (2000)
14. Colby, C.: Analyzing the Communication Topology of Concurrent Programs. In: Proceedings of the ACM SIGPLAN Symposium on Partial Evaluation and Semantics-Based Program Manipulation, pp. 202–213. ACM, New York (1995)

Combinators for Message-Passing in Haskell

Neil C.C. Brown

School of Computing, University of Kent, UK
neil@twistedsquare.com

Abstract. Much code in message-passing programs is tedious, verbose
wiring code. This code is error prone and laborious – and tends to be
repeated across many programs with only slight variations. By using
type-classes, higher-order and monadic functions in Haskell, most of this
code can be captured in re-usable high-level combinators that shorten
and simplify message-passing programs. We motivate the design and use
of these combinators via an example of a concurrent biological simulation, and explain their implementation in the Communicating Haskell
Processes library.

1   Introduction

Message-passing programming is a type of imperative concurrent programming
that eschews mutable shared state in favour of passing messages between concurrent processes. This paper is particularly concerned with systems featuring synchronous message-passing over point-to-point unbuffered channels (rather than
address-based systems such as mailboxes). This style of concurrent programming has recently been successfully applied to biological and complex systems
simulation [13], robotics [8], and can achieve good parallel speed-up on multicore
machines [16]. Implementations exist as libraries in several functional languages,
e.g. Concurrent ML [15] and Communicating Haskell Processes [2].

Message-passing programming supports a compositional model of programming, with processes comprised of sub-networks of communicating processes.
However, message-passing languages and libraries do not typically provide easy
ways in which to compose processes together, even when the composition is regular (e.g. a pipeline). Process wiring must be done "long hand", declaring channel variables/arrays and passing them to the appropriate process. This style of
wiring is tedious, verbose and error-prone.

In contrast, higher-order functional programming allows common coding patterns to be captured and re-used. For example, operations on lists can typically
be implemented using some combination of map, filter, or a fold. It is rare to
write a function that directly processes a list via pattern-matching, because the
operation can often be expressed using one of the aforementioned functions.

Haskell has seen a proliferation of further abstractions based on type-classes,
such as applicative functors [10], monads [12] and arrows [7]. These abstractions
capture particular patterns of computation, and allow general helper functions

R. Rocha and J. Launchbury (Eds.): PADL 2011, LNCS 6539, pp. 19–33, 2011.

(e.g. mapM) to act on all instances of this pattern; code re-use is supported by parameterising the helper functions with the type-class in question.

This paper contends that patterns in message-passing programming can be captured using functional programming techniques such as higher-order functions and type-classes. This paper's contribution is the introduction of new combinators for message-passing systems which **shorten and simplify code**: **wiring functions** for common process topologies (section 4), which can be generalised into **a composition monad** for more flexible wiring (section 5).

These abstractions are motivated and demonstrated using a central biological simulation example introduced in section 3. All of these new abstractions have been implemented using standard Haskell, and have been added to the Communicating Haskell Processes library, which is introduced in section 2.

2   Background: Communicating Haskell Processes

Communicating Haskell Processes (CHP) is a Haskell library that supports concurrent synchronous message-passing [2], and is based on the Communicating Sequential Processes calculus [6,17]. As with most imperative Haskell libraries, it provides a monad (named CHP) in which all of its actions take place. Its basic API provides channel creation and communication:

```
newChannelWR :: CHP (Chanout a, Chanin a)
writeChannel :: Chanout a -> a -> CHP ()
readChannel :: Chanin a -> CHP a
```

Note how the channels are used via two ends: the outgoing end (Chanout) on which values are sent, and the incoming end (Chanin) on which values are received. This separation between the two ends at the type level helps prevent mistakes – such as connecting two reading processes together with a channel, resulting in deadlock. It also promotes code clarity: making it clear from the type of a process whether it will send or receive on each channel.

We refer to something that has type CHP r as being a *complete* CHP process (one that is ready to run). Anything that will be a complete CHP process when given further arguments (e.g. Chanin a ->Chanout a ->CHP ()) is referred to simply as a CHP process. An example of a basic CHP process is the identity process that forwards values from one channel to another[1]:

```
idP :: Chanin a -> Chanout a -> CHP ()
idP input output = forever (readChannel input >>= writeChannel output)
```

CHP processes can be composed in parallel using the commutative, associative runParallel function which waits for all the parallel processes to terminate before returning a list of their results:

```
runParallel :: [CHP a] -> CHP [a]; runParallel_ :: [CHP a] -> CHP ()
```

---

[1] In this paper we suffix these simple processes with "P" to avoid confusion, here with the Haskell identity *function* (id ::a ->a).

The version with an underscore suffix discards the results of the parallel computations. The type of these functions exactly matches that of the standard monadic sequence functions, specialised to the CHP monad:

sequence :: [CHP a] -> CHP [a]; sequence_ :: [CHP a] -> CHP ()

2.1   Barriers and Enrolling

As well as channels, CHP also features barriers. A barrier is a synchronisation primitive that can only be used by processes enrolled on (i.e. members of) the barrier. When an enrolled process wishes to synchronise on the barrier, it must wait for all other enrolled processes to also do so. Barriers are created with an enrollment count of zero, using one of the functions:

newBarrier :: CHP Barrier; newBarrierPri :: Int -> CHP Barrier

The latter function features priority: the default is 0, and larger numbers indicate higher priority. When a process can choose between completing two barriers, the higher priority barrier will be chosen. Barriers feature a "scoped" API for enrolling, that eschews explicit enroll and resign (de-enroll) calls in favour of taking as an argument the block of code to execute while enrolled:

enroll :: Barrier -> (EnrolledBarrier -> CHP a) -> CHP a

The enroll function takes a barrier and a CHP process that operates on the enrolled barrier. The returned completed CHP process enrolls the given process on the barrier for the duration of its execution and resigns afterwards. To prohibit attempts to synchronise without first enrolling, synchronisation is only possible on the EnrolledBarrier type:

syncBarrier :: EnrolledBarrier -> CHP ()

As an example, the following code enrolls twice on a barrier, then runs two corresponding processes in parallel that repeatedly synchronise on the barrier:

```
do bar <- newBarrier
   enroll bar (\eb0 -> enroll bar (\eb1 ->
     runParallel [replicateM_ 100 $ syncBarrier eb0, replicateM_ 100 $ syncBarrier eb1]))
```

Note that it is crucial that both enrollments happen before the parallel composition (rather than in each parallel branch). Consider the alternative code:

```
do bar <- newBarrier
   runParallel [enroll bar (replicateM_ 100 . syncBarrier)
               ,enroll bar (replicateM_ 100 . syncBarrier)]
```

The barrier begins with an enrollment count of zero. When, in the above code, the first parallel branch runs, it will enroll, increasing the enrollment count to one. When it then tries to synchronise on the barrier, it may do so by itself. Thus one branch can enroll and (potentially) perform all 100 synchronisations before the other branch starts to run (and do the same). Thus, for the branches to synchronise together, the enrollment of both processes must occur before the parallel composition begins.

CHP already features two helper functions for enrolling, which hint at the combinator-based approach seen later in the paper. The enrollList function enrolls a single process on a whole list of barriers (nesting the process inside all the enrollments), while the enrollAll function enrolls each of a list of processes on a single barrier:

```
enrollList :: [Barrier] -> ([EnrolledBarrier] -> CHP a) -> CHP a
enrollList [] f = f []
enrollList (b:bs) f = enroll b (\eb -> enrollList bs (\ebs -> f (eb:ebs)))

enrollAll :: Barrier -> [EnrolledBarrier -> CHP a] -> CHP [a]
enrollAll b ps = enrollList (replicate (length ps) b) (runParallel . zipWith ($) ps)
```

The previous example can thus also be written as:

```
newBarrier >>= flip enrollAll [replicateM_ 100 . syncBarrier, replicateM_ 100 . syncBarrier]
```

3   Motivating Example: Blood Clotting Simulation

Section 2 introduced the existing Communicating Haskell Processes library. This section provides a motivating example for the design and inclusion of the new features in the library introduced in future sections. The example is a concurrent simulation of blood clotting, with "sticky" platelets moving down a one-dimensional pipeline of site processes. It is inspired by the example presented by Schneider et al. [19], and has been converted to CHP to use some advanced concurrency features such as conjunction [3].

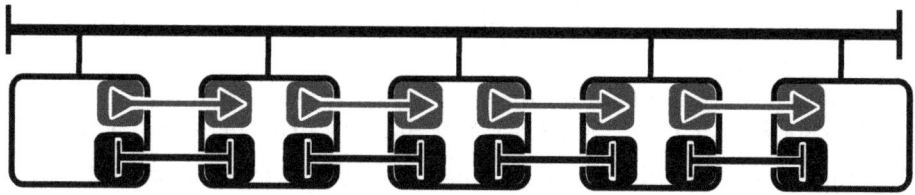

Fig. 1. Illustration of how the blood example is connected together. The first (left-most) process is a platelet generator, and the last (right-most) is a platelet consumer. The three processes in the centre are examples of the site processes (there are 100 in the real model). The processes are connected to their neighbours with a channel (the arrows) carrying platelets, and a barrier (drawn as a line with perpendicular ends). All the processes also enroll on a shared "tick" barrier (shown above the processes).

Platelets move (in a consistent direction) along a one dimensional pipeline. On each time-step a platelet may move or not move, with the following rule: if there are platelets immediately before or immediately after it in the pipeline, a platelet will only move forwards if they do so too. Each platelet may refuse to move on a given time-step with probability 5%. We model the sites (locations which can either hold a single platelet, or be empty) as active processes, and the platelets as passive data that passes between the sites. An illustration of their connectivity is given in figure 1.

The new features introduced later in this paper will demonstrate the power of a functional combinator-based approach. To provide a contrast to the existing methods that must be used in other imperative languages, such as occam or libraries for Java, we first present the example in figure 6 using idioms from imperative languages, such as numeric indexing. The exact definitions of the processes are not relevant in this paper and are thus omitted for brevity.

4   Wiring: Process Composition

In message-passing systems with typed channels, a substantial part of the programming model is the composition of processes using channels. For example, we may want to compose together the mapP and filterP processes (analogues of the standard list-processing functions) into a process that filters out negative numbers and then turns the remaining positive numbers into strings:

```
showPosP :: Chanin Int -> Chanout String -> CHP ()
showPosP input output = do (w, r) <- newChannelWR
                           runParallel_ [filterP (> 0) input w, mapP show r output]
```

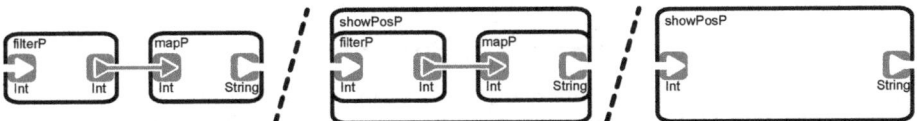

Fig. 2. The composition of filterP and mapP, as shown in the left-hand diagram. This composition becomes an opaque box to other components, as shown progressively in the middle and right diagrams. This component can then be further composed in a similar manner. The programming model used in CHP is thus compositional, allowing complex networks to be built from joining together different components without regard to their internal implementation.

This is shown diagrammatically in figure 2. It is instructive to note that the composition of two such processes with a single input channel and single output channel is itself a process with a single input channel and a single output channel. This component can then be re-used without requiring any knowledge of its internally concurrent implementation.

4.1   Simple Composition Operator

This composition of two single-input, single-output processes is so common that it is worth capturing in an associative operator:

```
(==>) :: (Chanin a -> Chanout b -> CHP ()) -> (Chanin b -> Chanout c -> CHP ())
      -> (Chanin a -> Chanout c -> CHP ())
(==>) p q r w = newChannelWR >>= \(mw, mr) -> runParallel_ [p r mw, q mr w]
```

The previous showPosP process can be written using this operator as follows:

```
showPosP = filterP (> 0) ==> mapP show
```

This point-free style is clearer and more elegant. By not introducing extra variable names we eliminate potential mistakes (mis-wiring). It can be seen that this process composition operator is an analogue of function composition.

We do not, however, always want to connect processes merely with a single unidirectional channel. We may want to connect processes with a pair of channels (one in each direction) or three channels, or a channel and a barrier, etc., as for example in the main function in our blood clotting example in figure 6 – which means that we need a more general operator than the one above.

4.2   Richer Composition Operator

Figure 3 shows another example of process composition, requiring different connections than figure 2. The types and directions of the channels needed to compose the processes are readily apparent – it should be just as easy to join these processes with two channels as it was to join filterP and mapP with one.

Fig. 3. An example of slightly different process composition than figure 2. The letters indicate the types of the channel-ends that each process takes. It is readily apparent, both that these processes *can* be composed, and *how* they should be composed: with a pair of channels.

To generalise the variety of composition possible, we use Haskell's type-class mechanism. We define a two parameter type-class, Connectable, an instance of which indicates that the two parameters can be wired together in some fashion, and provide a function that must be implemented to do so:

```
class Connectable l r where
  connect :: ((l, r) -> CHP a) -> CHP a
```

Instances for channels (in both directions) are trivial:

```
instance Connectable (Chanout a) (Chanin a) where
  connect p = newChannelWR >>= p
```

```
instance Connectable (Chanin a) (Chanout a) where
  connect p = newChannelWR >>= (p . swap)
    where swap (x, y) = (y, x)
```

We choose this style of function to compose the processes, rather than say connect :: CHP (l, r), because we may need to enroll the processes on the synchronisation object for the duration of their execution. Our chosen style of function allows us to do just that for an instance involving barriers:

```
instance Connectable EnrolledBarrier EnrolledBarrier where
  connect p = do b <- newBarrier
                 enroll b (\b0 -> enroll b (\b1 -> p (b0, b1)))
```

The instance that grants much greater power to the Connectable interface is the one that works for any pair of Connectable items:

```
instance (Connectable lA rA,Connectable lB rB) => Connectable (lA, lB) (rA, rB) where
  connect p = connect (\(ax, ay) -> connect (\(bx, by) -> p ((ax, bx), (ay, by))))
```

This instance means that two processes can easily be wired together if they need to be connected by a channel *and* a barrier, for example. Similar instances can also be constructed for triples and so on. Programmers may also create their own instances (as with any Haskell type-class) for synchronisation primitives not known to the library, or for compound data structures that feature several synchronisation primitives that need to be wired together differently.

A particularly powerful way to enhance this operator would be to use session types on CHP channels. Session types generalise from carrying a particular type on a one-way channel (as CHP currently does) to specifying the series of communications that can take place in both directions between two participants, encapsulating the entire protocol between two parties in the channel type. It has been shown that session types can be embedded well in a Haskell setting [14].

The Connectable interface is a suitable basic API, but it is too unwieldy to compose processes together. We can use it to define a more general version of the composition operator seen earlier:

```
(<=>) :: Connectable l r =>
    (a -> l -> CHP ()) -> (r -> b -> CHP ()) -> (a -> b -> CHP ())
(<=>) p q x y = connect (\(l, r) -> runParallel_ [p x l, q r y])
```

The type of this operator is very general. No restrictions are placed on the "outer" types a and b (which may be channels, but are not required to be so). This operator composes together any pair of two-argument processes where the second argument of the first process can be connected to the first argument of the second process. We can also trivially define other operators that are useful at the start and end of a process pipeline, respectively, and that compose just a start and end process:

```
(|<=>) :: Connectable l r => (l -> CHP ()) -> (r -> b -> CHP ()) -> (b -> CHP ())
(<=>|) :: Connectable l r => (a -> l -> CHP ()) -> (r -> CHP ()) -> (a -> CHP ())
(|<=>|) :: Connectable l r => (l -> CHP ()) -> (r -> CHP ()) -> CHP ()
```

We also provide a pipelineComplete function in the next section to support combining one start process and one end process with multiple middle processes.

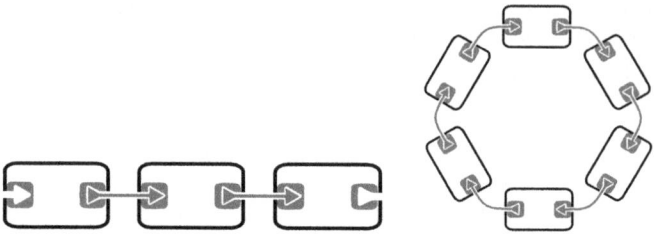

Fig. 4. The pipeline topology (left) and cycle topology (right). It can be seen that a cycle can be formed simply by connecting the two end points of a pipeline together. The processes are illustrated here by connecting them with a single channel, but any regular interface could be connected together using the Connectable class.

4.3   Capturing Common Topologies

We do not always want to simply compose two adjacent processes. Another common requirement is to wire together a pipeline of processes. We can do this by building on top of our connectable operator, meaning that the helper function is parameterised by the type of connection between processes, but fixes the topology – we can then easily extend this to a cycle (also known as a ring):

```
pipeline :: Connectable r l => [l -> r -> CHP ()] -> l -> r -> CHP ()
pipeline = foldr1 (<=>)
```

```
cycle :: Connectable r l => [l -> r -> CHP ()] -> CHP ()
cycle ps = connect (\(l, r) -> pipeline ps l r)
```

Both topologies are depicted in figure 4. We can also define a function for connecting a complete pipeline, as discussed at the end of the previous section:

```
pipelineComplete :: Connectable l r =>
  (l -> CHP ()) -> [r -> l -> CHP ()] -> (r -> CHP ()) -> CHP ()
pipelineComplete begin middle end = (begin l<=> pipeline middle) l<=>l end
```

This idea of capturing topology extends beyond such one-dimensional structures. A common requirement when building concurrent simulations with the CHP library is to form a regular two-dimensional (or three-dimensional) grid, either with or without diagonal connections. Producing such wiring, especially with diagonal connections, is verbose and error prone. Without the Connectable interface, it would have to be replicated for each type of channel used, increasing the possibility for error (this was originally the case in the CHP library [2]). But we can now write the function once, test it to show its correctness once, and re-use it repeatedly in different programs. We show an example type here but omit the lengthy definition[2]:

```
grid4way :: (Connectable right left, Connectable bottom top) =>
  [[above -> below -> left -> right -> CHP r]] -> CHP [[r]]
```

---

[2] It can be found in the library at http://hackage.haskell.org/package/chp-plus; an alternate short implementation is given in section 5.2 of this paper.

The parameter is a list of rows of processes (which must be rectangular); the result is a corresponding list of rows of results. The processes are wired together into a regular grid where the far right edge also connects to the far left edge, and the bottom edge to the top: this forms a torus shape.

Any topology (especially regular topologies) can be captured in helper functions like those given above, and re-used regardless of the channel types required to connect the processes.

4.4   Improved Process Wiring: Blood Clotting Example

The blood clotting example shown in figure 6 wired up its pipeline of processes by creating a list of channels and a list of barriers. List indexing was used to access the corresponding channels and barriers for each process. The connectable operators and functions introduced in the previous sections allow the processes to be wired together using a couple of the new operators and the pipeline combinator. This combinator is a list fold which replaces imperative-style list indexing.

The main feature of programming with CHP that enables the process wiring operators is the use of first-class processes[3]. In other languages where processes cannot be passed around, a function such as pipeline would not be possible to define. For example, the occam language does not have first-class processes. The C++CSP concurrent programming library allows complete processes (instances of classes that inherit from a CSProcess class) to be passed around, but processes still requiring channels is neither a straightforward nor natural idiom to support.

The revised version of the main process of the blood clotting example using the connectable operators where possible is shown in figure 7 and can be contrasted to figure 6. The new code using the connectable operators is much shorter. It is also instructive to note that there is no longer a call to the runParallel_ function in the main wiring function. The concurrency, which is a central primitive of CHP, has been captured in the pipelineComplete wiring function. This is indicative of the higher-level nature of the new process wiring, which abstracts away the details of the parallelism (and removes the channel declarations) in favour of operators that capture the connectivity pattern being used to join together the processes.

5   Compositional Wiring

Section 4 outlined ways to compose processes into a complete whole. We often have situations where a process needs not just one set of connections, but also some other cross-cutting connection. For example, a cycle of processes may all be connected to their neighbours with a channel – but they may also all be enrolled together on a barrier (as illustrated in figure 5). We have a similar situation in our blood clotting example, depicted in figure 1.

---

[3] Since a CHP process is a function/monadic action, these being first-class in Haskell means that CHP has first-class processes.

Consider how to implement such an arrangement with the combinators that we have introduced thus far; we have (with specialised types for illustration):

```
enrollAll :: Barrier -> [EnrolledBarrier -> CHP a] -> CHP [a]
pipeline :: [Chanin a -> Chanout a -> CHP ()] -> Chanin a -> Chanout a -> CHP ()
```

Both processes expect a list of processes that take exactly the required arguments (a barrier or a channel pair, respectively) and return a CHP process. Neither supports partial application that would return a process ready to be wired up by the other function: in short, these combinators do not compose.

We cannot simply create a function without the CHP monad, such as:

```
pipeline' :: [Chanin a -> Chanout a -> b] -> Chanin a -> Chanout a -> [b]
```

We require access to the CHP monad in order to run the processes in parallel, and to create the channels used to connect them together. This means that we need a different strategy in order to support composing these combinators in a useful way. To that end, we introduce a Composed monad.

5.1   The Composed Monad

We need to abstract over the return types of the processes being composed together while still allowing access to the functionality in the CHP monad. We therefore create functions such as (again with types specialised for illustration):

```
enrollAllR :: Barrier -> [EnrolledBarrier -> a] -> Composed [a]
pipelineR :: [Chanin a -> Chanout a -> b] -> Chanin a -> Chanout a -> Composed [b]
cycleR :: [Chanin a -> Chanout a -> b] -> Composed [b]
```

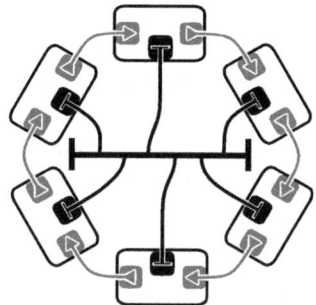

Fig. 5. A ring of processes connected to their neighbours with a single channel, and also all enrolled together on the same central barrier

Given a list of processes :: [EnrolledBarrier ->Chanin a ->Chanout a ->CHP ()], we can compose them, as depicted in figure 5, simply using:

```
enrollAllR b processes >>= cycleR
```

The meaning of composition in this monad is not intuitively the sequencing of actions as is often the case for monads (in fact, the monad is conceptually commutative in many cases). It is instead a form of nesting – the code above enrolls the processes on the barrier, and inside the scope of that enrollment it wires them together in a cycle. From a user's perspective the monad can be thought of as a series of wiring instructions. Each command composes the processes further until finally the complete processes are returned: the output of any Composed block is almost always such a list of complete CHP processes ready to be run in parallel. The type of the Composed monad is:

```
newtype Composed a = Composed { runWith :: forall b. (a -> CHP b) -> CHP b }
```

```
instance Monad Composed where
  return x = Composed (\r -> r x)
  (>>=) m f = Composed (\r -> m 'runWith' (('runWith' r) . f))
```

This type is not without precedence as a monad; it is equivalent to the continuation-passing monad transformer on top of CHP, forall b. ContT b CHP a, and is technically the codensity monad of CHP. The monad is not used to pass continuations, however. The intuition is that any type wrapped in Composed needs to be told how it can be turned into a CHP action, and then it becomes that CHP action. At the outer-level this is accomplished with runParallel:

```
run :: Composed [CHP a] -> CHP [a]
run ps = ps 'runWith' runParallel
```

5.2   Composed Wiring Functions

We can re-define all the wiring functions seen earlier in the new Composed monad. The most basic are the connectR and enrollR functions:

```
connectR :: Connectable l r => ((l, r) -> a) -> Composed a
connectR p = Composed (\r -> connect (r . p))
```

```
enrollR :: Barrier -> (EnrolledBarrier -> a) -> Composed a
enrollR b p = Composed (\r -> enroll b (r . p))
```

The latter can easily be expanded into an enrollAllR function:

```
enrollAllR :: Barrier -> [EnrolledBarrier -> a] -> Composed [a]
enrollAllR b ps = mapM (enrollR b) ps
```

The enrollAllR function enrolls a list of processes on the given barrier. Without the Composed monad it is an intricate recursive function, but with the Composed monad it is a non-recursive and straightforward mapM call.

We can define the pipelineR function as follows:

```
pipelineR :: Connectable l r => [r -> l -> a] -> Composed (r -> l -> [a])
pipelineR [] = return (\_ _ -> [])
pipelineR (firstP : restP) = foldM adj (\x y -> [firstP x y]) restP
  where adj p q = connectR (\(l, r) x y -> (p x l) ++ [q r y])
```

As before, the cycleR function is a small addition to the pipelineR function:

```
cycleR :: Connectable l r => [r -> l -> a] -> Composed [a]
cycleR [] = return []
cycleR ps = pipelineR ps >>= connectR . uncurry . flip
```

With these composition operators we can now easily define the 4-way grid composition discussed earlier in section 4.3:

```
grid4wayR :: (Connectable below above, Connectable right left) =>
    [[above -> below -> left -> right -> a]] -> Composed [[a]]
grid4wayR = (mapM cycleR . transpose) <=< (mapM cycleR . transpose)
```

The inherent symmetry, and regularity, of the combinator is exposed, and its cycleR-based definition trivial with the help of the standard list function transpose that swaps rows for columns in a list of lists and the (<=<) :: Monad m =>(b ->m c) ->(a ->m b) ->a ->m c function that composes two monadic functions.)

It is possible for users to define their own wiring functions using this monad. For example, a user may have a repeated pattern in their program, such as a list of processes where they wish to enroll all the processes at odd positions in the list on one barrier, but all the processes at even positions in the list on another barrier. They could write a function to do this, and use it in different situations in combination with other functions – for example, one such list may further be wired into a pipeline, while another may be wired into a star topology.

The use of wiring combinators avoids explicitly declaring and naming the channels and barriers required to construct the process network. This makes the code shorter, and prevents errors (such as passing the wrong channel-end to the wrong process, which will compile if they have the same type). It also means that common topologies (such as pipelineR) can be recognised by name when reading code – it is not straightforward to recognise wiring patterns when they are written out "long-hand" with individual named channels.

5.3   Further Improved Process Wiring: Blood Clotting Example

The motivation behind the Composed monad was that our original combinators did not easily compose. Certain combinators, such as enrollAll and pipeline, cannot easily be used together. For this reason our previous simplification of the blood platelets' wiring in figure 7 used enrollList instead. Often, nesting the combinators like this can lead to code nested many levels deep that is hard to follow, with many extra named parameters that are hard to track.

Our new Composed monad allows us to simplify the wiring in our blood clotting example even further by using two combinators: see figure 8 for the result. It can be seen that the only communication primitive that is named is the tick barrier. There are no manipulations involving list indexing as before. All of the creation of channels and barriers (except for tick) and all of the concurrency is hidden in the combinators for the Composed monad; pipelineCompleteR and enrollAllR create the channels and barriers, while the run function runs all the resulting processes concurrently.

```
plateletGenerator :: (Chanout Platelet, EnrolledBarrier) -> EnrolledBarrier -> CHP ()

plateletConsumer :: (Chanin Platelet, EnrolledBarrier) -> EnrolledBarrier -> CHP ()

site :: (Chanin Platelet, EnrolledBarrier) -> (Chanout Platelet, EnrolledBarrier)
        -> EnrolledBarrier -> CHP ()

numSites = 100

main :: IO ()
main = runCHP_ $ do
  (writers, readers) <- unzip <$> replicateM (numSites + 1) newChannelWR
  bars <- replicateM (numSites + 1) newBarrier
  tick <- newBarrierPri (-1)
  enrollList (replicate (numSites + 2) tick) $ \ticks ->
    enrollList bars $ \ebars -> runParallel $
      [site (readers !! i, ebars !! i)
            (writers !! succ i, ebars !! succ i)
            (ticks !! i) | i <- [0..numSites-1]] ++
      [plateletGenerator (writers !! 0, ebars !! 0) (ticks !! numSites)
      ,plateletConsumer (readers !! numSites, ebars !! numSites)
                        (ticks !! succ numSites)]
```

Fig. 6. An example version of the blood clotting example that uses array-like indexing idioms for wiring. The internal definition of the processes being wired together is not relevant (their types are given here to aid understanding), and the network is depicted in figure 1.

```
main = runCHP_ $ do
  tick <- newBarrierPri (-1)
  enrollList (replicate (numSites + 2) tick) $ \ticks ->
    pipelineComplete (flip plateletGenerator (ticks !! numSites))
                     (map (flip2 site) (take numSites ticks))
                     (flip plateletPrinter (ticks !! succ numSites))
  where flip2 f c a b = f a b c
```

Fig. 7. A revised version of the wiring code originally shown in figure 6, which uses the pipeline combinator and other new operators to simplify the wiring of the process network.

```
main = runCHP_ $ newBarrierPri (-1) >>= \tick -> run $
  pipelineCompleteR plateletGenerator (replicate numSites site) plateletConsumer
    >>= enrollAllR tick
```

Fig. 8. A further revised version of the wiring code shown originally in figure 6 (and previously revised in figure 7). This time the Composed monad is used to reduce the complete wiring code to just a few lines.

6   Related Work

Several other message-passing libraries exist in functional programming languages. Concurrent ML is the most obvious precursor [15], and it has since been converted to Haskell, too [18,4]. Given support for type-classes or a comparable mechanism, there is no reason why the programming patterns captured in this paper could not also be captured in Concurrent ML.

Erlang is a functional programming language with a strong message-passing component. However, Erlang uses asynchronous messages sent to a particular process address, rather than channels. This difference is vital with respect to the work described in this paper; the process composition described here does not apply to Erlang, and the styles of process that are composed in this paper are not common in Erlang. Additionally, Erlang is dynamically typed, which precludes the type-based connectable operators seen in this paper.

Lava is a hardware design domain-specific language embedded in Haskell [1]. Lava featured operators to compose together digital circuit components. This is an analogue of the Connectable operators seen in this paper – although Lava featured different combinators depending on data-flow direction, whereas the Connectable class abstracts away details such as directionality and types.

At an abstract level, CHP can be thought of as a way to represent interactive computations. Another way to do so is Functional Reactive Programming (FRP) [11]. There are various implementations of FRP [11,5,9], but broadly they represent interaction as a function from timed observations/inputs to timed outputs. This neatly removes explicit state and imperative constructs, but can cause problems with causality (where future events can affect past behaviour).

7   Conclusions

The Communicating Haskell Processes library is an imperative message-passing library built in a functional programming language. This paper has shown how the ideas of higher-order functions, type-class-based abstractions and re-usable combinators can be taken from functional programming and applied to message-passing programming, with all of the same benefits.

CHP programs are made up of many components composed together concurrently, and connected by channels and barriers. The "long-hand" way of composing these processes – manually declaring channels and passing the ends to the right processes – is tedious, verbose and error prone. The combinators discussed in this paper allow for an elegant and concise point-free style, composing processes together without ever naming the primitives that connect the processes.

The Connectable type-class allows the wiring functions to abstract away from the primitives used to compose processes and to instead focus on capturing topology. This allows complicated functions (such as two-dimensional grids with diagonal connections) to be written once and re-used. The Composed monad takes this further and allows complicated composition with several cross-cutting concerns to be done easily and compositionally, which makes for completely flexible wiring of processes. Both of these mechanisms could generalise to composing processes with any Haskell communication primitive such as MVar or TChan.

All of this work is only possible because functions and processes are first-class in CHP, and can thus be passed as arguments. Implementing these combinators in message-passing frameworks in other languages would either be overly verbose and awkward (e.g. using interfaces and classes in Java) or simply not possible (e.g. in the language occam, where higher-order programming is not possible).

References

1. Bjesse, P., Claessen, K., Sheeran, M., Singh, S.: Lava: hardware design in Haskell. In: ICFP 1998, pp. 174–184. ACM, New York (1998)
2. Brown, N.C.C.: Communicating Haskell Processes: Composable explicit concurrency using monads. In: Communicating Process Architectures 2008, pp. 67–83 (September 2008)
3. Brown, N.C.C.: Conjoined Events. In: Advances in Message Passing. ACM, New York (2010)
4. Chaudhuri, A.: A concurrent ML library in concurrent Haskell. In: ICFP 2009, pp. 269–280. ACM, New York (2009)
5. Elliott, C.M.: Push-pull functional reactive programming. In: Haskell 2009, pp. 25–36. ACM, New York (2009)
6. Hoare, C.A.R.: Communicating Sequential Processes. Prentice-Hall, Englewood Cliffs (1985)
7. Hughes, J.: Generalising monads to arrows. Sci. Comput. Program. 37(1-3), 67–111 (2000)
8. Jadud, M., Jacobsen, C.L., Simpson, J., Ritson, C.G.: Safe parallelism for behavioral control. In: 2008 IEEE Conference on Technologies for Practical Robot Applications, pp. 137–142. IEEE, Los Alamitos (2008)
9. Liu, H., Cheng, E., Hudak, P.: Causal commutative arrows and their optimization. In: ICFP 2009, pp. 35–46. ACM, New York (2009)
10. McBride, C., Paterson, R.: Applicative programming with effects. J. Funct. Program. 18(1), 1–13 (2008)
11. Nilsson, H., Courtney, A., Peterson, J.: Functional reactive programming, continued. In: Haskell 2002, pp. 51–64. ACM, New York (2002)
12. Peyton Jones, S.L., Wadler, P.: Imperative functional programming. In: POPL 1993, pp. 71–84. ACM, New York (1993)
13. Polack, F.A., Andrews, P.S., Sampson, A.T.: The engineering of concurrent simulations of complex systems. In: 2009 IEEE Congress on Evolutionary Computation (CEC 2009), pp. 217–224. IEEE Press, Los Alamitos (2009)
14. Pucella, R., Tov, J.A.: Haskell session types with (almost) no class. In: Haskell 2008, pp. 25–36. ACM, New York (2008)
15. Reppy, J.H.: Concurrent Programming in ML. Cambridge University Press, Cambridge (1999)
16. Ritson, C.G., Sampson, A.T., Barnes, F.R.M.: Multicore Scheduling for Lightweight Communicating Processes. In: Field, J., Vasconcelos, V.T. (eds.) COORDINATION 2009. LNCS, vol. 5521, pp. 163–183. Springer, Heidelberg (2009)
17. Roscoe, A.W.: The Theory and Practice of Concurrency. Prentice-Hall, Englewood Cliffs (1997)
18. Russell, G.: Events in haskell, and how to implement them. In: ICFP 2001, pp. 157–168. ACM, New York (2001)
19. Schneider, S., Cavalcanti, A., Treharne, H., Woodcock, J.: A Layered Behavioural Model of Platelets. In: ICECCS 2006, pp. 98–106. IEEE, Los Alamitos (2006)

Analysing a Publish/Subscribe System for Mobile Ad Hoc Networks with ProbLog

Theofrastos Mantadelis, Koosha Paridel, Gerda Janssens, Yves Vanrompay, and Yolande Berbers

Departement Computerwetenschappen, K.U. Leuven. Celestijnenlaan 200A, B-3001 Heverlee, Belgium
firstname.lastname@cs.kuleuven.be

Abstract. *Fadip* is a Publish/Subscribe system for Mobile Ad hoc Networks which uses probabilistic routing of messages to deal with the volatile nature of the network. It uses controlled propagation of publications and subscriptions, with the fading gossip technique to reduce the number of broadcasts. We present a probabilistic logic program in ProbLog that models Fadip. This allows us to calculate the probabilities that messages are successfully received by subscribers and to analyse the performance of the Fadip system.

Keywords: Probabilistic logic programming, ProbLog, Mobile Ad hoc Networks, Publish/Subscribe System.

1 Introduction

We use ProbLog [1], a probabilistic extension of Prolog, to analyse Fadip [2], a Publish/Subscribe protocol for Mobile Ad hoc Networks (MANETs). Publish/Subscribe systems for MANETs are used commonly in disaster recovery, smart city and vehicular networks. We model a MANET as a probabilistic graph representing connections between nodes by ProbLog's probabilistic facts. The Fadip protocol can be seen as a special kind of path finding in such a probabilistic graph. As there can be multiple non-mutually exclusive paths between two nodes, ProbLog is an appropriate probabilistic system to model this application.

Our main contribution is to show how a simple ProbLog program can encode this Fadip application for the case of one publisher and one subscriber, and how simple ProbLog queries can then compute the probabilities of message delivery for different parameter settings. Before, simulations were needed to estimate delivery ratios, while now they are inferred analytically.

We analytically investigate the delivery probability among random node pairs and show the effects of the fading gossip technique. We also evaluate different parameter settings and conclude on what their impact is.

2 Problem Statement

Publish/Subscribe systems have been intensively studied for wired networks and infrastructured mobile networks [3]. When used in MANETs they suffer from

R. Rocha and J. Launchbury (Eds.): PADL 2011, LNCS 6539, pp. 34–37, 2011.

scalability issues. Fadip [2] is a Publish/Subscribe system for MANETs and is designed to be lightweight in terms of the network topology (i.e. fixing routing information and maintaining logical structures of nodes) and the number of messages exchanged for communication. To achieve a reasonable delivery ratio, Fadip uses a hybrid model which propagates subscriptions and publications as bounded as possible and makes matching in intermediary nodes which act as undedicated rendezvous points. In Fadip, the routing is done probabilistically and neither the publishers nor the subscribers have any information about where their publication or subscription might be matched.

3   ProbLog

ProbLog [1] is a probabilistic framework that extends Prolog with probabilistic facts. A ProbLog program specifies a probability distribution over all possible non-probabilistic subprograms of the ProbLog program. The success probability of a query is defined as the probability that it succeeds in these subprograms.

ProbLog has been motivated by the real-life application of mining large biological networks where edges are labelled with probabilities. An edge represents a probabilistic link between the concepts represented by its nodes. The probabilistic links are mutually independent. ProbLog typically computes the probability of the existence of a path between two nodes [4]. The contribution of common parts in different paths between two nodes to the final probability is dealt according to the inclusion-exclusion principle from set theory.

4   Fadip Model in ProbLog

We model the MANET as a probabilistic graph. The graph nodes are the nodes of the mobile network. The graph edges model the connectivity between nodes. In a MANET this connectivity is not permanent. To model this, we attach to the edges probabilities which express the fraction of the time the connections are present. These probabilistic edges are represented by probabilistic facts.

We extend the path program to model the Publisher/Subscriber propagation of Fadip as a bounded bidirectional search of a path among two nodes. The parameters $MaxHop_p$ and $MaxHop_s$ are used as bounds when propagating the message of the Publisher and the subscription of the Subscriber, respectively. We used tabling as in [5] to avoid re-computations and to handle loops.

To integrate the fading gossip, we also need to express the fact that sending a message has a probability which decreases with the distance from its source [2]. We model this by flexible probabilistic facts, whose probability is determined at runtime. The delivery of a message between two nodes depends on the connection being present and the distance from the Publisher.

The model results in a relatively simple ProbLog program that allow us to query for the probability of a message delivery from a Publisher to a Subscriber[1].

---

[1] The ProbLog program and the analysis results can be found at:
http://people.cs.kuleuven.be/ theofrastos.mantadelis/appendixs/
PADL2011.pdf

5   Analysing the Model

We present how ProbLog can be used to analyse Fadip. The base operation is to calculate delivery probabilities. Fadip aims to reduce network traffic. For this it is beneficial to retain $MaxHop$ parameters as low as possible and to use fading gossip while retaining a good delivery probability. We used the OMNeT++ simulation log of a 150 node WiFi network, moving randomly at $1m/s$ in a playground of $1.5km \times 1km$. For the selection of Publisher and Subscriber, we considered two settings based on the distance between them. For the first, we randomly selected pairs of nodes which have paths with a minimum hop from 4 to 6 and for the second, pairs that have paths with a minimum hop from 8 to 10. We used ProbLog to query the delivery probability for these pairs with multiple values for $MaxHop_p$ and $MaxHop_s$ and activating or not fading gossip. The results of these queries are first used to evaluate the impact of the $MaxHop$ parameters. We observed that increasing $MaxHop_s$ has more effect on improving the delivery probability than increasing $MaxHop_p$. We also used the results to infer optimal values for $MaxHop_p$ and $MaxHop_s$. For example, in the first setting both are 3 and for the second setting are $4, 5$ respectively. Our analysis showed that fading gossip retains a high delivery probability for close distances up to $3-4$ hops and the delivery probability rapidly decreases for longer paths.

6   Conclusions

We presented an application of ProbLog that models and analyses the performance of Fadip. In [6] Bayesian Networks are used to analyse MANETs. By analysing the model one can infer delivery probabilities for different settings and use this information to chose optimal parameter settings and do evaluations. For our example network we concluded that $MaxHop_s$ is more important for obtaining a high delivery probability than $MaxHop_p$ and that the fading gossip technique has a good delivery probability for small hop counts while the message rapidly fades for larger hop counts. In [2] similar results are attained by simulating the behaviour of the network, in this work we attain them analytically. For future work we want to extend the ProbLog program to support multiple publishers and subscribers and study the impact of their interaction.

References

1. Kimmig, A., Santos Costa, V., Rocha, R., Demoen, B., De Raedt, L.: On the efficient execution of ProbLog programs. In: Proceedings of ICLP, pp. 175–189 (2008)
2. Paridel, K., Vanrompay, Y., Berbers, Y.: Fadip: Lightweight publish/Subscribe for mobile ad hoc networks. In: Meersman, R., Dillon, T., Herrero, P. (eds.) OTM 2010. LNCS, vol. 6427, pp. 798–810. Springer, Heidelberg (2010)
3. Baldoni, R., Virgillito, A.: Distributed event routing in publish/subscribe communication systems: a survey. DIS, Universita di Roma"La Sapienza", Tech. Rep. (2005)

4. De Raedt, L., Kimmig, A., Toivonen, H.: ProbLog: A probabilistic prolog and its application in link discovery. In: Proceedings of IJCAI, pp. 2462–2467 (2007)
5. Mantadelis, T., Janssens, G.: Dedicated tabling for a probabilistic setting. In: Technical Communications of ICLP, pp. 124–133 (2010)
6. Buchegger, S., Boudec, J.Y.L.: The effect of rumor spreading in reputation systems for mobile ad-hoc networks. In: Proceedings of WiOpt (2003)

Profiling for Run-Time Checking of Computational Properties and Performance Debugging in Logic Programs

Edison Mera[1], Teresa Trigo[2],
Pedro Lopez-García[2,3], and Manuel Hermenegildo[2,4]

[1] Complutense University of Madrid (UCM), Spain
[2] IMDEA Software Institute, Spain
[3] Spanish Research Council (CSIC), Spain
[4] School of Computer Science, Technical University of Madrid (UPM), Spain
edison@fdi.ucm.es, herme@fi.upm.es,
{teresa.trigo,pedro.lopez,manuel.hermenegildo}@imdea.org

Abstract. Although several profiling techniques for identifying performance bottlenecks in logic programs have been developed, they are generally not automatic and in most cases they do not provide enough information for identifying the root causes of such bottlenecks. This complicates using their results for guiding performance improvement. We present a profiling method and tool that provides such explanations. Our profiler associates cost centers to certain program elements and can measure different types of resource-related properties that affect performance, preserving the precedence of cost centers in the call graph. It includes an automatic method for detecting procedures that are performance bottlenecks. The profiling tool has been integrated in a previously developed run-time checking framework to allow verification of certain properties when they cannot be verified statically. The approach allows checking global computational properties which require complex instrumentation tracking information about previous execution states, such as, e.g., that the execution time *accumulated* by a given procedure is not greater than a given bound. We have built a prototype implementation, integrated it in the `Ciao/CiaoPP` system and successfully applied it to performance improvement, automatic optimization (e.g., resource-aware specialization of programs), run-time checking, and debugging of global computational properties (e.g., resource usage) in Prolog programs.

Keywords: profiling, run-time checking, performance debugging, resource usage estimation/verification, logic programming.

1 Introduction

Profilers have been developed in the context of several programming paradigms: imperative [5,16] (including object oriented [7]), functional [15,14], logic [3,9,4], or integrations of some of them, such as the functional logic languages Curry and Toy [1]. In this paper we focus our attention on profilers for logic programs, and in particular for the Prolog language. The implementation of Prolog profilers has

R. Rocha and J. Launchbury (Eds.): PADL 2011, LNCS 6539, pp. 38–53, 2011.

the added complexity w.r.t. more traditional paradigms of having to deal with its specific features such as non-determinism and the possibility of failure, which makes it necessary to deal with backtracking (and, hence, with choice points), and search pruning operators (like the cut). There exist some implementations of profilers for the Prolog language (e.g., [4,3]). However, in order to fill some gaps and to broaden the range of applications, we have developed a profiler for Prolog that has the following original features:

1. *It is based on the concept of cost center.* We have adapted the cost center definition of Morgan [14], developed in the context of functional programming, to support the unique features of logic programming. A cost center, as we will explain later in detail, is a program point (such as a procedure or a call in a clause body) where data about computational events is accumulated each time the point is reached by the program execution control flow. This allows measuring accumulated execution time of program procedures that do not overlap, i.e., the total resource usage of a program can be computed in a compositional way, by adding the execution time associated to each cost center. A cost center-based profiler with this property has been developed for functional programming [15], however, as far as we know, no implementation of this kind of profiler has been developed for logic programs.

2. It allows *preserving the precedence of cost centers in the call graph.* It provides separate accumulated resource usage information for a given procedure *depending on where it is called from,* i.e., it is a *call graph profiler* for Prolog. We have taken the call graph profiling approach of [16] as starting point and we have adapted it in order to deal with the more complex execution model of Prolog, taking failure, backtracking, and pruning operators into account. The SWI profiler is to our knowledge the only Prolog profiler that keeps the precedence between the caller and the callee, but it does not support the concept of cost center.

3. It *can measure a wide range of computational properties and events,* such as execution time, execution steps, numbers of calls, failures, exits, redos, choice point creations, cut executions, choice points removed by the cut operator, or the percentage of the accumulated cost of a predicate with respect to the total cost of the program. We use in the rest of the paper the term "resources" to refer to any of these properties. Although the current implementation is not fully parametric w.r.t. resources, it can be easily generalized as it was done with the static resource analysis integrated in CiaoPP [12].

4. It is *used for run-time checking of computational properties.* For this purpose, it is *tightly integrated in an advanced program development framework* which incorporates in a uniform way run-time checking, static verification, unit testing, debugging, and optimization. To our knowledge, no profiler has been used for this purpose or integrated in such an environment to date.

5. It includes a (configurable) *automatic method for detecting procedures that are performance bottlenecks* following several heuristics. The method automatically associates cost centers to procedures in an iterative process. Previous approaches are not automatic (e.g., [3,15,1]), so that the programmer is responsible for configuring cost centers iteratively based on the information

returned by the profiler until the root cause of the bottleneck is detected. We show that the configuration of cost centers can be automated, as we will explain further, by exploring a (static or dynamically) generated call graph until the root cause of the bottleneck is detected.

6. It is able to *point at the part of the program that is responsible for the bottleneck*, guided by any arbitrary resource (like time, event counts, etc.) and to provide explanations at different granularity levels. This information includes an automatically generated picture of (a sub-graph of) the call graph (see Section 6). Existing profilers only provide information about where the bottlenecks of the programs are without any kind of explanation about the root causes, requiring that additional techniques be applied in order to identify such causes.

7. It *combines time profiling with count profiling*, which has proved to be non-trivial [9], and supports modularity, allowing the specification of which modules should be instrumented for profiling. This feature of our profiler is possible thanks to the usage of Ciao's module system and the automatic code transformation provided through Ciao's semantic packages.

8. It *uses global static analysis* to reduce the overhead of the profiling process.

2   A Cost Center-Based Approach to Profiling

Fundamental to our approach to profiling is the concept of *cost center*, which is inspired by the one defined by Morgan [14] in the context of functional languages.

A *cost center* for us is a program point where data about computational events is accumulated each time the point is reached by the program execution control flow. In our current implementation both predicates and literals in body clauses can be marked as cost centers. However, for the sake of brevity, in this paper we will only describe cost centers at the predicate level. We also introduce a special cost center, named *remainder cost center* (denoted *rcc*), which is used for accumulating data about events not corresponding to any defined cost center.

In order to deal with the control flow of Prolog, we adopt the "box model" of Byrd [2], where predicates (procedures) are seen as "black boxes" in the usual way. Since the simple call/return view of procedures is not enough to capture backtracking, this model uses a "4-port box view." Namely, given a *goal* (i.e., a unique run-time call to a predicate), the four ports (events) in Prolog execution are: (1) *call* (start to execute the goal), (2) *exit* (succeed in producing a solution to the goal), (3) *redo* (attempt to find an alternative solution to the goal), and (4) *fail* (exit with failure, if no further solutions to the goal are found). Thus, there are two ports for "entering" the box (*call* and *redo*), and two ports for "leaving" it (*exit* and *fail*).

Definition 1 (Calls relation). *We define the* calls *relation between predicates in a program as follows: p calls q, written p $\leadsto$ q, if and only if a literal with predicate symbol q appears in the body of a clause defining p. Let $\leadsto^+$ denote the transitive closure of $\leadsto$.*[1]

---

[1] For simplicity we provide a static definition of the call graph. However, in practice, it is dynamically built, and thus it deals safely with meta-calls.

Definition 2 (Cost center set). *Given a program P to be profiled, the cost center set for P (denoted C_P), is defined as $C_P = \{p \mid p$ is a predicate of P marked as a cost center$\} \cup \{rcc\}$, where rcc is the remainder cost center.*

Definition 3 (Cost center graph). *The* cost center graph *of a program P (denoted G_P) is the graph defined by the set of nodes C_P and the set of edges $E = E' \cup \{(rcc, rcc)\}$, such that $(p,q) \in E'$ iff:*

1. *p is not the remainder cost center (i.e., $p \neq rcc$), $q \neq rcc$, and $p \rightsquigarrow^+ q$ through some path where all of its nodes (except the origin and destination) are not in C_P; or*
2. *$p = rcc$ and: (a) q is an entry point of program P such that $q \in C_P$, or (b) for some predicate r being an entry point of P, $r \rightsquigarrow^+ q$ through some path where all of its nodes (except the destination) are not in C_P.*

Definition 4 (Edge-accumulated resource usage). *Each edge $(c, d) \in G_P$ has a data structure R_{cd}, which contains the addition of resource usages over all the times that the cost center d was entered from cost center c, until a new cost center is entered or the computation finishes. This allows giving separate resource usage information for a given procedure depending on where it is called from.*

Our profiler is *parametric* w.r.t. the enter/leave ports, i.e., R_{cd} contains matrices of the form $Resource[enter][leave]$ ($enter \in \{call, redo\}$, $leave \in \{exit, fail\}$), whose elements are counters to keep track of the usage of several resources for the four possible "enter/leave" port combination (cf. the "4-port box" of node d). For example we keep track of the number of times that each of the four "enter/leave" port combination happens during program execution in $Counts[enter][leave]$. Execution times are also tracked in $Ticks[enter][leave]$.

Example 1. We are going to illustrate how the resource usage information is stored in the edges of the cost center graph during the profiling process. At any time in this process, only one edge is active. When execution enters a predicate which is defined as a cost center, the resource usage monitored so far is stored in the active edge, it is deactivated, and then another edge is activated. Consider program p, and its call graph and cost center graph in Figure 1. Before starting program execution, the active edge is (rcc, rcc). Then, when execution starts, the partial counters are reset and p is called. Since p is defined as a cost center, the resource usage monitored so far in the partial counters is accumulated in the active edge (rcc, rcc), the partial counters are reset, and the active edge changes to (rcc, p). Then, the execution of the body of p starts by executing q. Since q is not defined as a cost center, the active edge remains the same as before, (rcc, p) (and the partial counters are not reset). When the execution of q finishes, r is called. Since r is defined as a cost center, the resource usage monitored so far in the partial counters is accumulated in the active edge (rcc, p), the partial counters are reset, and the active edge changes to (p, r). Since r is the last call in the definition of p, when the execution of r finishes, the resource usage monitored so far in the partial counters is accumulated in (p, r) and program execution finishes.

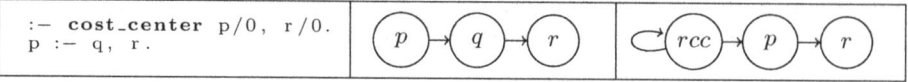

Fig. 1. Source code, call graph and cost center graph for Example 1

Definition 5 (Accumulated resource usage of a cost center). *The accumulated resource usage of a given cost center d (denoted R_d) is the sum of the resource usage for all times cost center d is entered either in forwards (i.e., via the* call *port) or backwards (i.e., via the* redo *port) execution, until a new cost center is entered or the computation finishes.*

The accumulated resource usage of a cost center can be obtained as the sum of the accumulated resource usages of its incoming edges: $R_d = \sum_{(c,d)\in E} R_{cd}$.

Our definition of accumulated resource of a cost center is compositional, in the sense that the total resource usage of a program P, denoted R_P, is the addition of the accumulated resource usage of all its cost centers: $R_P = \sum_{c \in C_P} R_c$. In contrast, in traditional profilers, the accumulated execution times for different predicates may overlap (and thus adding them may yield a result greater than their actual resource usage).

3   Integrating Profiling with Verification and Debugging

In this section we explain how our profiler is integrated within the Ciao/CiaoPP verification/debugging framework, which incorporates in a uniform way run-time checking, static verification, unit testing, debugging, and optimization [6,10]. The run-time checking of program state properties such as traditional types or modes can be performed relatively easily. This is in part due to the fact that properties are written in the source language and *runnable* (facilitated by the underlying logic engine), which simplifies the program transformation that adds run-time checks. However, the run-time checking of global computational properties requires monitoring, which is performed by our profiler. Figure 2 gives an overall

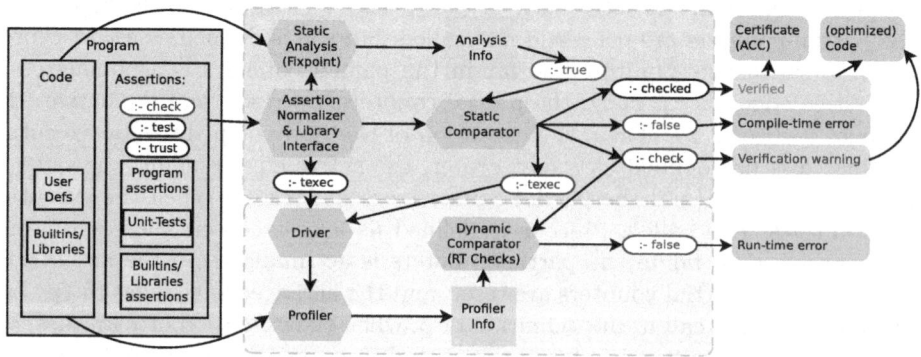

Fig. 2. The Ciao assertion framework (CiaoPP's verification/testing architecture)

```
:- cost_center qsort1/2, qsort2/2.

qsort1(A,B) :- qsort(A,B).
qsort2(A,B) :- qsort(A,B).

qsort([],[]).
qsort([X|L],R):-
        partition(L,X,L1,L2),
        qsort1(L1,R1),
        qsort2(L2,R2),
        append(R1,[X|R2],R).
```

```
partition([],_,[],[]).
partition([H|L],X,[H|L1],L2):-
    H < X, !,
    partition(L,X,L1,L2).
partition([H|L],X,L1,[H|L2]):-
    H >= X,
    partition(L,X,L1,L2).

append([],B,B).
append([H|A],B,[H|C]) :-
    append(A,B,C).
```

Fig. 3. Source code for qsort with cost center declarations (at predicate level)

view of such framework, placing the profiling tool in context. Hexagons represent the tools involved while arrows indicate the communication paths among them. The process input is the user program, *optionally* including a set of assertions that always includes the assertions present for predicates exported by any libraries used (left part of Figure 2), and, optionally, it can include unit tests.

In this paper we are interested in a subset of the versatile Ciao assertion language which allows expressing global computational properties whose run-time checking requires the use of our profiler. A detailed description of the full assertion language can be found in [6]. For brevity, we only introduce the class of **pred assertions**, which describes a particular predicate and, in general, follows the schema:

:- **pred** *Pred* [: *Precond*] [=> *Postcond*] [+ *Comp-Props*].

where *Pred* is a predicate symbol applied to distinct free variables and *Precond* and *Postcond* are logic formulae about execution states. An execution state is defined by the bindings of values to variables in a given execution step (in logic programming terminology, a substitution). *Precond* is the precondition under which the **pred** assertion is applicable. *Postcond* expresses that in any call to *Pred*, if *Precond* holds in the calling state and the computation of the call succeeds, then *Postcond* also holds in the success state. Finally, the *Comp-Props* field is used to describe properties of the whole computation of the calls to predicate *Pred* that meet *Precond* (e.g., resource usage properties). For example, the following assertion for the quick-sort program in Figure 3:

```
:- pred qsort(A,B) :(list(A,num),var(B)) => (list(A,num),list(B,num))
       +(cost(ub,steps,length(A)*log(length(A))), not_fails, is_det).
```

states that for any call to predicate qsort/2 with the first argument bound to a list of numbers and the second one a free variable, if the call succeeds, then the second argument is also bound to a list of numbers. It also states that (for any of such calls) an upper bound on the number of resolution steps required to execute qsort/2, is $length(A) \times log(length(A))$, a function on the length of list A. This is of course false, but we will see later in this section how we can detect it using our profiler. Additionally, not_fails and is_det express that the previous calls do not finitely fail (i.e., they produce at least one solution or do not terminate) and are deterministic (i.e., they produce at most one solution at most once), respectively. The `cost` construct for expressing resource usages, as illustrated in the previous sample assertion, follows the schema:

$$\textbf{cost}(\textit{Approx}, \textit{Res\_Name}, \textit{Arith\_Expr})$$

where the *Res_Name* field expresses which resource the assertion refers to. It is a user-provided identifier which gives a name to each particular resource that needs to be tracked, verified, or checked. *Arith_Expr* is an arithmetic function that expresses the resource usage of the predicate as a function of input data sizes. The *Approx* field states, for example, whether *Arith_Expr* is providing an exact value (**eq**), an upper bound (**ub**), or a lower bound (**lb**).

Each assertion can be in a particular *verification status*, marked with the keyword prefixes `check`, `checked`, `false`, `trust` or `true` (see the ellipses in Figure 2). The (default) status `check` determines that the assertion is to be checked. `checked` and `false` express that the assertion has already been proved correct or incorrect respectively by the system (a compile-time error is reported in the last case). `trust` expresses that the assertion is to be trusted (it provides information coming from the programmer), and `true` that the provided information is the result of static analysis and thus correct (safely approximated). We herein introduce a new status, `obs`, which means that an assertion expresses observed information (in this case, by the profiler).

In this paper we focus on the run-time checking of computational (resource-related) properties within the `CiaoPP` unified framework, giving an intuitive short description using the following example.

Example 2. Assume that we want the `CiaoPP` system to check whether the following assertion, which gives a logarithmic upper bound on the number of resolution steps of `qsort/2` as a function of the length of the input list, holds or not:

```
:- pred qsort(A,B):(list(A,num),var(B))
          + cost(ub,steps,length(A)*log(length(A))).
```

First, the `CiaoPP` system tries to statically verify the assertion. This is done by running a static resource usage analysis (see [12]) that computes *safe* lower and upper bounds on the resource usage (number of resolution steps in this case), and then by comparing the analysis results with the specification given in the assertion. A full description of the static verification of computational/resource-related properties is given in [8]. The quick-sort program is of the kind of divide-and-conquer programs that may cause the analysis to lose precision. As a consequence, the assertion cannot be proved to be false, since the lower bound resource usage function derived by the analysis (which is linear) is not greater than the upper bound function given in the assertion. Conversely, the assertion cannot be proved to hold, because the upper bound resource usage function derived by the analysis (which is exponential) is not less or equal than the upper bound function given in the assertion. Thus, the outcome of the static verification process is "unknown" and the assertion status remains as `check`.[2] However, if the run-time checking option is selected, `CiaoPP` instruments the program with checks to be performed at run-time

---

[2] This can optionally produce a *verification warning* (also known as an "alarm").

for (parts of) assertions which cannot be verified statically. Failure of these checks raises run-time errors referring to the corresponding assertion. In our example, using input data automatically generated (or taken from existing unit tests [10]) the profiler performs different calls to the quick-sort program. If for some of these calls the computed number of steps is greater than the one specified in the assertion, then such assertion is false (in fact, CiaoPP was easily able to prove it).

4   Proposing New Computational Properties

In order to support cumulative properties, we extend the set of properties used in the assertion language, starting with the addition of rel_cost, which expresses relative resource usages. For example, assuming that the qsort/2 procedure is part of a given main program, the assertion (with no postcondition):

```
:- pred qsort(A,B) : (list(A,num),var(B)) + rel_cost(ub,exectime,20).
```

expresses that the execution time of qsort/2 is at most 20% of the total execution time of the main program. The rel_cost construct follows the schema:

$$\textbf{rel\_cost}(\textit{Approx},\textit{Res\_Name},\textit{Percentage})$$

where *Approx* is as before, denoting an upper bound, a lower bound, or an exact value on the *Percentage* of the procedure resource (*Res_Name*) usage with respect to the total resource usage of the whole main program (from which the predicate is called) respectively.

We have also extended the cost and rel_cost property constructs with an extra argument *Type* specifying the kind of cost information we are interested in:

$$\{\texttt{cost},\texttt{rel\_cost}\}(\textit{Approx},\textit{Type},\textit{Res\_Name},\textit{Arith\_Expr})$$

defined as follows:

- **sol(I):** The cost of obtaining the I-th solution without considering the cost of obtaining the previous one. By definition, if I is greater than the number of solutions, then the related cost is zero.
- **allsols:** The cost of obtaining all the solutions. It is equivalent to the cost of applying findall/3 over the given predicate, but subtracting the cost of findall/3 itself.
- **call:** The cost of calling the predicate, regardless of whether it fails or succeeds (this is the value by default).
- **call_exit:** The cost of calling the predicate when it succeeds.
- **call_fail:** The cost of calling the predicate when it fails.
- **redo**: The cost of backtracking over the predicate, regardless of whether it fails or succeeds.
- **redo_exit:** The cost of backtracking over the predicate when it succeeds.
- **redo_fail:** The cost of backtracking over the predicate when it fails.

The following example illustrates how the CiaoPP system (with our profiler integrated and our extended run-time checking operations), monitors and checks relative resource usages at run-time.

Example 3. Consider again the `qsort/2` predicate in Figure 3, and assume that we want to know how the execution times of its recursive calls are distributed. Although as mentioned before it is possible to define cost centers at literal level, for the sake of clarity we have defined two bridge predicates (`qsort1/2` and `qsort2/2`) that are used in place of the recursive calls of `qsort/2`, and have marked them as cost centers using the following declaration:

```
:- cost_center qsort1/2, qsort2/2.
```

Assume that we profile the execution of `qsort/2` with an input list of 2500 randomly generated elements, and that our profiler outputs the assertions:

```
:- obs pred qsort1/2 + rel_cost(eq, exec_time, 48).
:- obs pred qsort2/2 + rel_cost(eq, exec_time, 47).
```

which mean that the observed execution times of `qsort1/2` and `qsort2/2` are 48% and 47% of the total execution time respectively.

Assume now that we want the `CiaoPP` system to check at run time whether the two (recursive) calls in the body of the (original) `qsort/2` are balanced (i.e., whether each recursive call consumes more or less 50% of the total execution time). For this purpose, we write the following assertions:

```
:- check pred qsort1/2 + rel_cost(ub, exec_time, 55).
:- check pred qsort2/2 + rel_cost(ub, exec_time, 55).
```

Assume that we call `qsort/2` with a non-uniformly distributed input list, and that the execution accumulates 65.01% and 8.16% of the time in the two cost centers associated to the two calls respectively. In this case, the `CiaoPP` dynamic comparator will throw a run-time checking error informing that the assertion for cost center `qsort1/2` is violated (because the monitored execution time is greater than the one expressed in the assertion), and, thus the two calls in the body of `qsort/2` are not balanced.

In contrast to non-cumulative global properties, the previously illustrated kind of cumulative properties cannot be checked immediately at run-time, but rather at the proper time instant in the program execution. In the current implementation, such checking is done at the end of the program execution (when the program control reaches an output port where there are no pending choice points). However, some scenarios require other rules for expressing the time instant in which the checking is performed. Consider for example a service that requires the check to be made periodically at certain time intervals, or when a certain number of client requests has been reached. Also, so far the operation for accumulating resource usages has been addition. However, it is desirable to have more complex operations. For example, old measurements could be discarded, or the events weighted according to their ages or other properties.

5   Program Transformation for Profiling

Source-to-Source Transformation for (High-Level) Profiling. A predicate marked as a cost center is transformed into an equivalent one that preserves its semantics while intercepting occurrences of events inside it, by using some

Program	Cost center transformation for profiling
:− **module**(ap,[append/3], [profiler]). :− **cost_center** append/3. append([],B,B). append([H|A],B,[H|C]) :− append(A,B,C).	'\$cc\$'(ap,append,3). append(E, L, R) :− hcc_call('ap:append',3,PrevCCE,CutTo), hcc_fail(PrevCCE,ChPt0), '\$cc\$append'(A,B,C), hcc_exit(PrevCCE,ActiveCCE,ChPt1), hcc_redo(ActiveCCE,ChPt0,ChPt1,CutTo). '\$cc\$append'([],B,B). '\$cc\$append'([H|A],B,[H|C]) :− '\$cc\$append'(A,B,C).

Fig. 4. Cost center transformation for profiling (at predicate level)

instrumentation procedures introduced by the transformation. For example, the predicate append/3 in Figure 4 is marked as a cost center (left hand side), and, in its transformation (right hand side), it is uniquely renamed to '\$cc\$append'/3. In order to avoid calls to instrumentation procedures along all recursive calls to append/3, the body of the recursive clause of '\$cc\$append'/3 is transformed so that it calls '\$cc\$append'/3 instead of append/3 (this also avoids the destruction of last call optimization.).

A brief description of the instrumentation predicates follows. They operate on the cost center graph. Any edge in such graph (CC-edge in the following), contains the already described (non backtrackable) arrays $Counts[enter][leave]$ and $Ticks[enter][leave]$ (Section 2). An implicit stack whose elements are pairs of CC-edges (variables PrevCCE and ActiveCCE) is used to keep the active CC-edge, and to restore the previous CC-edge when the control flow leaves the active one (so that the precedence of cost centers in the call graph is preserved):

- hcc_call(+Name,+Arity,-PrevCCE,-CutTo): activates the CC-edge whose destination is Name/Arity and origin the destination of the previous CC-edge. Unifies PrevCCE with a pointer to the previous CC-edge. Sets the flag named "*entryport*" (associated to the active CC-edge) to the value "call", in order to track that the predicate Name/Arity has been entered through the call port. Unifies CutTo with a pointer to the top of the current choice point stack.

- hcc_fail(+PrevCCE,-ChPt0): pushes a choice point on the stack in order to execute instrumentation code upon backtracking (after failure occurs), and unifies ChPt0 with a pointer to such choice point. The instrumentation code executed upon backtracking increments by one the value of $Counts[entryport][\texttt{fail}]$ associated to the active CC-edge, [3] and changes the active CC-edge to PrevCCE.

- hcc_exit(+PrevCCE,-ActiveCCE,-ChPt1): increments by one the value of $Counts[entryport][\texttt{exit}]$ associated to the active CC-edge. Unifies ActiveCCE with a pointer to the active CC-edge and ChPt1 with a pointer to the top of the current choice point stack. Changes the active CC-edge to PrevCCE.

- hcc_redo(+ActiveCCE,+ChPt0,+ChPt1,+CutTo): pushes a choice point on the stack to execute instrumentation code upon backtracking. Checks whether

---

[3] Note that the *entryport* flag can take the values call or redo.

ChPt0 and ChPt1 point to the same choice point, in which case the goal is deterministic (i.e., no choice points have been created during its execution), and all choice points up to CutTo are removed (namely, the ones introduced by hcc_fail/2 and hcc_redo/4 itself). The instrumentation code executed upon backtracking sets the "*entryport*" flag (associated to the active CC-edge) to the value "redo," and changes the active CC-edge to ActiveCCE.

Static Cost Center Optimization using CiaoPP. The overhead introduced by the transformation of cost centers described before can be reduced by using static analysis. There are situations where it can be ensured that some of the instrumentation predicates (or combinations of them) introduced by such transformation will never be reached. For example, when a predicate (or literal) marked as a cost center does not introduce choice points, always succeeds, or always fails. Thus, such unreachable instrumentation predicates can be removed. Our profiler detects these situations by using the information inferred by the CiaoPP analyzers [6] (such as non-determinism and non-failure). It also introduces specialized versions for reachable combinations of instrumentation predicates. Although these specialized versions increase the size of the instrumented program, they can significantly reduce the overhead introduced by the profiler. Figure 5 shows (right hand side) some of the optimized cost center transformations (which introduce specialized versions of the instrumentation predicates) performed by using information inferred by CiaoPP analyzers, that is expressed as assertions (left hand side).

Assertion	Specialized Cost Center Transformation
:− **true pred** Goal + (**no_choicepoint**, **not_fails**).	hcc_call_ncnf(Name, Arity, PrevCCE), call(Goal), hcc_exit_ncnf(PrevCCE).
:− **true pred** Goal + **no_choicepoint**.	hcc_call(Name, Arity, PrevCCE, CutTo), hcc_fail_nc(PrevCCE), call(Goal), hcc_exit_nc(PrevCCE, CutTo).
:− **true pred** Goal + **not_fails**.	hcc_call_nf(Name, Arity, PrevCCE, CutTo), call(Goal), hcc_exit(PrevCCE, ActiveCCE, ChPt1), hcc_redo_nf(ActiveCCE, ChPt1, CutTo).

Fig. 5. Cost center transformation optimization

Enriching Information with Low-level Profiling. We set up several hooks at some relevant points in the engine. Their implementation is located in a separate module. To avoid run-time overhead, such hooks are made available by compiling the engine with an option that enables them. For example, there are hooks that are called when a fail causes the next choice point to be tried (lph_fail_redo(wam)), when a cut is executed (lph_cut(wam)), and when a given predicate pred is called (lph_exit_call(wam, pred), where the variable wam is a structure that represents the current state of the virtual machine). Such hooks remain uninstantiated until the procedure profile/1 is used over a given goal, in which case they are instantiated to actual functions that perform the profiling itself. The end of the profiling leaves the hooks uninstantiated again. When performing low-level profiling, each edge of the cost center graph contains the following (non backtrackable) data structures: (1) the already described ones used in high-level profiling; (2) two matrices, $Cuts[enter][leave]$ and $SCuts[enter][leave]$, that keep the number of cut executions that remove or do not remove choice points respectively (which allows for example detecting useless pruning operations and checking that a cut actually prunes branches); and (3) a hash table used to track the execution of predicates. The key of each entry in the table is a predicate name/arity, and its fields are: (a) two matrices similar to the already described $Counts[enter][leave]$ and $Ticks[enter][leave]$), but referred to "predicate heads," and (b) a counter ($Skips$) to keep the number of choice points that are removed for that predicate by some pruning operator (cut) execution.

The low-level profiling allows tracking information on predicates that have not been marked as cost centers (e.g., library predicates), and therefore, to detect that certain low-level or library predicates are being used by our program without us being aware (which could happen if syntactic expansions are used). It also allows detecting backtracking in predicate heads (useful to detect predicates that do not succeed in the first clause, or that are not indexed by the first argument).

6   Automatic Performance Bottleneck Detection

Defining cost centers by hand in order to detect performance bottlenecks is a time-consuming task. As mentioned before, one of the original features of our profiling tool is a method for identifying performance bottlenecks in an automatic way, which uses an iterative process that defines cost centers at each iteration. For space reasons, we give a high-level description of the algorithm and refer the reader to [11] for details and examples. The method provides the sub-graph (a tree in fact) of the cost center graph that is responsible for the performance leak. It can be applied to modular programs and allows providing a list of modules whose predicates must be taken into account. The input call graph to the method is dynamically constructed (defining cost centers for all predicates in the selected modules, and executing once with profiling activated).

Starting with the initial goal as the current predicate, at each iteration the children of the current predicate in the call graph (i.e., its called predicates) are computed. They and *the previous cost centers* in the current branch of the cost center graph (including the current predicate), are marked as cost centers. Then, the goal is profiled, and, after that, the set of cost centers called by the current predicate and the amount of resource that each one consumes are computed. To ensure termination, any predicate previously defined as a cost center (including the current predicate) is removed from this set. If after this removal there are no cost centers left in the set, then the process finishes returning the graph built so far. Otherwise, it selects the relevant cost centers of the called cost centers set, according to a heuristic (which is a parameter of the method), provided by the user. Some examples of heuristic selection rules are: (1) select the N predicates that consume more resources, (2) select the ones whose resource consumption is larger than a given percentage of the total resource usage, or (3) select the predicates whose number is not larger than a percentage X of the number of program predicates, and which together consume a percentage of the total resource usage greater than a given bound Y. Independently of the heuristic used, a given predicate is selected at most once (and thus, the sub-graph returned is a tree).

We have also developed a method for drawing automatically the sub-graph of the cost center graph that is responsible for the performance leak, where different colors and sizes are used to express the accumulated resource usage in each cost center.

7 Experimental Results

We have performed an experimental assessment of our profiler. The results are shown in Table 1 for two different platforms with different processors and OS: an **Intel** Core i7, 4 cores x 2.67GHz (2 threads per core), 12GB of RAM, Ubuntu Linux 10.10 (kernel 2.6.35) and an Ultra**Sparc**-T1, 8 cores x 1GHz (4 threads per core), 8GB of RAM, SunOS 5.10. In both platforms, the execution has been *locked* to a single core in order to avoid erroneous execution time measurements. The profiler measures execution times using a high-resolution timer, which allows giving relevant values in situations where other methods would get a zero value. The first and second columns of the table show the benchmarks used[4] and the number of predicates defined in them respectively. For each platform, the Obs column shows the observed execution time without profiling (given in milliseconds). The following two columns grouped under (Est.Dev.) are meant to assess the accuracy of our profiler in monitoring execution times. They show the ratio between the execution time estimated by the profiler and Obs for two levels of profiling instrumentation: hl, which only performs the high level source-to-source transformation, and ll, which besides performing this transformation, also introduces hooks in the engine (i.e., it also performs low-level profiling). The columns grouped under Bot.D. refer to the automatic performance bottleneck detection process (described in Section 6), where the performance is measured in terms of execution time, the heuristic of selecting the goal with the largest execution time in each iteration has been followed, and the profiling has been performed without engine hooks (since they do not improve execution time measurements). Column #it shows the number of iterations needed to complete such process, and column ov_b shows its overhead, calculated as $ov_b = \frac{T_{tot} - T_{pr} - T_{co}}{\#it \times Obs}$, where the total time due to executing the program with profiling ($T_{pr} = \sum_{i=1}^{\#it} Prof_i$) and the total time due to its compilation ($T_{co} = \sum_{i=1}^{\#it} Comp_i$) have been subtracted from the total time (T_{tot}) in order to isolate the time due to the bottleneck detection process itself. Averages are also provided in the last row of the table.[5]

The columns under Profiling Ov. relate to the run-time overhead introduced by the different program transformations/instrumentations described in Section 5. They are grouped into two sub-columns, showing the results when the instrumentation has been optimized using CiaoPP's static analyzers (Optim.), and without such optimization (N.Op.). In both cases we present the results with (ll) and without (hl) engine hooks activated respectively. The overheads

---

[4] Source code for the examples is available at http://www.clip.dia.fi.upm.es/profiling/

[5] Weighted average taking the observed execution time as weight in all cases.

Table 1. Experimental assessment of the profiler

Program	# P.	Intel									Sparc								
		Obs (ms)	Est. Dev.		Bot.D.		Profiling Ov.				Obs (ms)	Est. Dev.		Bot.D.		Profiling Ov.			
							Optim.		N.Op.							Optim.		N.Op.	
			hl	ll	# it	ov$_b$ (%)	hl	ll	hl	ll		hl	ll	# it	ov$_b$ (%)	hl	ll	hl	ll
mem	5	67	1.0	1.4	4	2.40	1.0	4.6	1.0	4.6	377	1.0	1.4	4	4.65	1.0	7.8	1.0	7.8
guardians	9	182	1.0	1.6	4	0.95	1.0	3.8	1.0	3.8	959	1.0	1.3	4	1.31	1.0	6.1	1.0	6.1
color_map	5	99	1.0	1.8	2	1.26	1.0	4.3	1.0	4.3	558	1.0	1.3	2	2.24	1.0	6.4	1.0	6.4
bignums	4	102	1.0	2.4	3	1.46	1.0	2.6	1.0	2.6	2178	1.0	1.0	3	0.33	1.0	1.1	1.0	1.1
wumpus	65	211	1.0	1.6	4	1.53	1.0	5.6	1.0	5.6	1018	1.0	1.7	4	1.56	1.0	11.4	1.0	11.4
solve_jugs	6	255	1.0	1.6	4	0.52	1.0	4.0	1.0	4.0	1237	1.0	1.5	4	0.98	1.0	7.1	1.0	7.1
qsort	4	76	1.1	2.1	3	1.82	1.3	6.3	1.3	6.3	402	1.1	2.2	3	1.46	1.4	10.5	1.5	10.6
sudoku	12	72	1.3	1.7	7	2.42	1.5	5.3	1.6	5.6	359	1.2	1.5	7	4.44	1.7	8.7	1.8	9.4
zebra	5	40	1.3	1.5	3	3.53	1.5	5.7	1.5	5.7	184	1.4	1.4	3	7.16	1.9	10.6	1.9	10.6
hanoi	3	128	1.2	1.9	3	1.12	1.6	8.3	2.1	9.6	665	1.2	1.7	3	1.57	1.9	14.6	2.4	16.9
flat	4	65	1.5	1.8	4	2.41	2.9	10.0	4.2	14.2	323	1.5	1.6	4	2.54	3.8	17.2	5.4	24.7
substitute	3	187	2.0	2.3	3	0.71	2.9	12.7	2.9	12.6	1102	2.0	2.0	3	0.51	3.4	19.6	3.4	19.7
queens	16	92	2.0	2.2	6	1.79	3.1	15.7	3.1	15.7	429	2.3	1.9	6	4.30	4.4	28.4	4.4	28.4
Average		121	1.2	1.8	3	1.34	1.5	6.7	1.6	7.0	753	1.2	1.5	3	1.59	1.6	9.5	1.7	10.0

(ll and hl) are given as a ratio $\frac{Prof}{Obs}$, where $Prof$ refers to the execution time when the profiler is activated, with the cost centers assigned by the automatic bottleneck detection process reported in the columns grouped under Bot.D. (the number of selected cost centers is #it −1), and Obs is the value in the third column described before. The overhead ratio hl is very close to 1 (i.e., almost no overhead is introduced) for the first six programs in the table, while it is larger for the rest. This is because the latter perform recursive calls between cost centers. As expected, the overhead ratios (for both platforms) grow as we increase the degree of information that we want to obtain from the profiler.

It can be argued that the overhead introduced by our profiler is small for a reasonable level of profiling information, and that global static analysis indeed reduces such overhead. Interestingly, if we compare our results with those reported in [16] (which is the closest related previous work that we are aware of for which there is available data, although applied to imperative programs), the overheads of the hl columns under Profiling Ov./Optim. are of similar magnitude to those reported therein: 2.95 in the worst case, while in our results the worst overhead for the Intel platform is 3.1 (queens). However, our approach provides a richer (and more detailed) variety data.

8 Discussion and Future Work

Since its development our profiler has proved to be quite useful in practice by identifying the root causes of performance bottlenecks in several complex, real-life situations. For example, it was the key for identifying a difficult to locate performance bug in the (Ciao) CHR implementation (a complex and relatively large piece of code): a dereferencing chain for the attribute of a variable was constructed, instead of modifying the value of the attribute. Thus, the time needed for getting the value of such attribute was directly proportional to the number of times that the attribute was modified. Our profiler has also been successfully applied to resource-aware poly-controlled partial evaluation [13]. This technique combines different control strategies to obtain optimizations that cannot be obtained using a single control technique. Once the optimizations have been obtained they are compared using some values (called *fitness values*). Our implementation has been successfully used for estimating such values.

Note that in some cases, bottlenecks can only be detected using the fine-grain information provided by our low-level profiling (via engine hooks). For example, assume that we have a read-only library which is responsible for lack of performance. In this case we are unable to define cost centers on it to perform high-level profiling. Alternatively, we can activate the engine hooks to track information about all the subroutines invoked in such library, and use it to diagnose the performance problem. Engine hooks can also profile more properties, like the number of cut executions that remove (or do not remove) choice points, failures during head unification, or choice points removed for a given predicate (see Section 5).

Although our profiler already supports several computational properties and events, these are predefined. However, as future work, it should be straightforward to extend it to allow measuring user-defined resources, in the sense of the static resource analysis currently integrated in the `CiaoPP` framework [12].

Acknowledgments. This research has been partially funded by the EU 7th. FP NoE *S-Cube* 215483, FET IST-231620 *HATS*, MICINN TIN-2008-05624 *DOVES* and CM project P2009/TIC/1465 *PROMETIDOS*. Teresa Trigo has been supported by CAM grant CPI/0621/2008.

References

1. Brassel, B., Hanus, M., Huch, F., Silva, J., Vidal, G.: Run-Time Profiling of Functional Logic Programs. In: Etalle, S. (ed.) LOPSTR 2004. LNCS, vol. 3573, pp. 182–197. Springer, Heidelberg (2005)
2. Byrd, L.: Understanding the Control Flow of Prolog Programs. In: Tärnlund, S.-A. (ed.) Proceedings of the 1980 Logic Programming Workshop, Debrecen, Hungary, pp. 127–138 (July 1980)
3. Debray, S.K.: Profiling Prolog Programs. Software Practice and Experience 18(9), 821–839 (1983)
4. Ducassé, M., Noyé, J.: Tracing Prolog Programs by Source Instrumentation is Efficient Enough. Journal of Logic Programming 43, 157–172 (2000)
5. Graham, S.L., Kessler, P.B., Mckusick, M.K.: Gprof: a Call Graph Execution Profiler. In: SIGPLAN 1982: Proc. of the 1982 SIGPLAN Symp. on Compiler Construction, pp. 120–126. ACM, New York (1982)
6. Hermenegildo, M., Puebla, G., Bueno, F., López-García, P.: Integrated Program Debugging, Verification, and Optimization Using Abstract Interpretation (and The Ciao System Preprocessor). Science of Computer Programming 58(1-2), 115–140 (2005)
7. Kazi, I.H., Jose, D.P., Ben-Hamida, B., Hescott, C.J., Kwok, C., Konstan, J.A., Lilja, D.J., Yew, P.-C.: JaViz: A Client/Server Java Profiling Tool. IBM Syst. J. 39(1), 96–117 (2000)

8. López-García, P., Darmawan, L., Bueno, F.: A Framework for Verification and Debugging of Resource Usage Properties. In: Technical Communications of ICLP. LIPIcs, vol. 7, pp. 104–113. Schloss Dagstuhl (July 2010)
9. Matos, A.B.: A matrix model for the flow of control in prolog programs with applications to profiling. Software Practice and Experience 24(8), 729–746 (1994)
10. Mera, E., López-García, P., Hermenegildo, M.: Integrating Software Testing and Run-Time Checking in an Assertion Verification Framework. In: Hill, P.M., Warren, D.S. (eds.) ICLP 2009. LNCS, vol. 5649, pp. 281–295. Springer, Heidelberg (2009)
11. Mera, E., Trigo, T., López-García, P., Hermenegildo, M.: An Approach to Profiling for Run-Time Checking of Computational Properties and Performance Debugging. Technical Report CLIP3/2010.0, Technical University of Madrid (UPM), School of Computer Science, UPM (March 2010)
12. Navas, J., Mera, E., López-García, P., Hermenegildo, M.: User-Definable Resource Bounds Analysis for Logic Programs. In: Dahl, V., Niemelä, I. (eds.) ICLP 2007. LNCS, vol. 4670, pp. 348–363. Springer, Heidelberg (2007)
13. Ochoa, C., Puebla, G.: Poly-Controlled Partial Evaluation in Practice. In: ACM Partial Evaluation and Program Manipulation (PEPM 2007), pp. 164–173. ACM Press, New York (2007)
14. Jarvis, S.A., Morgan, R.G.: Profiling large-scale lazy functional programs. Journal of Functional Programing 8(3), 201–237 (1998)
15. Sansom, P.M., Peyton Jones, S.L.: Formally Based Profiling for Higher-Order Functional Languages. ACM Transactions on Programming Languages and Systems 19(2), 334–385 (1997)
16. Spivey, J.M.: Fast, accurate call graph profiling. Software Practice and Experience 34(3), 249–264 (2004)

Plato: A Compiler for Interactive Web Forms

Timothy L. Hinrichs

University of Chicago

Abstract. Modern web forms interact with the user in real-time by detecting errors and filling-in implied values, which in terms of automated reasoning amounts to SAT solving and theorem proving. This paper presents PLATO, a compiler that automatically generates web forms that detect errors and fill-in implied values from declarative web form descriptions. Instead of writing HTML and JavaScript directly, web developers write an ontology in classical logic that describes the relationships between web form fields, and PLATO automatically generates HTML to display the form and browser scripts to implement the requisite SAT solving and theorem proving. We discuss PLATO's design and implementation and evaluate PLATO's performance both analytically and empirically.

1 Introduction

Modern web forms, implemented using a combination of HTML and browser scripts (*e.g.*, JavaScript, Flash, Silverlight), solicit information from users on the World Wide Web. While many web forms are simple to build and maintain, the trend toward interactive web forms has significantly complicated web form development. For example, web forms are now routinely used as a platform for configuration management applications, which help users explore the permissible combinations of components for complex systems, *e.g.*, for a personal computer the processor, hard drive, and memory.

The two types of web-form interactions studied in this paper both occur each time the user changes the web form data: identifying errors and computing implied values. An error arises when the user data conflicts with the intended semantics of the web form, *e.g.*, a credit card's expiration date must be in the future, but the user entered a date in the past. Errors are often highlighted for the user in red. An implied value arises when all possible error-free completions of the form assign a specific value to a specific form field. Implied values are usually filled-in for the user automatically.

Browser scripts that detect errors and compute implied values are difficult to write because, in general, error-detection amounts to SAT solving (SAT), and implied value computation amounts to theorem proving (TP), *e.g.*, [32, 22]. Of course, not all error-detection/implied-value scripts implement the full machinery of SAT/TP; rather, the scripts for each form embody the fragment of SAT/TP necessary to address the form at hand. Conceptually, error-detection and implied-value scripts specialize SAT and TP algorithms to the web form's semantics. The specialization process, however, is error-prone and the resulting scripts can be difficult to maintain.

To complicate matters further, traditional TP is inadequate for computing implied values because web form errors amount to inconsistencies. Recall that in traditional TP an inconsistent premise set implies everything; hence, with traditional TP, all values would be implied for all web form fields anytime a single error was present. Instead,

R. Rocha and J. Launchbury (Eds.): PADL 2011, LNCS 6539, pp. 54–68, 2011.

implied values are computed using paraconsistent TP: where an inconsistent premise set does not necessarily imply every possible conclusion. Thus, in addition to specializing SAT/TP algorithms to implement error-detection/implied-value scripts, the web developer must choose an appropriate version of paraconsistent TP.

Techniques that can be applied to simplify web form construction and maintenance have been investigated by researchers in web engineering [33, 34, 30, 6], computer security [31, 8] formal methods [9], programming languages [19, 18, 5, 26, 10, 17], databases [7, 14], artificial intelligence [20, 23, 22], and configuration management [32, 28, 27, 1]. Most of the related work either prohibits web form users from causing errors or forces web form developers to define a paraconsistent version of implication by dictating which direction implied values can propagate (*e.g.*, through the syntax for form descriptions, through priorities, or by requiring web form fields to be structured hierarchically). Techniques that disallow errors are obviously inadequate for forms that allow errors, and forcing developers to dictate the direction implied values propagate results in forms where, for reasons unknown to the user, values only propagate in certain ways. Three notable exceptions [32, 22, 20] allow errors and utilize omni-directional versions of paraconsistent implication; however, [32] advocates approximate SAT/TP algorithms whose accuracy is unknown and [22] details only semantic definitions (for the special case where all form fields have a single value) without algorithmic results. The algorithms in [20] are the starting point for the work reported here; we have applied and tailored them to the web form domain and qualitatively improved their performance.

In this paper we describe PLATO, a tool that automatically constructs web forms from declarative descriptions provided by the web developer. Instead of writing HTML and browser scripts directly, the developer writes an ontology in classical logic that captures the constraints the web form data must satisfy. PLATO then compiles the ontology to (i) a SAT implementation customized to the ontology, (ii) a paraconsistent TP also customized to the ontology, and (iii) an HTML page that displays the form, highlights errors, and automatically fills-in implied values omni-directionally. The compilation process centers around the well-known resolution algorithm and utilizes an ontology-compression pre-processor to produce speed-ups of several orders of magnitude.

This paper is organized as follows. We begin with an example and our approach (Section 2). Our technical contributions, summarized below, follow.

– We report novel computational complexity results for a paraconsistent version of implication over a particular logical ontology language: the quantifier-free, function-free monadic fragment of first-order logic. (Section 3)
– We introduce the first compiler for web forms that generates error-detection and implied-value code specialized to the web form's ontology, outline its architecture, and discuss the challenges it addresses. (Section 4)
– We tailor and enhance existing compilation algorithms [20] to the web form problem. In particular, we introduce a compression algorithm that produces speed-ups of 10^5. (Section 5)
– We report the complexity for our algorithms, identify a special case for which our algorithms are optimal, and empirically evaluate our approach. (Section 6)

Subsequently, we report on related work (Section 7) and conclude (Section 8). Proofs have been omitted for lack of space but are available in the associated technical report.

2   Overview

Example. Figure 1 depicts a web form soliciting (a portion of) shipping and billing addresses for an e-commerce website. Notice that the shipping address is set to ⟨Chicago, Illinois⟩ and that the form includes a checkbox that indicates the shipping and billing addresses should be the same. If the user checks the checkbox, the form automatically copies ⟨Chicago, Illinois⟩ to the billing address. Had the user set the billing address instead of the shipping address, checking the checkbox would have propagated values in the opposite direction, exemplifying omni-directional implied value propagation.

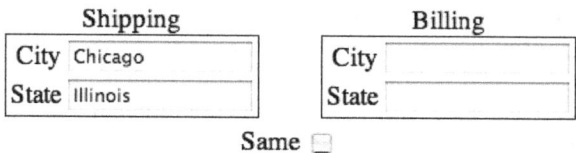

Fig. 1. Example web form

Starting with ⟨Chicago, Illinois⟩ for the shipping address and an empty billing address, suppose the user checks the checkbox, causing the form to fill-in ⟨Chicago, Illinois⟩ for the billing address. Now, suppose the user enters San Francisco for the billing city, thereby overriding the Chicago that was automatically filled-in. An error occurs because the two cities, Chicago and San Francisco, are supposed to be the same but are not. Without deleting one of three pieces of user-supplied data (Chicago, San Francisco, or the checkmark), there is no way to repair the error; hence, the form simply highlights the error for the user.

Approach. Traditionally, developers build such web forms by writing HTML to display the widgets and browser scripts to detect/highlight errors and compute/fill-in implied values. With PLATO, the developer provides a logical ontology describing the constraints the user-supplied data must satisfy (in addition to information about the display and range of permissible values for each field), and PLATO generates the corresponding HTML and browser scripts automatically.

For the example above, the developer provides PLATO with the following sentence that encodes the semantics of the checkbox. Below $Scity$ denotes the shipping address city, $Sstate$ the shipping state, $Bcity$ and $Bstate$ the billing city and state, and $same$ the checkbox. PLATO then generates the form described above.

$$same \Rightarrow \left(\bigwedge \begin{array}{c} Scity(x) \Leftrightarrow Bcity(x) \\ Sstate(x) \Leftrightarrow Bstate(x) \end{array} \right)$$

3   Logical Foundations of Web Forms

Here we give the logical foundations of web forms, errors, and implied values, and analyze the computational complexity of paraconsistent implication.

Fundamentally, the information web forms solicit from users is a set of key-value pairs[1]. Keys (form field names) are drawn from some predefined set F, and values are strings from some character set Σ (*e.g.*, Latin-1 or UTF-8). A web form submission, which we call a *payload*, is represented mathematically as a finite subset of $F \times \Sigma^*$. Logically, a payload is a set of sentences of the form $f(v)$ where $f \in F$ and $v \in \Sigma^*$. For example, the payload shown in Figure 1 is represented logically as $\{Scity(Chicago), Sstate(Illinois)\}$.

A server receiving a web form payload only accepts certain kinds of payloads, *e.g.*, those where the credit card's expiration date is in the future; all others are rejected. Mathematically, the set of *acceptable* payloads is simply a specific set of payloads, *i.e.*, a set of finite subsets of $F \times \Sigma^*$. Logically, the acceptable payloads correspond to the models satisfying a logical ontology.

In this paper we study a simple, first-order ontology language: monadic, quantifier-free, equality-free first-order logic. More precisely, the terms in our language are variables and object constants. Atoms take the form $p(t)$ where p is a predicate and t is a (single) term. Sentences are either atoms or $\{\wedge, \vee, \neg, \Rightarrow, \Leftarrow, \Leftrightarrow\}$ applied to sentences in the usual way. All variables are implicitly universally quantified. MON denotes all such sentences, and an ontology is a consistent subset of MON. The semantics are standard.

Web forms detect errors each time the user enters or edits data. A web form error arises whenever the current payload cannot be extended to an acceptable payload. Mathematically, a payload is *consistent* if it is a subset of some acceptable payload. All other payloads are *inconsistent*. A payload is *minimally inconsistent* if it is inconsistent and none of its subsets are inconsistent. There is one *error* in a payload for every minimally inconsistent subset contained within it. Logically, Λ is a consistent payload if it is logically consistent with the ontology Δ.

Web forms also fill-in implied values for the user automatically. For consistent payloads, implication is defined as usual. Suppose Δ is the web form ontology, and Λ is a consistent payload. The key-value pair $f(v)$ is positively implied by Λ with respect to Δ, written $\Lambda \models^\Delta f(v)$, if $f(v)$ belongs to every consistent superset of Λ. The key-value pair $f(v)$ is negatively implied, written $\Lambda \models^\Delta \neg f(v)$ if $f(v)$ belongs to no consistent superset of Λ.

Note that the above definition for implication is restricted to consistent payloads. When applied to an inconsistent payload (*i.e.*, a payload with errors), the definition results in all key-value pairs being both positively and negatively implied. Thus, for inconsistent payloads we say that a key-value pair is implied whenever there is a consistent fragment of the payload that implies the pair. Formally, an inconsistent Λ implies $f(v)$, written $\Lambda \models^\Delta_E f(v)$, if there is a consistent $\Lambda_0 \subseteq \Lambda$ such that $\Lambda_0 \models^\Delta f(v)$; likewise, $\Lambda \models^\Delta_E \neg f(v)$ if there is a consistent $\Lambda_0 \subseteq \Lambda$ such that $\Lambda_0 \models^\Delta \neg f(v)$.

Though strict implication was studied previously [22, 20], its computational complexity was unknown. Below we show that as long as $P \neq NP$, the optimal algorithm is singly exponential, even with a number of strong restrictions. More positively, we show that if the size of the ontology is constant, strict impliciation is in included in P because it is included in LOGSPACE and AC^0.

---

[1] HTML 4.01 form specification: http://www.w3.org/TR/html401/interact/forms.html

Theorem 1 (Strict Implication Complexity). *Suppose Δ is in* MON, *and Λ is a finite set of ground atoms. $\Lambda \models_E^\Delta p(a)$ is Π_2^P-hard and included in Σ_3^P. If the number of variables appearing in Δ is bounded by a constant, strict implication is both Σ_1^P- (NP-) and Π_1^P- (coNP-) hard and is included in Σ_2^P. If Δ is in clausal form, contains a single variable, and includes no object constants, strict implication is Π_1^P- (coNP-) hard. If Δ is of constant size, $\Lambda \models_E^\Delta p(a)$ is included in AC^0.*

Proof. (Sketch) For the polynomial hierarchy results, the inclusion proofs are straight-forward: guess a subset of Λ_0 (contributing an existential quantifier) and check if all models (contributing a universal quantifier) satisfy $\forall^*\Delta \Rightarrow p(a)$. (Since the language is monadic, each model is polynomial in the size of the signature.) If the number of variables is bounded by a constant, the check for satisfaction does not contribute a quantifier; otherwise, checking the satisfaction of $\exists^*\neg\Delta \lor p(a)$ (which is equivalent to the implication above) requires an additional existential quantifier.

For the polynomial hierarchy hardness proofs, we first show that strict implication is at least as hard as the well-known existential entailment. Then we embed the satisfiabil-ity of $\forall^*\exists^*.\phi$ into existential entailment over MON, where ϕ is monadic, quantifier-free, equality-free, function-free (which is Π_2^P-hard). For the restrictions, we embed both satisfiability and unsatisfiability of propositional logic.

For the AC^0 result, suppose Δ is of constant size. Slight modifications to the algo-rithms presented in this paper construct database queries by analyzing just Δ (which are therefore of constant size) that when evaluated over Λ compute strict implication. Since database query evaluation is included in AC^0 when the size of the queries is a constant, strict implication is included in AC^0. □

4   PLATO

PLATO is a tool that generates fully-functional web forms that provide real-time user feedback about errors (minimal inconsistencies) and implied values (strict implication). Below we discuss the high-level opportunities, challenges, and design decisions that lead to PLATO and follow up with PLATO's architecture. We describe PLATO's algo-rithms in Section 5.

4.1   Opportunities, Challenges, and Design Decisions

PLATO's design was dictated by two desires: (i) to provide users with a fast, powerful interface for entering web form data and (ii) to provide web developers with simple tools for constructing and maintaining such web forms. We begin by discussing the problem of programming the web browser to compute implied values.

Theorem proving versus knowledge compilation. Conceptually, the simplest way for the web browser to compute implied values is with a paraconsistent theorem prover written in JavaScript that takes as input the ontology, the current web form data, and a query. This approach fails to leverage a powerful property of the web form domain: the ontology is fixed for the lifetime of the form. Hundreds or thousands of users might all use the same form and in so doing pose millions of queries, all over the same ontology.

An implementation that analyzes the ontology anew for each query will repeat the same work over and over. Moreover, the computational complexity of implication when the ontology is fixed is strictly less than the complexity when it is not (see Theorem 1).

To leverage the static nature of the ontology, PLATO employs knowledge compilation [11] to construct JavaScript code that implements a paraconsistent theorem prover specialized to the given ontology. Intuitively, the manipulation of the ontology, which would normally happen at run time, happens at compile time, and the resulting code avoids performing that work for each query.

Compiling ontologies to JavaScript. Without errors, strict implication coincides with traditional implication; hence, constructing a theorem prover for paraconsistent implication specialized to a given ontology implicitly involves constructing a specialized theorem prover for traditional implication. Specializing a theorem prover for traditional implication requires generating JavaScript code that answers implication queries about that ontology. Despite the fact that an ontology can be interpreted as a set of boolean conditionals, this task is difficult because JavaScript and classical logic use disjunction differently. In JavaScript, once p and q are assigned values, p $||$ q is a query asking if either p or q (or both) is true; in contrast, in classical logic, $p \vee q$ is akin to an assignment that makes p or q (or both) true without specifying which.

To address this challenge, PLATO decomposes the compilation of an ontology to JavaScript into two steps: compiling the ontology to database queries and compiling those database queries into JavaScript. Database queries are a useful intermediary because the database and JavaScript meanings of disjunction are the same, and techniques for translating database evaluation to imperative code are well-known [25].

Traditional implication to paraconsistent implication. A compiler for traditional implication that generates database queries can easily be adapted to strict implication: augment each database query with an auxiliary consistency-checking query that ensures the data used to answer the original query is consistent with the ontology. The problem is that if the queries are evaluated top-down, the same consistency checks may be executed repeatedly; similarly, if the consistency checks are evaluated bottom-up, many irrelevant consistency checks might be computed.

While standard techniques such as memoization and magic sets are applicable, PLATO utilizes the fact that the web forms it generates always maintain a list of errors, *i.e.*, a list of minimally inconsistent data sets. Consistency can then be checked with special-purpose code that detects whether a given data set contains no errors.

4.2 Architecture

PLATO's architecture is shown in Figure 2. The web developer provides an ontology and the set of web form field predicates (along with display and typing information about those predicates). The Classical Compiler constructs database queries that compute minimal inconsistencies and strict implication when evaluated over a web form payload. The Database Compiler then translates those queries into JavaScript code, which is then embedded in the HTML produced by the HTML Generator.

The novel component of PLATO, the Classical Compiler, solves two conceptually distinct problems: database-query generation for error-detection and database-query

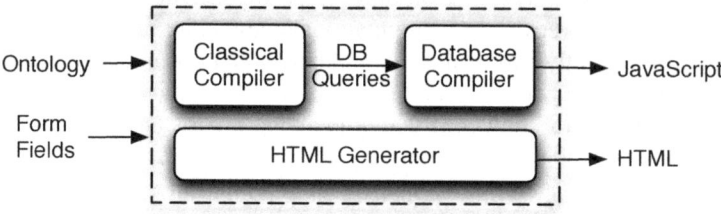

Fig. 2. PLATO architecture

generation for implied-values. However, our solutions to the two problems are almost identical; hence, we focus on the more complex of the two: implied-values.

Formally, the implied-value problem the compiler addresses closely resembles the notation we use for strict implication: $\Lambda \models_E^\Delta f(v)$. Given an ontology Δ, the compiler must compute database queries that implement $\models_E^\Delta$, i.e., when given a web form payload (the database), the queries must answer strict implication questions with respect to the ontology Δ. To simplify the exposition and proofs, we utilize the well-known equivalence of evaluating database queries on a database and evaluating first-order formulae on an interpretation.

Definition 1 (Web Form Constraint Compiler). *A web form constraint compiler is a function α that maps an ontology and a set of predicates to a set of first-order formulae. α is a compiler if for any ontology Δ, predicate set F, and predicate $f \in F$, there are sentences $\phi_f^+(x)$ and $\phi_f^-(x)$ in $\alpha[\Delta, F]$ such that for any payload Λ and any $v \in \Sigma^*$,*

$$\Lambda \models_E^\Delta f(v) \text{ if and only if } \models_\Lambda \phi_f^+(v) \text{ and}$$
$$\Lambda \models_E^\Delta \neg f(v) \text{ if and only if } \models_\Lambda \phi_f^-(v)$$

5   Algorithms

Here we explain the difficulty of compiling classical logic to database queries for error-detection and then discuss algorithms for strict implication and minimal inconsistency.

The naïve conversion of a classical ontology to database queries for detecting errors is straightforward: convert the ontology to conjunctive normal form, and treat each of the resulting clauses as a database query. For example, below is a simple ontology and the corresponding database (or logic programming) queries.

Ontology	Database Queries
$p(x) \Rightarrow q(x)$	$error :- p(x) \wedge \neg q(x)$
$q(x) \Rightarrow \neg r(x)$	$error :- q(x) \wedge r(x)$

This conversion fails to preserve the semantics of the ontology because classical logic uses the open world assumption, but databases use the closed world assumption (CWA); thus, classical logic allows form fields to be unknown, but databases require every form field value to be either true or false.

The queries above are unsound for the payload $\{p(a)\}$, *i.e.*, where p is assigned a and both q and r unknown. To see this, notice that the first database query evaluates to true, thereby signaling an error, because the CWA deems $\neg q(a)$ true; however, the payload is consistent with the ontology. Such errors can be eliminated by only evaluating queries whose form fields are all known.

Assuming the only evaluated queries are those with known form fields, the queries above are incomplete for the payload $\{p(a), r(a)\}$ (where q is unknown). Neither of the database queries above can be evaluated because both rely on q, an unknown value, yet the payload is inconsistent with the ontology. Such incompleteness can be eliminated by accounting for the interaction of the constraints.

PLATO's compilation algorithms expand the ontology to take constraint interaction into account. Whenever an error or implied value arises, the expanded ontology includes a single constraint that detects it without any unknown form fields. For the example above, PLATO generates an additional query: $error :- p(x) \lor r(x)$.

This example also illustrates an inadequacy of today's HTML forms: without using additional fields or special values, there is no way to differentiate selecting zero values for a field and leaving that field unknown. Both are communicated to the server in the same way. Currently, PLATO treats a field with zero values as unknown.

5.1 Strict Implication

PLATO's basic algorithm for constructing database queries implementing strict implication is a five-step process: compute the resolution closure of the web form ontology, compute the contrapositives of each clause in the closure, eliminate all rules with negation in the body, augment each contrapositive with a consistency check, and invoke predicate completion.

We illustrate with the ontology from above: $(\neg p(x) \lor q(x)) \land (\neg q(x) \lor \neg r(x))$. The resolution closure adds a single clause: $p(x) \lor \neg r(x)$. Computing the contrapositives, eliminating rules with negation in the body, and appending consistency checks is straightforward and produces the following rules.

$$q(x) \Leftarrow p(x) \land consistent_{p(x)}(x)$$
$$\neg q(x) \Leftarrow r(x) \land consistent_{r(x)}(x)$$
$$\neg r(x) \Leftarrow q(x) \land consistent_{q(x)}(x)$$
$$\neg p(x) \Leftarrow r(x) \land consistent_{r(x)}(x)$$
$$\neg r(x) \Leftarrow p(x) \land consistent_{p(x)}(x)$$

The consistency checks ensure that witnesses for implication are consistent with the entire ontology.

Definition 2 (*consistent*$_{\phi(\bar{x})}$ [20]). *For the ontology Δ and sentence $\phi(\bar{x})$, consistent*$_{\phi(\bar{x})}(\bar{t})$ *is true if and only if $\{\phi(\bar{t})\} \cup \Delta$ is consistent.*

Predicate completion then constructs the first-order formula defining strict implication for each signed predicate ρ: the disjunction of all the rules with ρ in the head.

$$\phi_q^+(x) \equiv p(x) \land consistent_{p(x)}(x)$$
$$\phi_q^-(x) \equiv r(x) \land consistent_{r(x)}(x)$$

$$\phi_r^-(x) \equiv (q(x) \wedge consistent_{q(x)}(x)) \vee (p(x) \wedge consistent_{p(x)}(x))$$
$$\phi_p^-(x) \equiv r(x) \wedge consistent_{r(x)}(x)$$
$$\bot \equiv \phi_p^+(x) \equiv \phi_r^+(x)$$

This basic algorithm is easy to implement, though there are obvious efficiency problems with computing the resolution closure. To mitigate the expense of resolution, PLATO first compresses the ontology. Consider the following example.

Ontology	Compression
$p(a) \wedge q(b) \wedge r(c)$ $\vee$ $p(b) \wedge q(d) \wedge r(e)$ $p(d) \wedge q(c) \wedge r(a)$	$p(x) \wedge q(y) \wedge r(z) \Rightarrow t(x,y,z)$ $t(a,b,c)$ $t(b,d,e)$ $t(d,c,a)$

The ontology on the left lists the possible combinations of p, q, and r in disjunctive normal form. The compression on the right represents the ontology as a single constraint over p, q, and r together with a new predicate t and a database table defining t's semantics as the permitted combinations of p, q, and r. Importantly, the database table t is not included when the resolution closure is computed; rather, it is treated as part of the database representing the web form data. Instead of computing the closure of 28 clauses, PLATO computes the closure of 1 clause; the drawback is that the 1 clause is not monadic because of $t(x, y, z)$.

Algorithm 1, named IMPLCOMPILE, formalizes the algorithm outlined here.

Algorithm 1. IMPLCOMPILE $[\Delta, F]$

Outputs: A set of first-order equivalences.
1: $\Delta := \text{RES}[\text{COMPRESS}[\Delta]]$
2: $\Gamma_p^s := \emptyset$ for all predicates $p \in F$ and all $s \in \{+, -\}$
3: **for all** contrapositives d in $\bigcup_{p \in F} \{p(x) \vee \neg p(x)\} \cup \Delta$ **do**
4:     write d as $\pm p(x) \Leftarrow \phi(x, \bar{y})$
5:     **if** $p \in F$ and $\neg$ does not occur in $\phi(x, \bar{y})$ **then**
6:         $\Gamma_p^{\pm} := \{\exists \bar{y}. \phi(x, \bar{y}) \wedge consistent_{\phi(x,\bar{y})}^{\Delta}\} \cup \Gamma_p^{\pm}$
7:     **end if**
8: **end for**
9: **print** $\phi_p^s \equiv \bigvee \Gamma_p^s$ for all predicates $p \in F$ and all $s \in \{+, -\}$

Theorem 2 (Soundness and Completeness). *Without compression, algorithm* IMPLCOMPILE *is a web form constraint compiler for* MON *ontologies.*

5.2 Minimal Inconsistencies

Computing minimal inconsistencies is useful for two reasons: to identify errors and to implement the consistency checks described above. PLATO's algorithm identifies the minimal inconsistent subsets by computing an over-approximation and then throwing out non-minimal subsets.

More precisely, the algorithm computes an *update* to the set of minimally inconsistent subsets as opposed to computing the entire set from scratch. The web form paradigm supports such updates naturally. Each time a user changes a form field, it is only the minimally inconsistent sets involving that field that need to be changed.

The algorithm, called CONSCOMPILE, is identical to IMPLCOMPILE except it adds no consistency check to the database queries that are generated and eliminates all rules with positive heads. It consists of five steps: compress the ontology, compute the resolution closure, compute the contrapositives of each clause in the closure, eliminate all rules with a positive head or with negation in the body, and perform predicate completion. For lack of space, we omit the formal definition.

The only difference between the queries generated by CONSCOMPILE and the error queries in the example at the start of the section is that instead of having a collection of statements of the form $error :- q(x) \wedge r(x)$, each form field is associated with a set of queries, *e.g.*, field q is associated with $\neg q(x) :- r(x)$ and field r is associated with $\neg r(x) :- q(x)$. If the user makes $q(a)$ true, the form evaluates $\neg q(a)$ using the queries associated with q, records all the form data subsets responsible for making $\neg q(a)$ true, adds $q(a)$ to each subset, and eliminates any subsets that are non-minimal.

6   Evaluation

Our evaluation of plato includes an analytical component, where we focus on resolution, and an empirical component, where we focus on ontology compression.

6.1   Analytical

PLATO's performance has two components: the performance of the compiler and the performance of the code the compiler produces. The performance of the compiler is polynomial in the performance of the resolution theorem prover; the performance of the code the compiler produces is directly related to the *size* of the resolution closure. Since the performance of the theorem prover is bounded from below by the size of the closure, the closure size (*i.e.*, output complexity of resolution) is of paramount interest.

The main reason PLATO's ontology language is no more expressive than MON is that the resolution closure of MON is finite. In particular, resolution's output complexity is either singly or doubly exponential in the size of the input.

Proposition 1 (Resolution Complexity). *The output complexity of resolution for* MON *is* EXPSPACE-*hard and included in* 2EXPSPACE. *When the premises are in clausal form, contain one variable, and include no object constants, the output complexity is* EXPSPACE-*complete.*

Proof. (Sketch) For inclusion in 2EXPSPACE, count the number of monadic clauses. Because a monadic clause may include multiple variables, *e.g.*, $p(x) \vee q(x) \vee \neg r(y)$, each such clause corresponds to a set of propositional clauses, *e.g.*, $\{p \vee q, \neg r\}$. The number of distinct sets of propositional clauses is 2^{3^n}, where n is the number of propositions (corresponding to the number of monadic predicates). Object constants only introduce a single exponential factor. For hardness, we embed propositional logic, where resolution proofs and therefore resolution closures are well-known to be exponential. For the special case, the closure is the same size as the closure of propositional logic.   □

This result has two consequences. The first is that the run-time of the compiler is exponential, which means it will not scale to large ontologies; however, that does not mean PLATO fails to scale to large web *forms*. Large web forms often have relatively small ontologies or have large ontologies that consist of many small, almost independent ontologies. Large web forms with large, complex ontologies are rare simply because people have trouble filling them out; those that exist (*e.g.*, TurboTax) are usually professionally designed to help people navigate them successfully.

Second, the set of database queries the compiler outputs is exponentially larger than the ontology. Fortunately, it turns out that evaluating one MON database query is singly exponential (in combined complexity), ensuring that the implementations of strict implication and inconsistency detection run in a singly exponential factor of the size of the resolution closure. Because strict implication and inconsistency detection are NP-hard, for any class of ontologies for which resolution's output complexity is EXPSPACE, PLATO produces singly exponential implementations of strict implication and inconsistency detection, which is optimal with respect to time if P $\neq$ NP. Furthermore, ontologies written in clausal form with a single variable and no object constants enjoy the EXPSPACE result.

Proposition 2. *For any class of* MON *for which resolution's output complexity is in* EXPSPACE, *without compression* PLATO *produces time-optimal implementations of strict implication and inconsistency detection, unless* P $=$ NP.

Corollary 1 (Optimality). *For ontologies written in clausal form with a single variable and no object constants, without compression* PLATO *generates time-optimal implementations of strict implication and inconsistency detection, unless* P $=$ NP.

6.2   Empirical

To test the effectiveness of the pre-resolution compression step of IMPLCOMPILE and CONSCOMPILE, we compared the performance of resolution both with and without compression on ontologies from CLib[2], a library of configuration management problems. We chose to test configuration management problems because they represent some of the most complex ontologies PLATO could be expected to handle. We analyzed all 5 of the problems in the Configit format that were supported by our Configit parser at the time of writing. Some Configit problems are decomposed into several components, each of which contains its own ontology. Moreover, for each ontology, we tested two versions: one requiring each form field to have a single value and one that does not. All told, the 5 Configit problems produced 26 distinct ontologies.

We tested both a compressed and an uncompressed version of each ontology. We timed both the conversion to clausal form (CNF), with a max of 900 seconds, and the computation of the resolution closure, again with a 900 second max. For 17 ontologies, either the compressed version, the uncompressed version, or both finished before timing out on either step; we report results for those 17 ontologies.

Figure 3(a) shows three ratios of uncompressed performance to compressed performance, where high numbers mean compression is beneficial: the time for computing

[2] http://www.itu.dk/research/cla/externals/clib/

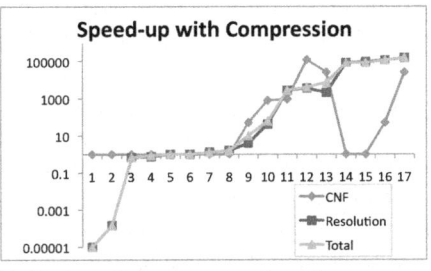
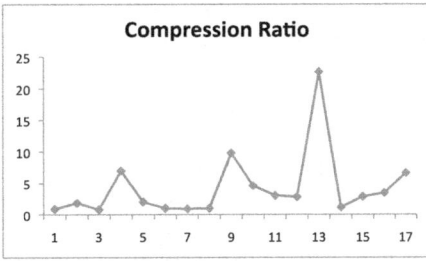

(a) Ratio of uncompressed performance to compressed performance

(b) Ratio of uncompressed size to compressed size

Fig. 3. Impact of compression

clausal form, the time for computing the resolution closure, and the total time. The 17 test cases are ordered from low to high in terms of total-time performance improvement. (Note there is no relationship between ontologies; however, we find the graphs easier to read when points are ordered and connected with lines.) The resolution and total-time results are virtually identical, indicating that the performance change in CNF conversion due to compression is negligible. The total-time results are mixed. For 9 ontologies, compression improves performance with speed-ups between 10x and 150,000x. For 6 ontologies, compression has little impact. For 2 ontologies, compression is harmful, with slow-downs of 7,000x and 100,000x. Slow downs arise because, despite the fact that the ontology is smaller, it contains predicates with more than one argument.

Compression is therefore sometimes quite useful, but it can also be harmful. Figure 3(b) shows the size ratio of the uncompressed to compressed ontologies for each of the 17 test cases, where size is measured as sentence complexity, *i.e.*, number of boolean connectives and atomic sentences. We conjectured that a high compression ratio would indicate high performance benefits, but some of the instances that benefited most from compression have ratios similar to those for the instances most harmed by compression.

Because it is unclear how to predict when compression will be beneficial, PLATO compresses every ontology and then attempts to compute the closure for some small period of time, *e.g.*, one minute. If the closure of the compressed ontology has not been computed before time expires, it computes the closure of the uncompressed ontology.

The current compression algorithm runs in time linear in the size of the ontology, and for all examples, compression time was negligible. To generate the resolution closure, we used the SNARK automated reasoning kit. All tests were run on a MacBook Pro with a 2.66 GHz Intel Core i7 and 8 GB of memory.

7   Related Work

Related work touches on three topics: web application development, inconsistency tolerance for classical logic, and knowledge compilation. See Section 1 for a discussion of work related to web application development.

Inconsistency tolerance for classical logic has received significant attention over the last decade (see [4] for a recent overview). Because this paper focuses on detecting and tolerating inconsistencies instead of repairing them (*e.g.*, [13, 2, 29]), the closest related work centers around definitions and implementations for paraconsistent implication. Perhaps the closest definition to our strict implication is the well-known existential entailment. Strict implication is better suited for the web-form setting because it differentiates the ontology from the data, whereas existential entailment does not; moreover, our implementation utilizes specific properties of the MON ontology language, which is better suited to the web form domain than propositional logic (the ubiquitous choice for studying existential entailment) but is more implementable than full first-order logic [12, 3]. Another related topic is argumentation theory. Whereas that work is usually concerned with establishing the relationships between all possible arguments with an argument tree, *e.g.*, [12, 4], PLATO constructs two arguments for each atomic conclusion: one supporting and one undermining.

In the context of knowledge compilation, our work is differentiated from most because it addresses inconsistency tolerance. The other efforts we are aware of that address both inconsistency and compilation [15, 21, 16, 20] fail to address the web form's real-time performance demands or fail to capitalize on the properties of the web form domain. Ignoring inconsistency tolerance, the most relevant knowledge compilation work transforms description logic ontologies into relational databases to efficiently reason about large data sets. In their terminology, the web form's constraints correspond to a TBox, the web form data corresponds to an ABox, and the web form domain only requires (positive and negative) instance queries. Our algorithms infuse the TBox into all possible instance queries at compilation-time but leave the database untouched; thus, according to [24], it is a form of *FO-rewriting*, as opposed to *combined FO-rewriting*.

8   Conclusion and Future Work

This paper introduced PLATO, a compiler for constructing web forms that detect errors and compute implied values. In essence, PLATO specializes an inconsistency-tolerant (*i.e.*, paraconsistent) theorem prover to a given ontology to capitalize on the fact that hundreds or thousands of users might combine to ask millions of queries all about the same ontology. We materialized this intuition in formal terms by showing that the parameterized complexity of the web form problem is polynomial when the size of the ontology is fixed. We introduced easy-to-implement compilation algorithms and analyzed how they scale under non-parameterized complexity assumptions. We identified a class of ontologies for which PLATO constructs time-optimal code and demonstrated compression algorithms yielding speed-ups of 10^5. PLATO is available online at
http://tlh.cs.uchicago.edu:5000/plato/.

Our long-term goal is to provide web developers with a practical tool for building and maintaining web forms. In the future we plan to investigate ontology languages that are more expressive than the monadic, first-order logic studied here but that retain some of the same computational properties. We hope to guide that work by investigating a version of PLATO that simplifies the construction of a common class of web forms: those that solicit data for a back-end database. The improved PLATO would accept a declarative description of the database view the user is intended to augment and would automatically extract the appropriate ontology from the database integrity constraints.

References

1. Axling, T., Haridi, S.: A tool for developing interactive configuration applications. Proceedings of the Journal of Logic Programming, 147–168 (1996)
2. Benferhat, S., Lagrue, S., Rossit, J.: An egalitarist fusion of incommensurable ranked belief bases under constraints. In: Proceedings of the AAAI Conference on Artificial Intelligence, pp. 367–372 (2007)
3. Besnard, P., Hunter, A.: Practical first-order argumentation. In: Proceedings of the AAAI Conference on Artificial Intelligence, pp. 590–595 (2005)
4. Besnard, P., Hunter, A.: Elements of Argumentation. MIT Press, Cambridge (2008)
5. Braßel, B., Hanus, M., Müller, M.: High-level database programming in curry. In: Hudak, P., Warren, D.S. (eds.) PADL 2008. LNCS, vol. 4902, pp. 316–332. Springer, Heidelberg (2008)
6. Brabrand, C., Moller, A., Ricky, M., Schwartzbach, M.: Powerforms: Declarative client-side form field validation. In: World Wide Web, pp. 205–214 (2000)
7. Brambilla, M., Ceri, S., Comai, S., Dario, M., Fraternali, P., Manolescu, I.: Declarative specification of web applications exploiting web services and workflows. In: Proceedings of the ACM SIG for the Management of Data, pp. 909–910 (2004)
8. Chong, S., Liu, J., Myers, A.C., Qi, X., Vikram, K., Zheng, L., Zheng, X.: Secure web applications via automatic partitioning. In: Proceedings of the ACM Symposium on Operating Systems Principles, pp. 31–44 (2007)
9. Cooper, E., Lindley, S., Yallop, J.: Links: Web programming without tiers. In: de Boer, F.S., Bonsangue, M.M., Graf, S., de Roever, W.-P. (eds.) FMCO 2006. LNCS, vol. 4709, pp. 266–296. Springer, Heidelberg (2007)
10. Cox, P.T., Nicholson, P.: Unification of arrays in spreadsheets with logic programming. In: Hudak, P., Warren, D.S. (eds.) PADL 2008. LNCS, vol. 4902, pp. 100–115. Springer, Heidelberg (2008)
11. Darwiche, A., Marquis, P.: A knowledge compilation map. Journal of Artificial Intelligence Research 17, 229–264 (2002)
12. Efstathiou, V., Hunter, A.: Algorithms for effective argumentation in classical propositional logic: A connection graph approach. In: Hartmann, S., Kern-Isberner, G. (eds.) FoIKS 2008. LNCS, vol. 4932, pp. 272–290. Springer, Heidelberg (2008)
13. Everaere, P., Konieczny, S., Marquis, P.: Conflict-based merging operators. In: Proceedings of the International Conference on Principles of Knowledge Representation and Reasoning, pp. 348–357 (2008)
14. Fernandez, M., Florescu, D., Levy, A., Suciu, D.: Declarative specification of web sites with strudel. The VLDB Journal, 38–55 (2000)
15. Flouris, G., Huang, Z., Pan, J.Z., Plexousakis, D., Wache, H.: Inconsistencies, negations and changes in ontologies. In: Proceedings of the AAAI Conference on Artificial Intelligence, pp. 1295–1300 (2006)
16. Gomez, S.A., Chesnevar, C.I., Simari, G.R.: An argumentative approach to reasoning with inconsistent ontologies. In: Proceedings of the KR Workshop on Knowledge Representation and Ontologies, pp. 11–20 (2008)
17. Gupta, G., Akhter, S.F.: Knowledgesheet: A graphical spreadsheet interface for interactively developing a class of constraint programs. In: Pontelli, E., Santos Costa, V. (eds.) PADL 2000. LNCS, vol. 1753, pp. 308–323. Springer, Heidelberg (2000)
18. Hanus, M., Kluß, C.: Declarative programming of user interfaces. In: Gill, A., Swift, T. (eds.) PADL 2009. LNCS, vol. 5418, pp. 16–30. Springer, Heidelberg (2008)
19. Hanus, M., Koschnicke, S.: An ER-based framework for declarative web programming. In: Carro, M., Peña, R. (eds.) PADL 2010. LNCS, vol. 5937, pp. 201–216. Springer, Heidelberg (2010)

20. Hinrichs, T.L., Kao, J.Y., Genesereth, M.R.: Inconsistency-tolerant reasoning with classical logic and large databases. In: Proceedings of the Symposium of Abstraction, Reformulation, and Approximation (2009)

21. Huang, Z., van Harmelen, F., ten Teije, A.: Reasoning with inconsistent ontologies. In: Proceedings of the International Joint Conference on Artificial Intelligence (2005)

22. Kassoff, M., Genesereth, M.R.: PrediCalc: A logical spreadsheet management system. Knowledge Engineering Review 22(3), 281–295 (2007)

23. Kassoff, M., Valente, A.: An introduction to logical spreadsheets. Knowledge Engineering Review 22(3), 213–219 (2007)

24. Kontchakov, R., Lutz, C., Toman, D., Wolter, F., Zakharyaschev, M.: Combined FO rewritability for conjunctive query answering in DL-Lite. In: Proceedings of the International Workshop on Description Logic (2009)

25. Levy, M.R., Horspool, R.N.: Translating Prolog to C: a WAM-based approach. In: Proceedings of the Compulog Network Area Meeting on Programming Languages (1993)

26. Serrano, M., Gallesio, E., Loitsch, F.: Hop, a language for programming the web 2.0. In: Proceedings of the International Conference on Object Oriented Programming, Systems, Languages and Applications, pp. 975–985 (2006)

27. Soininen, T., Niemelä, I.: Developing a declarative rule language for applications in product configuration. In: Gupta, G. (ed.) PADL 1999. LNCS, vol. 1551, pp. 305–319. Springer, Heidelberg (1999)

28. Subbarayan, S., Jensen, R., Hadzic, T., Andersen, H., Hulgaard, H., Moller, J.: Comparing two implementations of a complete and backtrack-free interactive configurator. In: Proceedings of the CP Workshop on CSP Techniques with Immediate Application, pp. 97–111 (2004)

29. Subrahmanian, V.S., Amgoud, L.: A general framework for reasoning about inconsistency. In: Proceedings of the International Joint Conference on Artificial Intelligence, pp. 599–604 (2007)

30. Suzuki, T., Tokuda, T.: Automatic generation of intelligent javascript programs for handling input forms in html documents. In: Proceedings of the International Conference on Web Engineering (2005)

31. Vikram, K., Prateek, A., Livshits, B.: Ripley: Automatically securing distributed web applications through replicated execution. In: Proceedings of the ACM Conference on Computer and Communications Security, pp. 173–186 (2009)

32. Vlaeminck, H., Vennekens, J., Denecker, M.: A logical framework for configuration software. In: Proceedings of the ACM SIGPLAN Symposium on Principles and Practice of Declarative Programming, pp. 141–148 (2009)

33. Yang, F., Gupta, N., Gerner, N., Qi, X., Demers, A., Gehrke, J., Shanmugasundaram, J.: A unified platform for data driven web applications with automatic client-server partitioning. In: Proceedings of the International World Wide Web Conference, pp. 341–350 (2007)

34. Yang, F., Shanmugasundaram, J., Riedewald, M., Gehrke, J.: Hilda: A high-level language for data-driven web applications. In: Proceedings of the International Conference on Data Engineering (2006)

On the Portability of Prolog Applications

Jan Wielemaker[1] and Vítor Santos Costa[2]

[1] VU University Amsterdam, The Netherlands
J.Wielemaker@cs.vu.nl
[2] DCC-FCUP & CRACS-INESC Porto LA
Universidade do Porto, Portugal
vsc@dcc.fc.up.pt

Abstract. The non-portability of Prolog programs is widely considered one of the main problems facing Prolog programmers. Although since 1995, the core of the language is covered by the ISO standard 13211-1, this standard has not been sufficient to support large Prolog applications. As an approach to address this problem, since 2007, YAP and SWI-Prolog have established a basic compatibility framework. The aim of the framework is running the same code on Edinburgh-based Prolog systems rather than having to migrate an application. This article describes the implementation and evaluates this framework by studying how it can be used on a number of libraries and an important application.

1   Introduction

Prolog has a long history, and its user community has seen a large number of implementations that evolved largely independently. This is in contrast to more recent languages such as Java, Python, or Perl. These language either have a single implementation (Python, Perl) or are controlled centrally (a language can only be called Java if it satisfies a set of standards [9]). The Prolog world knows dialects that are radically different, with different syntax and different semantics (e.g., Visual Prolog [12]). Arguably, this is a handicap for the language because every publicly available significant piece of code must be carefully examined for portability issues before it can be applied. As an anecdotal example, answers to questions on *comp.lang.prolog* typically include "on Prolog XYZ, this can be done using ..." or "which Prolog implementation are you using?".

In this work we propose an approach for improving the portability of applications in modern Prolog systems. Our approach has been implemented in the SWI-Prolog [22] and YAP [16] systems. The approach requires **(i)** support of the Prolog ISO standard to a large extent [2,18]; **(ii)** a module system close to Quintus Prolog module system; **(iii)** and a term-expansion approach; and, whenever this is not sufficient, **(iv)** a preprocessor, that allows one to explicitly state system-dependent regions of code. Except for the second requirement, we expect most of these features to be available or easy to implement in modern Prolog systems. On the other hand, arguably module support is a controversial issue in the Prolog community. Although any program larger than a few pages

R. Rocha and J. Launchbury (Eds.): PADL 2011, LNCS 6539, pp. 69–83, 2011.

requires modularity, the ISO standard for modules was never accepted by most Prolog developers. In our case, we follow the approach of using the Quintus module system, to better or worse arguably the closest to a standard in the Prolog community. This module system is supported by Quintus Prolog [1], SICStus Prolog [4], and Ciao [6], besides SWI-Prolog [22], and YAP [16]. Other Prolog systems, such as XSB-Prolog [15], have limited compatibility with this module system.

The key ideas of our approach are as follows. First, each program will belong to a dialect, such as `swi`, `yap`, or `sicstus`. Second, loading a program declared to belong to a dialect sets up a compile-time emulation layer that works as follows:

- load an extra set of built-ins and libraries;
- redefine conflicting built-ins;
- change system flags, if necessary.

The emulation layer will then be active while loading the file.

Our technique has been implemented in the SWI-Prolog [22] and YAP [16]. In YAP it has been used to implement a very extensive emulation layer for SWI-Prolog. This has allowed YAP to support a large number of SWI-Prolog packages, including the Java interface `jpl`, the `chr`, `clpfd` and `clpqr` extensions, several web interface packages, and the `plunit` package. SWI-Prolog includes emulation layers for several Prolog dialects, such as `yap`, `sicstus`, and `ciao`. The `sicstus` layer has been used to port a large natural language package from SICStus Prolog to SWI-Prolog, maintaining a single source for the package.

The paper is organized as follows. First, we discuss the key concepts in portability work. Second, we present our approach in more detail. Then, we present the YAP and SWI-Prolog case studies in more detail. We finish with some conclusions.

2   Portability Approaches and Related Work

Software portability is a problem since the day the second computer was built. In our case, we expect that at least basic portability requirements are fulfilled: there are few syntactic incompatibilities, and the core language primitives have to a large extent the same semantics. This is the case for the family of implementations that is subject in this study. Beyond that, the implementations vary widely; notably in **(i)** the organisation of the libraries; **(ii)** available library primitives; and **(iii)** access to external resources such as C-code, processes, etc.

Our problem is to some extent related to the problem of porting C-programs between different compilers and operating systems. Although today's C has made significant progress in standardizing the structure of the library (e.g., C99 internationalisation support) and POSIX has greatly simplified operating system portability, writing portable C-code still relies on judicious use of the C-preprocessor and a principled approach to portability. We therefore will take advantage of the underlying principles and choices that affect portability in the C-world, both because we believe the examples are widely known and because the C-community has a long-standing experience with portability issues.

The abstraction approach. A popular approach to make an application portable is to define an *interface* for facilities that are needed by the application and that are typically not portable. Next, the interface is implemented for the various target platforms. Targets that are completely different (e.g. Windows vs. X11 graphics) use completely distinct implementations, while small differences are handled using compile-time or run-time conditions. Typically, the "portable" part of the application still needs some conditional statements, for example if vital features are simply not available on one of the target platforms.

Abstractions come in two flavors: specifically designed and implemented in the context of an application; and designed as high-level general-purpose abstractions. We find instances of the latter class notably in areas where portability is hard, such as user-interface components (e.g., WxWindows, Qt, various libraries for threading).

Logtalk [10] is an example from the Prolog world: it provides a portable program-structuring framework (objects) and extensive libraries that are portable over a wide range of Prolog implementation. On the other hand, we could claim that Logtalk is a *language* developed by a community that just happens to be using a variety of Prolog implementations as backend. The portability of Logtalk itself is based on application-specific abstraction.

The emulation approach. Another popular approach is to write applications for environment X and completely *emulate* environment X on top of the target environment Y. Comparing with the previous approaches, arguably, one system can be seen as an abstraction to other. One of the most extreme examples here is *Wine*[1], that completely emulates the Windows-API on top of POSIX systems. The opposite is Cygwin [13], that emulates the POSIX API on Windows platforms. To the best of our knowledge, SEPIA was the first system to use this approach, in this case to emulate other Prolog systems [14].

Emulation has large advantages in reducing the porting effort. However, it comes at a price. Cygwin and Wine are very large projects because emulating one OS API can approach the complexity of an OS itself. This means that applications ported using this approach become heavyweight. Moreover, they tend to become slow due to small mismatches. For example, both Windows and POSIX provide a function to enumerate members of a directory and a function to get details on each member. The initial enumeration already provides more than just the name, but the set of attributes provided differs. This implies that a full emulation of the directory-scanning function also needs to call the 'get-details' function to fill the missing attributes, causing a huge slow-down. The real difficulty is that, often, the application is not interested in these painfully extracted attributes. Similar arguments hold for the differences between the thread-synchronisation primitives. For example, the initial implementation of SWI-Prolog message-queues that establish a FIFO queue between threads was based on POSIX thread 'condition variables' and ported using the pthread-win32[2] library. The Windows version was over 100 times slower than the POSIX

---

[1] http://www.winehq.org
[2] http://sourceware.org/pthreads-win32/

version. Rewriting the queue logic using Windows 'Event' object duplicates a large part of the queue-handling code, but provides comparable performance.

The conditional approach. Traditionally, (small) compatibility problems are 'fixed' using conditional code. There are two approaches: compile-time and run-time. In the Prolog world, we've seen mostly run-time solutions with the promise that partial evaluation can turn this into the equivalent of the compile-time approach.

Conditions themselves often come from version information (e.g. if (currentBrowser == IE && browserVersion == 6.0) ...). At some point in time, the variation in the Unix-world was so large that this was no longer feasible. Large packages came with a configuration file where the installer could indicate which features where supported by the target Unix version. Of course, most system managers found it hard to obtain a reasonable configuration. A major step forward was GNU `autoconf` [21], a package that provides clear guidelines for portability, plus a collectively maintained suite of tests that can automatically execute in the target environment (`configure`).

There is one important lesson to be learned from GNU autoconf: *do not test versions, but features.* E.g. if you want to know whether member/2 is available without loading library(lists), use a test like the one below rather than a test for a specific Prolog system:

```
catch(member(a, [a]), _, fail)
```

Feature tests work regardless of your knowledge of the availability of a predicate in a specific Prolog implementation and they keep working if implementations change this aspect or new implementations arrive on the market.

3   Prolog Portability Status

Before we can answer the question on the best approach for Prolog, we must investigate the current situation.

Our target Prolog systems have been influenced by the Edinburgh tradition, namely through Quintus Prolog, C-Prolog, DEC10-Prolog and its DEC10 Prolog library. They all at least partially support the ISO core standard. In addition, resources such as Logtalk, and the Leuven and Vienna constraint libraries have recently helped enhancing the compatibility of Prolog dialects due to a mutual interest of the resource developers (a wider audience) and Prolog implementors (valuable resources). Logtalk has pioneered this field, pointing Prolog implementors at non-compliance with the ISO standard and other incompatibilities. The constraint libraries have settled around the attributed variable and global variable API designed for hProlog ([5]). These APIs are either directly implemented or easily emulated.

The language. All systems can run programs satisfying the ISO standard as long as they do not depend on corner cases. There are cases where ISO demands an exception and implementations take the liberty to provide meaningful semantics.

Table 1. Core features provided by the target Prolog environment

	Ciao	SICStus	SWI-Prolog	YAP
ISO	yes	yes	yes	yes
module/2	yes	yes	yes	yes
module/3	yes	no	no	no
use_module/2	yes	yes	yes	yes
use_module/3	no	yes	no	no
operators and modules	local	global	both	both
export built-in	no	no	yes	yes
redefine built-in	yes	no	yes	yes
Term-expansion	yes	yes	yes	yes
Goal-expansion	yes	yes	yes	yes
Compilation-model[a]	file	direct	direct	direct
Directives	special	goal	goal	goal
Attributed variables	yes	yes	yes	yes
Coroutining (dif/2, freeze/2)	yes	yes	yes	yes
Global variables	yes	yes	yes	yes
Tabling	yes	no	no	yes
Threads	yes	no	yes[b]	yes[b]
Unicode	no	yes	yes	yes
Set unknown flag	fail	error	yes[c]	yes[c]
Get unknown flag	fail	fail	fail	fail
Provide unknown option[d]	error	error	ignore	error
Library license	GPL	Proprietary	GPL[e]	Artistic & GPL

[a] File: compile .pl to object and load object code.
[b] Provides create_prolog_flag/3.
[c] Following ISO technical report.
[d] E.g. write_term(foobar, [hello(true)]).
[e] With an additional statement that allows for use in proprietary code, based on the GCC runtime library.

E.g., SWI-Prolog supports the mode **arg**(-, +, ?); many systems support 'options' to predicates such as open/4 and write_term/4 that are not described by the ISO standard (e.g. 'encoding' in open/4 to indicate the character-set encoding of the file). Additional options are explicitly allowed by the standard, but there is no good mechanism to know which options are allowed by a specific implementation and it is not easy to find an elegant way to deal with different option-list requirements in different implementations. Similarly, most systems provide prolog-flags (current_prolog_flag/2) in addition to the standard flags. Finally, systems differ in the relation between operators and modules. Table 1 provides an overview of features that we consider most relevant to porting code in the four Prolog dialects considered. The table discusses approaches to modularity, term and goal expansion, major extensions in the code, and flag handling.

The libraries. The situation of the Prolog libraries is unfortunate. Although much of the code is derived from the public domain 'DEC10' library, a long period of independent development makes this barely recognizable. Currently, the way predicates are spread over the libraries and system built-ins differs enormously. Also different is the status of built-in predicates (can you redefine them, can you export them from a library, etc.) differs. Fortunately, there are only few cases where we find predicates with the same name but different semantics (e.g. delete/3[3]). In the last few years, cooperation around Logtalk and the CLP libraries as well as discussions in the community [11] have enhanced the situation somewhat.

Foreign code. As Bagnara ([3]) pointed out, the design of the foreign language interface is largely settled. All target systems use 'term-handles'; opaque handles to Prolog terms that must be allocated and thus ensure that the Prolog engine knows which terms are referenced by foreign code. On the other hand, the naming, coverage of the API functions to interact with terms as well as the way foreign code is made visible as Prolog predicates varies widely. We identify two problem areas.

- All Prolog systems allow binding external I/O channels to Prolog streams. The design of these interfaces however differs so widely that emulation is non-trivial and likely to cause severe performance degradation. See Sect. 5.
- The SWI-Prolog and YAP APIs allow for creating non-deterministic predicates in C. SICStus and Ciao require the non-determinism to be moved to Prolog. It is hard to make a SWI-Prolog/YAP non-deterministic implementation run of SICStus/Ciao without major work.

4   The YAP/SWI-Prolog Approach

Ideally, we would hope for a standardized full definition of the Prolog language and its libraries. However, getting agreement on such a library and proper implementations for all platforms has shown not to be trivial. Even if this library eventually exists, a lot of legacy applications may require extensive rewriting. In general, our goal is to run the same code on multiple Prolog systems, with the least possible rewriting effort.

As far as we are aware, there are none or very few cases where emulation leads to poor performance due to mismatches in the APIs as explained in Sect. 2. So, as a good shared abstraction is hard to achieve and application-abstractions are too limited in scope for our purposes, we follow *emulation* whenever possible. Note that, given a good framework, an emulation layer can be established incrementally and on 'as needed' basis.

The need for macro-expansion. Macro-processing is key to performing emulation efficiently. Dealing with incompatibilities only through runtime tests and, optionally, partial evaluation is insufficient. First of all, runtime tests can only deal with predicates and not with declarations (directives). Second, portable and

---

[3] http://www.cs.otago.ac.nz/staffpriv/ok/pllib.htm

adequate partial evaluation is not provided. Without partial evaluation, runtime testing is not acceptable for time-critical code and static analysis tools, even the simple cross-referencers available for SWI-Prolog, will complain about the code intended for other dialects. Term- and goal-expansion are provided by all target systems, but the details vary, making it rather awkward to use in application code. For example, Ciao requires special attention to make the rules available to the compiler. SWI-Prolog expansion follows its module-inheritance rules, first expanding in the module, then in the **user** module and finally in the **system** module. SICStus provides additional arguments to deal with source-location, and so on.

Conditional Compilation. Following the emulation-approach, compatibility libraries can use all machinery available to the hosting Prolog environment to emulate the target. Unfortunately, we still need a way to achieve portable conditional compilation in the application. As an example, features of one system allow for realizing a better (e.g., faster, more compact) implementation for a certain subsystem. In the case of SWI-Prolog, nb_setarg/3 allows for a clean reentrant and thread-safe implementation of counting proofs that is faster and requires less space than portable solutions. We will code this as below.

```
:- meta_predicate proof_count(0, -).
:- if(current_predicate(nb_setarg/3)).
proof_count(Goal, Count) :-
        State = count(0),
        (   call(Goal),
            arg(1, State, C0),
            C1 is C0 + 1,
            nb_setarg(1, State, C1),
            fail
        ;   arg(1, State, Count)
        ).
:- else.
proof_count(Goal, Count) :-
        findall(x, Goal, Xs),
        length(Xs, Count).
:- endif.
```

Notice the use of the if, else, and endif primitives for conditional compilation.

4.1   The SWI-Prolog/YAP Portability Framework

We can now present the key features of our framework:

- Support :- if(Goal). ...[:- else. ...] :- endif. conditional compilation. This is built-in in several systems, such as ECLiPSe [17], and can easily be provided on top of term-expansion for other systems.
- Provide :- expects_dialect(Dialect). to state that a module is designed for the given dialect. The effect of this directive is threefold.

1. Load and import library(dialect/Dialect), which provides emulation for built-ins of the dialect and term/goal expansion rules to resolve compatibility issues.
2. Make the current dialect available through **prolog_load_context**(*dialect, Dialect*) for term and goal-expansion.
3. Push a new library directory before the current library path. The new directory can provide additional and replacement libraries that provide the interface of the target and use the implementation techniques of the host (currently, we assume confliting libraries are not loaded yet).

- Synchronise some vital features, such as identifying the running dialect using the Prolog flag `dialect`.
- Provide a C-header to emulate the target foreign interface and C-code to implement the foreign interface.

5   Running SWI-Prolog Packages in YAP

YAP currently can run several SWI-Prolog packages, such as `clib`, `http`, `sgml`, `RDF`, `plunit`, `jpl`, `chr`, and `clpqr`. Some of these packages, such as `clib` and `jpl`, are mostly written in C. Other packages, such as `chr` and `clpqr` are Prolog code. The YAP library approach was as follows.

The C-Interface. The first step is to implement the SWI-Prolog C-interface. Notice that the SWI-Prolog interface contains significant duplicate functionality, as old functions are replaced by more powerful newer ones. Correctly implementing the whole functionality in a single go would have been a major endeavour. Instead, the YAP implementors have implemented functions as they are needed, and in some case only partially. Error messages are used to inform users that an interface function is only *partially* implemented.

A second challenge were the differences in internal objects that were exported through the interface. For example, YAP strings are 0-terminated C-strings. SWI-Prolog uses an additional length parameter to accommodate 0-bytes in atoms. SWI-Prolog internally supports an integer Prolog object that is always 64 bits long. YAP supports an integer that has word size.

There are also major differences in functionality between the two systems, that are simply almost impossible to cover. For example, the debugging infrastructure is much richer in SWI-Prolog. A second typical example are *blobs*. In SWI-Prolog, a blob is a symbol (like an atom) that is used to store external data, such as image-pixels or a handle to C-managed data. SWI-Prolog goes much further, and has a sizable infrastructure for blobs that accommodates user defined blobs with extensions over input, output, garbage-collection, etc. In contrast, in YAP a blob is an opaque object kept on the stacks. In cases such as this, supporting the SWI-Prolog interface will require defining a new type of objects and supporting them. The advantage is that YAP will benefit from the decisions made by SWI-Prolog. The drawback is that the YAP design is bound by these decisions.

PLStream. The next step was to support Input/Output. SWI-Prolog basically exports its Input/Output data structures, which are very different from YAP's. A first try at using the standard emulation layer approach was very painful: first because the interface is complex; and second because it involves reimplementing a large number of data structures that had to be working before anything could be experimented with. On the other hand, we could observe that SWI-Prolog's I/O was largely self-contained and almost exclusively written in C. This suggested an alternative approach, where it was decided to simply port the whole I/O subsystem as a C library. The process worked surprisingly well: the I/O routines are much independent of the rest of the system, and we only required reimplementing some internal interface functions. The interface layer required 800 lines of code, but much of this code is in fact reused from files in SWI-Prolog. We did observe several difficulties:

- some I/O functions build lists of characters using low-level abstract machine functionality; we just abstracted these operations without loss of efficiency.
- the code relies on the address of some atoms being known at compile-time. This required changes to the C-interface layer.
- SWI-Prolog and YAP streams are different: we allow limited access from YAP streams to SWI-Prolog streams, but not vice-versa.

The last challenge is simply keeping track of the changes in SWI-Prolog functionality. SWI-Prolog is a living object: new functions are being added in, and from time to time, preexisting functions do change. This is a good thing, and just a small problem with the external interface, but it is a major problem with the I/O library. As YAP-6 stabilises, we expect to be able to merge the YAP changes to the main SWI-Prolog distribution, and use `git` to track down changes in the SWI-Prolog distribution, with no negative impact on SWI-Prolog.

Evaluation. Table 2 gives an idea of the porting effort. There are about 200 Prolog source files, and a similar number of C source files. Altogether, we needed 28 `if` statements for cases of conditional code. We discuss some of these problems in more detail below.

The size of the C-code is similar to the size of the Prolog code. We only have 15 cases of conditional compilation, with most of these belonging to the `PLStream`

Table 2. Metrics on the SWI-Prolog Libraries

Prolog source-files	244
Prolog source-lines	67,532
Prolog clauses	≈14,000
`if` directives	≈28
C source-files	215
C source-lines	66,437
C predicates	267
`YAP` conditional compilation	15

package, which is unsurprising as this package is SWI-Prolog code. We believe this shows that most of the compatibility issues have been addressed at the emulation layer.

6   A First Case-Study: Portable Constraint Libraries

We have been able to share three major constraint libraries between the two systems using this framework: clpfd [19], clpr [7], and chr [8]. YAP originally implemented a SICStus mechanism for domain variables, so the first step was to also support the hProlog/SWI-Prolog mechanism [5]. From YAP-6.0.4, YAP implements the SICStus interface as mostly an extension of the SWI-Prolog interface (with some extra built-ins). Following SWI-Prolog, YAP now simply searches the global stack for attributed variables for realizing call_residue_vars/2, which is used by the toplevel to report residual constraints.

Given a common infrastructure, the goal was to reduce to a minimum the amount of effort in porting the constraint libraries between the two different systems. In the case of chr this was simplified because chr already supported by two systems: SICStus and SWI-Prolog. Difficulties had to do with the term expansion mechanism, which is different in the two systems, with SWI-Prolog having a more liberal syntax, and with supporting SWI-Prolog's *message-writing* mechanism.[4] Last, chr was originally implemented in hProlog and expects an hProlog compatibility library to provide list functionality. This forces YAP to be both compatible with SWI-Prolog and hProlog.

Markus Triska's clpfd is a SWI-Prolog native application. It was interesting that although the two applications were written independently, the challenges were very much similar: the term expansion mechanism, the message-writing system, and attribute predicates.

7   A Second Case-Study: The Alpino Dependency-Tree Parser Suite

The Alpino dependency-tree parser suite [20] is a large and complex program developed in SICStus Prolog over a long period of time. Table 3 gives some metrics of the application. The initiative to port Alpino came from the SWI-Prolog side based on a desire to use Alpino components as a library in a larger SWI-Prolog based application. On first contact, the Alpino team was interested, but had two major worries: "does SWI-Prolog support our current application without major rewrites", and "can we achieve one source that compiles and runs on both". The first was accompanied with a list of requirements. Most of these could be answered positively without hesitation. SWI-Prolog however lacks call_residue/2 and a Tcl/Tk interface. SWI-Prolog has a partial implementation of call_residue_vars/3.[5] Later copy_term/3 proved the correct and portable

---

[4] Based on Quintus Prolog. See print_message/2.

[5] The implementation may report variables that are inaccessible due to backtracking if the application uses non-backtrackable assignment as defined by nb_setarg/3 and nv_setval/2.

solution for the application's purposes. Tcl/Tk was no hard requirement and we hoped that the Ciao implementation might be able to solve this issue. A short summary of the SWI-Prolog/YAP portability framework convinced the Alpino team that future maintenance based on a common source could de dealt with.

Table 3. Metrics on the Alpino Parser

Prolog source-files	304
Prolog source-lines	473,593
Prolog predicates	$\approx 5,500$
Prolog clauses	$\approx 290,000$
C source-files	14
C++ source-files	27
C/C++-defined predicates	46

Below we summarize the non-trivial issues encountered and their resolution.

- The SICStus block directive declares predicates to suspend until an instantiation pattern is reached. SWI-Prolog has no such concept. Term-expansion was used to rename the clauses and generate a wrapper that implements the coroutining using when/2.[6]
- Operator declarations are mapped to declarations in the user module, SWI-Prolog's deprecated support for system-wide operators. The code below illustrates dialect handling here:

```
system:goal_expansion(op(Pri,Ass,Name),
                      op(Pri,Ass,user:Name)) :-
        \+ qualified(Name),
        prolog_load_context(dialect, sicstus).

qualified(Var) :- var(Var), !, fail.
qualified(_:_).
```

- Alpino depends on predicates from library(lists) that exist under a different name in SWI-Prolog and that we do not consider for including into SWI-Prolog. Therefore, we add library(dialect/sicstus/lists) with the following content

```
:- module(sicstus_lists,
          [ substitute/4,        % +Elem, +List, +NewElem, -List
            nth/3
          ]).
:- reexport('../../lists').

<implementation>
```

---

[6] Eventually, it was decided that using when/2 directly was more elegant and natively supported by both target Prolog systems.

Note that in addition, we must map explicitly qualified calls (e.g., lists: nth(N,L,E)) to sicstus_lists:nth(N,L,E) if the current dialect is sicstus. The mapping rule is in `sicstus.pl`, while clauses for the mapping are provided by the renamed modules.

- database references (assert/2, clause/3, recorda/3, erase/1) are safe in SICStus and goals fail if the reference does not exist. SWI-Prolog references used to be unsafe: references were heuristically tested for validity and an existence_error was raised if the reference was known to be invalid. In case the heuristics incorrectly claims that a reference is valid, the system could crash. Programming around this in Alpino was considered more effort than providing a compatible API in SWI-Prolog, so we decided for the latter.[7]
- We added support for the mode **recorded**(-,+,-) to the SWI-Prolog runtime. We also resolved that $\langle m \rangle$:clause(H,B) does not qualify H if the predicate is in module $\langle m \rangle$.
- SICStus (and Ciao) provide Prolog streams that can both be read and written to. SWI-Prolog's streams are either read or write. This makes it hard to provide a compatible emulation of the sockets library. We decided to support stream-pairs in the SWI-Prolog runtime system. All I/O predicates are aware of these pairs and will pick the appropriate member (close/1 addresses both streams). After this addition, emulating the required features of the socket library was simple.
- SICStus assert and friends can deal with attributed variables, as illustrated below.

```
?- dif(X, 3), assert(not_3(X)).
```

SWI-Prolog has no such support and adding this is a non-trivial exercise. As a work-around, we use the goal-expansion mechanism to map calls to the assert-predicates onto clp_assert. This predicate uses **copy_term(**)+Attributed, -Plain, -Constraints to extract the constraints from the term and inserts all constraints at the start of the body, creating the clause below.

```
not_3(X) :- dif(X, 3).
```

We consider the approach so specific that we decided to make the emulation part of the Alpino source-tree rather than the SWI-Prolog system.
- We provide an implementation for the libraries `arrays.pl`, `system.pl` and `timeout.pl` using SWI-Prolog primitives.
- At some places, we decided that both SICStus and SWI-Prolog provided already compatible alternatives for legacy SICStus code and adjusted the Alpino sources accordingly.
- We emulate the declaration of foreign predicates using the SICStus primitives foreign_resource/2, foreign/3 and load foreign_resource/1. The wrapper-generation is an extension of the older generator for Quintus (qpforeign.pl). In addition we wrote a script emulating the features of splfr that we need.

---

[7] The necessary infrastructure was developed several years ago.

This SICStus program extracts the foreign declaration from a Prolog file, generates a wrapper and calls the C-compiler to create a loadable foreign module. The SWI-Prolog replacement swipl-lfr.pl takes the same steps, using the C-compiler and linker front-end swipl-ld for the platform-specific linking.

In addition, we added sicstus.h to the SWI-Prolog include directory that provides the necessary mapping from SP_* API functions to PL_* API functions. The total amount of code involved is 664 lines of Prolog code and 244 lines of C-header (which satisfies our requirements, but is otherwise incomplete). No changes were required to the Alpino C-files, neither to the Prolog code. For the Alpino zlib-interface, creating a compressed serialization of a Prolog term based on SICStus fastrw.pl library and zlib, we decided on an alternative route for SWI-Prolog that was easier to realise than providing fastrw for SWI-Prolog. The Alpino code selects the implementation using the if/1 conditional compilation.

— Alpino uses the SICStus tcl/tk interface. License issues make it impossible to use the SICStus library here, while reimplementing from scratch is non-trivial. Initially, we ported library(tcltk) from Ciao Prolog using the same emulation-approach. Because Ciao uses a much finer grained module infrastructure, emulating enough of Ciao to run the tcltk library requires 17 files containing 971 lines of Prolog. In addition, SWI-Prolog's write_term/3 had to be modified to (by default) omit an extra space after a comma that separates two arguments (e.g., term(a,b) instead of term(a, b)).[8]

Unfortunately, Ciao's tcltk library could not sufficiently emulate the SICStus library for running Alpino. Eventually, the Ciao code was used to realise a new and portable tcl/tk interface that could support Alpino. This interface is part of the Alpino source-tree.

The above changes required about 20 person-days joint effort from the SWI-Prolog team and the Alpino team and resulted in a fully operational application running on the two target platforms. As mentioned above, SWI-Prolog was enhanced in several places. Also the Alpino code has been improved. It now relies less on SICStus legacy code; the application now supports UTF-8 on both Prolog platforms; the modularity was enhanced and the performance has been improved, also on SICStus.

The initial Alpino source contained 19 places of conditional compilation based of the if/1-directive. Since then, more conditional code was added to enhance performance on SWI-Prolog and use additional features of SWI-Prolog, such as (partial) support for multi-threading and its interface to GNU readline. The current code contains 59 places of conditional compilation. This small amount of conditional code has no significant impact of the maintainability of the Alpino code-base.

---

[8] This issue also affected Alpino, which contains C-code that relied on the exact term-layout. The 13211-1 standard describes spaces in the output of write_term to separate tokens where needed. Other spaces are not *explicitly* forbidden.

8   Conclusions

Portability of Prolog source-code is important. Portability prevents vendor lock-in, provides backup if an implementation is discontinued or is no longer suitable for sustaining an application because it lacks features that are important for future development. Portability is also needed if we want to combine packages developed on different Prolog implementations. For a long time, the Prolog community consisted of separated sub-communities associated to an implementation. The ISO standard has resolved many low-level compatibility issues. Logtalk and the Leuven/Vienna constraint libraries have created bridges, causing participating Prolog systems to resolve various incompatibilities. Currently, portability among four systems with common inspiration (YAP, SICStus, Ciao and SWI-Prolog) is comparable to other multi-vendor programming environments such as C on Unix in the 90s.

We present an approach for porting complex libraries and applications between systems. First, we make an argument for the need of an emulation layer between different systems. Often, such an emulation can not be complete. In this case, we propose using the reflexive approaches of Prolog in the fashion of the autoconf approach.

A number of issues that hinder the development of portable Prolog resources. Some of these involve major decisions and require major effort. Examples are non-portable types such as string-objects, advanced numeric types (unbounded, rationals, complex), and non-portable features (e.g., Unicode support, threads, tabling). There are a number of issues that are less involved and can greatly facilitate portability if agreement is reached and implemented. Examples are 'environment predicates', such as absolute_file_name/3, prolog_load_context/2, a mechanism to deliver (translated) messages to the user, further standardisation of Prolog flags, including a mechanism to define new flags and a clear vision on handling extensions to the option-list processed by predicates such as write_term/3.

We strongly advice anyone interested in porting a Prolog resource to get into contact with the vendors of the targeted Prolog systems. Many incompatibilities are much easier resolved by the vendor(s) and as a result both systems improve and get more compatible.

Acknowledgments. This work has been partially supported by the project STAMPA (PTDC/EIA/67738/2006), HORUS (PTDC/EIA-EIA/100897/2008), and by the Fundação para a Ciência e Tecnologia.

References

1. AI International ltd., Berkhamsted, UK. Quintus Prolog, User Guide and Reference Manual (1997)
2. Bagnara, R.: Is the ISO prolog standard taken seriously? ALP newsletter, 10–12 (February 1999)
3. Bagnara, R., Carro, M.: Foreign language interfaces for Prolog: A terse survey. ALP newsletter (May 2002)

4. Carlsson, M., Widén, J., Andersson, J., Anderson, S., Boortz, K., Nilson, H., Sjöland, T.: SICStus Prolog (v3) Users's Manual. SICS, PO Box 1263, S-164 28 Kista, Sweden (1995)
5. Demoen, B.: Dynamic attributes, their hProlog implementation, and a first evaluation. Report CW 350, Dep. of Comp. Science, K.U.Leuven, Leuven, Belgium (October 2002)
6. Hermenegildo, M.V., Bueno, F., Carro, M., López, P., Morales, J.F., Puebla, G.: An overview of the CIAO multiparadigm language and program development environment and its design philosophy. In: Degano, P., De Nicola, R., Bevilacqua, V. (eds.) Concurrency, Graphs and Models. LNCS, vol. 5065, pp. 209–237. Springer, Heidelberg (2008)
7. Holzbaur, C.: Metastructures versus attributed variables in the context of extensible unification. In: Bruynooghe, M., Wirsing, M. (eds.) PLILP 1992. LNCS, vol. 631, pp. 260–268. Springer, Heidelberg (1992)
8. De Koninck, L., Schrijvers, T., Demoen, B.: A flexible search framework for CHR. In: Schrijvers, T., Frühwirth, T. (eds.) Constraint Handling Rules. LNCS, vol. 5388, pp. 16–47. Springer, Heidelberg (2008)
9. SUN Microsystems. The java compatibility test tools (2001)
10. Moura, P.: Logtalk - Design of an Object-Oriented Logic Programming Language. PhD thesis, Department of Informatics, University of Beira Interior, Portugal (September 2003)
11. Pontelli, E., Schrijvers, T., Demoen, B., Moura, P., Swift, T.: Uniting the Prolog Community. ALP newsletter (February 2009)
12. Puls, T.L.: New features in Visual Prolog 7.2. In: Proceedings of the VIP-ALC 2008: Visual Prolog Applications And Language Conference, pp. 6–9. Prolog Development Center (July 2008)
13. Racine, J.: Review: The cygwin tools: A gnu toolkit for windows. Journal of Applied Econometrics 15(3), 331–341 (2000)
14. Meier, M., Aggoun, A., Chan, D., et al.: SEPIA An Extendible Prolog System. In: 11th World Computer Congress IFIP 1989 (August 2009)
15. Sagonas, K., Swift, T., Warren, D.S.: XSB as an Efficient Deductive Database Engine. In: Proc. of the ACM SIGMOD Int. Conf. on the Management of Data, pp. 442–453 (1994)
16. Costa, V.S., Damas, L., Reis, R., Azevedo, R.: YAP User's Manual (2002), http://www.ncc.up.pt/~vsc/Yap
17. Schimpf, J., Shen, K.: ECLiPSe by Example. Tutorial given at CP 2007 (2007)
18. Szabó, P., Szeredi, P.: Improving the ISO prolog standard by analyzing compliance test results. In: Etalle, S., Truszczyński, M. (eds.) ICLP 2006. LNCS, vol. 4079, pp. 257–269. Springer, Heidelberg (2006)
19. Triska, M.: Generalising constraint solving over finite domains. In: Garcia de la Banda, M., Pontelli, E. (eds.) ICLP 2008. LNCS, vol. 5366, pp. 820–821. Springer, Heidelberg (2008)
20. van Noord, G.: At Last Parsing is Now Operational. In: TALN 2006 Verbum Ex Machina, Actes De La 13e Conference sur Le Traitement Automatique des Langues Naturelles, Leuven, pp. 20–42 (2006)
21. Vaughan, G.V., Elliston, B., Tromey, T., Taylor, I.L.: GNU Autoconf, Automake, and Libtool. Pearson Education (October 2000)
22. Wielemaker, J.: SWI-Prolog: Reference Manual. University of Amsterdam, VU University Amsterdam, Kruislaan 419, 1098 VA Amsterdam/De Boelelaan 1081a, 1081 HV Amsterdam (1997-2010), http://www.swi-prolog.org/pldoc/index.html

Explicitly Recursive Grammar Combinators
A Better Model for Shallow Parser DSLs

Dominique Devriese and Frank Piessens

Distrinet, K.U. Leuven
{dominique.devriese,frank.piessens}@cs.kuleuven.be

Abstract. We propose a novel context-free grammar representation for parsing libraries in a pure programming language. Our representation explicitizes the recursion in the grammar, thus avoiding fundamental limitations of the grammar model currently employed by parser combinator libraries. Additionally, we decouple the grammar from its semantic actions using techniques from the Multirec generic programming library. The look and feel of the grammar and semantic actions remain close to traditional EBNF and syntax-directed definitions respectively.

In an accompanying technical report, we demonstrate that our representation supports more declarative implementations of grammar transformations than other work. The ideas described in this paper form the basis for our freely available **grammar-combinators** parsing library[1].

1 Introduction

1.1 Arithmetic Expressions

Let us start this paper with a standard example from the parser literature: a simple language of arithmetic expressions of the form "$(6 * (4 + 2)) + 6$". The following grammar defines this language in a formalism similar to (E)BNF [1, section 2.2]:

```
Line    →  Expr EOF
Expr    →  Expr ' + ' Term
        →  Term
Term    →  Term ' * ' Factor
        →  Factor
Factor  →  ' ( ' Expr ' ) '
        →  Digit+
Digit   →  ' 0 '  |  ' 1 '  |  ' 2 '  |  ...  |  ' 8 '  |  ' 9 '
```

The definitions of Expr and Term are such that "a+b*c" can only be interpreted interpreted as "a+(b*c)" and "a+b+c" only as "(a+b)+c". This modelling of operator precedence and left-associativity is idiomatic for LR-style grammars, but fundamentally relies on left-recursion: one of the productions of non-terminal Expr, for example, refers back to Expr itself in the first position.

---

[1] http://projects.haskell.org/grammar-combinators

R. Rocha and J. Launchbury (Eds.): PADL 2011, LNCS 6539, pp. 84–98, 2011.
© Springer-Verlag Berlin Heidelberg 2011

In order to obtain a parser for this grammar (without manually writing it ourselves), parser generators like Yacc [2] and ANTLR [3] are typically used to translate the grammar (provided in an EBNF-like formalism) into source code in the developer's programming language. This technique has proven succesful in practice, but suffers from various downsides: little assurance for syntax- and type-correctness of generated code, little reuse of the developer's existing programming environment (editor, type-checker, debugger, build system etc.) etc.

1.2   Parser Combinators

An elegant alternative are parser combinators. In this approach, the grammar is defined directly in a general purpose programming language. Parsers are considered first-class values and can be combined, extended, reused etc. With Swierstra and Duponcheel's well-known parser combinator library UUParse [4], our arithmetic expressions language can be expressed with the following definitions:

$$
\begin{aligned}
line &= expr \circledast pEnd \\
expr &= foldr\ (\$) \circledS term \circledast many\ exprTail \\
exprTail &= (+) \circledS pSym\ \text{'+'} \circledast term \\
term &= foldr\ (\$) \circledS factor \circledast many\ termTail \\
termTail &= (*) \circledS pSym\ \text{'*'} \circledast factor \\
factor &= read\ \textcircled{\tiny{R}}\ some\ digit \\
&\quad \textcircled{\tiny{1}}\ pSym\ \text{'('} \circledast expr \circledast pSym\ \text{')'} \\
digit &= pSym\ (\text{'0'},\text{'9'})
\end{aligned}
$$

For every non-terminal, a parser function is defined directly as a Haskell value, by combining primitive parser functions such as *pSym* (in this case produces a primitive parser for a single character in a given range). These are then combined using the *Applicative* and *Alternative* operators $\circledast$ (sequence, apply left result to right result) and $\textcircled{\tiny{1}}$ (disjunction) and shorthands $\circledS$ (apply value to result), $\circledS$ (substitute value for result), and $\circledast$ and $\circledast$ (sequence, ignore left resp. right result). The *many* and *some* combinators return parsers that respectively match zero or more or one or more times a given parser.

Note that the parser functions above mix semantic actions in the definitions of the parser functions. All parsers return the semantic value of the non-terminal they represent: the integer or char (for the *digit* parser) value of the matched string. We consider this mixing of grammar and semantics non-ideal and we will come back to this problem in section 2.4.

Important to notice about the definitions above, is that we have (manually) removed left-recursion from the grammar and replaced it with a different modelling of the left-associativity and precedence of the operators. This alternative modelling is typical for LL-style grammars and traditional parser combinator libraries indeed require the user to perform such a transformation by hand.

1.3   ω-Regular Grammars Considered Harmful

The UUParse parser definitions above express recursion between non-terminals using recursively defined Haskell values. Haskell supports this thanks to its call-by-need (lazy) evaluation strategy. At first sight, it seems that this allows the

UUParse parser to faithfully represent the recursive structure of the original grammar. However, closer inspection reveals that what the Haskell values represent is in fact not so much a graph than an infinite tree. We can see this by considering the *expr* parser function. Because of Haskell's purely functional nature [5], *expr* is observationally equivalent to what we get if we expand it to its definition, and likewise if we expand subexpressions to their definitions:

$$
\begin{aligned}
expr \equiv {} & foldr\ (\$)\ \$\ term \circledast many\ exprTail \\
\equiv {} & foldr\ (\$)\ \$\ (foldr\ (\$)\ \$\ factor \circledast many\ termTail) \circledast many\ exprTail \\
\equiv {} & foldr\ (\$)\ \$\ (foldr\ (\$)\ \$ \\
& (read\ \$\ some\ digit \oplus pSym\ '('\ \circledast exprTail \oplus pSym\ ')') \circledast \\
& many\ termTail) \circledast many\ exprTail
\end{aligned}
$$

In this way, we find an expansion of the definition of *expr* containing *expr* itself as a subexpression. We can continue expanding forever, obtaining an infinite number of expanded expressions, growing in size, and each indistinguishable from the original definition of *expr*. For any n, it is in fact possible to construct a different expression which cannot be distinguished from the original in less than n evaluation steps: simply take the original definition of *expr*, perform $n + 1$ expansions, and then make a change in the result of the final expansion.

These observations have very real practical consequences. A parser library working with such parser definitions, and respecting referential transparency (see section 4.3), is fundamentally limited. It cannot, for example, print a representation of the grammar in any finite number of evaluation steps n, because it might be looking at another grammar that can only be distinguished from the original after more than n computation steps. Similarly, no parsing library using this grammar model can calculate parsing tables upfront, fully execute a grammar transformation, or perform a sanity check for LL(1)-ness.

Because of the similarity of "infinite-tree" grammar definitions to infinite regular grammars, we will refer to this grammar model as ω-regular.

1.4   Toward Context-Free Grammars

Given these fundamental limitations, we define in this paper an alternative representation that does not suffer from them. We will do this without jeopardising the advantages of a parser combinator library (stay in the developer's programming language, keep the close relation of grammar definitions to the original grammar, ensure type safety, keep purely functional style).

The most important change is that we make the recursion in the grammar explicit. More concretely, we want to be able to distinguish the different expansions of the *expr* parser above. Even if they can all be considered functionally equivalent from a strict parsing point of view, we need to be able to treat them differently if we want to be able to print grammars, analyse or transform them.

So, what could be a better way to represent context-free grammars? A simple attempt to construct a better representation of our example grammar starts by defining the non-terminals as first class values:

data $Domain = Line \mid Expr \mid Term \mid Factor \mid Digit$

Our grammar can then be defined as a function that maps every non-terminal to its production rules. With unspecified primitive operations $token$, $endOfInput$, $\langle \cdot \rangle$, $|||$ and $\ggg$ in a $ProductionRule$ type class, we would like it to look somewhat like the following pseudo-code:

$grammarArith :: (ProductionRule\ p) \Rightarrow Domain \rightarrow p\ ()$
$grammarArith\ Line\ =\ \langle Expr \rangle \ggg endOfInput$
$grammarArith\ Expr\ =\ \langle Expr \rangle \ggg token\ \text{'+'} \ggg \langle Term \rangle$
$\qquad\qquad\qquad ||| \ \langle Term \rangle$
...

With non-terminals as first-class values, we avoid the problems related to ω-regular grammars discussed before: for a recursive position in a production rule, we do not embed that non-terminal's production rules directly (as we would do in traditional parser combinator libraries), but instead, we use an abstract $\langle \cdot \rangle$ operator that just marks the position where the recursion appears.

Let's now suppose that we want our grammar to generate an Abstract Syntax Tree (AST) using the following data types.

newtype $Line\ =\ SExpr\ Expr$
data $Expr\ \ =\ Sum\ Expr\ Term$
$\qquad\quad\ \ \mid\ STerm\ Term$
data $Term\ \ =\ Product\ Term\ Factor$
$\qquad\quad\ \ \mid\ SFactor\ Factor$
data $Factor = Paren\ Expr$
$\qquad\qquad\ \ \mid\ Number\ [Digit]$
newtype $Digit = MkDigit\ Char$

If the grammar produces AST result values, then it is not coupled to any concrete set of semantic actions. Semantic actions can be implemented as functions mapping parsed AST values to their semantic values.

$grammarArith :: (ProductionRule\ p) \Rightarrow Domain \rightarrow p\ ()$
$grammarArith\ Line\ =\ SExpr \ggcurly \langle Expr \rangle \ggg endOfInput$
$grammarArith\ Expr\ =\ Sum\quad \ggcurly \langle Expr \rangle \ggg^{*} token\ \text{'+'} \ggg \langle Term \rangle$
$\qquad\qquad\qquad ||| \ STerm \ggcurly \langle Term \rangle$
...

Unfortunately, the above grammar does not type check. Essentially, the problem is that all our non-terminals are of type $Domain$, so that all references $\langle idx \rangle$ must share a single result type. With the simple non-terminal representation above, we cannot express that non-terminal $Line$ corresponds to a different type of semantic values than non-terminal $Expr$.

Additionally, making the grammar produce AST result values is not necessarily a good idea. First, in cases where semantic values are small, it is not memory efficient, as the AST will be kept around in its entirety throughout the parsing process, even those parts which have already been processed by the semantic processor and are no longer needed. As long as the top node of the tree is being referenced, a garbage collector cannot deallocate any of the child nodes, since all of them are still being referenced. Secondly, this solution is also inherently linked to a top-down matching order, as it can only start producing semantic actions starting from the root node.

In this paper, we propose a solution to these problems based on a representation of non-terminals not all sharing the same type, which we present in section 2.1. In section 2.3, we define a well-typed primitive recursion operator $\langle \cdot \rangle$ and in section 2.4, we abstract grammars from their semantics without working with a full intermediate AST. Section 2.5 shows what the resulting grammar and semantic actions look like. In section 3, we discuss the expressive power and performance that can be expected from a library using our grammar model and in sections 4 and 5, we discuss related work and offer a conclusion.

In this text, we rely on a set of Haskell extensions that is currently only supported by the GHC Haskell compiler[2]. These are all well-accepted extensions that do not make type-checking undecidable. Our library supports the use of Template Haskell [6] for performing grammar transformations at compile-time (but TH is not needed if you don't use this).

2   An Explicitly Recursive Representation

2.1   Representing Non-terminals

We will model the set of non-terminals (the *domain*) as a "subkind" with proof terms, using the technique employed by Yakushev et al. to model indices into a set of mutually recursive data types in Multirec [7]. The GADT [8] ϕ_{arith} is a "subkind" that represents the domain of our arithmetic expressions grammar:

$$
\begin{aligned}
\textbf{data } \phi_{arith} \; ix \textbf{ where } & Line :: \phi_{arith} \; Line \\
& Expr :: \phi_{arith} \; Expr \\
& Term :: \phi_{arith} \; Term \\
& Factor :: \phi_{arith} \; Factor \\
& Digit :: \phi_{arith} \; Digit
\end{aligned}
$$

We use the previously defined AST types *Line*, *Expr*, *Term*, *Factor* and *Digit* to represent the non-terminals at the type-level. The GADT [8] ϕ_{arith} defines, for each non-terminal *ix*, a term of type $\phi_{arith} \; ix$, serving as a proof that *ix* is part of the domain ϕ_{arith}. With this "subkind" representation, we can express that a function is polymorphic over precisely the five non-terminal types in the domain, if it has type $f :: \forall ix \; . \; \phi \; ix \rightarrow \dots$ Note also that Haskell's separation between type and function name spaces allows the data constructor *Expr* and the type *Expr* to share the same name.

---

[2] TypeFamilies, GADTs, MultiParamTypeClasses, FunctionalDependencies, Flexible-Contexts and RankNTypes.

Because our non-terminal identifiers (*Line*, *Expr* etc.) all have different types, we can represent semantic values as a data family [9] over these types, associating each non-terminal type with the type of its semantic value. We will refer to such a family as a *semantic value family*. We define one such family for the ϕ_{arith} domain, written $[\![]\!]^{value}$.

data family $[\![]\!]^{value}$ ix
newtype instance $[\![]\!]^{value}$ $Line$ $= [\![\cdot]\!]^{value}_{Line}$ Int
newtype instance $[\![]\!]^{value}$ $Expr$ $= [\![\cdot]\!]^{value}_{Expr}$ Int
newtype instance $[\![]\!]^{value}$ $Term$ $= [\![\cdot]\!]^{value}_{Term}$ Int
newtype instance $[\![]\!]^{value}$ $Factor = [\![\cdot]\!]^{value}_{Factor}$ Int
newtype instance $[\![]\!]^{value}$ $Digit$ $= [\![\cdot]\!]^{value}_{Decimal}$ $Char$

This semantic value family specifies that for each non-terminal an *Int* value is kept (its calculated value), except for *Digit*, for which a character is kept.

2.2 Production Rules

We represent a grammar as a function mapping each non-terminal onto its production rules. To construct these production rules, we use combinators based on UUParse. We define them in type classes *ProductionRule* and *CharProductionRule*, so that algorithms can implement them as they need to.

class *ProductionRule* p **where**
$(\ggg)$ $:: p\ (a \to b) \to p\ a \to p\ b$
$(\|\|\|)$ $:: p\ va \to p\ va \to p\ va$
$\epsilon[\cdot]$ $:: a \to p\ a$
$endOfInput :: p\ ()$
die $:: p\ a$

class *CharProductionRule* p **where**
$token :: Char \to p\ Char$

Many of the functions above correspond directly to functions in the standard *Applicative* or *Alternative* type classes, but we avoid them for stylistic consistency, because we want to avoid the (ω-regular style) *some* and *many* operators in *Alternative* and for technical reasons related to a specific feature in our library (Template Haskell lifting of grammars). The $\ggg$ operator (corresponds to ⊛) represents sequencing of rules, applying the function result of the first rule to the result of the second (idiomatic for an *applicative* parser combinator style). The $\|\|\|$ operator (⊕) represents disjunction of parser rules, $\epsilon[v]$ (*pure v*) represents a rule matching the empty string and returning v as the parse result. The operator *die* (*empty*) returns a rule that always fails and *endOfInput* only matches the end of the string being parsed, returning a unit value. The *token* function in the *CharProductionRule* type class operator produces a rule that matches a single character and returns it. In the **grammar-combinators** library, a more complex version of the latter type class is used, that is polymorphic in the token type.

We omit the definitions for shorthand operators $\gg\!\!\ni$, $\ggg^*$ and $\ni\!\!\gg^*$, respectively applying a given function to the result of a rule, ignoring a sequenced rule's result, and replacing a rule's result with a given value.

2.3 A Different Take on Recursion

The crux to representing recursion properly in our grammars is the primitive recursion construct $\langle\cdot\rangle$, defined in the *RecProductionRule* type class below. The expression $\langle idx\rangle$ represents a recursive reference to non-terminal idx. Its result type is defined as $r\ ix$, where r is the semantic value family carried around by the production rule type p. The *RecProductionRule* class's functional dependencies ϕ and r will make sure that all rules in a grammar use the same domain and have consistent type requirements for references.

> **class** *RecProductionRule* $p\ \phi\ r\ |\ p \to \phi, p \to r$ **where**
> $\quad\langle\cdot\rangle :: \phi\ ix \to p\ (r\ ix)$

It is important to note that we do not define the $\langle\cdot\rangle$ operator in a type class just to add superficial polymorphism. On the contrary, it is this ability to overload the $\langle\cdot\rangle$ operator that will allow our algorithms to handle recursion in the way they need to. Some algorithms will simply unfold the recursion completely, effectively reverting back to the ω-regular representation, but others will handle the recursion in a fundamentally different way (e.g. limiting recursion depth, printing a string "<...>" in a grammar printer).

2.4 Semantic Value Family Polymorphism

Semantic value families allow us to impose a consistent typing of production rules in a grammar, but a remaining problem is that we do not actually want to couple a grammar to a single semantic value family. For example, for our arithmetic expressions grammar, we will further on define the *calcArith* set of semantic actions (we will refer to such a set as a *semantic processor*), that uses the $[\![]\!]^{value}$ family defined above to calculate the result of expressions as they are recognized. Other useful semantic processors could transform the same expressions into reverse polish notation, construct an AST or perform some form of side effects in a *Monad*. We will improve the modularity of grammars by decoupling them from their semantic processors.

As discussed in section 1.4, we do not want to solve this problem with the AST as a mandatory intermediate representation for parse results, because it is not memory efficient and limited to a top-down matching order. A better approach uses (again) techniques from the Multirec generic programming library[7]. They use a representation of mutually recursive data types as the fixed point of a *pattern functor* to manipulate them in generic algorithms. The AST data types shown previously are an example of such a family of mutually recursive data types, and the following is its pattern functor:

data PF_{arith} r ix **where**

$$
\begin{array}{lll}
SExprF & :: r\ Expr & \to & PF_{arith}\ r\ Line \\
SumF & :: r\ Expr & \to r\ Term & \to PF_{arith}\ r\ Expr \\
STermF & :: r\ Term & \to & PF_{arith}\ r\ Expr \\
ProductF & :: r\ Term & \to r\ Factor & \to PF_{arith}\ r\ Term \\
SFactorF & :: r\ Factor & \to & PF_{arith}\ r\ Term \\
ParenF & :: r\ Expr & \to & PF_{arith}\ r\ Factor \\
NumberF & :: [r\ Digit] & \to & PF_{arith}\ r\ Factor \\
MkDigitF & :: Char & \to & PF_{arith}\ r\ Digit \\
\end{array}
$$

type instance $PF\ \phi_{arith} = PF_{arith}$

The GADT PF_{arith} defines constructors analogous to the constructors of our AST data types, but recursive positions of type ix are replaced with values $r\ ix$ of the argument semantic value family r. As such, the semantic value family r plays the role of a *subtree representation functor* (our terminology), defining what values to keep for subtrees of AST nodes. Pattern functor values are tagged with the AST node type they represent. The type family instance registers PF_{arith} as the pattern functor for domain ϕ_{arith}.

Like for simply recursive types, data types isomorphic to our original AST data types can be recovered from this pattern functor by taking its fixed point using a type-level fixpoint combinator $HFix$. But the pattern functor also allows to do more with the AST values. Yakushev et al. demonstrate how to go back and forth between a type ix in a domain ϕ and its *one-level unfolding* of type $PF\ \phi\ I_*\ ix$ (where I_* is a wrapping identity functor: $I_*\ ix \sim ix$). For our example, they could convert a value of the AST type $Expr$ into an unfolded value of type $PF_{arith}\ I_*\ Expr$, exposing the top-level of its structure (similar, if you will, to the unfold operation for iso-recursive types [10, pp. 276-277]). Generic operations on instances of the pattern functor then allow them to implement various general-purpose generic algorithms. All of this gives an impressive, elegant and powerful generic programming machinery, but for our purposes, it is actually more useful to work with the pattern functor in a different way.

A powerful feature of the pattern functor is in fact the abstraction of the subtree representation functor r, allowing subtrees to be represented differently than as full subtrees. If we take our semantic value family $[\![\,]\!]^{value}$ as this subtree representation functor (instead of the wrapping identity functor I_*), then subtrees in the one-level unfolding of an AST are represented just by their calculated value (instead of a full sub-AST). For example, the value $(SumF\ [\![15]\!]^{value}_{Expr}\ [\![3]\!]^{value}_{Term})$ of type $(PF_{arith}\ [\![\,]\!]^{value}\ Expr)$ represents an $Expr$ value, constructed as the sum of another $Expr$ and a $Term$, where we only know that the value of the left hand side $Expr$ is 15 and the right hand side $Term$ has value 3. In general, the pattern functor PF_{arith} allows us to represent an AST where subtrees have already been processed into a semantic value, and this turns out to be precisely the vehicle we need for modelling the collaboration between a grammar, a parsing algorithm and a semantic processor.

Let us consider production rule Expr $\to$ Expr '+'Term as an example. Figure 1 shows a graphical illustration of this collaboration (for a semantic processor

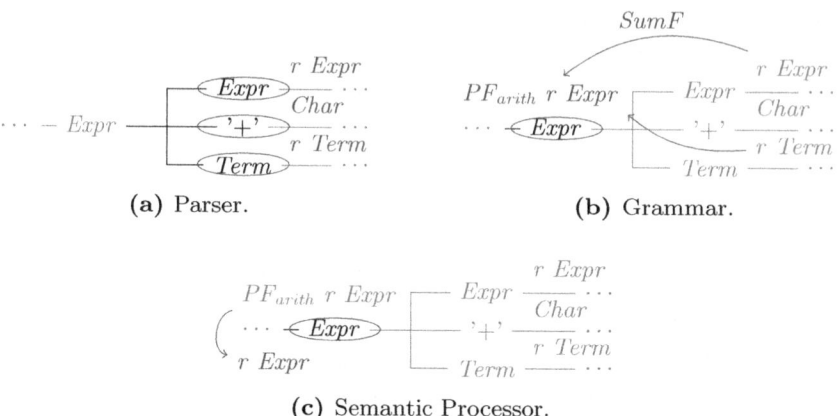

(a) Parser. (b) Grammar.

(c) Semantic Processor.

Fig. 1. A graphical representation of the collaboration between parser, grammar and semantic processor, using ϕ_{arith}'s pattern functor over a semantic value family r as an intermediate representation

working with a semantic value family r). In Figure 1a, the parser has matched the right-hand side elements of the production rule and has obtained their semantic values, typed r *Expr*, *Char* and r *Term*. In 1b, the grammar specifies how to combine these three values to the top of an AST, constructing a value of type PF_{arith} r *Expr*. For this production rule, the *SumF* constructor is used, throwing away the parse result for token '+'. Note that the grammar does not know anything about semantic value family r. In Figure 1c, the semantic processor accepts the constructed PF_{arith} r *Expr* value, calculates the combined semantic value and returns a processed value of type r *Expr* to the parser for use in subsequent matches. Note that nothing here assumes a top-down matching order.

2.5   So What Do We Get?

With all of this, the machinery for our context-free grammar combinators is in place, and we can define our running example grammar as follows:

type *ExtendedContextFreeGrammar* $\phi = \forall\, p\, r\, ix$. (*ProductionRule p*,
   CharProductionRule p, *RecProductionRule p* ϕ *r*,
   LoopProductionRule p ϕ *r*) $\Rightarrow \phi$ *ix* $\rightarrow$ *p* (*PF* ϕ *r ix*)
grammarArith :: *ExtendedContextFreeGrammar* ϕ_{arith}
grammarArith Line   = *SExprF* $\gg$ $\langle Expr \rangle$ $\ggg^*$ *endOfInput*
grammarArith Expr   = *STermF* $\gg$ $\langle Term \rangle$
     ||| *SumF* $\gg$ $\langle Expr \rangle$ $\ggg^*$ *token* '+' $\ggg$ $\langle Term \rangle$
grammarArith Term   = *SFactorF* $\gg$ $\langle Factor \rangle$
     ||| *ProductF* $\gg$ $\langle Term \rangle$ $\ggg^*$ *token* '*' $\ggg$ $\langle Factor \rangle$
grammarArith Factor = *NumberF* $\gg$ $\langle Digit \rangle^+$
     ||| *ParenF* $\gg^*$ *token* '(' $\ggg$ $\langle Expr \rangle$ $\ggg^*$ *token* ')'
grammarArith Digit = *MkDigitF* $\gg$ *tokenRange* ['0'..'9']

We first define a general *ExtendedContextFreeGrammar* type synonym, expressing that an extended context-free grammar is a function returning a production rule for every non-terminal. The $\forall \cdot$ quantification expresses that it must be defined for any production rule interpretation type p supporting the context-free grammar operations of type classes *ProductionRule*, *CharProductionRule* and *RecProductionRule*, and a type class *LoopProductionRule* that we have not encountered yet. It must also work with any semantic value family r, producing values of the pattern functor $PF\ \phi$ with r as the subtree representation type.

Our grammar *grammarArith* is typed *ExtendedContextFreeGrammar* ϕ_{arith}, neatly expressing exactly what it is: an extended context-free grammar for the domain ϕ_{arith}. The production rules are defined using combinators we saw before, and values of $PF_{arith}\ r$ are produced using the pattern functor's constructors. The one thing we have not yet discussed is the use of $\langle Digit \rangle^{+}$ in the production rule for *Factor*, representing one or more times the *Digit* non-terminal. The $\langle \cdot \rangle^{+}$ operator (and its companion $\langle \cdot \rangle^{*}$) is defined in the type class *LoopProductionRule*, and it is the use of this class that makes the grammar an *extended* context-free grammar. One of the algorithms we discuss in our technical report [11] automates the standard translation of such an extended grammar into a grammar using only normal references over an enlarged domain.

Stylistically, the pattern functor constructors end up at the beginning of each production rule, giving a nice visual tagging of the rules, and defining for each production rule what kind of AST node it corresponds with. The shorthand operators $\ggg^{*}$ and $\ggg^{*}$ allow us to indicate that the result of their right-hand side rules are not significant for the construction of the AST without distracting attention from the grammar. Note finally that this grammar is closer to the original grammar than the UUParse version on page 85, because we have done nothing to remove left recursion from the grammar and because semantics are kept separate from the grammar definition.

Our semantic processors become remarkably similar to syntax-directed definitions traditionally used with parser generators [1, pp. 303–323]:

$$\textbf{type } Processor\ \phi\ r = \forall\ ix\ .\ \phi\ ix \rightarrow PF\ \phi\ r\ ix \rightarrow r\ ix$$

$$calcArith :: Processor\ \phi_{arith}\ [\![]\!]^{value}$$

$$calcArith\ Line\quad (SExprF\ [\![e]\!]^{value}_{Expr}) = [\![e]\!]^{value}_{Line}$$

$$calcArith\ Expr\quad (SumF\ [\![e]\!]^{value}_{Expr}\ [\![t]\!]^{value}_{Term})\quad = [\![e+t]\!]^{value}_{Expr}$$

$$calcArith\ Expr\quad (STermF\ [\![t]\!]^{value}_{Term})\quad = [\![t]\!]^{value}_{Expr}$$

$$calcArith\ Term\quad (ProductF\ [\![e]\!]^{value}_{Term}\ [\![t]\!]^{value}_{Factor}) = [\![e*t]\!]^{value}_{Term}$$

$$calcArith\ Term\quad (SFactorF\ [\![t]\!]^{value}_{Factor})\quad = [\![t]\!]^{value}_{Term}$$

$$calcArith\ Factor\ (ParenF\ [\![e]\!]^{value}_{Expr})\quad = [\![e]\!]^{value}_{Factor}$$

$$calcArith\ Factor\ (NumberF\ ds)$$
$$= [\![read\ \$\ map\ (\lambda[\![d]\!]^{value}_{Decimal} \rightarrow d)\ ds]\!]^{value}_{Factor}$$

$$calcArith\ Digit\quad (MkDigitF\ c)\quad = [\![c]\!]^{value}_{Decimal}$$

This processor implements the direct calculation of *Int* values for subexpressions that we have previously described. Note its type *Processor* $\phi_{arith}\ [\![]\!].^{value}$, expressing that it is a processor for domain ϕ_{arith}, producing semantic values of family $[\![]\!]^{value}$. Like in traditional parser combinator libraries, a semantic processor can also produce side effects, simply by working with monadic calculations as semantic values instead of simple values.

Another example of a semantic processor, for which we do not need to provide any code, can be found in Yakushev et al.'s Multirec paper [7]. They define a function $to :: \phi\ ix \rightarrow PF\ \phi\ I_*\ ix \rightarrow ix$ in the *Fam* type class, transforming a single-level unfolding of an AST (as described earlier) back into the traditional AST data type. Serendipitously, composing to with the I_* constructor yields a ready-to-use and important semantic processor for our grammars. The function $(I_*\ .)\ .\ to$ (applying I_* to the result of applying to to two arguments) is precisely the semantic processor that produces a wrapped version of the AST as its semantic value. This elegant correspondence illustrates that our use of Multirec pattern functors to abstract semantic actions is a natural and powerful fit.

3   The Proof of the Pudding

3.1   Features

A grammar representation can only ever be as useful as the algorithms that it supports. Because of space constraints, we discuss the implementation of three important grammar algorithms in an accompanying technical report [11]:

printGrammar. Pretty-print a grammar definition in an (E)BNF like notation.
foldLoops. Perform the standard translation of an extended context-free grammar to a normal context-free grammar over an enlarged domain.
transformLeftCorner. Apply the left-corner transform [12] to convert a left-recursive grammar to an equivalent non-left-recursive grammar. Contrary to other work, our implementation of the transformation uses a functional style.

Furthermore, we have implemented an elaborate grammar analysis, transformation and parsing Haskell library called `grammar-combinators`, that is freely available online. This library is designed as a collection of independently usable, purely functional grammar algorithms that together form a comprehensive grammar library. The library provides various features that, to the best of our knowledge, are unavailable in any existing parser EDSL library.

Some practical features are a powerful transformation library (including the left-corner transform and a uniform version of Paull's left-recursion removal [1, p. 177], support for performing grammar transformations at compile time using Template Haskell [6]), a packrat parser [13] and basic compatibility components for UUParse[4] and Parsec[14].

A lot of interesting work remains to be done using the `grammar-combinators` library. It is published as an open source (GNU LGPL) library in the hope to attract people interested in parsing practice and/or EDSLs, both from research and practical perspectives. In the accompanying technical report [11], we discuss some ideas for future work (e.g. automatic inference of branches requiring backtracking for Parsec, checking LL(*)-ness and absence of left-recursion in grammars, penalty-based error handling for interactive scenario's).

3.2 Limitations

Defining the domain, pattern functor, semantic value family (families) and semantic processors for a grammar adds complexity, abstraction, and some extra work. On top of that, some limitations need to be taken into account.

A compelling feature of parser combinators that we have not looked at, is the ease with which you can combine unrelated parsers into new ones. We require a full view of grammars, and this makes us lose the simple compositionality of parser combinators. We think a grammar combination primitive can be introduced to partly recover this, but this remains future work.

Another limitation is that the added abstraction inevitably has a performance cost. In some initial tests, we have effectively noticed an important performance impact, even though general optimizations for generic code [15] seem to reduce it considerably. Performing grammar transformations at compile-time using Template Haskell limited the performance impact further. A more detailed performance analysis remains future work.

4   Related Work

For background material on context-free grammars, parsing and grammar transformations, we refer to Aho, Sethi and Ullman [1].

4.1   Parser Combinators

Parser combinators have a long history (see Leijen and Meijer [14] for references), but most work employs an ω-regular representation of grammars, with the associated downsides that we have discussed in section 1. Here, we limit ourselves to work that uses a representation of grammars in which recursion is observable.

TTTAS. Baars and Swierstra [16] (previous work [17]) implement the left-corner grammar transform [12] using type-level natural numbers as the representation of non-terminals. They ensure type-safety using a type environment encoded as a list of types. They propose a transformation library based on the arrows abstraction, which they use essentially for the generation of fresh type-level identifiers. Like ours, their grammar representation explicitly represents the grammar's recursion in a well-typed way and allows them to implement the left-corner transform and support left-recursive grammars.

Nevertheless, we believe our work provides significant improvements over theirs. Our representation of non-terminals as a "subkind with proof terms" [7] and type environments as data families is much less complex. We provide semantic value family polymorphism, which they do not. Contrary to their stateful *Trafo* transformation arrows, our grammar transformations do not require fresh non-terminal identifiers and feature a purely functional style [11].

Furthermore, Baars and Swierstra's grammars seem designed for compiler-generation in Viera et al.'s alternative for the standard Haskell *read*-function [18] and they are less easily human-readable than our grammars. Finally, Baars and Swierstra only discuss an implementation of the left-corner grammar transform, while we show the importance of our approach for a wider parsing library and discuss implementations of a variety of useful algorithms for grammar analysis, transformation and parsing [11].

Dependently typed parser combinators. Brink, Holdermans and Löh describe a dependently typed parser combinator library [19], implemented in the Agda programming language [20]. Agda's dependently typed nature simplifies the requirements on the representation of non-terminals (types of production rules can more simply depend on non-terminals). They implement the left-corner transformation in their formalism, and provide a machine-checkable proof of a language-inclusion property for the transformation.

The proof of correctness properties beyond type-safety is out of range in a language like Haskell and we think that Brink et al.'s provably correct grammar transformation shows that dependently typed functional programming is the way of the future, fulfilling old promises of practical provably correct programming. When looking at the modelling of grammars however, our model does provide some advantages over theirs, such as a nicer syntax for grammars and semantic value polymorphism.

4.2   Squiggolist Attribute Grammars

Our modelling of semantic processors (see section 2.5) is related to Fokkinga et al.'s account of attribute grammars as catamorphisms [21]. The functor F they define corresponds to our pattern functors $PF\ \phi$, but we do not need their third simplifying assumption (all non-terminals have the same semantic value) because of our use of Multirec. Their production and evaluation rule labels correspond (even visually) to AST pattern functor constructors in our model, which is a more meaningful concept. The main difference is that we do not model general attribute grammars with both upward and downward information flow, but only allow upward information flow (resulting in so-called *S-attributed grammars*), making our processors independent from a matching order.

4.3   Observable Sharing

Observing recursion in recursively defined values is sometimes referred to as "observable sharing". It is an open problem how this can be done in general in functional languages like Haskell. Several solutions have been explored, ranging from observing sharing within the *IO* monad [22] to adding referential identity as a fundamental language feature [23]. Our solution does not provide observable sharing for Haskell code but instead models the recursion in the parsing EDSL with a representation that is observable in Haskell. We think our approach is a compelling alternative for many of the applications of observable sharing.

4.4   Finally Tagless DSLs

Finally, our work is related to Carette, Kiselyov and Shan's tagless modelling of a typed object-language in a typed meta-language, in two interesting ways. First, if we look at our grammar definitions as expressions in a typed object language, then our *ProductionRule* and *CharProductionRule* type classes correspond directly to their *final tagless* model. From this point of view, our *RecProductionRule* type class improves upon their work by extending the final tagless model in a type-safe way to support meta-language-observable recursion in the object language. This extension achieves most of the benefits of their representation except that it depends on GADTs which they try to avoid.

On the other hand, if we consider the AST as the representation of an expression in an embedded typed object language, we see that the semantics of our grammars could also be expressed using a final tagless representations. In this model, the call to the *SumF* pattern functor constructor in the grammar would for example be replaced by a call to a *sum* function in a grammar-specific *ArithSemantics* type class. Such a final tagless encoding is more extensible than a standard encoding using GADTs, but our representation using the Multirec pattern functor features this extensibility as well (because the pattern functor is parametric in the representation of recursive sub-data). Additionally, it offers some benefits of its own that seem unavailable in a finally tagless style (e.g. supports generic algorithms using MultiRec [7]).

5   Conclusion

In summary, in this paper we make the following contributions:

- We discuss the fundamental limitations of the "ω-regular" grammar model used by current parser combinator libraries and argue for a richer model.
- We propose one novel such richer context-free grammar model, featuring type safety, referential transparency, natural grammar and semantic processor definitions and memory efficient semantic value family polymorphism.
- We discuss evidence that (contrarily to current parser combinator models) our representation supports a wide range of grammar algorithms, referring to an accompanying technical report and the implementation in our freely available `grammar-combinators` library.

Acknowledgements. This research is partially funded by the Interuniversity Attraction Poles Programme Belgian State, Belgian Science Policy, and by the Research Fund K.U.Leuven. Dominique Devriese holds a Ph. D. fellowship of the Research Foundation - Flanders (FWO). We thank Arie Middelkoop, Tom Schrijvers, Adriaan Moors, Doaitse Swierstra and the anonymous reviewers for their comments.

References

1. Aho, A.V., Lam, M.S., Sethi, R., Ullman, J.D.: Compilers: Principles, Techniques and Tools, 2nd edn. Addison-Wesley, Reading (2006)
2. Johnson, S.C.: YACC. Unix Programmer's Manual 2b (1979)
3. Parr, T., Quong, R.: ANTLR: A predicated-LL(k) parser generator. Software: Practice and Experience 25(7), 789–810 (1995)
4. Swierstra, S., Duponcheel, L.: Deterministic, error-correcting combinator parsers. In: Advanced Functional Programming, pp. 184–207 (1996)
5. Sabry, A.: What is a purely functional language? JFP 8(1), 1–22 (1998)
6. Sheard, T., Peyton Jones, S.: Template meta-programming for Haskell. SIGPLAN Notices 37(12), 75 (2002)
7. Yakushev, A., Holdermans, S., Löh, A., Jeuring, J.: Generic programming with fixed points for mutually recursive datatypes. In: ICFP, pp. 233–244 (2009)
8. Peyton Jones, S., Vytiniotis, D., Weirich, S., Washburn, G.: Simple unification-based type inference for GADTs. In: ICFP, pp. 61 (2006)
9. Schrijvers, T., Peyton Jones, S., Chakravarty, M., Sulzmann, M.: Type checking with open type functions. In: ICFP, pp. 51–62 (2008)
10. Pierce, B.: Types and programming languages. MIT Press, Cambridge (2002)
11. Devriese, D., Piessens, F.: Explicitly recursive grammar combinators - Implementation of some grammar algorithms. Technical Report CW594, KULeuven CS (2010)
12. Moore, R.: Removing left recursion from context-free grammars. In: NAACL, pp. 249–255 (2000)
13. Ford, B.: Packrat parsing: simple, powerful, lazy, linear time - functional pearl. In: ICFP, pp. 36–47 (2002)
14. Leijen, D., Meijer, E.: Parsec: Direct style monadic parser combinators for the real world. Technical Report UU-CS-2001-27, Universiteit Utrecht CS (2001)
15. Magalhaes, J., Holdermans, S., Jeuring, J., Löh, A.: Optimizing generics is easy! In: Workshop on Partial Evaluation and Program Manipulation, pp. 33–42 (2010)
16. Baars, A., Swierstra, S., Viera, M.: Typed transformations of typed abstract syntax. In: TLDI, pp. 15–26 (2009)
17. Baars, A., Swierstra, S.: Type-safe, self inspecting code. In: HASKELL (2004)
18. Viera, M., Swierstra, S., Lempsink, E.: Haskell, do you read me? constructing and composing efficient top-down parsers at runtime. In: HASKELL, pp. 63–74 (2008)
19. Brink, K., Holdermans, S., Löh, A.: Dependently typed grammars. In: Bolduc, C., Desharnais, J., Ktari, B. (eds.) MPC 2010. LNCS, vol. 6120, pp. 58–79. Springer, Heidelberg (2010)
20. Norell, U.: Towards a practical programming language based on dependent type theory. PhD thesis, Chalmers University of Technology (2007)
21. Fokkinga, M., Jeuring, J., Meertens, L., Meijer, E.: A translation from attribute grammars to catamorphisms. The Squiggolist 2(1), 20–26 (1991)
22. Gill, A.: Type-safe observable sharing in Haskell. In: Haskell, pp. 117–128 (2009)
23. Claessen, K., Sands, D.: Observable sharing for functional circuit description. In: Thiagarajan, P.S., Yap, R.H.C. (eds.) ASIAN 1999. LNCS, vol. 1742, p. 62. Springer, Heidelberg (1999)

Declarative Belief Set Merging Using Merging Plans*

Christoph Redl, Thomas Eiter, and Thomas Krennwallner

Institut für Informationssysteme, Technische Universität Wien
Favoritenstraße 9-11, A-1040 Vienna, Austria
{redl,eiter,tkren}@kr.tuwien.ac.at

Abstract. We present a declarative framework for belief set merging tasks over
(possibly heterogeneous) knowledge bases, where belief sets are sets of literals.
The framework is designed generically for flexible deployment to a range of applications, and allows to specify complex merging tasks in tree-structured *merging plans*, whose leaves are the possible belief sets of the knowledge bases that
are processed using *merging operators*. A prototype is implemented in MELD
(MErging Library for Dlvhex) on top of the dlvhex system for HEX-programs,
which are nonmonotonic logic programs with access to external sources. Plans
in the task description language allow to formulate different conflict resolution
strategies, and by shared object libraries, the user may also develop and integrate
her own merging operators. MELD supports rapid prototyping of merging tasks,
providing a computational backbone such that users can focus on *operator optimization and evaluation*, and on *experimenting* with merging strategies; this is
particularly useful if a best merging operator or strategy is not known. Example applications are combining multiple decision diagrams (e.g., in biomedicine),
judgment aggregation in social choice theory, and ontology merging.

1 Introduction

Merging knowledge from multiple knowledge bases has gained increasing attention
over the years, given that more and more knowledge from (possibly heterogeneous)
different sources must be combined into a coherent view. As knowledge bases are associated with sets of beliefs, i.e., statements an agent believes to be true (which need not
to be the case), in particular merging the belief sets of knowledge bases into a single
belief set is an issue. This problem has been widely studied, and there are many different approaches, e.g., [10]; for an introduction and a distinction from belief revision,
see [11].

Roughly, the merging approaches fall into two classes. The one class adheres to base-
oriented, syntactic strategies where the result of merging is a knowledge base, such that
its belief sets are the merged belief sets (e.g., [8]). The other class performs merging at
the semantic level, i.e., at the level of *models* of the knowledge bases, and aims to construct a merged set of models with associated syntactic belief sets (e.g., [13,16]). Several approaches are based on measuring distances between models resp. formulas [9];
however, appropriate distance functions are usually application dependent.

---

* Support: Austrian Science Fund P20841 and Vienna Science and Technology Fund ICT
08-020.

R. Rocha and J. Launchbury (Eds.): PADL 2011, LNCS 6539, pp. 99–114, 2011.

Apparently there is no single approach which is superior to all others in arbitrary scenarios and applications. Lack of domain knowledge may make it very hard to predict which choice will work out best. It is then reasonable, or also necessary, to experiment with various choices and to evaluate the results empirically. Furthermore, it may be necessary to combine different merging operators, taking the specific needs and criteria of some of the knowledge bases into account. However, despite many theoretical frameworks for belief merging, support for merging in practice is scarce, and the user has the burden to develop merging procedures and implement a workflow (e.g. perform syntactic alignment of the knowledge bases, apply a binary merging operator repeatedly, etc), as well as to cope with issues of heterogeneity. Changes for experimenting with different operators and workflows are cumbersome and require major efforts.

To alleviate this problem, we have developed a practical framework for belief set merging. It allows the declarative specification of a merging task in a formal and machine-readable way, using *merging plans* in a dedicated language. Application-dependent parts of the specification are defined by the user, i.e., the application developer, while routine tasks are managed by our framework. To encompass wide applicability, the framework is generically based on beliefs that are literals, i.e., possibly negated atomic formulas, following the semantic direction; via suitable encodings and operators, also sources with non-logical content may be handled (e.g., decision diagrams as we show).

Our main contributions are briefly summarized as follows.

- We define a simple, generic framework for belief set merging tasks where belief sets are sets of ground literals in predicate logic; they may also be viewed as models of the knowledge bases, which are sets of formulas (we will use the term *belief bases* synonymously) (Section 2). We provide the formal syntax and semantics of merging plans in a dedicated *merging task language* (Section 3). A merging plan is, like an arithmetic expression, a hierarchical arrangement of *merging operators* of arity $n \geq 1$ which describe how to merge n sets of belief sets into a single one; allowing $n = 1$ is convenient to accommodate also transformations (conversion, data cleaning, etc.) on sets of belief sets. An operator is either applied on merging sub-plans, i.e., the result of previous operator applications, or on the input knowledge bases.

- We have implemented the formal framework in the MELD system (*MErging Library for Dlvhex*) [14] (Section 4), which has been developed as plugin for the dlvhex reasoner.[1] The systems allows the automatic evaluation of merging plans written in our merging language, i.e., the computation of the merged belief sets according to the merging plans. MELD is based on HEX-programs [5], which are non-monotonic logic programs that allow to access external sources (for our concerns, knowledge bases at an extensional level). In fact, we extended HEX-programs to nested HEX-programs that allow to evaluate HEX-programs and access the resulting models as first class citizens; such an extension is novel and of independent interest for non-monotonic logic programs in general. Via abstract interfacing, also merging of heterogeneous knowledge bases can be handled in a flexible way.

- To explore the usefulness of the approach, we have considered various applications, which currently include decision diagram merging in life sciences (e.g., for DNA classification or screening tests), judgment aggregation, and merging of knowledge

---

[1] www.kr.tuwien.ac.at/research/systems/dlvhex/mergingplugin.html

bases in the Semantic Web (Section 6). We focus here on decision diagrams, which are encoded to belief sets via a natural encoding into a factual representation. The support for rapid prototyping and experimenting with merging scenarios could be fruitfully exploited to arrive for real-world data at a merging result that outperforms other results, and could have hardly been obtained without automated support.

To our knowledge, no comparable framework for belief merging in practice exists. MELD aims at providing a user-friendly interface for rapid prototyping of belief set merging tasks with large flexibility, such that the application developer can focus on the selection, optimization, and workflow of the merging strategy. The merging operators can be selected from a predefined library or defined by the user, using a simple plugin interface. We believe implementations of our framework like MELD will greatly alleviate to determine the right merging strategy in prototyping for a range of applications.

2 Preliminaries

We consider merging of belief sets that are close to model-based semantics of classical logic, in a finite setting. In our view, we abstract from a concrete language for knowledge bases and identify the latter with associated sets of belief sets. In this context, the term *belief bases* is used as a synonym for knowledge bases. To formulate beliefs, we assume a signature $\Sigma = (\Sigma_c, \Sigma_p)$ of a set Σ_c of constant symbols and a set Σ_p of predicate symbols of arity ≥ 0. For practical concerns, Σ is finite.

Definition 1. *A belief is an atomic formula $p(c_1, \ldots, c_n)$ or negated atomic formula $\neg p(c_1, \ldots, c_n)$ (i.e., a literal) over Σ. The set of all beliefs over Σ is denoted by Lit_Σ (i.e., the set of all literals over Σ). A belief set is a set $B \subseteq Lit_\Sigma$ of literals. The set of all belief sets is denoted by $\mathcal{A}(\Sigma) = 2^{Lit_\Sigma}$.*

The semantic abstraction of knowledge bases is then as follows.

Definition 2. *Given a knowledge base KB (in some language), it has associated belief sets $BS(KB) \subseteq \mathcal{A}(\Sigma)$.*

Intuitively, each belief set $B \in BS(KB)$ coherently collects conclusions from the knowledge base. There might be different possibilities, e.g., in a model-based view, or as common in non-monotonic logics. The following examples illustrate this.

Example 1. Consider the knowledge base $KB = \{dog(sue) \vee cat(sue), male(sue)\}$ in classical logic. Adopting as belief sets the maximal sets of literals consistent with KB (i.e., the Herbrand models of KB), we have $BS(KB) = \{\{dog(sue), \neg cat(sue), male(sue)\}, \{\neg dog(sue), cat(sue), male(sue)\}\}$. Alternatively, if a belief set consists of all classically entailed literals, we obtain $BS(KB) = \{\{male(sue)\}\}$.

Example 2. Consider the logic program $P = \{dog(sue) \vee cat(sue)., eat\_fish(X) \leftarrow cat(X), not\ abnormal(X).\}$. Adopting as belief sets the answer sets $AS(P)$ of this program [7], we obtain $BS(P) = AS(P) = \{\{dog(sue)\}, \{cat(sue), eat\_fish(sue)\}\}$.

While we abstract from concrete languages, it will be convenient to refer with KB^Σ to the implicitly defined signature of $BS(KB)$.

HEX-**programs.** Our implementation employs HEX-programs [5], which consist of rules

$$a_1 \vee \cdots \vee a_n \leftarrow b_1, \ldots, b_m, \text{not } b_{m+1}, \ldots, \text{not } b_n,$$

where each a_i is a classical literal and each b_j is either a classical literal or an *external* literal of the form $\&p[q_1, \ldots, q_k](t_1, \ldots, t_l)$, where p is the name of an external predicate, the q_i are predicate names, and the t_j are terms;[2] intuitively, p is evaluated externally, where the value of $q_1, \ldots, q_k$ is passed as input. The atom succeeds for variable binding if the external evaluation succeeds. Via such atoms, in particular abstract belief set computation is conveniently facilitated, also across the Web.

Example 3. Suppose an external knowledge base consists of an RDF file located on the web at "$http:// \ldots / data.rdf$." Using an external atom $\&rdf[<url>](X, Y, Z)$, we may access all RDF triples (s, p, o) at the URL specified with $<url>$. To form belief sets of pairs that drop the third argument from RDF triples, we may use the rule

$$bel(X, Y) \leftarrow \&rdf[``http:// \ldots / data.rdf"](X, Y, Z).$$

The semantics of HEX-programs generalizes the answer set semantics of logic programs [7], but we omit a further account (as it is less relevant) and refer to [5,6] for background and details. For execution, we use the dlvhex system [6], which implements HEX-programs providing a plugin mechanism for library and user defined external atoms.

3   Belief Set Merging Using Merging Plans

We now develop our formal framework for merging belief sets, which introduces merging plans and merging tasks. In the following, we suppose to have a collection $KB = KB_1, \ldots, KB_n$ of knowledge bases with associated sets of belief sets $BS(KB_1), \ldots, BS(KB_n)$. For illustration, we use logic programs under answer set semantics.

Recall that we aim at merging the belief sets $BS(KB_i)$ as such, rather than the underlying knowledge bases KB_i. This may be necessary if the knowledge base access is limited, for instance in the Web context. There also frequently the source formats may be not aligned, such that beliefs and belief sets are similar but not identical. Possible mismatches have to be overcome and conflicts resolved.

A closer look at the problem reveals that two basic types of mismatches need attention, viz. *language (syntactic) incompatibilities* and *logical inconsistencies*.

Syntactic Incompatibilities. A first problem is that the belief sets may use different vocabularies to encode the same information. For example, the programs $P_1 = \{degree(john, ``MSc") \leftarrow\}$ and $P_2 = \{deg(john, ``Master\ of\ Science") \leftarrow\}$ have a single answer set with a single fact encoding the same information, but syntactically their answer sets are different. The problem may concern constants or predicate names.

---

[2] Strictly, [5] considers only positive literals but the extension to negative literals is trivial; furthermore, [5], also allows variables for predicate names which we do not need.

We resolve this problem by introducing a so called common signature, which acts as a vocabulary shared by all sources, and applying mapping functions.

The *common signature* $\Sigma^C = (\Sigma_c^C, \Sigma_p^C)$ is a signature which suffices to define mappings from the collections of belief sets $BS(KB_i)$ over Σ^{KB_i} to new collections of belief sets $\mathcal{B}_i'$ over Σ^C, such that $\mathcal{B}_i' = \mathcal{B}_j'$ if and only if the user considers $\mathcal{B}_i'$ and $\mathcal{B}_j'$ to represent equivalent information, with respect to the application in mind. A *belief set conversion* is then a function $\mu_i : 2^{\mathcal{A}(\Sigma^{KB_i})} \rightarrow 2^{\mathcal{A}(\Sigma^C)}$. Informally, μ_i maps the semantics of KB_i, expressed in the signature Σ^{KB_i}, to a semantics in the common signature Σ^C. The mapping has to provided by the user, who must ensure that converted sets of belief sets are identical only if she wishes them to be treated the same for merging.

Continuing our previous example, suitable mapping functions are

$$\mu_1(\mathcal{B}) = \mathcal{B},$$
$$\mu_2(\mathcal{B}) = \{\{degree(X, \text{``}MSc\text{''}) \mid deg(X, \text{``}Master\ of\ Science\text{''}) \in B\}\cup$$
$$\{degree(X, Y) \mid deg(X, Y) \in B, Y \neq \text{``}Master\ of\ Science\text{''}\} \mid B \in \mathcal{B}\};$$

i.e., the belief sets of P_1 are unchanged while all occurrences of "*Master of Science*" in the belief sets of P_2 are changed to "*MSc*", and predicate *deg* is changed to *degree*.

The above notion of conversion is very general, but as in the example, often simple modular conversions at the level of belief sets ($\mu_i(\mathcal{B}) = \bigcup_{B \in \mathcal{B}} \mu_i'(B)$) or even at the level of atoms ($\mu_i'(B) = \{\tau_i(b) \mid b \in B\}$), for instance by mapping Σ^{KB_i} via τ_i to Σ^C) may be used. More involved mappings may exploit schema matching and alignment (if possible), which however we omit here. After the mappings have been applied, we can safely assume that all sources are given over the same vocabulary.

Logical Inconsistencies. The second and more complicated type of conflicts concerns logical mismatches. While syntactic incompatibilities could be resolved by translating each source *independently* into the common language, logical inconsistencies only appear when multiple belief sets with contradicting contents are united.

We abstractly model application-dependent integrity constraints on sets of belief sets $\mathcal{B}$ as a set $\mathcal{C} \subseteq 2^{\mathcal{A}(\Sigma^C)}$, such that $\mathcal{B} \subseteq \mathcal{A}(\Sigma^C)$ satisfies the integrity constraints iff $\mathcal{B} \in \mathcal{C}$. Then, collections $\mathcal{B}_1, \mathcal{B}_2 \subseteq \mathcal{A}(\Sigma^C)$ of belief sets over the common signature Σ^C violate the constraints (i.e., are inconsistent) iff $(\mathcal{B}_1 \cup \mathcal{B}_2) \notin \mathcal{C}$.

The resolution of such inconsistencies is only possible during the incorporation of the sources. For this purpose we introduce the concept of *merging operators*.

Definition 3. *An n-ary operator with parameters from $\mathcal{D}_1, \ldots, \mathcal{D}_m$, $m \geq 0$, is a function*

$$\circ^{n,m} : \underbrace{\left(2^{\mathcal{A}(\Sigma^C)}\right)^n}_{collections\ of\ belief\ sets} \times \underbrace{\mathcal{D}_1 \times \ldots \times \mathcal{D}_m}_{additional\ parameters} \rightarrow 2^{\mathcal{A}(\Sigma^C)} .$$

The first n arguments are the collections of belief sets the operator is applied on. We assume that they have already been mapped to the common signature by applying the functions μ_i. The other m arguments over arbitrary domains $\mathcal{D}_i$ (like integers, enum types or strings) may provide additional information to control the behavior of the operator, e.g., by guiding it in special cases. The result of the operator is a further set of belief sets over the common signature Σ^C.

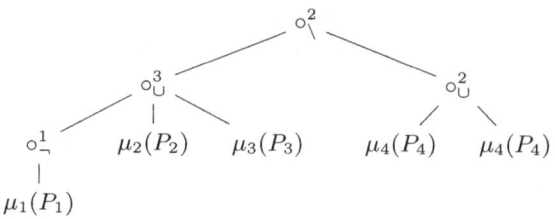

Fig. 1. Merging plan

Example 4. The naive union operator, which has no parameter ($m = 0$), is defined as

$$\circ_U^{2,0}(\mathcal{B}_1, \mathcal{B}_2) = \{B_1 \cup B_2 \mid B_1 \in \mathcal{B}_1, B_2 \in \mathcal{B}_2, \nexists A : \{A, \neg A\} \subseteq (B_1 \cup B_2)\} \ ,$$

where the parameters $\mathcal{B}_1$ and $\mathcal{B}_2$ are sets of belief sets. The operator unions the belief sets of both sources pairwise, where classically inconsistent pairs are skipped.

If this operator is applied on the belief sets of the programs $P_1 = \{p \vee \neg p \leftarrow ; q \leftarrow\}$ and $P_2 = \{p \vee r \leftarrow ; s \leftarrow\}$ under the answer set semantics, the result is

$$\circ_U^{2,0}(AS(P_1), AS(P_2)) = \{\{p, q, s\}, \{p, q, r, s\}, \{\neg p, q, r, s\}\} \ .$$

The belief sets of the knowledge bases are $AS(P_1) = \{\{p, q\}, \{\neg p, q\}\}$ and $AS(P_2) = \{\{p, s\}, \{r, s\}\}$. This yields four pairs $B_1 \cup B_2$; one is inconsistent and thus skipped.

3.1 Merging Plans and Tasks

The result of an operator could be input to a further operator, similar as sub-expressions and numbers in complex arithmetic expressions. This leads to a hierarchical tree-structure with the converted belief sets $\mu_i(BS(KB_i))$ at the leaf nodes, and merging operators at the inner nodes. We call such a structure a *merging plan*, formally defined next.

Definition 4. *The set $\mathcal{M}_{KB,\Omega}$ of merging plans over knowledge bases $KB = KB_1, \ldots, KB_n$ and a set $\Omega = \{\circ_1, \ldots, \circ_n\}$ of operators is the smallest set such that*
  (i) each $M \in KB$, called atomic *merging plan, is in $\mathcal{M}_{KB,\Omega}$;*
  (ii) if $\circ_i^{n,m} \in \Omega, s_j \in \mathcal{M}_{KB,\Omega}$ and $a_k \in \mathcal{D}_i$ for $1 \leq j \leq n, 1 \leq k \leq m$, then $(\circ_i^{n,m}, s_1, \ldots, s_n, a_1, \ldots, a_m) \in \mathcal{M}_{KB,\Omega}$.

Example 5. Fig. 1 shows a graphical representation of a merging plan over logic programs $P_1, \ldots, P_5$ with primitive merging operators of different arities. It informally computes the negation of P_1 using the unary operator $\circ_\neg^1$, and unions this with P_2 and P_3 (using a ternary version of the operator). It then subtracts from this the union of P_4 and P_5, using set difference. The formal expression for this merging plan is

$$M = (\circ_\setminus^2, (\circ_U^3, (\circ_\neg^1, P_1), P_2, P_3), (\circ_U^2, P_4, P_5)).$$

With merging plans available, we now formalize *merging tasks*.

Definition 5. *A merging task is a quintuple* $T = \langle KB, \Sigma^C, \mu, \Omega, M \rangle$, *where* $KB = KB_1, \ldots, KB_n$ *are knowledge bases,* Σ^C *is a common signature,* $\mu = \mu_1, \ldots, \mu_n$ *are belief set conversions* $\mu_i : 2^{\mathcal{A}(\Sigma^{KB_i})} \rightarrow 2^{\mathcal{A}(\Sigma^C)}$, Ω *is a set of operators, and* $M \in \mathcal{M}_{KB,\Omega}$ *is a merging plan over* KB *and* Ω.

The set of merging operators Ω is the only component that is, even though it is part of the formal task definition, usually not specific for a certain merging task in practice. It rather consists of approved operators which are probably useful in many different scenarios. The knowledge bases KB will mostly exist before merging is planned and are often provided by third parties. The components Σ^C, μ_i and M must be defined by the user as part of he merging scenario formalization.

Using our previous definitions, we define the outcome of a merging task next.

Definition 6. *The* result *of a merging task* $T = \langle KB, \Sigma^C, \mu, \Omega, M \rangle$, *denoted as* $[\![T]\!]$, *is*

$$[\![T]\!] = \begin{cases} [\mu_i(BS(M))]_{\Sigma_p^C}, & \text{if } M \in KB, \\ [\circ^{n,m}([\![T_1]\!], \ldots, [\![T_n]\!], a_1, \ldots, a_m)]_{\Sigma_p^C}, & \text{if } M = (\circ^{n,m}, s_1, \ldots, s_n, a_1, \ldots, a_m), \end{cases}$$

where $[\mathcal{B}]_{\Sigma_p^C} = \{\{p(a_1, \ldots, a_n) \in BS \mid p = (\neg)p', p' \in \Sigma_p^C\} \mid BS \in \mathcal{B}\}$ *denotes the projection of* $\mathcal{B}$ *to the atoms over* Σ_p^C, *and* $T_i = \langle KB, \Sigma^C, \mu, \Omega, s_i \rangle$, $1 \le i \le n$.

Informally, if M is an atomic merging plan (i.e., a knowledge base), then it can be evaluated directly and the result is just the associated set of belief sets, mapped to the common signature. Otherwise, M contains at least one operator application, and the result is the one of the topmost operator, applied on the results of the merging sub-plans.

Example 6 (cont'd). Let M be the merging plan from Example 5 and consider programs

$$P_1 = \{a., b.\}, P_2 = \{x., y.\}, P_3 = \{\neg a., c.\}, P_4 = \{a., x.\}, P_5 = \{c., x., y.\}$$

that consist only of facts (rules $p \leftarrow$, omitting $\leftarrow$). The complete merging task is $T = \langle \{P_1, \ldots, P_5\}, \Sigma^C, \mu_{id}, \Omega, M \rangle$, where the common signature contains the propositional (0-ary) atoms a, b, c, x and y, all mappings in μ_{id} are identity functions (since all knowledge bases use already the common vocabulary), and $\Omega = \{\circ^3_{\cup}, \circ^2_{\curlywedge} \circ^1_{\neg}\}$.

Now we compute the result $[\![T]\!]$ of this merging task as follows. For the sake of readability, we use $[\![M]\!]$ as an abbreviation for $[\![\{P_1, \ldots, P_5\}, \Sigma^C, \mu_{id}, \Omega, M]\!]$:

$$[\![\langle \{P_1, \ldots, P_5\}, \Sigma^C, \mu_{id}, \Omega, M \rangle]\!] =$$
$$\circ^2_{\curlywedge} \left([\![(\circ^3_{\cup}, (\circ^1_{\neg}, P_1), P_2, P_3)]\!], [\![(\circ^2_{\cup}, P_4, P_5)]\!] \right) =$$
$$\circ^2_{\curlywedge} \left(\circ^3_{\cup}([\![(\circ^1_{\neg}, P_1)]\!], [\![P_2]\!], [\![P_3]\!]), [\![(\circ^2_{\cup}, P_4, P_5)]\!] \right) =$$
$$\cdots = \circ^2_{\curlywedge}(\{\{\neg a, \neg b, c, x, y\}\}, \{\{a, c, x, y\}\}) = \{\{\neg a, \neg b\}\}.$$

We may view a merging task T as a knowledge base per se by casting it into a knowledge base in some logic language; e.g., T may be cast to the classical formula $\neg a \wedge \neg b$.

The examples above are trivial and involve only simple set operations, but still illustrate the principles. We clearly can use advanced belief merging operators, showing the usefulness of the framework. We will see this in the following sections.

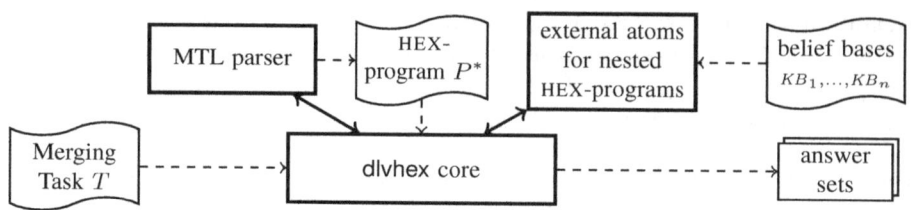

Fig. 2. MELD System Architecture (control flow ⟶, data flow ⇢)

4 The MELD System

We have implemented our framework in MELD (*MErging Library for Dlvhex*), using the infrastructure and possibilities of the dlvhex system to transparently access heterogeneous (possibly dispersed) knowledge sources. In MELD, we assume that the knowledge bases KB_i are given as HEX-programs [6]. This has the great advantage that by using external atoms, the belief sets (which then are answer sets) may contain information from virtually any knowledge source, e.g. the tuples of a relational database, the triplets of an RDF ontology, or a model of a propositional formula. The HEX-programs only serve as an interface to these sources, enabling access to their belief sets (in fact, using nested HEX-programs described below).

The architecture of MELD is shown in Fig. 2. Essentially the system consists of three major components: (1) a language for specifying merging tasks in a machine-readable format; (2) a compiler which translates declarative task descriptions into semantically equivalent *nested* HEX-*programs*, i.e., HEX-programs with program nesting. The program constructed computes the merged belief sets in its answer sets; and (3) a suite of specific external atoms developed in dlvhex which allow for executing nested HEX-programs.

The system is realized as a plugin to dlvhex, and provides a user-friendly interface for the specification of a merging task $T = \langle KB, \Sigma^C, \mu, \Omega, M \rangle$ as defined above. The knowledge bases KB are given as (nested) HEX-programs, and the merging operators Ω are implemented as C++ classes. MELD comes with a few predefined operators, and can be easily extended, using a plugin-mechanism, with user-defined operators in C++. The components Σ^C, μ_i and R are the most specific parts of a certain merging scenario. All components are declaratively specified in an INI-style text file (we use here filename extension .mt), in a dedicated *merging task language (MTL)*, which we discuss below. Then MELD can be used to compute merging task result according to the semantics above by executing the command: dlvhex --merging task.mt. The evaluation of merging tasks will be described below.

Merging Task Language (MTL). To specify merging tasks in a machine-readable way, we defined the *merging task language* (MTL). For space reasons, here an in depth presentation is not possible, and we will illustrate it on examples. More details, including the complete syntax, can be found on the system's website (see footnote 1).

```
[common signature]
predicate:foo/1; predicate:bar/3;

[belief base]
name: input1;
mapping: "bar(X, Y, Z) :- &rdf[\'http://...\'](X, Y, Z).";
mapping: "foo(Y) :- &rdf[\'http://...\'](X, Y, Z).";

[belief base]
name: input2;
source: "P2.lp";

[belief base]
name: input3;
mapping: "foo(X) :- &dlC[\'http://...\',a,b,c,d,\'student\'](X)";

[merging plan] {
    operator: setminus;
    source: {
        operator: setunion;  source: {input1};  source: {input2};
    };
    source: {input3};
}
```

Fig. 3. Merging Task Description

Example 7. Consider the merging task description in Fig. 3. It consists of three parts.

- [common signature]: The first part is the common signature, which is a list of all predicate names with associated arities. Only atoms over these predicates will be regarded during belief set merging.
- [belief base]: The second part is the declaration of the belief bases. For each belief base, a unique name and the mapping function to the common signature are specified, via arbitrarily many mapping rules under the HEX-semantics. The mapping may be done directly, as for belief bases input1 and input3, or outsourced as in case of input2. Note that the actual belief sources are *not* defined directly, as they are given implicitly and accessed by queries in the rule bodies. E.g., in input1 we access an RDF file on the web using the external atom &rdf. The mapping rules can derive arbitrary atoms in the heads (also intermediate atoms), but only those using predicates listed in the common signature will be regarded during merging.
- [merging plan]: The third part is a tree-structured merging plan, which defines how to combine the sources, described as a nested expression, with names of belief bases at the bottom and operators applied to inputs (source). In the example, we first compute the union of input1 and input2, and subsequently subtract input3.

MELD allows the automatic computation of the merged belief sets according to a merging plan of this kind a more elaborate example is discussed in Section 5.

Translation to Nested HEX-Programs. We briefly describe how merging task description are evaluated in MELD. The key concept are *nested* HEX-*programs*.

We designed a suite of external atoms which allow to evaluate a (possibly nested) HEX-program P given as input, and to access each answer set of P like an object in the host program. Thus, processing the answer sets and reasoning over them, inside another program, is possible. To our knowledge, this is the first ASP language featuring this and of independent interest. The sub-programs can be executed *independently* of the host program, such that their answer is imported into the main program and computation continued afterwards. We realized nested HEX-programs using *handles* that refer to sub-programs, answer sets and their constituents; this is best explained with an example.

Example 8. Consider the following two rules.

$$h(H, S) \leftarrow \&hex[\text{``}node(a).\ node(b).\ edge(a, b).\text{''}, \text{``''}](H), \&answersets[H](S).$$
$$p(P, A) \leftarrow h(H, S), \&predicates[H, S](P, A).$$

The external atom $\&hex$ in the first rule is used to execute the sub-program Q given as string literal "$node(a).\ node(b).\ edge(a, b).$". It will "return" a unique integer value H that can be used later on to investigate the answer to Q. Here, this done in the evaluation of the external atom $\&answersets$, which in turn returns, one by one, a set of unique handles S that point to the answer sets of Q. In the second rule, we pass each pair (H, S) retrieved by the first rule to the external atom $\&predicates$ which finds out the names and arities of the predicates contained in the respective answer set. This well lead to the atoms $p(node, 1)$ and $p(edge, 2)$. We could go a step further and also retrieve the arguments of the atoms in Q's answer sets, using further external atoms provided by our plugin. Moreover, by using $\&hexfile$, sub-programs in external files can be included.

Evaluation of merging tasks. We have implemented a transformation which parses a declarative merging task, specified in MTL, and assembles a semantically equivalent HEX-program P^* that uses program nesting, reflecting the merging plan structure. The translation is complex and we omit the details here.

Briefly, $\&hex$ resp. $\&hexfile$ atoms serve as starting point for evaluating atomic merging plans, i.e., merging plans which consist of a single belief base without operator applications. For non-atomic merging plans, we compute the result bottom-up like an arithmetic expression. To this end, we realized an external atom $\&operator$ which allows us to call operators implemented as C++ classes. As answer sets are accessible objects in our extension, we can pass them from operator to operator until we finally retrieve the result of the topmost operator, which yields the outcome of the merging plan.

Our implementation automatically assembles and evaluates P^* when dlvhex is started with the `--merging` option. The input files must contain a merging task description. For details of the transformation and a proof of the correctness, we refer to [14].

5   Belief Merging in Action

We now consider a more realistic belief merging example in fault diagnosis, which is a classical KR problem. In the course of this, we consider different merging operators, which are based on distance functions and give rise to a hierarchically constructed a family of such operators, and we report how the problem can be solved in MELD.

Example 9 (Circuit Diagnosis). Consider the full adder circuit shown in Fig. 4. Given input values $x = y = 1$ and carry input $c_{in} = 1$, the value of the output carry $c_{out} = 1$ is correct, but the output sum s should be 1 instead of 0. Any component in the

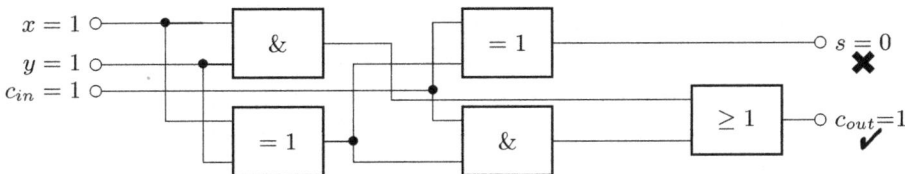

Fig. 4. Malfunctioning full adder (expected output: $s = 1$ and $c_{out} = 1$)

circuit may be broken, leading to different possible abductive explanations (i.e., fault assumptions that logically entail the observation): either (1) the XOR gate on the lower left (xor_1), (2) the XOR gate located middle top (xor_2), or (3) both xor_1 and xor_2 are malfunctioning; the result is not unique.

Here our framework comes into play: different experts may find different explanations. For a collective diagnosis, we must integrate the individual opinions such that (i) the group explanation is still a valid explanation, and (ii) it is close to the individual opinions (under a suitable notion).

Suppose we have three experts inspecting the malfunctioning full adder, with individual explanations $AS(P_1) = \{ab(xor_1)\}$, $AS(P_2) = \{ab(xor_2)\}$ and $AS(P_3) = \{ab(xor_1), ab(xor_2)\}$. Informally, expert 1 believes that xor_1 is broken, expert 2 suspects xor_2 is broken, and expert 3 believes both are broken. Clearly, besides on these opinions, the overall result depends on the merging operator.

Distance-based merging operators. A popular class of operators is defined using a distance function for between two interpretations resp. sets of literals. We call such operators *distance-based operators*. An example is an adaption of Dalal's distance between interpretations [2] (which is their Hamming distance) to $|B_1 \triangle B_2|$, the cardinality of the symmetric difference of belief sets B_1 and B_2. For more discussion, see [9].

We build a distance function $D_{d,\underline{d}}(B, KB)$ between a belief set B and knowledge bases $KB = KB_1, \ldots, KB_n$ in three steps:

1. We start from a distance function $\underline{d}(B_1, B_2)$ between two belief sets. Besides the adapted Dalal distance, which we denote with $\underline{dal}$, many other choices are possible (e.g., weighted distance; we consider two other options below).
2. Next, we define a distance function d on top of $\underline{d}$ to measure the distance of belief set B to a knowledge base KB, denoted $d_{\underline{d}}(B, KB)$, by aggregating the values $\underline{d}(B, B')$ for all belief sets of $B' \in BS(KB)$. Here a popular choice is $d = min$:

$$min_{\underline{d}}(B, KB_i) = \min_{B' \in BS(KB_i)} \underline{d}(B, B')$$

i.e., we informally take the distance of B to the closed belief set of KB.
3. For each $1 \leq i \leq n$, the function $d_{\underline{d}}(B, KB_i)$ yields a distance value; these n values are aggregated into a single value $D_{d,\underline{d}}(B, KB)$. A popular choice for D is the sum:

$$sum_{\underline{d},d}(B, KB) = \Sigma_{i=1}^{n} d_{\underline{d}}(B, KB_i)$$

Summarizing, in each step some parameter ($\underline{d}$, d, D) can be chosen to arrive at $D_{\underline{d}}(B, KB)$. Given the latter, the following merging operator is straightforward:

$$\Delta_{\underline{d},d,D}(KB, \mathcal{C}) = \arg\min_{B \in \mathcal{C}} D_{\underline{d},d}(B, KB),$$

```
[common signature]                  [belief base]
predicate:ab/1;                     name: expert3;
                                    source: "P3.lp";
[belief base]
name: expert1;                      [merging plan] {
source: "P1.lp";                        operator: dbo; bsdistance: "ignoring";
                                        constraintfile: "fulladder.lp";
[belief base]                           constraintfile: "fault.obs";
name: expert2;                          {expert1}; {expert2}; {expert3};
source: "P2.lp";                    }
```

Fig. 5. Group decision problem

i.e., selecting among all possible belief sets that satisfy the (application dependent) constraints $\mathcal{C}$, a belief set B which is at minimum overall distance to KB.

Solving the group decision problem. In MELD, a group decision of the three experts can be obtained using the above operator $\Delta_{\underline{d},d,D}(KB,\mathcal{C})$ (named dbo for *distance-based operator* there), where the constraints $\mathcal{C}$ ensure that the result is still an abductive explanation. The merging task is specified as follows.

The belief bases with respective belief sets (as answer sets) are in external files Pj.lp. with answer sets as described above (either hard-coded or suitable computed). As all external programs deliver belief sets over predicate ab, no mapping functions are specified; this makes the implementation use identity mappings. The merging plan applies the previously defined operator on the three individual belief sets, where in MELD $d_{\underline{d}} = min_{\underline{d}}$ and $D_{d,\underline{d}} = sum_{d,\underline{d}}$ by default, and $\underline{d}$ (the distance between two belief sets) is defined in the bsdistance-statement. Setting bsdistance to dal gives us the adapted Dalal distance $\underline{dal}$. The group decision is then $\{\{ab(xor_1)\}, \{ab(xor_2)\}\}$; either xor_1 or xor_2 is defect. Omitting formal details, the value ignoring for bsdistance penalizes situations where atoms from individual belief sets are missing in the group decision candidate. This results in the group decision $\{\{ab(xor_1), ab(xor_2)\}\}$: it satisfies all three experts completely - no beliefs are ignored, thus has distance 0.

Besides ignoring and dal, MELD supports the option unfounded, which penalizes situations where the group decision candidate contains atoms *not* occurring in an individual belief set. This will yield the result $\{\{ab(xor_1)\}, \{ab(xor_2)\}\}$. Each explanation is minimal, as its single atom is unfounded for only one of the experts.

This example demonstrates the advantages of the framework and its implementation compared to hard-coding: It is easy to prototype merging scenarios and quickly change merging operators and parameters. If we would like to add further expert opinions or sub-divide the group into sub-groups and aggregate the decisions hierarchically, this could be easily done by modifying the .mt file accordingly.

6   Evaluation and Experiments

We take a closer look at MELD regarding performance and usefulness in practice. The runtime behavior is less an issue for two reasons. First, the system is intended to serve as a rapid prototyping tool to support the user when experimenting and evaluating different merging strategies. For a production version, a hard-coded implementation can be considered after an optimal setting has been found. Second, the behavior is largely determined by the merging operators in use, as the information flow in between and the translation of formal merging tasks to nested HEX-programs are both linear in the number of belief bases and the sizes of their answer sets. Also evaluating the assembled program P^* is not a big issue as its structure is fairly simple. The merging operators are application dependent and can be implemented and optimized by the user, so our framework does not cause notable overhead. We now describe real world tasks which can be solved by MELD with merging task descriptions similar to Example 9.

Decision diagram merging. Decision diagrams are an important tool for decision making in many fields of science. This is because compared to other formalisms (e.g. production rules) they are intuitive even for non-professionals in knowledge engineering. Biomedical examples include severity ratings of diseases depending on patient data (in particular tumor staging systems [19]), DNA classification (coding vs. junk DNA), and aids for therapy selection. Another frequent application domain is business and economy (e,g., liquidity appraisal in economics [1]).

Informally, a *decision diagram* is are rooted directed acyclic graph $D = (V, R)$. Each edge in E is labeled with a condition $X \diamond Y$, where $\diamond$ is a comparison operator and X and Y are variables or values from suitable domains. For example, $b \leq 12.5$ may compare a blood value b of a patient to the maximum value for healthy people, and each leaf (a node without out-edges) of D is tagged with a class label. Clearly, D must satisfy further structural and semantic conditions, but we simply omit this here.

To classify an instance, one starts at the root (the only node without in-edges) and follows an edge iff its condition is satisfied. This is repeated until a leaf is reached; there one reads the assigned class. Sometimes we have multiple similar but non-equivalent diagrams, e.g. due to different expert opinions or different training sets if the diagrams stem from machine-learning tools. It becomes then necessary to incorporate the input classifiers into a single one. If we encode decision diagrams as sets of facts (e.g., over predicates $leaf(X, C)$, $innernode(X, Y)$, etc.) and provide merging operators tailored for decision diagrams (and decode the encodings internally), the merging can clearly be done automatically using MELD. This is a great advantage if it is not clear right from the beginning which training algorithms and merging strategies behave best.

As a concrete example we consider a popular approach to classify protein-coding DNA sequences [17]. One first computes numerical features of the sequences in a large annotated training set T, which are known to vary significantly between coding and non-coding DNA for biological reasons. We used 20 numerical features proposed by [12]. They are computed for a set of sequences of 54 bases each. Subsequently, one trains a decision diagram D over these features; we will work with decision *trees* here, which are a special form of decision diagrams. When a new sequence needs to be classified, one computes the feature values and runs through D.

Here our framework comes into play, realizing an idea discussed in [18]. Instead of training a single decision tree over T, first split T into subsets $T_1, \ldots, T_n$ and train classifiers $D_1, \ldots, D_n$ on them (thus fostering parallelization); then merge the D_i into a single tree D. We found that combining several classifiers trained by different machine-learning algorithms may significantly improve the final result. This is not always true, but depends on the training set T, the selection of learners, and the merging procedure.

Some combinations may increase the accuracy compared to a single tree trained over T, while others decrease it. However, this exactly demonstrates the strengths of our framework: it is easy to try out several different scenarios and evaluate the results empirically, while the technical details of the merging process are managed by MELD.

For training data extracted from the Human-Genome Project, we achieved our optimal result using a merging operator inspired by the algorithm in [1] and three input trees trained over only 10 sequences each (hence each tree queried only the feature with highest entropy), gaining an accuracy increase from 48.85% to 65.25%; see [15] for details. Many other approaches based on statistical features were developed; in comparison, our result is fairly good. Most of them produce a classifier with accuracy only slightly above 70%, see e.g., [17], including recent ones [20,21]; this suggests that there may be a close by natural limit for statistical features.

A further finding of our experiments is that by training multiple classifiers and merging them afterwards, mostly a much smaller training set (in total) suffices to gain the same accuracy as by training a single classifier; e.g., for an accuracy of 65.25%, the latter needed several hundred sequences (compared to 30). Furthermore, the merged decision tree usually has a lower depth than a tree created over a single, but larger training set. Obtaining these results would have been much harder without the framework, since the merging of the classifiers had to be done by hand after each change of parameters.

Our merging operator implements an algorithm developed in [18] and realized in the MORGAN system. But in contrast to MORGAN, where the algorithm is implemented directly as part of the main system, MELD sources it out into an operator library. This simplifies the implementation of further merging strategies and exchanging them easily.

Judgment aggregation. In Section 4 we have seen how to incorporate individual beliefs into a group decision; this is a common problem in social choice theory [3]. Realistic applications include planning of group activities with individual preferences, and diagnosis making by teams of several doctors.

Syntactic belief merging. We distinguished syntactic belief merging approaches, i.e., merging sets of formulas or programs, and semantic approaches. Even if our framework is essentially semantic, we may also use it for syntactic tasks by using an appropriate encoding of formulas or programs. That is, we encode the knowledge base as sets of literals. This allows us to use MELD for (e.g. talking about the same domain but focusing on different details), we need to combine them into a single ontology [22]. Given appropriate merging operators which decode the ontologies represented by literal sets internally, this task can clearly be supported by MELD. To vary the ordering of the sources is then easy. If the merging operator is not commutative and associative or if we have multiple alternative operators, the quality of the final ontology can vary as well, and we may find the best one by empirically using MELD.

7   Related Work and Conclusion

While the theory of belief merging has a rich literature, only few implemented systems are available. In [8], the authors present an implementation of Removed Set Fusion based merging of logic programs by translating sets of logic programs into a single logic program, whose answer sets correspond to removed sets. Compared to our approach, this method uses a syntactic strategy for merging belief bases and has a fixed semantics.

COBA [4] handles belief *revision* rather than merging. Its approach to finding consistent models is similar to our implementation of distance-based operators in Section 4. In contrast to our generic framework, COBA uses a fixed semantics.

The MORGAN system [18] was used to merge DNA classification trees. The merging operator we used for our experiments is almost equivalent to this system. However, while we implemented the algorithm as merging operator for our flexible framework, MORGAN is hard-coded. Therefore it is easy to modify parameters and make experiments with different settings in our system. The changes only concern the declarative task description, while in MORGAN one needs to rewrite the main source files.

Our approach works semantically, i.e., it does not merge logic programs but interpretations of the programs. Nevertheless, by encoding formulas as literals one can also implement syntactic strategies within the framework. Future work will include addressing performance issues which was neglected so far since the main goal was flexibility. Another possible extension is the implementation of additional merging operators. This increases the chance that the user will find a suitable one and avoids that she needs to implement it on his own. Also support for syntactic strategies for belief merging may be fruitfully deployed in our framework. Additionally, the merging task language may be extended by further language constructs like iterative application of operators.

References

1. Bahar, R.I., Frohm, E.A., Gaona, C.M., Hachtel, G.D., Macii, E., Pardo, A., Somenzi, F.: Algebraic decision diagrams and their applications. In: ICCAD 1993, pp. 188–191 (1993)
2. Dalal, M.: Investigations into a theory of knowledge base revision. In: AAAI, pp. 475–479 (1988)
3. Dasgupta, P.S., Hammond, P.J., Maskin, E.S.: The implementation of social choice rules: Some general results on incentive compatibility. Rev. Econ. Stud. 46(2), 185–216 (1979)
4. Delgrande, J.P., Liu, D.H., Schaub, T., Thiele, S.: COBA 2.0: A Consistency-Based Belief Change System. In: Mellouli, K. (ed.) ECSQARU 2007. LNCS (LNAI), vol. 4724, pp. 78–90. Springer, Heidelberg (2007)
5. Eiter, T., Ianni, G., Schindlauer, R., Tompits, H.: A uniform integration of higher-order reasoning and external evaluations in answer-set programming. In: IJCAI 2005, pp. 90–96 (2005)
6. Eiter, T., Ianni, G., Schindlauer, R., Tompits, H.: dlvhex: A system for integrating multiple semantics in an answer-set programming framework. In: WLP 2006, pp. 206–210 (2006)
7. Gelfond, M., Lifschitz, V.: Classical negation in logic programs and disjunctive databases. New Generat. Comput. 9(3-4), 365–385 (1991)
8. Hué, J., Papini, O., Würbel, E.: Merging belief bases represented by logic programs. In: Sossai, C., Chemello, G. (eds.) ECSQARU 2009. LNCS, vol. 5590, pp. 371–382. Springer, Heidelberg (2009)
9. Konieczny, S., Lang, J., Marquis, P.: DA^2 merging operators. AIJ 157(1-2), 49–79 (2004)
10. Konieczny, S., Pérez, R.P.: On the logic of merging. In: KR 1998, pp. 488–498 (1998)
11. Liberatore, P., Schaerf, M.: Arbitration (or how to merge knowledge bases). IEEE Trans. Knowl. Data Eng. 10(1), 76–90 (1998)

12. Liew, A.W.C., Wu, Y., Yan, H.: Selection of statistical features based on mutual information for classification of human coding and non-coding DNA sequences. In: ICPR, pp. 766–769 (2004)
13. Lin, J., Mendelzon, A.: Knowledge base merging by majority. In: Dynamic Worlds: From the Frame problem to Knowledge Management. Kluwer, Dordrecht (1999)
14. Redl, C.: Development of a belief merging framewerk for dlvhex. Master's thesis, Vienna University of Technology, A-1040 Vienna, Karlsplatz 13 (June 2010), http://media.obvsg.at/AC07808210-2001
15. Redl, C.: Merging of biomedical decision diagrams. Master's thesis, Vienna University of Technology, A-1040 Vienna, Karlsplatz 13 (October 2010), http://media.obvsg.at/AC07808795-2001
16. Revesz, P.: On the semantics of arbitration. Intl. J. Algebra Comput. 7(2), 133–160 (1997)
17. Salzberg, S.: Locating protein coding regions in human DNA using a decision tree algorithm. J. Comput. Biol. 2, 473–485 (1995)
18. Salzberg, S., Delcher, A.L., Fasman, K.H., Henderson, J.: A decision tree system for finding genes in DNA. J. Comput. Biol. 5(4), 667–680 (1998)
19. Sobin, L., Gospodarowicz, M., Wittekind, C.: TNM Classification of Malignant Tumours, 7th edn. Wiley, Chichester (2009)
20. Sree, P.K., Babu, I.R., Murty, J.V.R., Rao, P.S.: Towards an artificial immune system to identify and strengthen protein coding region identification using cellular automata classifier. Intl. J. Comput. Commun. 1(2), 26–34 (2007)
21. Sree, P.K., Babu, I.R.: Identification of protein coding regions in genomic DNA using unsupervised FMACA based pattern classifier. Intl. J. Comp. Sci. Netw. Secur. 8(1), 305–309 (2008)
22. Stumme, G., Maedche, A.: FCA-MERGE: Bottom-Up Merging of Ontologies. In: IJCAI 2001, pp. 225–230 (2001)

Using Constraints for Intrusion Detection: The NeMODe System

Pedro Salgueiro[1], Daniel Diaz[2], Isabel Brito[3], and Salvador Abreu[1]

[1] Departamento de Informática, Universidade de Évora
and CENTRIA FCT/UNL, Portugal
{pds,spa}@di.uevora.pt
[2] University of Paris 1-Sorbonne, Paris, France
Daniel.Diaz@univ-paris1.fr
[3] Departamento de Engenharia, Escola Superior de Tecnologia e Gestão,
Instituto Politécnico de Beja, Portugal
isabel.sofia@estig.ipbeja.pt

Abstract. In this work we present NeMODe a declarative system for Computer Network Intrusion detection which provides a declarative Domain Specific Language for describing computer network intrusion signatures that could spread across several network packets, which allows to state constraints over network packets, describing relations between several packets, and providing several back-end detection mechanisms which relies on Constraint Programming (CP) methodologies to find those intrusions.

Keywords: Constraint Programming, Intrusion Detection Systems, Domain Specific Languages.

1 Introduction

Network Intrusion Detection Systems are one of the most important tools in computer network management to maintain the security, integrity and quality of computer networks and keep the users data safe. To maintain the quality and integrity of the services provided by a computer network, some aspects must be verified in order to maintain the security of the users data. The description of those conditions, together with a verification that they are met can be seen as an Intrusion Detection task. These conditions, specified in terms of properties of parts of the (observed) network traffic, will amount to a specification of a desired or an unwanted state of the network, such as that brought about by a system intrusion or another form of malicious access.

Those conditions can naturally be described using a declarative programming approach, such as Constraint Programming [1], enabling the description of these situations in a natural, declarative and expressive way. To help the description of those network situations, we created a declarative, very expressive, Domain Specific Language (DSL) [2], enabling an easy description of intrusion signatures that spread across several network packets, allowing to state constraints

R. Rocha and J. Launchbury (Eds.): PADL 2011, LNCS 6539, pp. 115–129, 2011.

over network entities and express relations across several network packets. This DSL will then translate the *program* into constraints that will be solved by more than one constraint solving techniques, including Constraint Based Local Search and Propagation-based systems such as Gecode [3]. It also have the capabilities of running several solvers in parallel, in order to benefit from the earliest possible solution. We have already made some preliminary work on using network constraints to perform intrusion detection [4], and have also developed a preliminary implementation of such a DSL[5,6]. In this work we present a new and more complete version version of such a DSL (NeMODe) as well as a its complete specification to a better comprehension.

This paper is organized as follows. Section 2 presents the state of the art and a brief description of Intrusion Detection Systems, Constraint Based Local Search, Adaptive Search and Domain Specific Languages. Section 3 demonstrates how to model and perform Intrusion Detection using Constraint Programming. Section 4 details the DSL provided by NeMODe and provides some examples. Section 5 shows the experimental results obtained by NeMODe. Section 6 evaluates NeMODe and Section 7 presents the conclusions and future work. Throughout this paper, we mention technical terms pertaining to TCP/IP and UDP/IP network packets, such as *packet flags ,URG, ACK, PSH, RST, SYN, FIN, acknowledgment, source port, destination port, source address, destination address, payload*, which are described in [7].

2   State of the Art

2.1   Intrusion Detection Systems

Intrusion Detection Systems(IDS) play a very important role in computer network security, which focus on traffic monitoring trying to inspect traffic to look for anomalies or undesirable communications in order to keep the network a safe place. There are two major methods to detect intrusions in computer networks; (1) based on the network intrusion signatures, and (2) based on the detection of anomalies on the network [8]. With Signature Based Intrusion Detection, intrusions are described using their signatures, particular properties of network packets used by the intrusion. These properties are then looked in the network traffic to find the desired intrusion. In Anomaly-Detection Based, the systems models the *normal* behavior of the network using statistical methods and/or data mining approaches. The network behavior is then monitored, and if it is considered anomalous according the network model, there is a great probability of and attack. In this work, we adopted an approach based on signatures.

Snort [9] is a widely used Intrusion Detection System that relies on efficient pattern-matching techniques to detect the desired intrusion signature. Snort is primarily designed to detect signatures that can be identified in a single network packet. Although it provides some basic mechanisms to write rules that spread across several network packets, the relations between those network packets are very simple and limited.

Snort presents some pre-processors that help to relate separate network packets; `Stream4` is such a pre-processor: it gives Snort the ability to be stateful, allowing the trace of network packets on its session and use its state on the given session to create a rule that describes the desired signature. The `Flow` pre-processor also allows snort rules to relate with other rules by using the *flowbits* keyword, allowing one rule to set some flag, and later other rule can check if that flag is set, and, if so, complete the rule to describe the desired signature.

These two pre-processors help Snort to describe network attack signatures that span several network packets, but they do so in a very limited way, not allowing the description of more complex relations between packets, such as the temporal distance between two packets. Also, the way that the relation between several rules is expressed is awkward and often counter-intuitive.

Most of the work in the area of Intrusion Detection Systems consists in the development of faster detection methods [10]. The work described in [11] is such an example, which implements a regular expression matching algorithm using graphics hardware (GPUs) to perform intrusion detection. There is also some work focused on how the network signatures are described detected. [10] presents an algorithm and an implementation method for performing flow aware content search based on Bloom Filters which allows to search signatures that spread across several packets. In [12], the authors present a declarative approach to specify intrusion signatures which are represented as a specialized graph, allowing the description of signatures that spread across several network packets.

2.2   Constraint Programming

Constraint Programming (CP) is a declarative programming paradigm which consists in the formulation of a solution to a problem as a *Constraint Satisfaction Problem* (CSP) [1], in which a number of variables are introduced, with well-specified domains and which describe the state of the system. A set of relations, called *constraints*, is then imposed on the variables which make up the problem. These constraints are understood to have to hold true for a particular set of bindings for the variables, resulting in a *solution* to the CSP.

There are several types of constraint solvers, in this work we use: (1) Propagation Based solvers; and (2) Constraint Based Local Search(CBLS).

Propagation-Based solvers. Using Propagation-Based [1] solvers, the problem is described by stating constraints over each variable that composes the problem, which states what values are allowed to be assigned to each variable, then, the constraint solver will propagate all the constraints and reduce the domain of each network variables in order to satisfy all the constraints and instantiate the variables that compose the problem with valid results, thus reaching a solution to the initial problem. Gecode [13] is a constraint solver library based on propagation, implemented in C++ and designed to be interfaced with other systems or programming languages.

Constraint Based Local Search. CBLS [14] is a fundamental approach to solve combinatorial problems such as Constraint Satisfaction Problems. CBLS is a method that can solve very large problems, although not a complete algorithm and unable to provide a complete or optimal solution. Usually, this approach initiates with an initial, candidate solution to the problem which is then iteratively improved though small modifications until some criteria is satisfied. The modifications to the candidate solution is usually driven by heuristics that guide the solver to a solution.

Adaptive Search (AS) [15] is a Constraint Based Local Search [14] algorithm, taking into account the structure of the problem and using variable-based information to design general heuristics which help solve the problem. The iterative repairs to the candidate solution in Adaptive Search are based on variable and constraint error information which seeks to reduce errors on the variables used to model the problem. AS computes the error of all constraints in which it appears, projecting the errors on each individual variables. Based on this information, the variable with the highest cost is the one that will be chosen to change its value. After the variable with the highest cost have been calculated, the *min_ conflict* [1] heuristic is used to select the new value to that variable, which is the value that provides the minimum total error to the next solution. Adaptive Search has recently been ported to Cell/BE, presented in [16].

2.3 Domain Specific Languages

Domain Specific Languages(DSLs) [2] allows to easily create programs to a specific and well defined domain with efficiency, generating easy to understand and maintain programs, by using a specific *jargon*. Most IDSs, like Snort and Bro [17], also a widely used IDS, provide custom languages to describe the signatures, but they are usually scripting languages, based mostly on pattern matching and regular expressions, *counter-intuitive*, and don't use a declarative approach, making them less expressive.

3 Intrusion Detection with Constraints

Our approach to intrusion detection relies on describing the desired signatures through the use of constraints and then identify a set of packets that match the target network situation in the network traffic window, which is a log of the network traffic in a given time interval.

The network intrusion needs to be modeled as a Constraint Satisfaction Problem (CSP) in order to use the constraint programming mechanisms. A CSP which models a network situation is composed by a set of variables, V, which represents the network packets involved necessary to describe the network situation; the domain of the network packet variables, D; and a set of constraints, C, which relates the variables in order to describe the network situation. We call such a CSP a network CSP. On a network CSP, each network packet variable is a tuple of integer variables, 19 variables for TCP/IP [1] packets and 12 variables for UDP packets [2], which represent the significant fields of a network packet necessary to model the intrusion signatures used in our experiments.

---

[1] Here, we are only considering the "interesting" fields in TCP/IP packets, from an IDS point-of-view.

[2] Here, we are only considering the "interesting" fields in UDP packets, from an IDS point-of-view.

The domain of the network packet variables, D, are the values actually seen on the network traffic window, which is a set of tuples of 19 integer values (for the TCP variables) and 12 integer values (for the UDP variables), each tuple representing a network packet actually observed on the traffic window and each integer value represents each field relevant to intrusion detection. The packets payload is stored separately in an array containing the payload of all packets seen on the traffic window. The correspondence between the packet and its payload is achieved by matching the packet number, i, which is the first variable in the tuple representing the packets and the ith position of the array containing the payloads.

Listing 1 shows a representation of such CSP, where P represents the set of network packet variables, where $P_{n,z}$, is each of the individual integer variables of the network packet variable, in a total of z fields for each network of the n variables, with $z = 19$ for TCP packets and $z = 12$ for UDP packets.

D is the network traffic window, where $D_i = (V_{i,1}, \ldots, V_{i,z}) \in D$ is one of the real network packets on the network traffic window, which is part of the domain of the packet variables P.

$Data$ is the payloads of the network packets present in the network window, where $Data_i$ is the payload of the packet $P_i = (V_{i,1}, \ldots, V_{i,z}) \in D$.

The associated domains of the network packet variables is represented by $\forall P_i \in P \Rightarrow P_i \in D$, forcing all variables belonging to P to obtain values from the set of packets in the network window D.

A solution to a network CSP, if it exists, is an assignment of network packet values, $D_i = (V_{i,1}, \ldots, V_{i,z}) \in D$, to each packet variable, $P_i = (P_{j,1}, \ldots, P_{j,z}) \in P$, that models the desired situation, thus identifying the network packets that identify the intrusion being detected.

Listing 1. Representation of a network CSP

$$P = \{(P_{1,1}, \ldots, P_{1,z}), \ldots, (P_{n,1}, \ldots, P_{n,z})\}$$
$$D = \{(V_{1,1}, \ldots, V_{1,z}), \ldots, (V_{x,1}, \ldots, V_{x,z})\}$$
$$Data = \{Data_1, \ldots, Data_x\}$$
$$\forall P_i \in P \Rightarrow P_i \in D$$

---

4   NeMODe - A DSL to Describe Network Signatures

In this work we present a declarative, intuitive domain-specific programming language for the Network Intrusion Detection [2] of NeMODe, which talks about network entities, their properties and relations between them, allowing to describe network intrusion signatures, and, with base on those descriptions, generate Intrusion Detection mechanisms.

The key characteristic of this DSL is to ease the way how network attack signatures are described using constraint programming, hiding from the user all the constraint programing aspects and complexity of modeling network signatures in a Constraint Satisfaction Problem(CSP), but still using the methodologies of

CP to describe the problem at a much higher level, describing how the network entities should relate among each other and what properties they should verify.

Maintaining the declaritivity and expressiveness of the CP, allows an easy and intuitive way of describing the network attack signatures, by describing the properties that must or must not be seen on the individual network packets, as well as the relationships that should or should not exist between each of the network packets.

The DSL is a front-end to several back-ends, one to each intrusion detection mechanism. This allows to generate several recognizers based on different constraint solver methods, from a single description. With several recognizers, it is possible run each of them in parallel, allowing to select the first produced solution, as the behavior of each solver depends on the problem being solved.

NeMODe provides two back-end detection mechanisms; (1) based on the Gecode constraint solver; and (2) based on the Adaptive Search algorithm. Each of these detection mechanisms are based on Constraint Programming techniques, but they are completely different in the way they perform the detection, and also the way the signatures are described. In Sec. 2.2 each of these approaches are explained.

4.1   NeMODe Specification

A NeMODe program is composed by an optional set of initial declarations, followed by a network *case*(line 1 of Listing 2), which describes the network situation to be modeled.

Those initial declarations is a comma separated list of declarations port numbers and/or hostnames, which can later be used later on the description of the problem, making the program more *readable*, by referring to hostnames instead of ip addresses, and port or service names instead of port numbers.

A network *case* is the main part of a NeMODe program and is composed by two parts; (1) the *solver_list*, (line 3 of Listing 2) containing the description of the intrusion signature to be found and the identification of the tool which will be used to solve the problem; and (2) the actions to take when the desired network situation is detected, the *stmt_action_list*(line 1 of Listing 6). There are two types of solvers,(line 5 of Listing 2), the *filter* and the *solver*. The *solver* is used to describe and solve complex network intrusion signatures, while the *filter* is only used to perform simple filtering tasks, accomplished by using a packet analyzer tool, such as *tcpdump* [18].

A *solver*(line 5 of Listing 2) is composed by 3 parts; (1) the network traffic source; (2) the identification of the tools that will be used to perform the filtering; and (3) the description of the filtering/solving process. The result of this filtering process is then stored in a variable, which could later be used as an input to other filtering stage. The most important part of a NeMODe program is the list of statements, *stmt_list* (line 8 of Listing 2), where the signatures are described.

Listing 2. NeMODe simplified grammar - The beginning of a program

```
1  case → ID { solver_list } => { stmt_action_list };
2
3  solver_list → solver | solver_list , solver
4  solver → ID = filter ( ID , ID ) { primitive_list }
5         | ID = solve ( ID , ID ) { stmt_list }
6
7  stmt_list → stmt | stmt_list , stmt
8  stmt → primitive | connective | ID  = { stmt_list } | ID  | macro_stmt | logic_stmt
```

There are 6 types of statements(line 8 of Listing 2); (1) the *primitive* statements; (2) the *connective* statements; (3) the *definition* statements; (4) the *use* statements; (5) the *macro* statements; and (6) the *logical* statements.

Listing 3. NeMODe simplified grammar - The most important statements

```
1   primitive → primitive_type ( var  )
2             | data ( var ) ~= STRING  | data ( var , NUMBER ) == STRING
3             | address eq_op ID | address eq_op ip_address
4             | port eq_op NUMBER | port eq_op ID
5
6   primitive_type → tcp_packet | udp_packet | urg | ack | psh | rst | syn | fin | nak
7
8   connective → ack ( var ) eq_op var
9             | port eq_op port | address eq_op address
10            | time rel_op time
11            | data ( var , NUMBER , NUMBER ) == data ( var , NUMBER , NUMBER )
```

The *primitive* statements (line 1 of Listing 3) allows to force some specific properties of a network packets to hold true. This statements allows to force a network packet to be tcp/udp packet; to have any of its tcp flags set; not to acknowledge another tcp packet; force a packet to have a specific data on its payload; and assure that a network packet have a specific source/destination address or a specific source/destination port.

The *connective* statements (line 8 of Listing 3) allows to relate two network packets by forcing the existence of some relations between the two of them. They allow to force: (1) a tcp packet to acknowledge other tcp packet; (2) a destination/source port of a packet to be equal/different to other destination/source port of other packet; (3) a destination/source address to be equal/different to a destination/source address of other packet; (4) the payload of two network packets to be equal/different at specific positions; and (5) two network packets to have a temporal relation, such as their temporal distance to be inferior to a given amount of time.

The *primitive* and *connective* can describe most of network intrusion signatures, but NeMODe provides some more types of statements to help the description of such signatures, the *definition* statements, the *use* statements and the *macro* statements.

The *definition* statements (line 8 of Listing 2) allows to define a variable as a group of statements, which can later be used in the description of a network situation. This type of statements have no effect on the program unless they are used latter on the program, being only the definition of a variable.

The **use** statement (line 8 of Listing 2) is just the simple use of a definition previously defined. As for the **macro** statements (line 1 of Listing 4), these are built with the purpose of avoiding the repetition of unnecessary code.

Listing 4. NeMODe simplified grammar - The *macro* statements

```
1  macro_stmt → ID := repeat
2               | interval ( var ) eq_op time | duration ( var ) eq_op time
3               | connection ( var , var )
4
5  repeat → repeat ( NUMBER , var )
```

The **repeat**(line 5 of Listing 4) statement is one of the available **macro** statements, which allows to repeat a previously defined variable a given number of times. That *repetitions* are then stored under a variable, i.e. *R := repeat(3,C)*, so that later be possible to state constraints over a specific variable of an *iteration* of the *repetition*.

The *macro* statement **duration** (line 2 of Listing 4) forces the overall duration of a *repetition* to a be higher or lower than a certain amount o time, i.e. duration(R) < secs(60). As for the *macro* statement **interval**(line 2 of Listing 4), it forces the time between two *iterations* of a *repetition* to be higher/lower than a given amount of time, i.e. interval(R) < secs(60). Finally, the last *macro* statement, **connection**(line 3 of Listing 4), forces two network packets to be related, so that the source/destination of one packet be the destination/source of other packet.

The last type of statements is the **logical** statements(line 1 of Listing 5), which allows to specify logic operations(**and**, **or**) over **primitives** and **connective** statements.

Listing 5. NeMODe simplified grammar - Logic statements

```
1  logic_stmt → logic_stmt logic_op logic_stmt | ( logic_stmt )
2               | primitive | connective
```

The **stmt_ action_ list**(line 1 of Listing 6) part of a **case**, allows to describe the actions to take when an intrusion is detected, which is a coma separated list of statements, being allowed to use a previously described **primitive** and/or **connective** statements, as well as the **alert** statement. This list of statements allows to specify a set of properties over a set of network packets, being possible to relate them with variables used in the description of the network intrusion signature. Those new variables can later be used in the **alert** statement, together with some *strings* to alert the network administrator for an intrusion.

Listing 7 describes some basic entities, such as port addresses, ip address and time, used in several types of statements.

Variables

NeMODe variables, (line 1 of Listing 8), are always upper case, and can be categorized in several types: (1) the initial **declarations** variables; (2) the **solver/-filters** variables; (3) the **definitions** variables; (4) the **repetitions** variables

Listing 6. NeMODe simplified grammar - Action statements

```
1  stmt_action_list → stmt_action | stmt_action_list , stmt_action
2  stmt_action → primitive | connective | actions
3
4  actions → alert ( alert_arg_list )
5  alert_arg_list → alert_arg | alert_arg_list , alert_arg
6  alert_arg → var | STRING
```

Listing 7. NeMODe simplified grammar - Basic entities

```
1  port → dst_port ( var )  | src_port ( var )
2  address → src ( var ) | dst ( var )
3  time → usecs ( NUMBER ) | secs ( NUMBER ) | time_arith
4  time_arith → time ( var ) | NUMBER
5             | time ( var ) arith_op time_arith
```

Listing 8. NeMODe simplified grammar - Variables

```
1  var → ID | repeat_var | filter_var
2  repeat_var → ID [ NUMBER ] : ID
3  filter_var → ID . ID | ID . repeat_var
```

and the network packet variables. The declaration of the variables is implicit, being defined the first time they are referenced or used.

Variable scope

A NeMODe program is composed by several scopes, the first one the program itself, then, a second scope for the *solvers/filters*, and inside each solver there might exist a third scope, the repetition of a definition. At each scope level, it might be necessary to access a variable of a higher scope level. Accessing a higher scope level variable is transparent if there is no other variable with the same name on the current scope level, otherwise there is the need to access that variable using a special syntax.

Accessing a variable inside a *repetition*. To access a variable defined in a *definition*, assigned to a variable, one starts to refer the *repetition* variable, then the number of the *iteration* and finally the variable name, e.g. r[2].A.

Accessing a variable inside a *solver*. Sometimes it is necessary to access a variable defined inside a *solver* or *filter*, to do this, one starts to refer the filter and then the desired variable, which can be either a simple variable, e.g. gecode.A or a variable inside a *repetition*, e.g. gecode.R[2].A.

4.2   Examples

So far, we have worked with some simple network intrusion signatures: (1) a DHCP spoofing, (2) a DNS spoofing and (3) a SYN flood attack. All of these intrusion patterns can be described using NeMODe and the generated code was successful in finding the desired situations in the network traffic logs. A Portscan attack and an SSH Password brute-force attack are further explained in [5].

DHCP spoofing. DHCP Spoofing is a Man in The Middle(MITM) attack, where the attacker tries to reply to a DHCP request faster than the legit DHCP server of the local network, allowing the attacker to provide false network configurations to the target host, such as the default gateway, forcing all traffic from/to the target to pass though an attacker controlled machine, allowing it to capture or modify the important data. This kind of intrusion can be detected by looking for several answers to a single DHCP request, originated in different machines, although, if the attacker spoofs its addresses, invalidates this detection method. A NeMODe program to model a DHCP spoofing is shown in Listing 9. Line 2 describes the packet that initiates a requests a DHCP, line 3 the first reply to the request and line 4 the second reply the DHCP request. Finally, on line 6 is stated that packets B and C(the first and second reply) should have different source addresses.

Listing 9. A DHCP Spoofing attack programmed in NeMODe

```
1  dhcp_spoofing {
2      udp_packet(A), dst_port(A)==67,
3      udp_packet(B), dst_port(B)==68,
4      udp_packet(C), dst_port(C)==68,
5
6      src(B) != src(C)
7  } => {
8      alert('DHCP Spoofing attempt')
9  };
```

DNS spoofing. DNS Spoofing is also a Man in The Middle (MITM) attack. In this attack, the attacker tries to provide a false DNS query posted by the victim, if succeeded the victim could access a machine under the control of the attacker, thinking that it is accessing the legit machine, allowing the attacker to obtain crucial data from the victim. In order to arrange this attack, the attacker tries to respond with a false DNS query faster than the legit DNS server, providing a false IP address to the name that the victim was looking for. This kind of attacks is possible to detect by looking for several replies to the same DNS query. Listing 10 shows how this attack can be programmed using NeMODe. Line 2 describes the packet that makes the DNS request. Lines 4-5, describes a first reply to the DNS request and lines 7-8 describes the second reply. Lines 10-12 states that packets B and C should be different and that the *DNS id* of the replies should be the equal to the DNS request, which is the first two bytes of the packets data.

SYN flood attack. A SYN flood attack happens when the attacker initiates more TCP/IP connections than the server can handle and then ignoring the replies from the server, forcing the server to have a large number of half open connections in standby, which leads the service to stop when this number reach the limit of number of connections. This attack can be detected if a large number of connections is made from a single machine to other in a very short time interval. Listing 11 shows how a SYN flood attack can be described using NeMODe.

Listing 10. A DNS Spoofing attack programmed in NeMODe

```
1  dns_spoofing {
2      udp_packet(A), dst_port(A) == 53
3
4      udp_packet(B), src_port(B) == 53,
5      dst(B) == src(A), dst_port(B) == src_port(A),
6
7      udp_packet(C), src_port(C) == 53,
8      dst(C) == src(A), dst_port(C) == src_port(A),
9
10     B != C,
11     data(B,0,2) == data(A,0,2),
12     data(C,0,2) == data(A,0,2)
13 } => {
14     alert('DNS Spoofing attempt')
15 };
```

Lines 2-3 describes a TCP/IP packet with the SYN flag and assigns those properties to variable C. In line 4, the *macro* statement **repeat** is used to repeat the properties of definition C 30 times, and assign it to variable R. Line 5 states that the time interval between each repetition of C should be less than to 500 micro-seconds.

Listing 11. A SYN flood attack programmed with NeMODe

```
1  syn_flood {
2    C = { tcp_packet(A),
3          syn(A), nak(A) },
4    R := repeat(30,C),
5    max_interval(R) < usecs(500)
6  } => {
7    alert('SYN flood attack attempt')
8  };
```

4.3   Code Generation

The current implementation of NeMODe is able to generate code for the Gecode solver and for the Adaptive Search algorithm. These two approaches to constraint solving are completely different as well as the description of the problems, forcing us to have several code generators for each of back-end available. We were able to minimize this difference by creating custom libraries for each constraint solver so that the code generation process is not completely different for each back-end. Fig. 1 represents the architecture of the system; starting with a NeMODe program, which is parsed into a semantic model, then it is generated code to the appropriate back-ends used. Them, the generated code receives as input the network traffic and produces a valid solution, if the described intrusion exists on the current network traffic.

Generating a Gecode program: This goal is achieved by generating code based on Gecode constraint propagators that describe the desired network signatures. We created a custom library that defines functions that combine

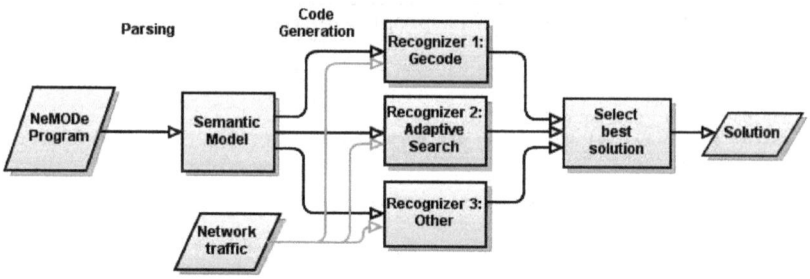

Fig. 1. NeMODe system architecture

several stock arithmetic Gecode constraints with element and extensional constraints to define custom, network related *macro* constraints. The same library includes definitions for a few network-related constraint propagators useful to implement some of the constraints needed to describe and solve IDS problems.

Generating an A.S. program: The task of generating Adaptive Search resumes to create the proper error functions so that Adaptive Search be able to solve the problem; the `cost_of_solution` and `cost_on_variable`. To ease the generation of this functions, a small library was created which implements small error functions, specific to the network intrusion detection domain, which are then used to generate the code for the error functions.

5   Experimental Results

While developing this work, several experiments were done. We have tested the examples of Sect. 4.2, a DHCP Spoofing attack, a DNS Spoofing attack and a SYN flood attack. All these network intrusions were successfully described using NeMODe and valid Gecode and Adaptive Search code was produced for all network signatures and then executed in order to validate the code and ensure that it could indeed find the desired network intrusions.

The code generated for Gecode was run on a dedicated computer, an HP Proliant DL380 G4 with two Intel(R) Xeon(TM) CPU 3.40GHz and with 4 GB of memory, running Debian GNU/Linux 4.0 with Linux kernel version 2.6.18-5. As for the Adaptive Search code, it run on an IBM BladeCenter H equipped with QS21 dual-Cell/BE blades, each with two 3.2 GHz processors, 2GB of RAM, running RHEL Server release 5.2. The reason to run both detection mechanisms in different machines with a completely different architecture is because Adaptive Search has recently been ported to Cell/BE, and we choose this version of Adaptive Search to run our experiments, forcing us to use the QS21 dual-Cell/BE blades, which is incompatible with the implementation of Gecode, forcing us to use a machine with x86 architecture to run Gecode.

In all the experiments we used log files representing network traffic which contains the desired signatures to be detected. These log files were created with the help of *tcpdump*, which is a packet sniffer, during actual attacks to a computer to simulate the real attacks described in this work.

DHCP and DNS spoofing attacks: We programmed these two attacks using the DSL of The attack was provided by NeMODe, which successfully generated code for Adaptive Search as well as for Gecode and successfully detected the intrusions. Both problems were modeled using 3 udp network packets, each one composed of 12 integer variables, in a total of 36 integer variables. The search space for both this problems was a set of 400 udp network packets, each composed of 12 integer values, in a total of 4800 values.

SYN flood attack: In the SYN flood attack, we programmed with the DSL of NeMODe which in turn generated code for Adaptive Search and Gecode. This code was then used to successfully detect the intrusion. The problem was modeled by 30 tcp network packet variables, each comprised of 19 integer variables, in a total of 570 integer values. The the search space of the problem was composed by 100 tcp network packets, each composed of 19 integer values, in a total of 1900 values.

Table 1 presents the time(user time, in seconds) required to find the desired network situation for the attacks presented in the present work, using both detection mechanisms, Gecode and Adaptive Search. The times presented are the average of 128 runs.

Table 1. Average time(in seconds) necessary to detect the intrusions using Gecode and Adaptive Search

Intrusion to detect	Gecode (seconds)	A.S (seconds)
DHCP Spoofing	0.0082	0.3924
DNS Spoofing	0.0069	0.3512
SYN flood	0.0566	0.0466

6 Evaluation

The experimental results described in Sec. 5 shows that the performance varies in a great scale depending on the problem and the recognizer. Table 1 shows that that Gecode usually performs better than Adaptive Search, except in the SYN flood attack. The SYN flood attack performed better in Adaptive Search due to the fact that the network packets of the attack are close together and there aren't almost any other packets between the packets of the attack. The results obtained with Gecode, are quite good, allowing us to start the detection of intrusions in real network traffic instead of log files. Adaptive Search inferior performance figures are explained by the lack of good heuristic, as precise tuning of the sensitive algorithm of AS has yet to be done.

As for the DSL provided by NeMODe, it revealed to be very expressive and powerful, allowing an easy description of all the three network intrusions and generate valid code that could detect the desired network situation. Although other intrusion detection systems like Snort could detect the attacks presented in this work, they don't allow to describe the problems with the expressiveness used by NeMODe or even relate the several packets that make part of the attack.

7   Conclusions and Future Work

The work presented in this paper presents NeMODe, a system for Network Intrusion detection, which provide a declarative Domain Specific Language that generates intrusion detection recognizers based on Constraint Programming, more specifically, using Gecode and Adaptive Search. NeMODe presents a very expressive DSL that allows to describe network intrusion signatures by expressing relations between network packets simply by stating constraints over network packets.

This work shows that it is possible to use a single signature description based on CP to generate several recognizers, each one based on a different CP paradigms, and with that recognizers detect the desired intrusions.

We proved that we can easily describe network signature attacks that spread across several network packets, which can not me done in friendly and declarative way in systems like Snort. Although the intrusions mentioned in this work can be detected with other intrusion detection systems, they are modeled/described with out relating the several network packets of the intrusion, much of the times using a single network packet to describe the intrusion, which could in some situations produce a large number of false positives.

A very important future work is to model more network situations as a CSP in order to evaluate the performance of the system while working with a larger diversity of problems. Although the DSL allows to describe a broad range of attacks, it still needs more flexibility to cope with more types of signatures and include more back-ends. We also need to better evaluate the the work presented in this paper by comparing the obtained results with systems like Snort.

Also a very important future step is to start performing network intrusion tasks on live network traffic link, allowing to apply this method in a real network to assess its performance.

Acknowledgments

Pedro Salgueiro acknowledges FCT –Fundação para a Ciência e a Tecnologia– for supporting him with scholarship SFRH/BD/35581/2007. The IBM QS21 dual-Cell/BE blades used in this work were donated by IBM Corporation, in the context of a SUR (Shared University Research) grant awarded to Universidade de Évora and CENTRIA.

References

1. Rossi, F., Van Beek, P., Walsh, T.: Handbook of constraint programming. Elsevier Science, Amsterdam (2006)
2. Van Deursen, A., Visser, J.: Domain-specific languages: An annotated bibliography. ACM Sigplan Notices 35(6), 26–36 (2000)
3. Gecode Team: Gecode: Generic constraint development environment (2008), http://www.gecode.org
4. Salgueiro, P., Abreu, S.: Network Monitoring with Constraint Programming: Preliminary Specification and Analysis. In: Proceedings of the 18th International Conference on Applications of Declarative Programming and Knowledge Management (2009)
5. Salgueiro, P., Abreu, S.: A DSL for Intrusion Detection based on Constraint Programming. In: SIN 2010: Proceedings of the 3rd International Conference on Security of Information and Networks. ACM, New York (2010)
6. Salgueiro, P., Abreu, S.: On using Constraints for Network Intrusion Detection. In: INForum 2010 - Simpósio de Informática, Braga, Portugal (2010)
7. Comer, D.: Internetworking With TCP/IP, 5th edn. Principles Protocols, and Architecture, vol. 1. Prentice Hall, Englewood Cliffs (2006)
8. Zhang, Y., Lee, W.: Intrusion detection in wireless ad-hoc networks. In: Proceedings of the 6th Annual International Conference on Mobile Computing and Networking, p. 283. ACM, New York (2000)
9. Roesch, M.: Snort - lightweight intrusion detection for networks. In: LISA 1999: Proceedings of the 13th USENIX Conference on System Administration, Berkeley, CA, USA, pp. 229–238. USENIX Association (1999)
10. Arun, K.S.P.: Flow-aware cross packet inspection using bloom filters for high speed data-path content matching. In: IEEE International Advance Computing Conference, IACC 2009, pp. 1230–1234 (June 6-7, 2009)
11. Vasiliadis, G., Polychronakis, M., Antonatos, S., Markatos, E.P., Ioannidis, S.: Regular Expression Matching on Graphics Hardware for Intrusion Detection. In: Balzarotti, D. (ed.) RAID 2009. LNCS, vol. 5758, pp. 265–283. Springer, Heidelberg (2009)
12. Kumar, S., Spafford, E.H.: A software architecture to support misuse intrusion detection. In: Proceedings of the 18th National Information Security Conference, pp. 194–204 (1995)
13. Schulte, C., Stuckey, P.J.: Speeding up constraint propagation. In: Wallace, M. (ed.) CP 2004. LNCS, vol. 3258, pp. 619–633. Springer, Heidelberg (2004)
14. Van Hentenryck, P., Michel, L.: Constraint-based local search. MIT Press, Cambridge (2005)
15. Codognet, P., Díaz, D.: Yet another local search method for constraint solving. In: Steinhöfel, K. (ed.) SAGA 2001. LNCS, vol. 2264, pp. 73–90. Springer, Heidelberg (2001)
16. Abreu, S., Diaz, D., Codognet, P.: Parallel local search for solving constraint problems on the cell broadband engine (preliminary results). CoRR, abs/0910.1264 (2009)
17. Paxson, V.: Bro: a system for detecting network intruders in real-time* 1. Computer networks 31(23-24), 2435–2463 (1999)
18. tcpdump web page at http://www.tcpdump.org (April 2009)

A Declarative API for Particle Systems

Pavel Krajcevski[1] and John Reppy[2]

[1] Disney Interactive Studios
Pavel.Krajcevski@disney.com
[2] University of Chicago
jhr@cs.uchicago.edu

Abstract. Recent trends in computer-graphics APIs and hardware have made it practical to use high-level functional languages for real-time graphics applications. Thus we have the opportunity to develop new approaches to computer graphics that take advantage of the high-level features of functional languages. This paper describes one such project that uses the techniques of functional programming to define and implement a combinator library for *particle systems*. Particle systems are a popular technique for rendering fuzzy phenomena, such as fire, smoke, and explosions. Using our combinators, a programmer can provide a declarative specification of how a particle system behaves. This specification includes rules for how particles are created, how they evolve, and how they are rendered. Our library translates these declarative specifications into a low-level intermediate language that can be compiled to run on the GPU or interpreted by the CPU.

Keywords: Computer Graphics, Embedded DSL, Particle Systems.

1 Introduction

In recent years, real-time computer graphics APIs, such as OpenGL, have shifted from working in terms of individual vertices to working with large batches of geometry. Furthermore, the computational load has shifted from the CPU to specialized GPUs that have supercomputer performance at commodity prices. These trends make it practical to use high-level functional languages to program real-time graphics and to take advantage of features like higher-order functions and polymorphic type systems [2]. This paper describes one such project: a declarative library for defining *particle systems*.

Particle systems are a technique for animating and rendering fuzzy phenomena such as fire, smoke, explosions, *etc.* in 3D graphics [9]. Because these phenomena have a fluid and dynamic appearance, traditional polygon-based rendering techniques are not well suited for rendering them. A particle system is a stochastic system that represents these phenomena as a cloud of simple *particles*. Each particle has state, *i.e.*, position, color, velocity, *etc.*, that is evolving over time according to some "physics" model [13].

Many animation systems today (*e.g.*, Blender [1] and Terminal Reality's Infernal Engine [2]) provide support for particle effects by requiring the user to specify a set of properties that are the interpreted by the underlying architecture. These methods for creating

---

[1] http://wiki.blender.org/index.php/Doc:Manual/Physics/Particles
[2] http://www.infernalengine.com/tech_particles.php

R. Rocha and J. Launchbury (Eds.): PADL 2011, LNCS 6539, pp. 130–144, 2011.

particle systems are designed to give artists much more creative control through a large variety of properties but discourage the creation of quick, dynamic particle systems that are easily simulated with many particles. In contrast, McAllister has described a C++ library for particle systems that provides a higher level of abstraction than hand-written effects and is more flexible than the canned systems found in animation tools [8]. In his system, one uses a sequence of *action* functions to specify how the state of the current particle system is modified. But his system has some limitations: it is not declarative, does not use runtime compilation techniques, and does not (yet) support running particle systems on the GPU.

This paper presents a declarative approach to implementing particle systems, which is inspired by McAllister's work, but which addresses the limitations of his library. Using our API, one specifies the physics of a particle system as the composition of actions, which represent particle state to state functions. These functions are then compiled to run on either the CPU or GPU (via OpenCL [5]). Our library is implemented as part of the SML3d library [12], which is a library for OpenGL-based graphics for the MLton version of Standard ML.

The remainder of the paper is organized as follows. In the next section, we provide a more detailed description of how particle systems work and give a simple example of such a system in pseudo code. In Section 3, we describe our combinator library for particle systems and illustrate its use with several examples. This section is followed by a description of the implementation, which includes a discussion of the optimizations that we perform. We then discuss related work in Section 6 and conclude in Section 7.

2 Particle Systems

A **particle system** is a technique in computer graphics that is used to render *fuzzy phenomena*, such as rain, fire, explosions, *etc.* [9]. Particle Systems consist of a set of individual particles that each have their own **state**. The state of a particle is defined by a list of variables defining attributes that are used in either the physical simulation of the particle or in its rendering. A typical implementation of a particle system executes the following steps for each frame of animation:

1. New particles are generated by means of a stochastic process that determines the number of new particles and their initial states.
2. Particle states are updated.
3. Particles that have exceeded the qualifications for their existence are deleted.
4. Particles are rendered in the scene.

The most common state variables of a particle system are position, velocity, color, and age. A particle is considered *alive* if it exists within some predetermined boundary of the particle system and its age is below the maximum age of a particle.

The physical simulation of the particle system is defined by a set of rules that affect the particles. Some rules may be applied to only a subset of the particles while others affect all of the particles. An example of this is having particles bounce off of a platform versus gravity. In order to get the particle state for frame $i + 1$, we apply these rules to the state of the particles for frame i in relation to the time elapsed between rendering.

2.1   A Simple Particle System

As a simple example, let us consider a particle system that models a geyser or fountain.[3] In this system, particles represent water that is being ejected into the air from the ground. Particles will be emitted from a ground plane (the XZ plane) with some initial velocity vector pointing mostly up. As their state evolves, gravity slows their upward velocity until they eventually fall to earth and die when they reach the ground. For visual effect, we also want the color of the particle to evolve as it ages (*i.e.*, starting as white and then darkening to blue).

Simulating the basic physics of particle motion requires tracking the particle's velocity (**vel**) and position (**pos**) and checking to see if the particle has outlived its lifespan or hit the ground. The SML code for updating the physics state of a particle is as follows, where NONE is returned if the particle has died:

```
fun updateParticle ({pos, v, life} : particle, dt) =
      if (life = 0) then NONE
      else let
         val pos = Vec3f.add(pos, Vec3f.scale(dt, v))
         in
            if (#y pos <= 0.0) then NONE
            else SOME{
                pos = pos,
                v = Vec3f.sub(v, Vec3f.scale(dt, gravity)),
                life = life-dt
            }
         end
```

Using our library, the physics of this particle system is specified as follows:

```
P.sequence [
    P.accelerate gravityVec,
    P.inside {
        d = groundPlane,
    thenStmt = P.move,
    elseStmt = P.die
    }
]
```

The physics is defined as a sequence (composition) of two actions (an action is just a function from particle states to particle states). The first action applies gravitational acceleration to the particle's state and the second tests to see if the particle is in the half-space defined by the ground plane. If it is, then the particle is moved (*i.e.*, its position is updated), otherwise it dies. The lifetime of the particle is set when it is created and is tracked automatically.

---

[3] SML source code for this example can be found in the SML3d source code.

2.2 Specifying Particle Systems

Specifying a particle system using our library is a staged process. First, the components for birth, simulation, and rendering are conglomerated into a single program. Each of these variables will be discussed in detail in Section 3

```
val create : {emit: emitter, physics : action, render : renderer}
        -> program
```

To run the program on a specific target (*e.g.*, CPU or GPU), we must first compile it to an executable. This involves breaking down the higher level combinators into a form representable on the target. In order to execute the program, it is instantiated with its own set of run-time variables. Each target supports a standard interface for compiling, instantiating, and running a program.

```
type exec   (* executable program *)
type psys   (* instance of an exec *)

val compile : Particles.program -> exec
val new : {exec : exec, maxParticles : int} -> psys
val step : {psys: psys, t : Time.time} -> unit
val render : psys -> unit
```

Lastly, we have a mechanism to delete a particle system when it is no longer needed.

```
val delete : psys -> unit
```

3   Particle-System Combinators

An SML3d particle system is specified by three components: an *emitter*, which describes the generation of new particles, an *action*, which describes how the state of a particle evolves, and a *renderer*, which defines how a particle's state is visualized. This section describes how these components are specified and gives an example of a complete specification.

3.1   Variables

Particle systems are parameterized by *variables*, which have one of four possible types.

```
type 'a ty

val boolTy   : bool ty
val intTy    : int ty
val floatTy  : float ty
val vec3fTy  : Vec3f.vec3 ty
```

We use phantom types [7] to ensure type correctness for particle-system variables.

```
type 'a var

val new : string * 'a ty -> 'a var
```

Whenever a new variable is created, its type is specified. Subsequent uses of variables must match the specified type.

Our system has two kinds of variables: constants and parameters. Constants are variables that are created with an initial value.

```
val constb  : bool -> bool var
val consti  : int -> int var
val constf  : float -> float var
val const3f : (float * float * float) -> Vec3f.vec3 var
```

Parameters are initially created without values associated to them. The act of associating a value with a variable is called *binding*. Variables that are bound before a program is compiled are treated as constants; unbound variables are bound on a per-instance basis.

The binding of variables can be done at any point during the execution of the particle system and must be done prior to execution. The program will abort at runtime if it encounters any unbound variables, and there are no static guarantees at runtime to detect unbound variables. Due to this freedom in variable definition, anything that is defined in terms of particle system variables can be made time-varying by re-binding the variable after given time intervals.

3.2   Domains

We use McAllister's notion of a *domain* to specify many of the properties of a particle system. In the abstract, a domain is a subset of $\Re^3$; examples of domains include line segments, discs, cylinders, and half-spaces (*i.e.*, planes). Domains are created by specifying a series of particle system variables as parameters to a constructor. Domains are used to specify three dimensional objects that the particles interact with and random vector generators by defining a space containing all possible values. Some examples of how domains are specified are

```
type domain
val point : vec3f var -> domain
val plane : {pt: vec3f var, n : vec3f var} -> domain
val sphere : {c : vec3f var, r : float var} -> domain
```

3.3   Emitters

In our particle system definition, we use the notion of an *emitter* to denote a collection of domains from which the particle state variables generate their values. Since the domains are specified using particle system variables, whose values are not fixed, the conditions under which particles are generated can change over the course of a particle system's lifetime. Along with the domains, the emitter also takes a particle system variable parameter that defines the rate at which the particles should be created.

One example in which these variables may change is a geyser that emits particles in bursts. Over the course of the animation, the domain specifying the initial velocity of the particles could be specified by a cylinder whose radius changes with the rate of particle creation. Both of the radius of the cylinder and rate of emission would be specified by particle system variables.

```
type action

val move : action
val die : action
val nop : action
val accelerate : Vec3f.vec PSV.var -> action

val bounce : {
     friction : float PSV.var,
     resilience : float PSV.var,
     cutoff : float PSV.var,
     d : domain
   } -> action
```

Fig. 1. Common actions used in SML3D particle systems

Particle state. The state of a particle consists of a number of properties. The initial domain of each of the following properties is specified upon the creation of an emitter:

position a vector of three floats that specifies the current position of the particle
velocity a vector of three floats that specifies the current velocity of the particle
size a vector of three floats that specifies the size of the particle for each axis.
color a vector of four floats that specifies the color (RGB plus alpha) of the particle
lifetime a float which represents the number of seconds left for this particle to live. If
   this value is less than or equal to zero, then the particle does not get rendered.

3.4 Actions

The main part of a particle system is the specification of its physics. An *action* represents a function from particle states to particle states. We have three kinds of action combinators: basic actions, such as move a particle; sequences of actions; and predicate actions. The semantics of particle-physics simulation can be described by applying the physics action to the state of each particle to get a new state (or $\perp$ if it dies; we assume that for an action a, $a(\perp) = \perp$).

Basic actions. Basic actions are operations that modify the state of the particle. Figure 1 gives a few examples of common actions that are used by particle systems. These include move, which updates the particle's position by adding its scaled velocity, die, which kills the particle, and accelerate, which adds a vector to the particle's velocity. A more complicated example is bounce, which reflects the particle's velocity when it reaches the edge of the specified domain.

Sequences. Sequences of actions are combined using the sequence combinator

```
val sequence : action list -> action
```

which returns the composition of its arguments.

```
val inside : {
      d : domain, thenStmt : action, elseStmt : action
    } -> action

val faster : {
      t : Time.time, thenStmt : action, elseStmt : action
    } -> action
```

Fig. 2. Some predicate actions

Predicates. Predicates are constructs that take a high level conditional statement and use it to determine which sub-action to apply. Figure 2 gives an example of two predicates. The first tests to see if a particle's position is inside a domain and the second tests the particle's speed. Each predicate has two subactions: the `thenStmt` is applied if the predicate's condition is true for the particle and the `elseStmt` is applied if the predicate's condition is false.

The `die` action is often used in combination with predicates to mark particles as dead when they meet certain conditions such as their velocity gets too high or they enter (or exit) a specified domain.

3.5   Renderers

Renderers describe the mechanisms used to render the particle system. These are not complex in terms of particle systems and do not take any parameters (except perhaps textures). The main function of the renderer is to translate the particle state into pixels on the screen. The mechanisms required to do this vary based on the renderer, *e.g.*, the points renderer maps particles to points rendered at the particle's position with its color. Some examples of renderers are

```
type renderer
val points : renderer
val texQuads : Texture.texture_id list -> renderer
```

3.6   A Complete Example

To illustrate the use of these combinators in practice, we examine an example of a fountain implemented as a particle system. Figure 3 gives a screen shot of this system in action. The fountain consists of an emitter just above the XZ plane that launches particles into the air, a disc on the XZ plane that the particles bounce off of when they fall, and a cutoff plane three units below the XZ plane.

First, we define variables for the parts of the particle system that vary between instances.

```
val gravityVec = PSVar.new ("g", PSVar.vec3fTy)
val bounceFriction = PSVar.new ("bf", PSVar.floatTy)
val bounceRes = PSVar.new ("br", PSVar.floatTy)
val emitterRate = PSVar.new ("er", PSVar.intTy)
```

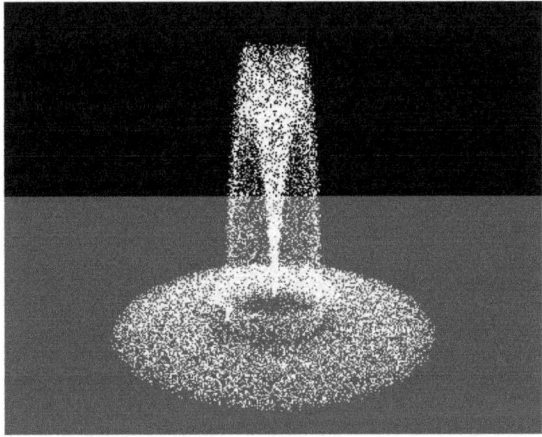

Fig. 3. The fountain particle system in action

Next, we specify the emitter. Each of the values of the emitter specifies a domain for vector properties and constants for the scalar variables. Note that these values do not all have to be constants. For example, the `emitterRate` variable, which specifies the number of particles to generate per-frame, is not a constant variable. Hence, we may change the variable to simulate higher or lower water pressure of the fountain.

```
val emitterFountain = P.newEmitter {
    maxNum = emitterRate, (* emission rate *)
    positionD = P.line(
      const3f (0.0, 0.01, 0.0), const3f (0.0, 0.4, 0.0)),
    velocityD = P.cylinder(
      const3f (0.0, 0.25, ~0.01), const3f (0.0, 0.27, ~0.01),
      constf 0.021, constf 0.019),
    colorD = P.line(
      const3f (0.8, 0.9, 1.0), const3f (1.0, 1.0, 1.0))
    sizeD = P.point(const3f (1.0, 1.0, 1.0 )),
    lifetime = PSVar.constf 100.0
  }
```

Each of the values that are specified by a domain uses the 3D primitive to randomly generate a point within the domain using a uniform distribution. Following the emitter, the action list describes the physics simulation of the particle system. For this system, we simulate a fountain that bounces off of the ground plane. Hence, since the emitter provides the initial upwards velocity, we specify gravity, the bounce off of the ground, and finally death.

```
val bounceDisc = P.disc(
    const3f (0.0, 0.0, 0.0), const3f (0.0, 1.0, 0.0),
    constf 5.0, constf 0.0)

val actionFountain = P.sequence [
    P.accelerate gravityVec,
```

```
P.bounce {
    fiction = bounceFriction,
    resilience = bounceRes,
    cutoff = constf(0.0),
    d = bounceDisc
    },
P.inside {
  d = P.plane(
     PSVar.const3f (0.0, ~3.0, 0.0),
     PSVar.const3f (0.0, 1.0, 0.0)),
  thenStmt = P.move,
  elseStmt = P.die
}
]
```

Finally, we create the hooks that will incorporate the particle system into the desired runtime environment. First, we package all three components by calling the P.create function. Then, we compile the particle system for the desired environment. At this point, the system is converted first to an internal representation and then to a representation that caters to the chosen runtime. Finally, we create an instance of the particle system, specifying the total number of particles that we want to use for that particular instance.

```
val fountain = P.create {
    emitter = emitterFountain,
    physics = actionFountain,
    render = P.points
  }

val fountainExe = PsysCL.compile fountain

val fountainPsys = PsysCL.new {
    exec = fountainExe,
    maxParticles = 10000
  }
```

Before we are ready to enter the main loop of the program, some of the variables need to be initialized. First, we bind values to the particle system variables that were not initialized during compilation but will not be changing during the actual program execution.

```
PsysCL.bind3f (fountainPsys, gravityVec, (0.0, ~9.8, 0.0));
PsysCL.bindf (fountainPsys, bounceFriction, ~0.05);
PsysCL.bindf (fountainPsys, bounceRes, 0.35);
```

Then, we define a function that renders the system at the current time.

```
fun runsOnce (inst, emitRate) = (
    PsysCL.bindi (inst, emitterRate, emitRate);
    PsysCL.step {inst=inst, t = Time.now()};
    PsysCL.render inst)
```

In order to actually animate the particle system, all we need to do is update it with our desired emitter rate. Since the emitter rate is bound each time the system runs, we are free to vary the value dynamically.

4   Implementation

Once the particle system has been compiled into an internal representation (IR), we perform a number of optimizations on the IR itself before we go to code generation. During code generation, we allow the user to specify different backends on which the particle system will run: OpenCL, GLSL, or the CPU.

4.1   Internal Representation

Execution of the particle system is handled in a number of steps. First, the emitter and physics components are compiled down into an internal representation. The IR represents programs as a DAG of *blocks*, where each block is a list of *statements*. Variables in the IR are single assignments and we use explicit parameter passing (instead of ϕ-nodes) to represent live variables in control-flow between blocks. Each block contains a list of *statements*, which are procedures used to manipulate *IR variables*. Then, if applicable, the IR is compiled down onto the host runtime environment, *e.g.* OpenCL on the GPU.

Due to the nature of the variables in the particle state, all of the operations performed by the particle system's emitter and physics can be described by primitive vector and scalar operations. This is another reason why this representation of a particle system lends itself to the GPU. But more importantly, it means that all of our higher level constructs involving domains can be represented by a relatively minor set of vector operations.

Variables. The IR has its own class of variables to parameterize its operations. Some of these variables correspond to the user-defined variables described in Section 3.1 and others are internal. Similar to the particle system variables, the IR variables have a name, type, and scope associated with them. The scope of the IR variables is restricted to the following:

Constant — a variable that represents a constant value. These variables have global scope and correspond to either user-defined constants and internal constants.
Global — a variable whose value is defined outside the IR and has global scope. These include the unbound user variables and the particle state variables.
Parameter — a parameter to a block. The scope of the variable is its block.
Local — a variable defined by an IR binding in a block. The scope of the variable is the remainder of the block (*e.g.*, similar to a let-bound variable in a lexically-scoped language).

The translation to the IR generates a mapping from user-defined variables to IR globals. This mapping is used to supply instance-specific values for these variables when the particle system is run.

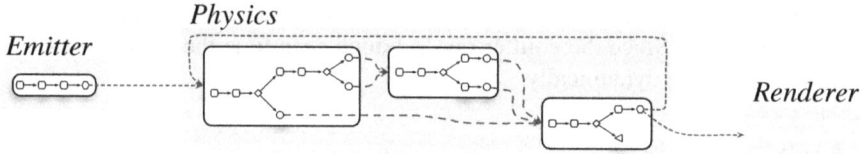

Fig. 4. The IR graph for a simple particle system

Blocks. The IR representation of an emitter or physics component is a DAG of *blocks*. Each block has a list of parameter variables and a body, which consists of a tree of statements. The five basic types of statements are:

PRIM(y, p, xs, s)
> is a binding of y to the result of applying primitive operator p to the argument variables xs. The scope of y is the statement s.

IF(x, s1, s2)
> is a conditional where x is a boolean variable that is tested, s1 is the *then* branch, and s2 is the *else* branch.

GOTO(b, xs)
> is an unconditional control transfer to block b with arguments xs.

RETURN(xs)
> is a statement that marks the completion of the component's execution. The variables xs represent the results of the computation and correspond to the particle state variables.

DISCARD
> is a statement that terminates the particle and discards its state.

State variables. State variables are a specific set of IR variables used by the implementation to track the state of the particle. These variables are special because they are passed to the root block as parameters. Then, after the processing is completed, a RETURN statement is called with parameters matching those that were passed into the root block of the program.

The state variables are those specified by the emitter (position, velocity, size, color, and life) plus an extra one, called *secondary position*, which contains the value of the particle's position on the previous frame. As described below, some of these variables may be eliminated by optimzation.

4.2   Optimizations

We perform a number of optimizations on the IR to eliminate unused computations and reduce the memory requirements of representing particles. These optimizations are performed in light of the *implicit* data and control-flow between the components. Figure 4 illustrates these dependencies for a simple example. The dashed edge from the return node of the emitter code to the entry of the physics code represents the fact that the particle state created by the emitter is used by the physics. Likewise, the backedge from the return node in the physics code to its own entry represents the fact that the resulting state from one physics step is the input to the next. Lastly, there is an edge from the physics return node to the renderer, which represents the fact that the renderer renders the particle state.

Contraction. Our optimization performs a number of standard *contractive* optimizations that serve to simplify and reduce the code. These include eliminating unused local variables, merging blocks that have only one predecessor into their predecessor, and constant folding.

Useless variable elimination. One of our most important optimizations is *useless variable elimination* (UVE). Many particle systems only use a subset of the state variables, but the translation to the IR must be conservative and include code to support all of them. We use UVE to prune out state variables that cannot possibly affect the rendering of the system.

We use a simplified version of Shivers' UVE algorithm [11], that starts by marking the inputs to the renderer as *useful* (*e.g.*, if we are rendering the system as points, then the position and color are marked as useful). This information is then propagated back through the physics code's control flow, with the right hand side variables of a PRIM node being marked as useful if the left hand side is useful, arguments to conditionals are marked as useful, and the useful parameters of a block cause the corresponding arguments to GOTOs to be marked useful. Because the physics code is implicitly in a loop, we must propagate usefulness from the root block's parameters back to the corresponding arguments of the RETURN statements. Once a fixed point is reached, we propagate the useful variable information into the RETURN statements of the emitter and apply the analysis to the emitter code. Since the emitter is run only once per particle, we do not need to iterate to a fixed point. Once the analysis is complete, we rewrite the code to remove any variable that is not marked as useful.

Domain-specific optimizations. Many optimizations can be performed on geometric operations to simplify the actual execution of the code. For example, if we take the dot product of a vector v and the unit vector pointing along the y-axis, this is identical to just extracting the y-coordinate from v. We can avoid many superfluous operations in this manner. This optimization is mostly useful in conjunction with constant folding, since many of the available optimizations do not become apparent until one or the other happens.

5   Targetting GPUs

Our system is designed to support multiple backend targets for executing particle systems. These include a CPU target that interprets the IR, a planned backend that translates the IR to GLSL [10] to run on the GPU, and a backend that generates OpenCL [5] code that can run on either the CPU or GPU. These backends implement the standard interface that was described in Section 2.2. In this section, we discuss some of the issues in generating code for the OpenCL target.

Code Generation. Generating OpenCL code from the IR is complicated by the fact that the IR is a control-flow graph, while the OpenCL is a block-structured language. Fortunately, however, our combinators do not produce cyclic graphs, so the process is possible. We do a prepass that matches blocks with the IF statements (if any) that they are a join continuation for. We then use this information to translate the IR into an AST representation that can be pretty printed as OpenCL code. The code generation also deals with mapping IR variables to OpenCL variables, *etc.*.

Representing particles. Particles are represented as an array of OpenCL structs, where each field corresponds to a particle state variable. We also create arrays of OpenGL attributes to hold those particle state variables that are used by the renderer. While using separate arrays for the renderer results in some redundancy, it is necessary because some rendering methods require multiple vertices, each with their own set of attributes, per particle. For example, line segments require two vertices per particle, which are defined by the position and secondary position state variables.

Random numbers. To support random-number generation, each particle has a random seed as part of its state. The OpenCL translation uses a functional random-number generator that takes a seed and produces both a random number and a new seed. We then thread the seed state through the generated code and save it back in the particle state at the end of the execution.

Particle birth and death. Another tricky issue is managing particle birth and death, since the size of the total population affects the number of new particles generated each iteration. Because we want to avoid moving data from the GPU back to the CPU, we have to use a parallel-scan algorithm to compute for each particle the number of live particles with lower IDs [4]. This information can then be used to manage births as follows. Assume that we want to add k new particles, then a dead particle with ID i is reborn if $i - j \leq k$, where j is the number of live particles with IDs lower than i.

6   Related Work

Reeves was the first researcher to suggest the combination of stochastic processes and particles to render fuzzy phenomena. His seminal paper describes the basic ideas that underlie all modern particle systems [9]. He describes several applications, including the use of particle systems to render the wall of fire caused by the "Genesis bomb" in the movie *Star Trek II: The Wrath of Kahn* (Paramount 1982).

Our work was inspired by McAllister's C++ library for building particle systems [8]. In this library, McAllister introduced the notion of domains as a type associated with particle systems. From this, we were able to abstract a functional approach to creating particle systems at a high level. Another contribution was Kipfer *et al.*'s method of simulating particles on the GPU [6]. In their paper, they used the GPU to handle both sorting and particle interaction, motivating the design for how we should present our data in order to streamline it on the GPU. Finally, Yi and Froemke's Ticker Tape library provided an example for how particle systems can be created using more intuitive methods [14]. In this library, each operation on a particle system was defined by having a user-defined creation, physics, and rendering operation, which was later composted into one system.

Animation tools, such as Blender, define particle systems by manipulating their properties directly. Many of these tools specify particle systems in similar ways. They require the user to define methods for creation and rendering, and then have mechanisms by which the appearance of the particle system is specified. For example, Blender's particle system animation allows for splines and other user-defined particle paths. This method is useful for artists, but it also is limited in that the animations generally target non-real time rendering. As a result, performance and ease of creation are not measures by which we judge the tool's effectiveness.

7   Conclusion

In this paper we have presented a declarative approach to defining particle systems. Our implementation provides a set of combinators for specifying the physics of a particle system; these combinators are then compiled into an internal representation that can either be interpreted on the CPU or translated to code that can run on the GPU. This approach takes advantage of the high-level features of functional languages and demonstrates a way that high-level languages can provide a better programming model for computer graphics.

In practical environments, this method of defining particle systems could be used to create tools that provide a much more visual approach to creating particle systems to be used in the field. Visual programming languages have been used to create procedural animations before, such as Apple's Quartz Composer [1]. Such a programming tool would increase the ease of creating particle systems in both video game and movie production.

7.1   Future Work

There are many features of particle systems that are not implemented in the programming model that we have introduced in this paper. Most notably, there is no way to specify the sorting of particles in our programming model. Also, allowing the user to pass state variables into the particle system run-time environment would introduce many new opportunities for more dynamic definitions of particle systems.

User-defined state variables. Actions, such as `accelerate` and `move`, are specific cases of the vector operation $x_{i+1} = x_i + ty_i$, where the x and y are bound to specific state variables. By exposing state variables to the user, we can use a smaller set of actions to support our current behaviors. Furthermore, we can allow user-defined state variables and renderers to increase the flexibility of the system. This generalization only requires changes to the user API, since the IR and backends already deal with the general case.

Sorting. When rendering a group of translucent polygons, it is generally assumed that the polygons are sorted by their distance from the camera. Kipfer *et al.* introduced a nice way to sort particles on the GPU using a bitonic sort [6]. This sorting algorithm lends itself fairly well to the GPU and would not require an extensive overhaul of our current system. Their implementation, however, leverages the technical aspects of GLSL and does not provide a platform independent way of representing the sorting of particles.

Particle-particle interaction. Finally, one last feature of particle systems that should be supported is the idea of particle-particle interaction. Such interactions are a challenge to GPUs, but there are techniques for spatial sorting that can be applied to handle them, such as Kipfer *et al.*s Uberflow system [6]. Using the particles' sorting to determine proximity would allow for many other effects as well, such as flocking.

References

1. Apple Inc.: Quartz Composer Programming Guide (October 2008), http://developer.apple.com
2. Elliott, C.: Programming graphics processors functionally. In: Haskell 2004. ACM Press, New York (2004)
3. Elliott, C., Hudak, P.: Functional reactive animation. In: ICFP 1997, pp. 263–273. ACM Press, New York (1997)
4. Harris, M.: Parallel prefix sum (scan) with CUDA. In: GPU Gems 3. Addison-Wesley, Reading (2007)
5. Khronos OpenCL Working Group: The OpenCL Specification (Version 1.1) (2010), http://www.khronos.org/opencl
6. Kipfer, P., Segal, M., Westermann, R.: Uberflow: a gpu-based particle engine. In: HWWS 2004, pp. 115–122. ACM, New York (2004)
7. Leijen, D., Meijer, E.: Domain specific embedded compilers. In: DSL 1999, pp. 109–122. ACM, New York (1999)
8. McAllister, D.K.: The design of an API for particle systems. Tech. rep., University of North Carolina (January 2000), www.particlesystems.org
9. Reeves, W.T.: Particle systems—a technique for modeling a class of fuzzy objects. ACM Trans. Graph. 2(2), 91–108 (1983)
10. Rost, R.J., Licea-Kane, B.: OpenGL Shading Language, 3rd edn. Addison-Wesley, Reading (2010)
11. Shivers, O.: Useless-variable elimination. In: WSA 1991 (October 1991)
12. The SML3d library, http://sml3d.cs.uchicago.edu
13. Witkin, A.: An introduction to physically based modeling: Particle system dynamics (1997), http://www.cs.cmu.edu/~baraff/pbm/constraints.pdf
14. Yi, M., Froemke, Q.: Ticker tape: A scalable 3d particle system with wind and air resistance (May 2010), http://software.intel.com/en-us/articles/tickertape

Integrating XPath with the Functional-Logic Language Toy

Rafael Caballero[1], Yolanda García-Ruiz[1], and Fernando Sáenz-Pérez[2],[*]

[1] Departamento de Sistemas Informáticos y Computación,
[2] Departamento de Ingeniería del Software e Inteligencia Artificial
Universidad Complutense de Madrid, Spain

Abstract. This paper presents a programming framework for incorporating XPath queries into the functional-logic language $\mathcal{TOY}$. The proposal exploits the language characteristics, including non-determinism, logic variables, and higher-order functions and patterns. Our setting covers a wide range of standard XPath axes and tests. In particular reverse axes are implemented thanks to the double nature of XPath queries, which are both higher-order functions and data terms in our setting. The combination of these two different worlds, the functional-logic paradigm and the XML query language XPath, is very enriching for both of them. From the point of view of functional-logic programming, the language is now able to deal with XML documents in a very simple way. From the point of view of XPath, our approach presents several nice properties as the generation of XML test-cases for XPath queries, which can be useful for finding bugs in erroneous queries.

Keywords: Functional-Logic Programming, Non-Deterministic Functions, XPath Queries, Higher-Order Patterns.

1 Introduction

In the last few years the Extensible Markup Language XML [12] has become the *de facto* standard for the exchange of different types of data. Thus, querying XML documents from different languages as become a convenient feature. XQuery [14,15] has been defined as a query language for finding and extracting information from XML documents. It extends XPath [13], a domain-specific language that has become part of general-purpose languages. Although less expressive than XQuery, the simplicity of XPath makes it a perfect tool for many types of queries. In this paper, we address the task of incorporating XPath into the functional-logic system $\mathcal{TOY}$ [8]. The usual approach for integrating XPath in an existing programming language first represents the XPath query by means of some suitable data type, and then employs some evaluator which takes the XPath query and the XML document as inputs, and produces the desired result

---

[*] This work has been supported by the Spanish projects TIN2008-06622-C03-01, S-0505/TIC/0407, S2009TIC-1465, and UCM-BSCH-GR58/08-910502.

R. Rocha and J. Launchbury (Eds.): PADL 2011, LNCS 6539, pp. 145–159, 2011.
© Springer-Verlag Berlin Heidelberg 2011

as output. However, in functional and functional-logic languages, a different approach is possible: XPath queries can be represented by higher-order functions connected by higher-order combinators. Using this approach, an XPath query becomes at the same time implementation (code) and representation (data term). In this paper we follow this idea, which has been used in the past, for instance for defining parsers in functional and functional-logic languages [3,7].

The specific characteristics of functional-logic languages match perfectly the nature of XPath queries:

- *Non-deterministic functions* are used to nicely represent the evaluation of an XPath query, which consists of fragments of the input XML document.
- *Logic variables* are employed for instance when obtaining the contents of XPath text nodes. Also, they play an important role when defining XML test-cases for XPath queries, one of the most appealing features of our setting.
- By defining rules with *higher-order patterns* XPath queries become truly first-class citizens in our setting. This allows us to define the transformation for introducing reverse axes as `parent` or checking that the query is constructed using XPath standard components.

The rest of the paper is organized as follows. Section 2.1 briefly introduces the functional-language $\mathcal{TOY}$ and the XPath subset considered in this work. Section 3 defines the basic components of XPath queries in $\mathcal{TOY}$. Section 4 shows how XML test-cases for XPath queries can be readily generated, while Section 5 takes advantage of higher-order patterns for introducing some improvements in our framework. Finally, Section 6 presents some conclusions.

2   Preliminaries

Next we introduce briefly the functional-logic language $\mathcal{TOY}$ and the subset of XPath that we intend to integrate with $\mathcal{TOY}$.

2.1   The Functional-Logic Language $\mathcal{TOY}$

All the examples in this paper are written in the concrete syntax of the lazy functional-logic language $\mathcal{TOY}$ [8], but most of the code can be easily adapted to other similar languages as Curry [5]. We start explaining a possible representation of basic XML documents in $\mathcal{TOY}$. A $\mathcal{TOY}$ program is composed of data type declarations, type alias, infix operators, function type declarations and defining rules for functions symbols. Data type declarations and type alias are useful for representing XML documents in $\mathcal{TOY}$, as illustrated next:

```
data node      = txt     string
               | comment string
               | tag     string [attribute] [node]
data attribute = att     string string
type xml       = node
```

```
<?xml version='1.0'?>              tag "root" [att "version" "1.0"] [
<food>                            tag "food" [] [
 <item type="fruit">               tag "item" [att "type" "fruit"] [
   <name>watermelon</name>           tag "name" [] [txt "watermelon"],
   <price>32</price>                 tag "price" [] [txt "32"]
 </item>                           ],
 <item type="fruit">               tag "item" [att "type" "fruit"] [
   <name>oranges</name>              tag "name" [] [txt "oranges"],
   <variety>navel</variety>          tag "variety" [] [txt "navel"],
   <price>74</price>                 tag "price" [] [txt "74"]
 </item>                           ],
 <item type="vegetable">           tag "item" [att "type" "vegetable"] [
  <name>onions</name>                tag "name" [] [txt "onions"],
  <price>55</price>                  tag "price" [] [txt "55"]
 </item>                           ],
 <item type="fruit">               tag "item" [att "type" "fruit"] [
   <name>strawberries</name>         tag "name" [] [txt "strawberries"],
   <variety>alpine</variety>         tag "variety" [] [txt "alpine"],
   <price>210</price>                tag "price" [] [txt "210"]
 </item>                           ]
</food>                           ]]
```

Fig. 1. XML example (left) and its representation in $\mathcal{TOY}$ (right)

The data type **node** represents nodes in a simple XML document. It distinguishes three types of nodes: texts, tags (element nodes), and comments, each one represented by a suitable data constructor and with arguments representing the information about the node. For instance, constructor **tag** includes the tag name (an argument of type **string**) followed by a list of attributes, and finally a list of child nodes. The data type **attribute** contains the name of the attribute and its value (both of type **string**). The last type alias, **xml**, renames the data type **node**. Of course, this list is not exhaustive, since it misses several types of XML nodes, but it is enough for this presentation. Notice that in this paper we do not consider the adequacy of the document to its underlying *Schema* definition [11]. This task has been addressed in functional programming defining regular expression types [10]. However, in this work we assume well-formed input XML documents.

The $\mathcal{TOY}$ primitive **load_xml_file** loads an XML file returning its representation as a value of type **node**. Figure 1 shows an example of XML file and its representation in $\mathcal{TOY}$.

Each rule for a function f has the form:

$$\underbrace{f\ t_1 \ldots t_n}_{\text{left-hand side}} \rightarrow \underbrace{r}_{\text{right-hand side}} \quad \text{where } \underbrace{s_1 = u_1, \ldots, s_m = u_m}_{\text{local definitions}}$$

where u_i and r are expressions (that can contain new extra variables) and t_i, s_i are patterns. The overall idea is that a function call $(f\ e_1 \ldots e_n)$ returns an instance $r\theta$ of r, if:

- Each e_i can be reduced to some pattern a_i, $i = 1 \ldots n$, such that $(f\ t_1 \ldots t_n)$ and $(f\ a_1 \ldots a_n)$ are unifiable with most general unifier θ, and
- $u_i\theta$ can be reduced to pattern $s_i\theta$ for each $i = 1 \ldots m$.

In $\mathcal{TOY}$, variable names must start with either an uppercase letter or an underscore (for anonymous variables), whereas other identifiers start with lowercase. Infix operators are also allowed as particular case of program functions. Consider for instance the definitions:

```
infixr 30 /\           infixr 30 \/           infixr 45 ?
false /\ X = false     true \/ X = true       X ? _Y = X
true /\ X = X          false \/ X = X         _X ? Y = Y
```

The /\ and \/ operators represent the standard conjunction and disjunction, respectively, while ? represents the non-deterministic choice. For instance the infix declaration infixr 45 ? indicates that ? is an infix operator that associates to the right (the r in infixr) and that its priority is 35. The priority is used to assume precedences in the case of expressions involving different operators. Computations in $\mathcal{TOY}$ start when the user inputs some goal as

Toy> 1 ? 2 ? 3 ? 4 == R

This goal asks $\mathcal{TOY}$ for values of the logical variable R that make true the (strict) equality 1 ? 2 ? 3 ? 4 == R. This goal yields four different answers $\{R \mapsto 1\}$, $\{R \mapsto 2\}$, $\{R \mapsto 3\}$, and $\{R \mapsto 4\}$. The next function extends the choice operator to lists: member [X|Xs] = X ? member Xs. For instance, the goal member [1,2,3,4] == R has the same four answers that were obtained by trying 1 ? 2 ? 3 ? 4 == R. $\mathcal{TOY}$ is a *typed* language. Types do not need to be annotated explicitly by the user, they are inferred by the system, which rejects ill-typed expressions. However, function type declarations can also be made explicit by the user, which improves the clarity of the program and helps to detect some bugs at compile time. For instance, a function type declaration is: member :: [A] -> A which indicates that member takes a list of elements of type A, and returns a value which must be also of type A. As usual in functional programming languages, $\mathcal{TOY}$ allows partial applications in expressions and higher order parameters like apply F X = F X.

A particularity of $\mathcal{TOY}$ is that partial applications with pattern parameters are also valid patterns. They are called *higher-order patterns*. For instance, a program rule like foo (apply member) = true is valid, although foo (apply member []) = true is not because apply member [] is a reducible expression and not a valid pattern. Higher-order variables and patterns play an important role in our setting. Functional-logic programming share with logic programming the possibility of using logic variables as parameters. For instance, the goal member L == 3 asks for lists containing the value 3. The first solution is L -> [3 | _A], which indicates that L can be a list starting by 3 and followed by any list (represented by the anonymous variable _A). The second answer is L -> [_A, 3 | _B], indicating that 3 can be the second element of the list as well. In this way a (potentially) infinite number of answers can be obtained. The possibility of generating values for the parameters is employed for generating test-cases in Section 4.

2.2   The XML Query Language XPath

XPath is a typed functional language. We consider XPath queries of the form (a complete description of XPath 2.0 can be found at [13]):

$$
\begin{aligned}
XPath &= \text{doc(file)} \; / \; Relative \\
Relative &= Step_1 \; / \; \dots / \; Step_n \; \mid \; Relative \mid Relative \\
Step &= Axis :: Test \mid Axis :: Test[XPath] \\
Axis &= \text{self} \mid ForwardAxis \mid ReverseAxis \\
ForwardAxis &= \text{child} \mid \text{descendant} \mid \text{descendant-or-self} \mid \dots \\
ReverseAxis &= \text{parent} \mid \text{ancestor} \mid \text{ancestor-or-self} \mid \dots \\
Test &= \text{node()} \mid name \mid \text{text()} \mid \text{comment()} \mid *
\end{aligned}
$$

The grammar above specifies a subset of the XPath language, enough for representing easily most XPath queries. There are other axes that can be used in XPath, as following-sibling, but according to [15], implementations are not required to support them. *Absolute* XPath location paths start with doc(*file*), which loads the XML *file*, and sets the context node to the root, followed by a relative location path. A relative location path can be either a sequence of steps or two relative location paths combined by the disjunction operator |. Each step takes as starting node the context node, and it is composed by an *axis* that changes the context node, and by a test that returns only those nodes satisfying the test. Tests can be *kind tests* as comment() which holds for comment nodes, or *name tests* which check the name of the node. A special kind test is * which holds for *element* nodes. For instance, the query:

```
doc("food.xml")/child::food/
            child::item[child::name/child::text()="onions"]/
            child::price/child::text()
```

returns the price of onions in file "food.xml". Assuming the XML document of Figure 1, this query returns in a XQuery/XPath system the value "55". Observe the presence of the filter [child::name/child::text()="onions"]. Filters select some context nodes that verify certain conditions. In this case it means that we select all the element nodes item such that they have a children element with tag name containing a text "onions". However, filters do not change the context node, that is, the item node verifying the filter is kept as context after the step. The rest of the location path navigates to the children of the item node with tag price, returning its text value. XPath allows also abbreviated forms. For instance the previous query can be written as:

```
doc("food.xml")/food/item[name="onions"]/price/text()
```

3   XPath Queries in $\mathcal{TOY}$

In this section we present the basis of our setting, including the type for XPath queries, the step combinators, tests and forward axes. Reverse axes are considered in Section 5.

3.1   The Type xPath

Typically, XPath expressions return several fragments of the XML document. Thus, the expected type for XPath could be `type xPath = xml -> [xml]` meaning that a list or sequence of results is obtained. This is the approach considered in [1] and also the usual in functional programming [4]. However, in our case we take advantage of the non-deterministic nature of our language, returning each result individually and avoiding the introduction of lists. We define an XPath expression as a function taking a (fragment of) XML as input and returning a (fragment of) XML as its result: `type xPath = xml -> xml`.

3.2   Loading XML Documents and Combining XPath Queries

In order to apply an XPath expression to a particular document, we use the following infix operator definition:

```
(<--) :: string  -> xPath -> xml     S <-- Q = Q (load_xml_file S)
```

The input arguments of this operator are the string S representing the file name and an XPath query Q. The function applies Q to the XML document contained in file S. This operator plays in $\mathcal{TOY}$ the role of doc in XPath.

Next, we define the XPath combinators / and :: which correspond to the connection between steps and between axis and tests, respectively. In $\mathcal{TOY}$, these symbols are defined simply as function composition:

```
infixr 55 .::.                      infixr 40 ./.
(.::.) :: xPath -> xPath -> xPath (./.) :: xPath -> xPath -> xPath
(F .::. G) X  = G (F X)            (F ./. G) X = G (F X)
```

We use the function operator names .::. and ./. because :: and / are already defined in $\mathcal{TOY}$. The variable X represents the input XML fragment (the context node). The rules specify how the combinator applies the first XPath expression (F) followed by the second one (G). Observe that due to the precedence and associativity, an expression like: A.::.B ./. C.::.D ./. E.::.F is understood by $\mathcal{TOY}$ as: (A.::.B) ./. ((C.::.D) ./. (E.::.F)) . The disjunction operator | of XPath is is represented in $\mathcal{TOY}$ simply by the choice operator ? defined in Subsection 2.1.

3.3   Basic Axes and Tests

Figure 2 shows the representation in $\mathcal{TOY}$ of some basic axes. The first one is self, which returns the context node. In our setting, it corresponds simply to the

```
self,child,descendant :: xPath
descendant_or_self :: xPath
self X = X
child (tag _ _ L) = member L
descendant X = child X
descendant X = if child X == Y
               then descendant Y
descendant_or_self =
               self ? descendant
```

```
nodeT,elem :: xPath
nameT,textT,commentT::string->xPath
nodeT X = X
nameT S (tag S Att L ) = tag S Att L
textT S (txt S) = txt S
commentT S (comment S) = comment S
elem = nameT _
```

Fig. 2. XPath axes and tests in $\mathcal{TOY}$

identity function. A more interesting axis is `child` which returns, using the non-deterministic function `member`, all the children of the context node. Observe that in XML only *element nodes* have children, and that these nodes correspond in $\mathcal{TOY}$ representation to terms rooted by constructor `tag`. Once `child` has been defined, `descendant` is just a generalization. The first rule for this function specifies that `child` must be used once, while the second rule corresponds to two or more applications of `child`. In this rule, the `if` statement is employed to ensure that `child` succeeds applied to the input XML fragment, thus avoiding possibly infinite recursive calls. Finally, the definition of axis `descendant-or-self` is straightforward. The first test defined in Figure 2 is `nodeT`, which corresponds to *node()* in the usual XPath syntax. This test is simply the identity. For instance, here is the XPath expression that returns all the nodes in an XML document, together with its $\mathcal{TOY}$ equivalent:

XPath → `doc("food.xml")/descendant-or-self::node()`
$\mathcal{TOY}$ → `("food.xml" <-- descendant_or_self.:::.nodeT)==R`

The only difference is that the $\mathcal{TOY}$ expression returns one result at a time in the variable R, asking the user if more results are needed. If the user wishes to obtain all the solutions at a time, as usual in XPath evaluators, then it is enough to use the primitive `collect`. For instance, the answer to the $\mathcal{TOY}$ goal:

`Toy> collect ("food.xml" <-- descendant_or_self.:::.nodeT) == R`

produces a single answer, with R instantiated to a list whose elements are the nodes in `"food.xml"`. The *name* test checks if the context node is an element with a certain name S. The test either returns as output the same XML fragment received as input, or fails. An example of a relative location path using this test:

XPath → `child::food/child::item`
$\mathcal{TOY}$ → `child.:::.nameT "food"./.child.:::.nameT "item"`

Notice that the expression in $\mathcal{TOY}$ is longer in length due to the presence of the identifier `nameT`, which is not required in XPath. In the next subsection we see how this situation improves when introducing abbreviated forms. Other useful tests are `textT` and `commentT`, which correspond to *text()* and *comment()*, respectively, in XPath. In the case of $\mathcal{TOY}$, the text (respectively comment) string is obtained by means of a logic variable as, for instance, in:

```
XPath → child::food/child::item/child::price/child::text()
TOY → child.::.nameT "food"./.child.::.nameT "item" ./.
         child.::.nameT "price"./.child.::.textT P
```

The logic variable `P` obtains the prices contained in the example document. Finally, the text `elem` represents in $\mathcal{TOY}$ the XPath test `*` which is satisfied only for *element* nodes. Notice in its definition (cf. Figure 2) the use of the anonymous variable `_` in its right-hand side indicating that any tag name is accepted.

3.4   Abbreviations

A number of abbreviations are used frequently in XPath expressions. The most important abbreviation is that `child::` can be omitted from a location step. This is usually done when `child::` is followed by a name test. Thus, the query `child::food/child::price/child::item` becomes simply `food/price/item`. In $\mathcal{TOY}$ we cannot do that directly because we are in a typed language and the combinator `./.` expects xPath expressions and not strings. However, we can introduce a similar abbreviation by defining new unitary operators `name` and `text`, which transform strings in XPath expressions:

```
name :: string -> xPath      name S = child.::.(nameT S)
```

An example:

```
XPath → food/item/price
TOY  → name "food"./.name "item"./.name "price"
```

The same idea can be applied to `commentT` and `textT`. Another XPath abbreviation is `//` which stands for `/descendant-or-self::node()/`. In $\mathcal{TOY}$:

```
infixr 30 .//.
(.//.) ::  xPath -> xPath -> xPath
A .//. B = append A (descendant_or_self .::. nodeT ./. B)
append :: xPath -> xPath -> xPath
append (A.::.B) C = (A.::.B) ./. C
append (X ./.Y) C = X ./. (append Y  C)
```

Notice that a new function `append` is used for concatenating the XPath expressions. This function is analogous to the well-known `append` for lists, but defined over xPath terms. This is our first example of the usefulness of higher-order patterns since for instance pattern (`A.::.B`) has type xPath, i.e. `xml -> xml`.

The next example uses both name, .//. and the disjunction operator, asking for all the elements with name either "price" or "variety":

XPath → food//(price | variety)
$\mathcal{TOY}$ → name "food".//.(name "price" ? name "variety")

Another possible improvement is to define a new version of ./. whose left-hand side is an XML name (a string):

```
infixr 35 /.
(/.) :: string -> xPath -> xPath        S /. X = name S ./. X
```

For instance:

XPath → food/item/price/text()
$\mathcal{TOY}$ → "food"/."item"/."price"/.text P

Now the queries in XPath and in $\mathcal{TOY}$ look quite similar. In XPath we obtain the output: 32 74 55 210, while in $\mathcal{TOY}$ we get the associated four solutions: P ↦ 32, P ↦ 74, P ↦ 55, and P ↦ 210.

3.5 Filters

Optionally, XPath tests can include a predicate or filter. Filters in XPath are enclosed between square brackets. In $\mathcal{TOY}$, they are enclosed between round brackets and connected to its associated XPath expression by the operator .#:

```
infixr  60 .#
(.#) :: xPath -> xPath -> xPath
(Q .# F)  X =  if F Y == _ then Y  where Y = Q X
```

This definition can be understood as follows: first the query Q is applied to the context node X, returning a new context node Y. Then the if condition checks whether Y satisfies the filter F, simply by checking that F Y does not fail, which means that it returns some value represented by the anonymous variable in F Y == _. Although XPath filter predicates allow several possibilities, in this presentation we restrict to XPath expressions. As in the previous subsection, it is convenient to define a version of .# accepting strings instead of XPath queries:

```
infixr 60 #
(#) :: string -> xPath -> xPath    S # F = child.::.(nameT S) .# F
```

Filters in XPath are defined usually by means of comparison operators, as = or >. For instance, the following XPath query asks for the price of watermelons: food/item[name="watermelon"]/price. The expression name="watermelon" means: check whether the context node has a children name, which has a children text watermelon. In $\mathcal{TOY}$ we can mimic this behavior by defining:

```
(.=) :: string -> string -> xPath
(.=) A B  = (A /. text B)
```

This operator takes as input parameters both sides of the equality, represented by the strings A and B, and the input XML context X. The strict equality with anonymous variable at the right-hand side is used to check whether A has a text child B in the XPath context X. An example of application of this operator:

```
XPath → food/item[name="onions"]
TOY  → "food"/."item"#("name".="onions")
```

The same approach can be used for other operators, as >. Filters selecting attributes with certain values are of particular interest, and are represented in XPath by symbol @. In $\mathcal{TOY}$ they are represented by the operator @=:

```
(@=) :: xmlName -> xmlName -> xPath
(@=) S V X = if (xmlAtt S V == member Attr) then X
           where (xmlTag _Name Attr _L) = X
```

This filter checks if the attribute S of the context element takes the value V. The next example shows the items of type fruit:

```
XPath → food/item[@type="fruit"]
TOY  → "food"/."item"#("type"@="fruit")
```

Or course, other comparison operators as @> can be defined analogously. As $\mathcal{TOY}$ is a typed language, several versions of the operators would be needed for the different involved types (strings, numbers, ...).

4   Generating Test-Cases for XPath Expressions

Suppose that we wish to know the price of onions as stored in our XML document. According to the previous section, we can write in $\mathcal{TOY}$:

```
Toy>("food.xml" <--
     name "food"./."item"#("type"@="onions")./.name "price" ) == R
```

The goal returns no answer, but we know that "food.xml" includes the price of onions. Where is the error? Sometimes it is useful to have a test-case, i.e., an XML file which contains some answer for the query. Comparing the test-case and the original XML document can help to find the error. In our setting, such test-cases are obtained for free. For instance, we can submit the goal:

```
Toy>(name "food"./."item"#("type"@="onions")./.name "price") X== _
```

asking for an XML document X such that the query succeeds. The anonymous variable at the right-hand side of the strict equality indicates that we are not interested in the output. However, the answer is difficult to read and understand:

```
X -> tag _A _B [tag  "food" _C [
      tag  "item" [att  "type"  "onions" | _D ]
                  [tag  "price" _E _F | _G ] | _H ] | _I ]
```

The logic variables indicate that replacing them by any valid XML fragment produces a valid XML test-case for the query. In particular, in the case of lists, they indicate that other elements can be added, and the smaller test-case corresponds to substituting these variables by the empty list. In order to enhance the readability of the result we define a function:

```
generateTC :: xPath -> string -> bool
generateTC F S = if (F X == _) then write_xml_file X S
```

This function receives the XPath expression and the file name S as input parameters, looks for an XML test-case X, and writes it to the file using the primitive write_xml_file. The goal:

```
Toy> generateTC (name "food"./."item"#("type"@="onions")./.
                 name "price") "tc.xml" == R
```

produces the following XML file "tc.xml":

```
<food>
 <item type="onions">
  <price />
 </item>
</food>
```

It is worth noticing that the primitive has replaced the logic variables by empty elements. Comparing this file and our example "food.xml", we see that "onions" is not an attribute, but a child node. Therefore, the correct query should be:

```
Toy> ("food.xml"<--
      name "food"./."item"#("name".="onions")./.name "price")==R
```

which returns the answer: R → tag "price" [] [text "55"].

5   Higher Order Patterns

The possibility of employing higher order patterns in $\mathcal{TOY}$ allows the user to consider XPath queries as truly data terms. Queries can be examined and modified before and during its evaluation, as any constructed term. In this section, we take advantage of this feature in two ways. First, we define a function that checks if an XPath query follows the XPath standard. Then, we apply a transformation similar to those described in [9] for introducing the reverse axis parent.

5.1   Validating XPath Queries

So far, we have described several different tests and axes that can be combined for defining XPath queries. Moreover, our setting allows the user to define their own combinators, axes and tests, or to use the existing ones in a non-standard way. For instance, the query `nodeT.:::.child` is allowed, although it does not follows the XPath grammar (it should be `child.:::.nodeT`, first the axis and then the test). The reason is that the expression is well-typed from the point of view of a $\mathcal{TOY}$ expression. Although in principle such unusual queries can work and even be useful in some cases, it is convenient to define a function that indicates whether a query conforms to the XPath standard or not. However, in the previous sections we have defined many different abbreviations. Should we consider all of them for detecting standard queries? Fortunately, the answer is 'no'. It is enough to recognize the few basic axes and tests, because the abbreviations are automatically reduced to these basis forms during computations. For instance, the goal `Toy> ("name" /. text T) == R` yields:

```
R ->   child.:::.nameT "name" ./. child.:::.textT T
```

Now we are ready to define the function `standard` using higher-order patterns:

```
standard,step,test:: xPath -> bool
simpleTest,axis::xPath -> bool
```

```
standard A               = step A
standard (A ./. B)       = step A /\ standard B
step (Axis.:::.Test)     = (axis Axis) /\ (test Test)
axis A                   = (A==child)\/(A==self)\/(A==descendant)
test A                   = simpleTest A
test (A .# B)            = simpleTest A /\ standard B
simpleTest nodeT         = true
simpleTest (nameT S)     = true
simpleTest (textT S)     = true
simpleTest (commentT S)= true
```

Function `standard` succeeds if the query is either a single step of several steps combined by the operator `(./.)`. Steps are defined by an axis and a test connected by `(.:::.)`. Finally, the definition of functions `test`, `simpleTest` and `axis` is self-explanatory. For instance, the goal: `Toy> standard ("food" /. name "item")` produces the answer `yes`, but `standard (nodeT.:::.child)` produces the answer `no`, meaning that the query is not standard.

5.2   Reverse Axes

The queries defined so far only use forward axes such as `descendant` or `child`. However, in XPath reverse axes such as `parent` are also allowed. Implementing these axes is not trivial in our approach, since each `xPath` function receives

```
delParent :: xPath -> xPath ->xPath
delParent (X./.self.::.T1) T2 = addFilter (delParent X T2) (self.::.T1)
delParent (X./.child.::.T1) T2 = X./.self.::.(T2.#(child.::.T1)
delParent (X./.descendant.::.T1) T2= X./.self.::.T2.#(child.::.T1)
delParent (X./.descendant.::.T1) T2= X./.descendant.::.T2.#(child.::.T1)


preprocess :: xPath -> xPath
preprocess A = rev (foldl transform (self.::.nodeT) A)


foldl :: (xPath -> xPath -> xPath) -> xPath -> xPath -> xPath
foldl F Z (A.::.T) = F Z (A.::.T)
foldl F Z (G ./. H) = foldl F (F Z G) H


transform :: xPath -> xPath -> xPath
transform X (self.::.T) = X ./.(self.::.T)
transform X (child.::.T) = X ./.(child.::.T)
transform X (descendant.::.T) = X ./.(descendant.::.T)
transform X (parent.::.T) = delParent X T


addFilter :: xPath -> xPath -> xPath
addFilter (X./.A.::.(T.#F)) G = X ./. (A.::. (T.# (F ./. G)))


rev :: xPath -> xPath
rev (A.::.B) = A.::.B
rev (F./.G) = rev' F G
rev' (A.::.B) G = (A.::.B) ./. G
rev' (X ./. Y) G = rev' X (Y./. G)
```

Fig. 3. Preprocessing **parent** axis

as input the fragments of the XML document that satisfied the previous steps. These fragments corresponds to a subtree of the XML document and thus it is not possible to obtain the **parent** of the current XML fragment. A possible solution is to include the whole XML document and a representation of the path leading to the context node as input parameters, following by instance the ideas in [6]. Nevertheless, this complicates the implementation, and the simple definitions of the previous sections would be no longer valid. An alternative is to preprocess the query, replacing the reverse axes by predicate filters including forward axes, as shown in [9]. For the sake of space we only include the rules for removing **parent** outside filter predicates, although the same approach can be extended to **parent** in filter predicates, to **ancestor**, and to **following-sibling**.

(P_1) child::T_1/S/parent::T_2 $\equiv$ self::T_2[child::T_1/S]
(P_2) descendant::T_1/S/parent::T_2 $\equiv$ self::T_2[child::T_1/S]
(P_3) descendant::T_1/S/parent::T_2 $\equiv$ descendant::T_2[child::T_1/S]

where T_1 and T_2 are tests that optionally can include filters, and S is a (possibly empty) sequence of steps using the **self** axis. For instance the relative location path **child::variety/parent::node()** is transformed by (P_1) into the equivalent expression **self::node()[child::variety]**. The equations are implemented in $\mathcal{TOY}$ through the program rules for `delParent` which can be found in Figure 3. The first program rule is used for skipping the sequence S, while the three following rules resemble closely $(P_1), (P_2), (P_3)$ when S is the empty sequence. In order to apply this function, we change the definition of the operator $<--$, which now preprocesses the query before applying it to the XML document: `S <-- F = (preprocess F) (load_xml_file S)`. Then we define an initial version of `parent` that indicates that it fails without preprocessing:

```
parent::xPath          parent S =  if false then S
```

Function `preprocess` uses a version of the well-known catamorphism `fold` acting over XPath queries to apply a function `transform` to each individual steps, which in turn employs `delParent` as auxiliary function. The result is obtained with the steps associated to the left, as in $(S_1 \,./. \, S_2) \,./. \, S_3$. This is corrected by function `rev` which is the analogous to the reverse function used in functional program for lists. All this code is possible thanks to the use of higher-order patterns. The next example looks for nodes having at least one "variety" child.

```
XPath → doc("food.xml")/food//variety/parent::node()
TOY  → name "food".//."variety"/.parent.:::.nodeT
```

6   Conclusions

We have shown how the declarative nature of the XML query language XPath fits in a very natural way in functional-logic languages. XPath queries are represented in this setting by non-deterministic higher-order expressions, thus becoming first-class citizens of the language that can be readily extended and adapted by the programmer. In the case of the functional-logic language $\mathcal{TOY}$, the possibility of using higher-order patterns make this affirmation even more valid, since XPath expressions manipulated directly as data terms. The result is enriching for both XPath and $\mathcal{TOY}$ users:

- For the users of the functional-logic $\mathcal{TOY}$ the advantage is clear: they can use XPath queries in their programs in a natural way. The queries are written in $\mathcal{TOY}$ and thus using them requires little effort. Moreover, since the combinators, tests and axes are written in $\mathcal{TOY}$ they can be freely modified and extended. The situation can be analogous to the introduction of parsers in functional [7] and functional-logic languages [3].
- From the point of view of the XPath apprentices, the tool can be useful, specially if they have some previous knowledge of declarative languages. The possibility of generating test-cases for XPath queries is an easy and powerful tool that can be very helpful for understanding the basics of XPath.
- The framework can also be interesting for designers of XPath environments, because it allows the users to easily define prototypes of new features such as new combinators or functions.

Our proposal also contains some drawbacks that deserve to be discussed. First of all, the syntax of the queries resembles quite closely XPath, but the differences can be confusing at first. However, in our experience this difficulty is soon overcome by practice, and in any case is easy to write a parser converting standard XPath format to the format explained in this paper. Another difficulty arises from the implementation of features using the position of the node in the sequence. This features can be introduced in our non-deterministic setting, but only using some impure primitive like `collect` that bundles in a list the results of a non-deterministic expression. The problem with this impure primitive is that cannot deal with logic variables, which can be a problem for instance for the generation of test-cases.

A description of how to download and install the $\mathcal{TOY}$ system including the source code of the XPath library, and a description of some extensions like the `ancestor` axis, position filters, and more, can be found at [2].

References

1. Almendros-Jiménez, J.M.: An Encoding of XQuery in Prolog. In: Bellahsène, Z., Hunt, E., Rys, M., Unland, R. (eds.) XSym 2009. LNCS, vol. 5679, pp. 145–155. Springer, Heidelberg (2009)
2. Caballero, R., García-Ruiz, Y., Sáenz-Pérez, F.: Integrating XPath with the Functional-Logic Language Toy (Extended Version). Technical Report SIP-05/10, Facultad de Informática, Universidad Complutense de Madrid (2010), http://federwin.sip.ucm.es/sic/investigacion/publicaciones/pdfs/SIC-5-10.pdf
3. Caballero, R., López-Fraguas, F.J.: A functional-logic perspective on parsing. In: Middeldorp, A. (ed.) FLOPS 1999. LNCS, vol. 1722, pp. 85–99. Springer, Heidelberg (1999)
4. Guerra, R., Jeuring, J., Swierstra, S.D.: Generic validation in an XPath-Haskell data binding. In: Proceedings Plan-X (2005)
5. Hanus, M.: Curry: An Integrated Functional Logic Language (version 0.8.2) (March 28, 2006), http://www.informatik.uni-kiel.de/~mh/curry/ (2003)
6. Huet, G.: The zipper. J. Funct. Program. 7(5), 549–554 (1997)
7. Hutton, G., Meijer, E.: Monadic parsing in Haskell. J. Funct. Program. 8(4), 437–444 (1998)
8. López-Fraguas, F.J., Hernández, J.S.: TOY: A Multiparadigm Declarative System. In: Narendran, P., Rusinowitch, M. (eds.) RTA 1999. LNCS, vol. 1631, pp. 244–247. Springer, Heidelberg (1999)
9. Olteanu, D., Meuss, H., Furche, T., Bry, F.: XPath: Looking forward. In: Chaudhri, A.B., Unland, R., Djeraba, C., Lindner, W. (eds.) EDBT 2002. LNCS, vol. 2490, pp. 109–127. Springer, Heidelberg (2002)
10. Sulzmann, M., Lu, K.Z.: Xhaskell — adding regular expression types to haskell. In: Chitil, O., Horváth, Z., Zsók, V. (eds.) IFL 2007. LNCS, vol. 5083, pp. 75–92. Springer, Heidelberg (2008)
11. W3C. XML Schema 1.1
12. W3C. Extensible Markup Language, XML (2007)
13. W3C. XML Path Language (XPath) 2.0 (2007)
14. W3C. XQuery 1.0: An XML Query Language (2007)
15. Walmsley, P.: XQuery. O'Reilly Media, Inc., Sebastopol (2007)

Sloth – A Tool for Checking Minimal-Strictness

Jan Christiansen

Christian-Albrechts-Universität Kiel
jac@informatik.uni-kiel.de

Abstract. We present a light-weight tool called Sloth which assists programmers in identifying unnecessarily strict first order functions. Sloth reports counterexamples in form of a partial value, the corresponding result of the tested function and a recommended result. We present examples where the hints reported by Sloth can be used to improve a function with respect to memory behaviour, non-termination, and performance in the context of functional-logic programming. Furthermore we give an example-driven introduction into the basics of the implementation of Sloth. To improve the results in comparison to an existing approach we use additional constraints to assure that Sloth's suggestions are implementable without employing parallelism.

Keywords: Haskell, Curry, testing, non-strictness, minimal-strictness, sequentiality.

1 Introduction

In a non-strict programming language like Haskell the production of data by one function and the consumption of this data by another function can be interleaved. As soon as the data is consumed the memory can be freed by the garbage collector. This way, functions in a modular programming style, which is very commonly used in Haskell, often have a small memory footprint (Hughes 1989). In contrast, in a strict programming language data is always produced completely by one function before it is consumed by another function.

But, although Haskell is a non-strict language, functions may be unnecessarily strict. Consider the function *intersperse* from the standard library *Data.List*. It intersperses an element between all pairs of succeeding elements of a list.

$$
\begin{array}{ll}
intersperse :: \alpha \rightarrow [\alpha] \rightarrow [\alpha] \\
intersperse \ \_ \quad [\,] \quad\ \ = [\,] \\
intersperse \ \_ \quad [x] \quad = [x] \\
intersperse \ sep \ (x : xs) = x : sep : intersperse \ sep \ xs
\end{array}
$$

Furthermore consider the function $chop :: (\alpha \rightarrow Bool) \rightarrow [\alpha] \rightarrow [[\alpha]]$ from the hackage package *utility-ht* by Thielemann, which splits a list into a list of sublists. For example, we have $chop \ (==\ \text{'a'}) \ \text{"abcada"} \equiv [\text{""}, \text{"bc"}, \text{"d"}, \text{""}]$. By means of *intersperse* and *chop* we define a function *replaceBy* which replaces all occurrences of a specific element in a list by a given list.

R. Rocha and J. Launchbury (Eds.): PADL 2011, LNCS 6539, pp. 160–174, 2011.
© Springer-Verlag Berlin Heidelberg 2011

$$replaceBy :: Eq\ \alpha \Rightarrow \alpha \to [\alpha] \to [\alpha] \to [\alpha]$$
$$replaceBy\ x\ sep\ xs = concat\ (intersperse\ sep\ (chop\ (== x)\ xs))$$

Let us consider an application of this function. In HTML you have to replace all occurrences of German umlauts by a specific HTML encoding. For this example we only replace all occurrences of the character '\228' which is the German umlaut ä by the corresponding encoding "ä". We process a large file (about 6MB), namely the collected works of Shakespeare. The run-time system of the Glasgow Haskell Compiler (ghc) reports a maximum memory usage of 40MB for this task.

```
40,339,120 bytes maximum residency (7 sample(s))
```

This is quite contrary to the expectations about memory behaviour in a non-strict programming language. Unexpected consumption of memory like this is called a *space leak*. In this case the space leak is caused by an unnecessarily strict implementation of *intersperse*. We can use Sloth to observe that the presented implementation of *intersperse* is too strict.

Sloth provides a function called *strictCheck* to check whether a function is as non-strict as possible for inputs up to a specific size. The size of a term is the number of constructors in the term. That is, *strictCheck* (*intersperse* :: *Bool* → [*Bool*] → [*Bool*]) 2 checks whether the Boolean instance of *intersperse* is as non-strict as possible for inputs whose size in sum is at most two. We can employ free theorems (Wadler 1989) and quite a lot of reasoning to show that a polymorphic function is minimally strict if and only if its monomorphic Boolean instance is minimally strict. But for the lack of space we do not present these results here.

```
> strictCheck (intersperse :: Bool -> [Bool] -> [Bool]) 2
2: \⊥ (⊥:⊥) -> ⊥:⊥
4: \⊥ (⊥:⊥:⊥) -> ⊥:⊥:⊥:⊥
Finished 4 tests.
```

Sloth presents two argument result pairs which show that *intersperse* is unnecessarily strict. The first counterexample states that *intersperse* yields ⊥ if it is applied to ⊥ and ⊥ : ⊥ while a minimally strict implementation yields ⊥ : ⊥ instead[1]. Sloth <u>highlights</u> the subterm on the right hand side of -> where the tested function is too strict. That is, it highlights a non-bottom term which is bottom for the current implementation while there exists a less strict implementation that yields the highlighted value instead.

We can define a less strict implementation of *intersperse* by yielding the first element of the list "before" performing pattern matching on the tail.

$$intersperse' :: \alpha \to [\alpha] \to [\alpha]$$
$$intersperse'\ \_\ \ [] \quad = []$$
$$intersperse'\ sep\ (x : xs) = x : go\ xs$$
where
$$go\ [] \quad\ = []$$
$$go\ (y : ys) = sep : y : go\ ys$$

---

[1] For readibility we use ⊥ in the output while Sloth actually uses the symbol _ instead.

The run-time system reports a maximum memory usage of only 12KB for processing Shakespeare's work using this less strict implementation of *intersperse*.

```
12,312 bytes maximum residency (91 sample(s))
```

That is, one delay of a pattern matching improves the memory usage by a factor of 3,000. Obviously, you seldomly generate HTML from a 6MB text file. Furthermore we did not choose a file that does not contain any umlauts by accident. The presented space leak is linear in the size of the longest substring that does not contain the character that is replaced. Nevertheless this is not an artificial example. The presented space leak is a modification of a space leak discovered by Fischer (2010) in his *searchstring* package (Fischer et al.). This example is supposed to emphasise that being too strict can have a tremendous effect with respect to memory behaviour when processing large amounts of data.

The rest of this paper is organized as follows.

– In Section 2 we present the less-strict relation which has originally been introduced by Chitil (2006). Besides the basic idea Chitil (2006) has presented a light-weight tool, called StrictCheck, to check whether a function is least strict. We argue that, in practice, least strict implementations are often not desirable as they have to employ features like concurrency.
– In Section 3 we present the definition of sequentiality by Vuillemin (1974). We use this definition to avoid functions that require the use of concurrency. In this case we have to consider minimal-strictness instead of least-strictness. Furthermore we give an example-driven explanation of the basics of the implementation of Sloth.
– In Section 4 we present some examples of unnecessarily strict functions. First, we present two non-standard functions, one from functional programming and one from functional logic programming. These examples demonstrate benefits of less strict functions besides memory behaviour. Furthermore we discuss some standard functions which are not minimally strict.

2   Least-Strictness

Chitil (2006) has originally presented the idea of checking whether a function is as non-strict as possible. In this section we present his approach and argue that his least-strictness is often not desirable in practice.

For the sake of simplicity we do not strictly separate syntax and semantics. For example, we use the less strict ordering on syntactic objects rather than semantic objects although its formal definition is based on semantics. We as well relate syntactic objects by the cpo ordering $\sqsubseteq$, which relates elements of the interpretation of a data type . Furthermore, $\equiv$ denotes semantic equivalence and $\bot$ denotes a non-terminating expression.

Two functions f and g of the same type are related by the less-strict ordering $\preceq$ if and only if f and g yield the same results for total inputs and the results for partial inputs are related by the semantic ordering $\sqsupseteq$[2]. For an n-ary function

---

[2] Note that we use the reversed order $\sqsupseteq$ on purpose as $\prec$ denotes "less strict than".

by partial input we denote n values of which at least one is a partial value. As two functions are only related by $\preceq$ if they agree for total inputs we assume that non-total results for total inputs are intended. For example, the division yields a non-total result for a total input, namely if it's second argument is zero. Thus the division is least strict (with respect to the presented definition of less-strictness) although it could yield a more defined result if its second argument is zero.

Example 1 (Less-Strictness). Let us consider the Boolean conjunction *andL*, like it is implemented in Haskell (where it is called (&&)) and the strict Boolean conjunction *and*.

$$andL :: Bool \rightarrow Bool \rightarrow Bool$$
$$andL\ False\ y = False$$
$$andL\ True\ y = y$$
$$and :: Bool \rightarrow Bool \rightarrow Bool$$
$$and\ False\ False = False$$
$$and\ False\ True = False$$
$$and\ True\ False = False$$
$$and\ True\ True = True$$

For all total inputs, namely for *False* and *False*, *False* and *True*, *True* and *False*, and *True* and *True*, *andL* yields the same results as *and*. For the partial input *False* and $\perp$, *andL* yields *False* while *and* yields $\perp$. For all other partial inputs *andL* yields the same results as *and*. Therefore, *andL* is less strict than *and*, that is, $andL \prec and$.

Let us consider the symmetric counterpart of *andL*, called *andR*. While *andL* performs pattern matching on its first argument, *andR* performs pattern matching on its second argument.

$$andR :: Bool \rightarrow Bool \rightarrow Bool$$
$$andR\ x\ False = False$$
$$andR\ x\ True = x$$

Like we have shown that *andL* is less strict than *and* we can show that *andR* is less strict than *and*. But *andL* and *andR* are incomparable. While *andL* yields a more defined result than *andR* for the input *False* and $\perp$, *andR* yields a more defined result than *andL* for the input $\perp$ and *False*. Summing up, we have $andL \prec and$ and $andR \prec and$, but $andR \not\preceq andL$ and $andL \not\preceq andR$.

So how can we check whether a function is least strict? We consider a function f of type $\tau \rightarrow \tau'$. Because f is monotonic, for every value v of type τ and every total value tv of type τ with $v \sqsubseteq tv$ we have $f\ v \sqsubseteq f\ tv$. Therefore, $f\ v$ is a lower bound of the set $\{f\ tv \mid tv$ total value$, v \sqsubseteq tv\}$. Thus, $f\ v$ is less or equally defined than the corresponding greatest lower bound, in other words, $f\ v \sqsubseteq \bigsqcap\{f\ tv \mid tv$ total value$, v \sqsubseteq tv\}^{3}$. Chitil (2006) employs this inequality to

---

[3] An analogous statement holds for functions with an arbitrary number of arguments.

check whether a function is least strict. For all inputs a least strict function is supposed to agree with the corresponding greatest lower bound.

If the argument type of f has infinitely many values Sloth has to approximate the infimum. As the infimum operator is monotonically decreasing the infimum may be smaller if we consider a larger set for the approximation. Therefore a counterexample may not be a counterexample if we consider a more precise approximation.

Consider the following definition.

$$potential :: [Bool] \to Bool$$
$$potential\ [] \qquad = True$$
$$potential\ (\_ : xs) = potential\ xs$$

Obviously this function is too strict. It performs pattern matching although it yields *True* for all total inputs. Sloth reports the following counterexamples if we check *potential* for Boolean lists up to size one.

```
> strictCheck potential 1
1: \⊥ -> True
2: \(⊥:⊥) -> True
Finished 2 tests.
```

In contrast to the counterexamples for *intersperse* from the introduction these counterexamples are highlighted differently. We refer to counterexamples highlighted this way as potential counterexamples. A potential counterexample might be no counterexample if we consider inputs of larger sizes. That is, there might be a size greater than one such that Sloth does not report some of the counterexamples it reports for size one. One way to confirm a potential counterexample is to increase the size. But, for example, Sloth reports only potential counterexamples for the function *potential* no matter what size we use.

We can verify a potential counterexample by hand. A potential counterexample is definitely a counterexample if all more defined total inputs lead to results that are at least as defined as the recommended result. For example, consider the first counterexample. For all total inputs that are more defined than ⊥ the function *potential* yields *True*, which is as defined as the recommended value *True*. Therefore, the first counterexample is definitely a counterexample.

Nevertheless there are cases in which a finite approximation is sufficient to identify a definite counterexample. For example, consider the following function.

$$definite :: [Bool] \to [Bool]$$
$$definite\ [] \qquad = [True]$$
$$definite\ (\_ : xs) = True : definite\ xs$$

Both counterexamples reported by Sloth are definite.

```
> strictCheck definite 1
1: \⊥ -> True:⊥
2: \(⊥:⊥) -> True:True:⊥
Finished 2 tests.
```

Sloth employs the monotonicity of the tested function to identify definite counterexamples. Let us consider the first counterexample. Sloth observes that the evaluation of *definite* [ ] yields *True* : [ ] and the evaluation of *definite* $(\bot : \bot)$ yields *True* : $\bot$. As *definite* is monotonic we have *definite bs* $\sqsupseteq$ *True* : $\bot$ for all total Boolean lists *bs* with *bs* $\sqsupseteq \bot : \bot$. Therefore we have $\bigsqcap \{$*definite tv* | *tv* total value, $\bot \sqsubseteq tv\} \sqsupseteq$ *True* : $\bot$. Furthermore we have *definite* $\bot \equiv \bot \sqsubseteq$ *True* : $\bot$. Thus, we know that *definite* is too strict for the input $\bot$ by only considering two applications of *definite*[4].

The definition of least-strictness, as it is used by StrictCheck, has a shortcoming. Some functions that one would consider to be as non-strict as possible are not least strict.

Example 2 (Least-Strictness). Let us consider the function *andL* from Example 1 again. On the one hand we have *andL* $\bot$ *False* $\equiv \bot$. On the other hand we consider the infimum $\bigsqcap \{$*andL False False*, *andL True False*$\}$. As this infimum equals *False*, *andL* is not least strict since *andL* $\bot$ *False* does not agree with the corresponding infimum.

In fact, *andL* is not as non-strict as possible. We can define a Boolean conjunction in Haskell that yields *False* for *False* and $\bot$ as well as for $\bot$ and *False*. For example, we can use the *unamb* operator, presented by Elliott (2009), which employs concurrency and *unsafePerformIO*.

In practice we often want to know whether there is a less strict implementation that avoids the use of such features. In fact, many functions are not least strict because there is often a bias towards one argument with respect to non-strictness. For example, StrictCheck identifies (&&), (||), (++), *and*, *or*, *zip*, as well as the list instances of (==) and *compare* as too strict. In contrast, Sloth does identify these functions as minimally strict as it checks whether a function is too strict without considering features like concurrency. To restrict the considered functions we employ the concept of sequentiality by Vuillemin (1974).

3   Sequentiality and Minimal-Strictness

The definition of sequentiality employs contexts, which we only informally introduce here. Let Σ be the set of constructor and function symbols. A context is a term over Σ and the additional symbol [], called hole. Let c be a context with n holes, that is, n occurrences of the symbol [] and $e_1, \ldots, e_n$ be expressions. Then $c[e_1, \ldots, e_n]$ denotes the context c where the i-th hole is filled in with expression e_i. Vuillemin (1974) has given the following definition of sequentiality.

Definition 1 (Sequentiality). *A functional language is sequential if the following holds. Let c be a context with n holes such that $c[\bot, \ldots, \bot] \equiv \bot$. Then there exists at least one $i \in \{1, \ldots, n\}$, called sequential position, such that*

$$c[e_1, \ldots, e_{i-1}, \bot, e_{i+1}, \ldots, e_n] \equiv \bot$$

for all expressions $e_1, \ldots, e_n$ of appropriate types.

---

[4] Note that StrictCheck does not distinguish potential and definite counterexamples.

By distinguishing three cases we illustrate that there in deed always exists a sequential position. If the evaluation of $c[\bot, \ldots, \bot]$ causes a pattern matching on position i, then, if the term at position i is $\bot$, the result is $\bot$. That is, position i is a sequential position. If the context c projects to position i then position i is a sequential position. If the evaluation of $c[\bot, \ldots, \bot]$ neither causes a pattern matching nor c projects to one of the positions then the semantics of $c[e_1, \ldots, e_n]$ is independent of the terms e_1 to e_n and therefore all positions are sequential.

We refer to the first two cases of sequential positions as demanded positions of the term $c[\bot, \ldots, \bot]$ in the following. Note that there are sequential positions that do not fall in any of the three cases above. That is, there are sequential positions which are neither demanded positions of $c[\bot, \ldots, \bot]$ nor the semantics of $c[e_1, \ldots, e_n]$ is independent of the terms e_1 to e_n. For example, consider the strict Boolean conjunction *and* again. We have *and* $\bot$ $\bot \equiv \bot$ and consider the context *and* [] [] which has two holes. We have *and* $\bot$ $b \equiv \bot$ for all values of type *Bool* because *and* performs pattern matching on its first argument[5]. That is, position 1 is a demanded position of *and* $\bot$ $\bot$. But obviously we have *and* b $\bot \equiv \bot$ for all values of type *Bool*, too. That is, position 1 as well as position 2 are sequential positions of *and*. Note that position 2 is not a demanded position of *and* $\bot$ $\bot$.

In the following we consider a sequential sublanguage of Haskell.

Example 3 (Sequentiality). Let us consider the Boolean conjunction *andL* from Example 1 again. We have *andL* $\bot$ $\bot \equiv \bot$ and can apply Definition 1 with the context *andL* [] [] which has two holes. The definition states that one of the arguments of *andL* is a sequential position, that is, we have

$$\forall b :: Bool. \; andL \; b \; \bot \equiv \bot \qquad \text{or} \qquad \forall b :: Bool. \; andL \; \bot \; b \equiv \bot.$$

As we have *andL* *False* $\bot \equiv$ *False* $\not\equiv \bot$ the former statement is false and, therefore, the latter statement is true. Thus, position 1 is a sequential position. That is, by sequentiality we have *andL* $\bot$ *False* $\equiv \bot$ and *andL* $\bot$ *True* $\equiv \bot$.

The idea behind the implementation of Sloth is to search for witnesses that prove, that a certain position is *not* sequential. For example, *andL* *False* $\bot$ is a witness that the second position is not a sequential position of *andL*. If we do not discover a witness we assume that the position is sequential.

Besides the function *strictCheck*, which we have used in the introduction already, Sloth provides the function *verboseCheck*, which additionally reports successful test cases. When we check *andL* using *verboseCheck* Sloth reports the following test cases.

```
> verboseCheck andL 4
1: \⊥ ⊥ -> ⊥
2: \True ⊥ -> ⊥
Finished 2 tests.
```

---

[5] This is due to the left to right pattern matching order used in Haskell.

Sloth does not check *andL* $\perp$ *False* as well as *andL* $\perp$ *True* as the witness *andL False* $\perp$ $\equiv$ *False* shows that position 2 is not a sequential position of *andL* $\perp$ $\perp$. Therefore the only sequential position of *andL* $\perp$ $\perp$ is position 1 and *andL* $\perp$ *False* as well as *andL* $\perp$ *True* are determined by sequentiality. Furthermore, Sloth does not check *andL False* $\perp$ as *andL* yields a total value and it obviously cannot be too strict in this case.

In Example 2 we have observed that *andL* is not least strict. According to the criterion for least-strictness a least strict Boolean conjunction *and'* has to satisfy the following equations.

$$and' \perp \perp \equiv \perp \qquad and' \ False \perp \equiv False \qquad and' \perp False \equiv False$$

In Example 3 we have observed that, if *and'* is sequential, the first two equations imply *and'* $\perp$ *False* $\equiv$ $\perp$. Thus there is no sequential, least strict Boolean conjunction.

Let us consider *andL* again. We have *andL* $\perp$ $\perp$ $\equiv$ $\perp$ and *andL False* $\perp$ $\equiv$ *False*. Furthermore these equations imply *andL* $\perp$ *False* $\equiv$ $\perp$ and *andL* $\perp$ *True* $\equiv$ $\perp$ by sequentiality. As *andL* satisfies all these equations and obviously all Boolean conjunctions yield $\perp$ for the input *True* and $\perp$ there is no sequential Boolean conjunction that is less strict than *andL*. A similar argument shows that there is no sequential Boolean conjunction that is less strict than *andR*. As *andL* and *andR* are incomparable (see Example 1) we are looking for minimally strict Boolean conjunctions in the context of sequentiality and not for a least strict Boolean conjunction.

Example 4 (Multiple Sequential Positions). In the following we consider *and* from Example 1 again. Argument position 1 as well as argument position 2 are sequential positions. In contrast to the previous examples, we cannot exclude any test cases as all positions are sequential. Although, when we check *and* using *verboseCheck* only position 1 is considered in the test cases.

```
> verboseCheck and 4
1: \⊥ ⊥ -> ⊥
2: \False ⊥ -> False
3: \True ⊥ -> ⊥
Finished 3 tests.
```

The counterexamples reported by *strictCheck* and *verboseCheck* are satisfiable by a single sequential function. If there is more than one sequential position we cannot satisfy the counterexamples with respect to both positions. Therefore, if there are counterexamples with respect to multiple sequential positions, Sloth applies a heuristic. If one of the positions is a demanded position it chooses this position. For example, as *and* performs pattern matching on its first argument Sloth considers position 1 in the presented test cases. This way the suggested minimal strict implementation preserves the pattern matching order if possible. For example, the minimally strict Boolean conjunction that satisfies the counterexamples presented above is *andL* and *andL*, as well as *and*, performs pattern matching on its first argument. If none of the considered sequential positions is a demanded position Sloth chooses the leftmost position.

Sloth identifies demanded positions of a function by "attaching" unique labels to errors which are passed to the function. By exception handling Sloth checks which of the errors is evaluated by the function. For example, if we consider the application $andL \perp_1 \perp_2$ the evaluation of this application yields $\perp_1$. That is, position 1 is the demanded position of $andL \perp \perp$. The block-box test tool Lazy SmallCheck (Runciman et al. 2009) uses a similar approach to efficiently generate test cases.

So far we have only consider examples with flat result types. When we consider a function that yields a non-flat type like a tuple or a list we have to instantiate the context in Definition 1 with the function and a projection to a $\perp$-position to apply the definition of sequentiality.

Example 5 (Non-Flat Result Types). Consider the following function.

$$andTuple :: Bool \rightarrow Bool \rightarrow (Bool, Bool)$$
$$andTuple\ x\ y = (andL\ x\ y, andR\ x\ y)$$

If we consider $andTuple \perp \perp \equiv (\perp, \perp)$ we can use the context $fst\ (andTuple\ []\ [])$ as well as $snd\ (andTuple\ []\ [])$ to apply Definition 1. That is, a function may have different sequential positions for the same input but with respect to different result positions. Sloth handles non-flat types by applying the approach presented so far to every result position that is $\perp$. The check of $andTuple$ using *verboseCheck* yields the following result.

```
verboseCheck andTuple 4
1: \⊥ ⊥ -> (⊥,⊥)
2: \True ⊥ -> (⊥,⊥)
3: \⊥ True -> (⊥,⊥)
Finished 3 tests.
```

Sloth additionally highlights subterms that have been checked by coloring the corresponding underscores. We omit these highlights for readability. Here, both underscores on the right hand side of -> of the first test case are highlighted. Furthermore the first component of the tuple of the second test case as well as the second component of the tuple of the third test case are highlighted. Thus, the test cases with respect to the first tuple component resemble the test cases for $andL$. The test cases with respect to the second tuple component resemble the test cases for $andR$.

As we have already observed the set of demanded positions is a subset of the set of sequential positions. That is, instead of considering all sequential positions we may consider only demanded positions. The following example shows that we get false positives if we only consider demanded positions.

Example 6 (Demanded Positions). Consider the following function.

$$second :: Bool \rightarrow Bool \rightarrow Bool$$
$$second\ False\ y = y$$
$$second\ True\ y = y$$

We have *second* $\perp$ b $\equiv$ $\perp$ for all values of type *Bool* because *second* performs pattern matching on its first argument. But obviously we have *second* b $\perp$ $\equiv$ $\perp$ for all values of type *Bool*, too. That is, position 1 as well as position 2 are sequential positions of *second*. If we check *second* using *verboseCheck* we get the following result.

```
verboseCheck second 4
1: \⊥ ⊥ -> ⊥
2: \⊥ False -> False
3: \⊥ True -> True
Finished 3 tests.
```

Sloth additionally checks *second* for the input *False* and $\perp$ as well as *True* and $\perp$. It does not report these test cases as it presents only test cases with respect to one sequential position. The application *second False* $\perp$ as well as *second True* $\perp$ are as non-strict as possible. If Sloth would only consider demanded positions it would not check the applications *second* $\perp$ *False* and *second* $\perp$ *True*. That is, Sloth would state that *second* is minimally strict although it is not.

4 Case Studies

In this section we present case studies for the application of Sloth. First we present two monomorphic functions that are not part of the standard Haskell libraries. These functions demonstrate examples for benefits of less strict functions beside memory behaviour. Furthermore we present some results for Haskell functions from the *Prelude* and from the standard library *Data.List*.

Consider the following data type of Peano numbers.

data *Peano* = *Zero* | *Succ Peano*

We define multiplication of Peano numbers by means of a standard implementation of the addition.

$$multP :: Peano \rightarrow Peano \rightarrow Peano$$
$$multP \; Zero \qquad \_ = Zero$$
$$multP \; (Succ \; x) \; y = addP \; y \; (multP \; x \; y)$$

Furthermore we define an infinite Peano number as follows.

$$infinity :: Peano$$
$$infinity = Succ \; infinity$$

This is a standard implementation of Peano numbers. For example, the numbers package by Augustsson provides an identical Peano implementation.

The evaluation of *multP Zero infinity* yields *Zero* in a non-strict programming language like Haskell. On the contrary the evaluation of *multP infinity Zero* does not terminate. But do all implementations of the multiplication of Peano numbers behave this way? That is, can we give an implementation of Peano multiplication in Haskell that yields *Zero* in both cases (without using parallelism)?

We use Sloth to check whether *multP* is minimally strict. Sloth enumerates partial values to check a function for all values up to a specific size. To enumerate values we use instances of the type class *Data*. Therefore we have to provide instances of the type classes *Typeable* and *Data* for *Peano*[6].

Sloth reports two counterexamples if we check *multP* up to size three.

```
> strictCheck multP 3
3: \(Succ ⊥) Zero -> Zero
5: \(Succ (Succ ⊥)) Zero -> Zero
Finished 7 tests.
```

As the counterexamples presented by Sloth are potential counterexamples we have to verify them. For all total inputs that are more defined than *Succ* ⊥ and *Zero* the function *multP* yields *Zero*, which is as defined as the recommended result *Zero*. Therefore, the counterexamples presented by Sloth are definitely counterexamples.

In particular the counterexamples show that a minimally strict implementation of Peano multiplication yields *Zero* for the arguments *infinity* and *Zero*. Thus, now we are able to answer the question. There is an implementation of the multiplication of Peano numbers that terminates no matter whether it is applied to *Zero* and *infinity* or to *infinity* and *Zero*.

The evaluation of *multP infinity Zero* does not terminate because *multP* is inductively defined over its first argument. Hence, even if the second argument is *Zero*, the first argument is completely evaluated. Note that it therefore takes linear time in the size of *p* to evaluate *multP p Zero* for any Peano number *p*.

We can define an improved implementation by simply adding an additional rule to the definition of *multP*. We could replace the pattern *Succ* _ by _, but we use the former to emphasize that there is still a bias towards the second argument with respect to non-strictness.

$$multP' :: Peano \rightarrow Peano \rightarrow Peano$$
$$multP'\ Zero \qquad \_\ = Zero$$
$$multP'\ (Succ\ \_)\ Zero = Zero$$
$$multP'\ (Succ\ x)\ y \quad = addP\ y\ (multP'\ x\ y)$$

Sloth does not report any counterexamples if we check *multP'* for Peano numbers up to size 50. Note that for any Peano number *p* it takes only constant time to evaluate *multP' p Zero* rather than linear time as for *multP p Zero*.

In contrast, StrictCheck identifies *multP'* as unnecessarily strict. For the input *Succ (Succ Zero)* and *Succ* ⊥, *multP'* yields *Succ* ⊥ while StrictCheck suggests *Succ (Succ* ⊥). This "improvement" can only be achieved by employing an operator like *unamb* (Elliott 2009).

The next example is supposed to emphasize that the presented tool is of interest for all kinds of non-strict declarative programming languages. A functional logic programming language like Curry (Hanus 2006) can be considered as a functional language with non-determinism and free variables. The syntax

---

[6] By using the option *DeriveDataTypeable* the ghc can derive these instances.

of Curry is very similar to the syntax of Haskell and the deterministic subset of Curry resembles Haskell.

Let us consider an algebraic data type for binary natural numbers like it is defined by Brassel et al. (2007).

data $Nat = One \mid O\ Nat \mid I\ Nat$

This is a little-endian representation of binary numbers without leading zeros. For example, the term $O\ (I\ One)$ represents the decimal number six. Note that in contrast to $Peano$ the data type Nat does not include zero. Brassel et al. (2007) furthermore define the following multiplication of binary numbers where $addN$ is the addition of binary numbers.

$$multN :: Nat \rightarrow Nat \rightarrow Nat$$
$$multN\ One\quad y = y$$
$$multN\ (O\ x)\ y = O\ (multN\ x\ y)$$
$$multN\ (I\ x)\ \ y = addN\ (O\ (multN\ x\ y))\ y$$

We use Sloth to check whether $multN$ is minimally strict for inputs up to size three. Note that we, in fact, check the corresponding Haskell implementation as Sloth is implemented in Haskell. As $multN$ is deterministic it behaves identically in Haskell and Curry.

```
> strictCheck multN 3
27: \(I ⊥) (O One) -> O (I ⊥)
28: \(I ⊥) (O (O ⊥)) -> O (O ⊥)
29: \(I ⊥) (O (I ⊥)) -> O (I ⊥)
Finished 32 tests.
```

Sloth reports two counterexamples. As these counterexamples are definite we do not have to verify them by hand. For lack of space we do not provide a detailed explanation why $multN$ is unnecessarily strict. Instead we only present a minimally strict implementation. If we swap the arguments of the recursive application of $multN'$ in the last rule the resulting function is minimally strict.

$$multN' :: Nat \rightarrow Nat \rightarrow Nat$$
$$multN'\ One\quad y = y$$
$$multN'\ (O\ x)\ y = O\ (multN'\ x\ y)$$
$$multN'\ (I\ x)\ \ y = addN\ (O\ (multN'\ y\ x))\ y$$

Sloth does not report any counterexamples for $multN'$ for inputs up to size ten.

But why do we bother whether $multN$ is too strict? Brassel et al. (2007) have introduced the Nat data type to guess numbers. In a functional logic programming language you can non-deterministically guess elements of a specific type by employing free variables. But no Curry system can guess values of the primitive integer type. By employing the data type Nat it is possible to guess numbers while the performance of the arithmetic operations for Nat is still reasonable.

As an example, consider the following implementation of the generation of Pythagorean triples in Curry.

$pythagorean :: (Nat, Nat, Nat)$
$pythagorean \mid addN\ (multN\ a\ a)\ (multN\ b\ b) == multN\ c\ c = (a, b, c)$
   where a, b, c *free*

Here a, b, and c are defined to be free variables by the keyword *free*. You can consider free variables as generators that non-deterministically enumerate all possible values of a type (Antoy and Hanus 2006). That is, *pythagorean* yields all triples of binary numbers a, b, and c such that $a * a + b * b = c * c$. For all numbers that do not satisfy this equation the guard yields a failure, that is, the empty result set.

Because of non-strict evaluation, free variables are only evaluated as far as necessary. That is, if a function is more strict than necessary, it leads to more non-determinism. Note that this never leads to more non-deterministic results. In fact, if a function is too strict, we only get the same result more than once or more derivations fail.

For example, consider the following implementations of constant functions. When we apply *const1* to a free variable we get the result 1 twice, while *const2* applied to a free variable yields only a single result.

$const1 :: Bool \rightarrow Int$ $const2 :: Bool \rightarrow Int$
$const1\ False = 1$ $const2\ \_ = 1$
$const1\ True\ = 1$

Thus, minimally strict functions are advantageous in a functional logic programming language. We can observe this advantage when we compare run-times for the generation of Pythagorean triples, using *multN* and *multN'* respectively[7].

number of triples	100	200	300
multN	3.87s	17.81s	33.42s
multN'	1.10s	5.87s	12.78s

It takes three times as long to enumerate Pythagorean triples if we use the unnecessarily strict implementation of multiplication. In fact, using Sloth we have discovered that most of the functions presented by Brassel et al. (2007) are more strict than necessary.

Because neither StrictCheck nor Sloth can handle higher order functions we only consider first order functions[8] in the following.

The *Prelude* functions, *splitAt*, *unzip*, *reverse*, *unlines* and *unwords* are too strict. Furthermore, in the module *Data.List* the first order functions *inits*, *tails*, *intersperse* and *intercalate* are too strict. As an interesting example we only consider *reverse* in the following. For example, we can improve *inits* in a similar way as we have improved *intersperse* in the introduction.

Let's consider the tail recursive, linear complexity implementation of *reverse*. If we check *reverse* Sloth reports two potential counterexamples.

---

[7] The run-times are measured with the Curry compiler KiCS (Brassel and Huch 2007).
[8] Note that we consider type class contexts as higher order types.

```
> strictCheck (reverse :: [Bool] -> [Bool]) 2
2: \(⊥:⊥) -> ⊥:⊥
4: \(⊥:⊥:⊥) -> ⊥:⊥:⊥
Finished 4 tests.
```

If we check *reverse* for Boolean lists up to size ten all these potential counterexamples remain potential counterexamples. And indeed *reverse* is not minimally strict. When we apply *reverse* to a total list that is more defined than $\perp : \perp$, that is, a total list with at least one element, the result is always a list with at least one element.

We can easily define a minimally strict reverse function with quadratic complexity by employing *last* and *init*. We can also define a minimally strict implementation of *reverse* with linear complexity if we employ that a minimally strict implementation of *reverse* preserves the shape of a list. But, in most cases the memory behaviour of this implementation is worse than the behaviour of the original implementation. This shows that we should not blindly aim for minimally strict implementations but have to consider every case individually.

5   Directions for Future Research

While Sloth tries to identify as many sequential positions as possible, we could as well consider demanded positions only. The resulting criterion is computationally less intensive but for the price of more false positives. We plan an empirical evaluation to check whether it is worth to pay this price.

An obvious improvement of the presented approach is the integration of higher-order functions. This extension is of particular interest as it enables the handling of type classes. For example, consider the Haskell function *intersect*.

$$intersect :: Eq\ \alpha \Rightarrow [\alpha] \rightarrow [\alpha] \rightarrow [\alpha]$$
$$intersect\ xs\ ys = [\,x \mid x \leftarrow xs, any\ (x ==)\ ys\,]$$

This function shows a similar behavior as *multP* presented in Section 4. While the evaluation of *intersect* [] [0..] yields [], the evaluation of *intersect* [0..] [] does not terminate. Furthermore the evaluation of *intersect xs* [] takes linear time in the size of *xs*. We can improve both aspects by adding an additional rule to the definition like we have done for *multP*.

There are a couple of other interesting observations with respect to minimal-strictness that are worth to investigate. For example, default definitions in type classes are not aware of type-specific information and, therefore, sometimes, cannot be as non-strict as type-specific implementations. The function $(<=) ::$ *Bool* $\rightarrow$ *Bool* $\rightarrow$ *Bool*, which implements the Boolean implication, is too strict because it is implemented by means of *compare* :: *Bool* $\rightarrow$ *Bool* $\rightarrow$ *Ordering*. That is, we have *False* $<= \perp \equiv \perp$ as well as $\perp <= $ *True* $\equiv \perp$, while a naive implementation would yield a defined value in one of these cases. For the same reason most instances of $(<=)$ are too strict, for example, the instances for (*Bool*, *Bool*), *Maybe Bool*, and [*Bool*] are too strict. Note that this also implies that *min* and *max* for these data types are unnecessarily strict. But this is a very fine line because we have to trade modularity for minimal-strictness.

Last but not least Sloth provides lots of space for improvements. For example, Sloth treats all potential counter examples equally. But if the number of values that were used for the approximation of the infimum is very small it is very likely that a potential counterexample is not a counterexample. In these cases it might be a good choice to not present these unlikely counter examples. Furthermore, we assume that there is room for improvements with respect to the presentation of counter examples.

Acknowledgement. I wish to thank Daniel Fischer for discovering and sharing the space leak in his *searchstring* package.

References

Antoy, S., Hanus, M.: Overlapping rules and logic variables in functional logic programs. In: Etalle, S., Truszczyński, M. (eds.) ICLP 2006. LNCS, vol. 4079, pp. 87–101. Springer, Heidelberg (2006)

Augustsson, L.: numbers Package, `hackage.haskell.org/package/numbers/` (Version 2009.8.9)

Brassel, B., Huch, F.: The Kiel Curry System KiCS. In: WLP 2007 Preproceedings, Technical Report 434 (2007)

Brassel, B., Fischer, S., Huch, F.: Declaring Numbers. In: WFLP 2004 Proceedings (2007)

Chitil, O.: Promoting Non-Strict Programming. In: IFL 2006 Draft Proceedings (2006)

Elliott, C.: Push-pull functional reactive programming. In: Haskell Symposium 2009 Proceedings (2009)

Fischer, D.: Unnecessarily strict implementations. Haskell-Cafe Mailing List (September 2010)

Fischer, D., Kuklewicz, C., Bailey, J.: Sringsearch Package, `http://hackage.haskell.org/package/stringsearch/` (Version 0.3.1)

Hanus, M.: Curry: An Integrated Functional Logic Language, Vers. 0.8.2 (2006), `curry-language.org`

Hughes, J.: Why Functional Programming Matters. Computer Journal (1989)

Runciman, C., Naylor, M., Lindblad, F.: Smallcheck and lazy smallcheck: automatic exhaustive testing for small values. In: Haskell Workshop 2008 Proceedings (2009)

Thielemann, H.: Utility-ht Package, `http://hackage.haskell.org/package/utility-ht/` (Version 0.0.5.1)

Vuillemin, J.E.: Proof-techniques for recursive programs. PhD thesis, Stanford University (1974)

Wadler, P.: Theorems for free! In: FPCA 1989 Proceedings (1989)

The F# Asynchronous Programming Model

Don Syme[1], Tomas Petricek[2], and Dmitry Lomov[3]

[1] Microsoft Research, Cambridge, United Kingdom
[2] Faculty of Mathematics and Physics, Charles University in Prague, Czech Republic
[3] Microsoft Corporation, Redmond WA, USA
{dsyme,dmilom}@microsoft.com, tomas@tomasp.net

With one breath, with one flow, you will know, asynchronicity. [The Police, 1983, adapted]

Abstract. We describe the asynchronous programming model in F#, and its applications to reactive, parallel and concurrent programming. The key feature combines a core language with a non-blocking modality to author lightweight asynchronous tasks, where the modality has control flow constructs that are syntactically a superset of the core language and are given an asynchronous semantic interpretation. This allows smooth transitions between synchronous and asynchronous code and eliminates callback-style treatments of inversion of control, without disturbing the foundation of CPU-intensive programming that allows F# to interoperate smoothly and compile efficiently. An adapted version of this approach has recently been announced for a future version of C#.

1 Introduction

Writing applications that react to events is becoming increasingly important. A modern application needs to carry out a rich user interaction, communicate with web services, react to notifications from parallel processes, or participate in cloud computations. The execution of reactive applications is controlled by events. This principle is called *inversion of control* or *the Hollywood principle* ("Don't call us, we'll call you").Even the internal architecture of multi-core machines is approaching that of an event-based distributed computing environment [2].

For this paper, asynchronous (also called "non-blocking" or "overlapped") programming is characterized by many simultaneously pending reactions to internal or external events. These reactions may or may not be processed in parallel. Today, many practically-oriented languages have reached an "asynchronous programming impasse":

- **OS threads are expensive, while lightweight threading alone is less interoperable.** Despite many efforts to make them cheap, OS threads allocate system resources and large stacks [16] and their use is insufficient for problems that require a large number of pending reactions of outstanding asynchronous communications. For this reason many advocate either complete re-implementations of OS threading [3] or language runtimes supporting only light-weight threads. However, both are difficult without affecting performance of CPU-intensive

R. Rocha and J. Launchbury (Eds.): PADL 2011, LNCS 6539, pp. 175–189, 2011.
© Springer-Verlag Berlin Heidelberg 2011

native code, and in any case interoperating with OS threads is a fundamental requirement for languages that interoperate smoothly with virtual machines such as
C#, F#, Scala [12, 19], so in this paper we assume it as an axiom. So these languages must look to add an additional light weight-tasking model that is not 1:1
with OS threads, a starting point for this paper.

- **Asynchronous programming using callbacks is difficult.** The usual approach
  to address asynchronous programming is to use callbacks. However, without language support, callback-based code inverts control, is awkward and is limited in
  expressivity. In normal use, asynchronous programming on .NET and Java leads
  to a tangle of threads, callbacks, exceptions and data-races.

What is to be done about this? The answer proposed in this paper, and adopted by F#
since 2007[1], is to add an *asynchronous modality* as a first-class feature to a general
purpose language design. By "modality" we mean reusing the control flow syntax of a
host language with a different computational interpretation.[2] The key contribution of
this paper is to give a recipe for how to augment a core language (e.g. an ML-like
language, with no threading or tasks) with a non-blocking modality to author
lightweight asynchronous tasks in a relatively non-intrusive way. The modality has
control constructs that are syntactically a superset of the core language and these are
given an asynchronous semantic interpretation. For F#, this allows asynchronous code
to be described fluently in familiar language syntax, without disturbing the foundation
of CPU-intensive programming that allows F# to compile efficiently to Common IL,
and hence to native code, and to interoperate well with .NET and C libraries.

2   An Overview of F# Asynchronous Programming

In this section we give an overview of the elements of F# asynchronous programming, element by element. We assume familiarity with ML-like core languages and
use *expr* to indicate ordinary expressions in F# programming [17]. The F# asynchronous programming extension adds a new syntactic category *aexpr* to indicate the added
syntax of asynchronous expressions:

   expr := async { *aexpr* }

The foundation of F# asynchronous programming is the Async<T> type, which
represents an asynchronous computation. All expressions of the form async { ... }
are of type Async<T> for some T. When executed, an async value will eventually produce a value of type T and deliver it to a continuation.

   In asynchronous expressions, control-flow constructs can be used to form values
that represent asynchronous computations, and additions are made to this syntax to
await the completion of other asynchronous computations and bind their results. The

---

[1] This paper describes the asynchronous support in F# 2.0. While the core idea was released and
  published in book form 2007, the model has not been described in the conference literature.
  This paper aims to rectify this and to help enable replication in other languages.
[2] Other examples of language modalities are C# iterators (where the control syntax of C# is
  used to write programs that generate sequences) and F# sequence expressions (a similar use).

grammar of asynchronous expressions for F# is shown below[3]. Importantly, this is a superset of F# core language syntax, where control flow constructs are preferred to have an asynchronous interpretation.

```
aexpr :=
    | do! expr                          execute async
    | let! pat = expr in aexpr          execute & bind async
    | let pat = expr in aexpr           execute & bind expression
    | return! expr                      tailcall to async
    | return expr                       return result of async expression
    | aexpr; aexpr                      sequential composition
    | if expr then aexpr else aexpr     conditional on expression
    | match expr with pat -> aexpr      match expression
    | while expr do aexpr               asynchronous loop on synchronous guard
    | for pat in expr do aexpr          asynchronous loop on synchronous list
    | use val = expr in aexpr           execute & bind & dispose expression
    | use! val = expr in aexpr          execute & bind & dispose async
    | try aexpr with pat -> aexpr       asynchronous exception handling
    | try aexpr finally expr            asynchronous compensation
    | expr                              execute expression for side effects
```

The signatures of the library functions used in this section are:

```
Async.RunSynchronously    : Async<'T> → 'T
Async.StartImmediate      : Async<unit> → unit
Async.StartInThreadPool[4] : Async<unit> → unit
Async.Parallel            : Async<'T>[] → Async<'T[]>
Async.Sleep               : int → Async<unit>
```

We also assume a function that takes a URL address and fetches the contents of a web page – we show later in this section how this function is defined.

```
getWebPage: string -> Async<string>
```

2.1 Writing, Composing and Running Asynchronous Computations

Asynchronous computations form a monad and can bind a result from another asynchronous computation using **let! v = *expr* in *aexpr***. To return a result, we use the **return *expr*** syntax, which lifts an expression into asynchronous computation. The following example downloads a web page and returns its length:

```
async { let! html = getWebPage "http://www.google.com"
        return html.Length }
```

The expected types are as follows:

$$\text{let! } pat_T = expr_{\text{Async<T>}} \text{ in } aexpr_{:\ \text{Async<U>}} \qquad : \textbf{Async<U>}$$
$$\text{return } expr_T \qquad : \textbf{Async<T>}$$

The syntax **do! expr** indicates the execution of a subordinate asynchronous operation of type **Async<unit>**, the type of an asynchronous operation that does not return a

---

[3] F# indentation aware syntax allows the omission of the **in** keyword.

[4] `Async.StartInThreadPool` is called `Async.Start` in F# 2.0. We use the former for clarity.

useful result.The following example sleeps 5sec., resumes, performs a side effect, and sleeps another 5 sec. Note F# is an impure, strict functional language, and, as with other operations in F#, asynchronous computations may have side effects.

```
async { do! Async.Sleep 5000
        printfn "between naps"
        do! Async.Sleep 5000 }
```

The typings for the syntactic elements used here are as follows:

$$\textbf{do! } \textit{Expr }_{\text{Async<unit>}} \qquad\qquad\qquad\qquad : \textbf{Async<unit>}$$
$$\textit{aexpr }_{\text{Async<unit>}} \textbf{; } \textit{aexpr }_{\text{Async<T>}} \qquad\qquad : \textbf{Async<T>}$$
$$\textit{expr }_{\text{unit}} \qquad\qquad\qquad\qquad\qquad\qquad : \textbf{Async<unit>}$$

Asynchronous computations can also bind the results of core language expressions using **let** v = *expr* in *aexpr*, executed using normal expression evaluation:

```
async { let! html = getWebPage "http://www.bing.com"
        let words = html.Split(' ', '\n', '\r')
        printfn "the number of words was %d" words.Length }
```

For the F# version of asynchronous programming, a value of type **Async<_>** is best thought of as a "task specification" or "task generator". Consider this:

```
let sleepThenReturnResult =
    async { printfn "before sleep"
    do! Async.Sleep 5000
    return 1000 }
```

This declaration does not start a task and has no side effects. An **Async<_>** must be explicitly run, and side effects will be observed each time it is run. For example, we can explicitly run an asynchronous computation and block for its result as follows:

```
let res = Async.RunSynchronously sleepThenReturnResult
printfn "result = %d" res
```

This runs, as a background operation, a task that prints "before sleep", then does a non-blocking sleep for 5 sec., and then delivers the result 1000 to the blocking operation. In this case, the function is equivalent to standard blocking code with a pause, but we'll see a more interesting use in Section 3. The choice to have asyncs be task generators is an interesting one. Alternatives are possible: "hot tasks" that run immediately, i.e. futures, or "cold tasks" that must be started explicitly, but can only be run once. Task-generators are more suitable for a functional language as they eliminate state (e.g. whether a task has been started).

When an asynchronous computation does not produce a result, it can be started as a co-routine, running synchronously until the first point that it yields:

```
Let printThenSleepThenPrint =
    async { printfn "before sleep"
            do! Async.Sleep 5000
            printfn "wake up" }

Async.StartImmediate printThenSleepThenPrint
printfn "continuing"
```

This program runs a task that prints "before sleep", then schedules a callback and prints "continuing". After 5 sec., the callback is invoked and prints "wake up".

This raises the question of how the callback is run: is it on a new thread? In a thread pool? Fortunately, .NET has an answer to this. Each running computation in .NET implicitly has access to a *synchronization context*, which for our purposes is a way of taking a function closure and running it "somewhere". We use this to execute asynchronous callbacks. Contexts feature in the semantics in Section 3.

An asynchronous computation can also be started "in parallel" by scheduling it for execution using the .NET thread pool. The operation is queued and eventually executed through a pool of OS threads using pre-emptive multi-tasking.

```
Async.StartInThreadPool printThenSleepThenPrint
```

2.2 Asynchronous Functions

An asynchronous function is a design idiom where a normal F# function or method returns an asynchronous computation. The typical type signature of an asynchronous function f is $ty_1 \rightarrow \ldots \rightarrow ty_n \rightarrow$ Async<ty_{return}>. For example:

```
let getWebPage (url:string) =
    async { let req = WebRequest.Create url
            let! resp = req.AsyncGetResponse()
            let stream = resp.GetResponseStream()
            let reader = new StreamReader(stream)
            return! reader.AsyncReadToEnd() }
```

This uses additional .NET primitives. It is common that functions are written entirely in this way, i.e. the whole body of the function or method is enclosed in async { ... }. (Indeed, in Java/C# versions of an asynchronous language modality, it is natural to support only asynchronous *methods*, and not asynchronous *blocks* or *expressions*).

The above example uses several asynchronous operations provided by the F# library, namely AsyncGetResponse and AsyncReadToEnd. Both of these are I/O primitives that are typically used at the leaves of asynchronous operations. The key facet of an asynchronous I/O primitive is that it does not block an OS thread while executing, but instead schedules the continuation of the asynchronous computation as a callback in response to an event.[5] Indeed, in the purest version of the mechanism described here, every composite async also has this property: asyncs don't block at all, not even I/O, except where performing useful CPU computations.

Tail Recursive Functions and Loops. A very common pattern in functional programming is the use of recursive functions. Let's assume we have a function receive of type unit -> Async<int> that asynchronously returns an integer, for example by awaiting a message. Now consider an asynchronous function that accumulates a parameter by repeatedly awaiting a message:

---

[5] The .NET library provides operations through the "Asynchronous Programming Model" (APM) pattern of BeginFoo/EndFoo methods. The F# library provides Async.FromBeginEnd to map these to functions and uses this to wrap primitives to await basic operating signals such as semaphores, toread and write socket connections, and to await database requests.

```
let rec count n =
    async { printfn "count = %d" n
            let! msg = receive()
            return! count (n + msg) }
```

Here, **return!** *expr* is an asynchronous tailcall that yields control to the sub-ordinate async, with finite overall resource usage (neither the stack nor the heap holding continuations grows indefinitely).Note *expr* has type **Async<T>** for some **T**.

Recursive asynchronous functions with asynchronous tailcalls give a very general way to define asynchronous loops. However, the F# and OCaml syntax also allows the direct use of **for** and **while** loops, often combined with the use of imperative data structures such as reference cells. It is useful to extend these to asynchronous code. A variation on a **count** function can be defined as follows:

```
let count =
    async { let n = ref 0
            while true do
                printfn "count = %d" n.Value
                let! msg = receive()
                n := n.Value + msg }
```

2.3 Exception Handling and Resource Compensation

Without a language support, the exception handling in asynchronous computations is extremely difficult [10]. With language support it becomes simple: the **try...with** and **try...finally** constructs can be used in async expressions in the natural way:

```
async { try
            let! primary = getWebPage "http://primary.server.com"
            return primary.Length
        with e ->
            let! backup = getWebPage "http://backup.server.com"
            return backup.Length  }
```

Here, a failure anywhere in the download from the primary server results in the execution of the exception handler and download from the backup server.

Deterministic resource disposal is a language construct that ensures that resources (such as file handles) are disposed at the end of a lexical scope. In F# this is the construct **use** *val* **= expr in expr**, translated to **let** *val* **= expr in try** *expr* **finally** *val*.**Dispose()**. The resource *val* is freed on exit from the lexical scope.

Resource cleanup in asynchronous code is also difficult without language support [10]. Many OO design patterns for async programming use a "state" object to hold the state elements of a composed asynchronous computation, but this is non-compositional. With language support, state becomes implied by closure, and resource cleanup becomes simple. For example, the **getWebPage** function defined above can be improved as follows:

```
let getWebPage (url:string) =
    async { let req = WebRequest.Create url
            use! resp = req.AsyncGetResponse()
            use stream = resp.GetResponseStream()
            use reader = new StreamReader(stream)
            return! reader.AsyncReadToEnd() }
```

Here the connection, the network stream and reader are closed regardless of whether the asynchronous computation succeeds, fails or is cancelled, even though callbacks and asynchronous responses are implied by the use of the asynchronous syntax.

2.4 Cancellation

A *cancellation mechanism* allows computations to be sent a message to "stop" execution, e.g. "thread abort" in .NET. Cancellation mechanisms are always a difficult topic in imperative programming languages, because compiled, efficient native code often exhibits extremely subtle properties when pre-emptively cancelled at arbitrary machine instructions. However, for asynchronous computations we can assume that primitive asynchronous operations are the norm (e.g. waiting on a network request), and it is reasonable to support reliable cancellation at these operations. Furthermore, it is reasonable to implicitly support cooperative cancellation at specific syntactic points, and additionally through user-defined cancellation checks.

One test of asynchronous programming support in a language is whether cancellation of asynchronous operations is handled without additional plumbing. F# async supports the implicit propagation of a *cancellation token* through the execution of an asynchronous computation. Each cancellation token is derived from a *cancellation capability* (a `CancellationTokenSource` in .NET), used to set the overall cancellation condition. A cancellation token can be given to `Async.RunSynchronously`, `Async.StartImmediate`, `Async.StartInThreadPool` and `Agent.Start`, e.g.

```
let capability = new CancellationTokenSource()
let tasks = Async.Parallel [ getWebPage "http://www.google.com"
                             getWebPage "http://www.bing.com" ]
// Start the work...
Async.Start (tasks, cancellationToken=capability.Token)
// OK, the work is in progress, now cancel it...
capability.Cancel()
```

Cancellation is checked at each I/O primitive, subject to underlying .NET library and O/S support, and before the execution of each `return`, `let!`, `use!`, `try/with`, `try/finally`, `do!` and `async { ... }` construct, and before each iteration of an asynchronous `while` or `for` loop. For `getWebPage` this means cancellation can occur at several places. But it *cannot* occur during core-language code (e.g. expressions such as library calls, executed for side-effects), and it *cannot* occur in such a way that the resource-reclamation implied by the `use` and `use!` expression constructs is skipped. Cancellation is not necessarily immediately effective: in a multi-core or distributed setting it may take arbitrarily long to propagate the cancellation message.

3 Semantics

We now present a semantics for a simplified version of F# async programming, with the following aims:

- To give a formal reference model that is close to an ideal implementation, yet fairly neutral w.r.t. the core language.

- To differentiate between computations that are *pending on I/O, waiting in work queues*, and *actively burning the CPU*. These are the operational characteristics that matter most to working programmers, as they have different cost models.
- To give a semantics that can be reduced to (a) the "single-threaded" model, where one thread serves all reactions, or the "thread-pool" model, where a pool of threads serves all reactions.

We do not present formal proofs based on the given semantics. The semantics is as follows. We first perform a CPS conversion to reduce async expressions to core language expressions (Fig. 1). We assume the "core" language has appropriate contextual reduction rules (see Fig. 2). An async expression becomes a function $\lambda(sc, ec, cc, t).$ body accepting success, exception and cancellation continuations sc, ec and cc, and a cancellation token t. The only asynchronous action is *asyncsleep* which raises a wake-up event after an arbitrary time period. Starting an async provides continuations to reify errors and cancellation as exceptions in the core language.

Fig. 2 presents semantics for our asynchronous extension. We assume a core language whose semantics is given as a standard small-step reduction relation $e \leadsto e'$. The semantics for the asynchronous extension is then specified as a relation on $(A, Q, P) \leadsto (A', Q', P')$, where

(a) A is a set of active computations $e@ctxt$. Each conceptually corresponds to an active OS thread contending for the CPU, evaluating e. Each is labeled with a synchronization context $ctxt$ indicating how suspended async operations are requeued. Multiple computations may share the same context (e.g. a thread pool).

(b) Q is a set of queued computations $e@ctxt$. Each conceptually corresponds to a queued work item awaiting execution in $ctxt$. For each context we assume an operation $\text{dequeue}_{ctxt}(Q, A) \rightarrow (Q', A')$ which activates one queued evaluation.

(c) P is a set of pending reactions $ev \rightarrow e@ctxt$. Each conceptually corresponds to a pending callback when ev occurs, e.g. pending reactions to UI events. We assume event descriptors are unique strings indicating a wakeup signal.

REDUCTION performs one step of an active computation in A. SUSPENSION schedules a pending reaction to an event. ACTIVATION activates a queued computation in Q. EVENT queues a pending reaction in response to an event. Evaluation is non-deterministic: more than one reduction rule may apply to a given triple. We do not specify when events are raised: we assume they happen at an arbitrary number of steps once created by evaluations of asyncsleep.

Some important ramifications of the semantics is as follows:

- When there is one *ctxt*, with one thread, the semantics degenerates to a deterministic queue of event reactions, each run to completion or to an asyncsleep.
- When there is one *ctxt*, and multiple threads, the semantics degenerates to a thread pool, running reactions to events in parallel.

- Cancellation cannot be caught, though `finally` clauses are run when cancellation occurs. If an exception happens in a `finally` clause, then if the `finally` is being executed during cancellation, the exception is ignored, otherwise it is propagated.
- Cancellation checks are implicit at specific, well-defined places. Regular non-asynchronous expressions can be used for non-interruptible operations.

$$async \{ ae \} \equiv \lambda(sc, ec, cc, t). \emptyset; \Delta \, ec \, [\![ae]\!] \, (sc, ec, cc, t)$$
$$asyncsleep \equiv \lambda conts. \, suspend \, (conts, fresh)$$
$$StartImmediate(e, t) \equiv e \, ((\lambda x. x), (\lambda exn. \, raise \, exn), (\lambda exn. \, raise \, exn), t)$$
$$[\![let! \, x = e \, in \, ae]\!] = \lambda(sc, ec, cc, t). \emptyset; \, e \, ((\lambda x. [\![ae]\!] \, (sc, ec, cc, t)), ec, cc, t)$$
$$[\![return \, e]\!] = \lambda(sc, ec, cc, t). \emptyset; \, sc \, e$$
$$[\![if \, e \, then \, ae_1 \, else \, ae_2]\!] = if \, e_1 \, then \, [\![ae_1]\!] \, else \, [\![ae_2]\!]$$
$$[\![let \, v = e \, in \, ae]\!] = let \, v = e \, in \, [\![ae]\!]$$
$$[\![try \, ae \, finally \, e]\!]$$
$$= \lambda(sc, ec, cc, t). \emptyset; \Delta \, ec [\![ae]\!] ((\lambda x. \Phi \, e \, sc \, ec \, x), (\lambda x. \Phi \, e \, ec \, ec \, x), (\lambda x. \, Ke; \, cc \, x), t)$$
$$[\![try \, ae_1 \, with \, x \to ae_2]\!] = \lambda(sc, ec, cc, t). \emptyset; \Delta \, ec \, [\![ae_1]\!] \, (sc, (\lambda x. [\![ae_2]\!] \, (sc, ec, cc, t)), cc, t)$$
$$[\![while \, e \, do \, ae]\!] = let \, rec \, f() = if \, e \, then \, [\![ae; \, return! \, f()]\!] \, else \, [\![return()]\!] \, in \, f()$$
$$[\![return! \, e]\!] = e$$
$$[\![e]\!] = \lambda(sc, ec, cc, t). \, sc \, x$$
$$\emptyset; e \equiv if \, t. \, Cancelled \, then \, c \, \text{"cancel"} \, else \, e$$
$$\Phi \, e \, sc \, ec \, x \equiv match \, (try \, Ok \, e \, with \, err \to Err \, err) \, with \, Ok \, v \to sc \, x \mid Err \, err \to ec \, err$$
$$\Delta \, ec \, f \, x \equiv match \, (try \, Ok \, (f \, x) \, with \, err \to Err \, err) \, with \, Ok \, v \to v \mid Err \, err \to ec \, err$$
$$K \, e \equiv try \, e \, with \, err \to nil$$

Fig. 1. CPS Translation of Asynchronous Expressions[6,7]

4 Patterns for Concurrent and Reactive Programming

We now present some common patterns built on top of the F# asynchronous model.

4.1 Parallel Composition

Parallel composition of asynchronous computations is efficient because of the scalability properties of the .NET thread pool and the controlled, overlapped execution of operations such as web requests by modern OSs. The F# library provides two simple options for parallel composition, though it is easy to author additional patterns, particularly through the use of agents (see below).

Fork-join parallelism. The library function `Async.Parallel` takes a list of asynchronous computations and creates a single asynchronous computation that starts the individual computations in parallel and waits for their completion:

---

[6] $\emptyset$ indicates a cancellation check, given a cancellation continuation c and a cancellation token t. Φ and K indicate detecting and ignoring an exception in core-language code respectively. Δ represents catching an exception and passing it to an exception continuation.

[7] We omit **do!**, **aexpr; aexpr** and **expr**: they are syntactic sugar for **let!**. No cancellation check is inserted for the sub-case **expr; aexpr**. For **match**, **for** and **use** see the F# spec [17].

$e = e\ e\ |\ \lambda x.e\ |\ \textbf{let}\ x = e\ \textbf{in}\ e\ |\ \textbf{raise}\ e\ |\ \textbf{try}\ e\ \textbf{with}\ v{\to}e\ |\ \textbf{suspend}(e,ev)$ – some core language
expressions and results (let rec, tuples, primitive values, conditionals, pattern matching omitted)

$A = \{e@ctxt\}$ – sets of active computations

$Q = \{e@ctxt\}$ – sets of queued computations

$P = \{ev \to e@ctxt\}$ - sets of pending reactions

$e \leadsto e'$ – small-step evaluation relation for the core language

Start state is $A_0 = \{\overline{e_i@ctxt_i}\}$ for some $\overline{e_i}$ and $\overline{ctxt_i}$, $Q_0 = \emptyset$, $P_0 = \emptyset$

$\boxed{(A, Q, P) \leadsto (A', Q', P')}$ evaluation relation for asynchronous extension:

REDUCTION: $e \leadsto e' \implies (\{e@ctxt\} \cup A, Q, P) \leadsto (\{e'@ctxt\} \cup A, Q, P)$

SUSPENSION: $(\{\textbf{suspend}(e, ev)@ctxt\} \cup A, Q, P) \leadsto (A, Q, P \cup \{ev \to e@ctxt\})$

ACTIVATION: $dequeue_{ctxt}(Q, A) \to (Q', A')$, $ctxt$ is in $Q \implies (A, Q, P) \leadsto (A', Q', P)$

EVENT: $(A, Q, P \cup \{ev \to e@ctxt\}) \leadsto (A, Q \cup \{e@ctxt\}, P)$

Fig. 2. Expression Reduction

```
let task =
    Async.Parallel [ getWebPage "http://www.yahoo.com";
                     getWebPage "http://www.bing.com" ]
let result = Async.RunSynchronously task
```

It is possible to create computations that fetch tens of thousands of web pages in parallel. Assuming that `urls` is a list of URLs:

```
let all = Async.Parallel [ for url in urls -> getWebPage url ]
```

Promise-based parallelism. The F# library primitive for parallel execution is `Async.StartChild`. Its type is:

```
Async.StartChild  : Async<'T> → Async<Async<'T>>
```

It takes an async representing a child task and returns an async that represents the completion of the task, a form of promise [5]. Two-way parallel composition is then:

```
let parallel2 (job1, job2) =
    async { let! task1 = Async.StartChild job1
            let! task2 = Async.StartChild job2
            let! res1 = task1
            let! res2 = task2
            return (res1, res2)
```

On the first bind, `StartChild` starts the computation and returns a promise, also represented as an async, which is awaited on the second bind. The inferred type is:

```
val parallel2 : Async<'T> * Async<'U> -> Async<'T * 'U>
```

4.2 Reactive Agents Using State Machines

One primary motivation for including the async modality in F# is that it allows a faithful and simple representation of asynchronous message-receiving agents. An agent encapsulates a message queue and asynchronously reacts to messages received from other components. The signature of the F# library type for agents is as follows:

```
type Agent<'T> =
    static member Start: (Agent<'T> -> Async<unit>) -> Agent<'T>
    member Receive : Async<'T>
    member Post : 'T -> unit
```

(**Agent<T>** is a recommended type alias for the type **MailboxProcessor<T>** in F# 2.0.)
One litmus test of an asynchronous programming modality is writing reactive state
machines using a set of mutually recursive asynchronous functions. This is a common
pattern for reactive agents [20]. For example, consider an agent that adds numbers and
can be activated and deactivated. The type of messages sent to the agentis:

```
type Message =
    | Toggle
    | Add of int
    | Get of AsyncReplyChannel<int>
```

The agent has states *active* and *inactive*, which are represented as functions. Both
states are parameterized by the current number maintained by the agent. The following example creates and starts the agent (initially *active* with value 0):

```
let agent = Agent<Message>.Start (fun inbox ->
    let recactive n =
        async { printfn "active %d" n
                let! msg - inbox.Receive()
                match msg with
                | Toggle->return! inactive n
                | Add m  ->return! active (n + m)
                | Get ch -> ch.Reply n; return! active n }
    and inactive n =
        async { printfn "inactive %d" n
                let! msg = inbox.Receive()
                match msg with
                | Toggle ->return! active n
                | Add _  ->return! inactive n
                | Get ch -> ch.Reply n; return! inactive n }
    active 0 )
```

We can use the **Post** member of the agent to send messages to the state machine, e.g.

```
agent.Post (Add 10)    // Prints "active 10"
agent.Post Toggle      // Prints "inactive 10"
agent.Post (Add 20)    // Prints "inactive 10"
```

Results can be retrieved by agents using **PostAndAsyncReply**:

```
async { agent.Post (Add 30)                    // prints: "active 30"
        let! n = agent.PostAndAsyncReply Get // calls & waits
        printfn "got: %d" n }                  // prints: "got: 30"
```

4.3 Reactive User Interface Programming

Typical reactive GUI code should not perform CPU intensive calculations, but needs
to promptly react to the user activity. This is an area where the F# asynchronous
model works well as it enables a co-routine style of programming with a rich set of

control constructs [13]. Most of GUI frameworks allow accessing widgets only from a single thread (or do not support threads at all, e.g. JavaScript), making cooperative resumption-based asynchronous tasks are a perfect match for GUI programming.

In F#, user interface events are exposed as values [18] and we can use the `Async.AwaitObservable` primitive to use them as asyncs that will resume as soon as an event occurs. For example, assume an event `wnd.LeftButtonDown` representing clicks on a window. The following prints information about the first click event:

```
Async.StartImmediate
    async { let! me = Async.AwaitObservable wnd.LeftButtonDown
            printfn "clicke at (%d, %d) in %s" me.X me.Y wnd.Text }
```

The code registers a callback that will be called when the event occurs. The callback is scheduled through the GUI message queue. The example above waits only for the first occurrence of the event. To implement more complex logic, we can use control flow constructs available in the asynchronous modality. For example, consider a computation that reactively loops through three colors, in response to mouse clicks.

```
let semaphoreStates =
    async { while true do
                for light in [green; orange; red] do
                    let!_ = Async.AwaitObservable wnd.LeftButtonDown
                    wnd.BackgroundColor <- light }

Async.StartImmediate semaphoreStates
```

5 Implementation

At its core, the F# 2.0 implementation of the F# async model is as follows:

- The `async` syntax is de-sugared by the compiler as a "computation expression".
- The `Async<T>` type is represented as a function that, when run, is given three continuations for success, exceptions and cancellation, and will eventually call one of these. A cancellation token is also supplied as an argument.

Together these perform a localized continuation-passing translation of control-flow and a heap-based allocation of the closures. This is a simple and efficient implementation that also builds on the uniform tailcall support of .NET 4.0.This is in essence a direct implementation of the semantics described in Section 3, though many local optimizations are added, and additional protection is made against some cases where .NET does not guarantee tailcalls, e.g. in some partial-trust execution.

The `async { ... }` construct is an instance of an F# *computation expression* [19], a form of *retargetable syntacticcontrol-flow*, c.f. Haskell monadic syntax and LINQ query syntax [11]. We have de-emphasized this here, as adding an asynchronous syntactic modality to a language is independent of its implementation. For example:

```
async { let l = ref []
        for url in urls do
            let! result = getWebPage url
            l := result :: !l
        return !l }
```

is de-sugared to

```
async.Delay(fun () ->
    let l = ref []
  async.Combine(
      async.For(urls, fun url ->
          async.Bind(getWebPage url, fun result ->
              l := result :: l
              async.Zero() )),
        async.Delay(fun () -> async.Return(!l)))))
```

5.1 Some Usability and Performance Indicators

The role of F# async is to replace the direct use of OS threads in scalable .NET programming, and to be a "nicer" way of writing the event-based code necessary to achieve true scalability. This is hard to quantify, but one way to see this is to look at the results of a small study [10]. This implements a TCP server using four techniques: C#+OS threads, C#+callback async, F#+OS threads and F# + F# async. Approximate coding time and code lengths were recorded, and the developer was an expert in all areas. This study keeps many variables constant: the VM, GC, OS and underlying library, only the language support changes. The results are below:

	max clients	C# LoC	C# coding	F# LoC	F# coding
OS Threads	~1200	~90 lines	~20 mins	~60 lines	~20 mins
Async	> 8000	~330 lines	+ ~3 hours	~60 lines	+ ~10 mins

Comparing scalability and development time for a .NETpseudo-stock quote server
[10], .NET 3.5, Dell Optiplex 745, Win 7 Enterprise, 4 GB, 32-bit

The advantages of F# async are clear: > 7x improvement in scalability, and ~18x decrease in time to transition to event/async implementation. This is consistent with the authors' experience of using the mechanism in practice.

The above illustrates the primary benefits of F# async programming against its immediate comparison point on .NET. It is also somewhat useful to compare to other systems implementing agent models. Some comparison points are shown below.

	pingpong10^5, 1msg	pingpong1, 10^7 msg
F# 2.0 async actors	8.2s/211Mb	5.9s/5.6Mb
Scala 2.8.1 actors	5.5s/166Mb	21.4s/23Mb
Erlang 5.8 processes	(exceeds max agents)	16.8s/6Mb

Agent creation and messaging statistics, Windows 7.
pingpong n creates n pairs of agent and bounces messages between them. Memory use is steady state private working set. Dell E6400, Intel P9500 2.53Ghz, 2 Core, .NET 4.0, Win7 Enterprise

F# 2.0 per-agent overheads are marginally higher, but message processing is faster. However, a word of caution! *In reality, for all these languages, the in-memory processing costs are nearly always "good enough" for real-world asynchronous programming.* In real-world applications the overheads are often swamped by I/O latencies, I/O waits, graphical rendering or other CPU computations. Further, in client-tapps, a non-blocking UI can be much more important than reducing CPU usage.

6 Summary

Two major themes run through today's programming landscape: Web and Multi-core. Asynchronous/overlapped/non-blocking network programming is a critical problem for optimizing today's web programming, and compositional, functionally-oriented parallel programming is critical for multi-core programming. The F# async model makes significant practical contributions in both these areas, delivering a clean, efficient and scalable implementation of a compositional asynchronous programming model in the context of a viable applied functional programming language, without disturbing compilation via .NET and interoperability with .NET libraries.

To recap, why is such a modality useful? There are three ways to look at this:

- **Expressivity:** Compositional asynchronous reactions are expressed using sequencing, recursion, pattern matching, conditionals and exception handling. State machines, reactive UIs and agents are simple instantiations of these.
- **Semantic Separation:** Adding an asynchronous modality gives language support to a methodology that separates network I/O and asynchronous message passing from "local" effects such as memory access and console I/O.
- **Scalability:** Event-based programming is still essential to scaling for server-side systems which use OS threads. The performance indicators of Section 5 show how using F# async allows both scaling and efficient coding in this domain.

In practice, the F# asynchronous programming model has consistently proved itself to be an effective tool for multi-core, I/O and agent-programming problems [19, 13, 10].

6.1 Related Work

The topics of parallel, reactive, concurrent and distributed programming have given rise to a vast literature. Some of the key techniques are co-routines, promises, futures and actors [20, 1], synchronous languages [4], functional reactive programming, Join-based thread co-ordination, orchestration languages [22]and light-weight threading, especially Erlang [20]. Task, event, async and fork-join libraries abound, with no language integration. Using monadic delimited continuations for event-based programming is not new [9, 7, 15, 21]. Events v. threads is a major topic in systems research, with papers highlighting the duality of the two approaches, or advocating each [8, 9, 3]. The focus is mostly on systems performance, and less on expressivity.

The F# model ranks as a language integrated implementation of a lightweight task mechanism specifically designed to fluently integrate with high-performance code and interoperate well with existing virtual machines. Others with similar goals include Thorn, the "react" and "continuation" models of Scala and Kilim [6, 14, 16] and the F# model shares much in common with the latter two in the use of a localized CPS transform. This achieves conceptual efficiency by re-utilizing the control syntax of the core language with an asynchronous interpretation.

Acknowledgements. We thank Brian McNamara, Nikolaj Bjorner, Niklas Gustafsson, Simon Peyton Jones, Gregory Neverov, Laurent le Brun, Luke Hoban, Jomo Fisher, Tobias Gedell, and others for their help and advice on the design of the F# async model, and LAMP EPFL for a 2006 sabbatical where this work started.

References

[1]   Agha, G.: Actors: a model of concurrent computation in distributed systems. MIT Press, Cambridge (1986)

[2]   Baumann, A.: et al.: The multikernel: a new OS architecture for scalable multicore systems. In: SOSP 2009: Proc. of the ACM SIGOPS 22nd Symp. on OS Principles (2009)

[3]   von Behren, R., Condit, J., Brewer, E.: Why events are a bad idea (for high-concurrency servers). In: HOTOS 2003: Proc. of the 9th Conf. on Hot Topics in OS (2003)

[4]   Berry, G., Gonthier, G.: The ESTEREL synchronous programming language: design, semantics, implementation. Sci. Comput. Program. 19(2), 87–152 (1992)

[5]   Friedman, D.P., Wise, D.S.: Aspects of applicative programming for parallel processing. IEEE Trans. Computers 27(4), 289–296 (1978)

[6]   Haller, P., Odersky, M.: Scala actors: Unifying thread-based and event-based programming. Theor. Comput. Sci. 410(2-3), 202–220 (2009)

[7]   Kiselyov, O.: Delimited control in OCaml, abstractly and concretely. In: Blume, M., Kobayashi, N., Vidal, G. (eds.) FLOPS 2010. LNCS, vol. 6009, pp. 304–320. Springer, Heidelberg (2010)

[8]   Lauer, H.C., Needham, R.M.: On the duality of operating system structures. SIGOPS Oper. Syst. Rev. 13(2), 3–19 (1979)

[9]   Li, P., Zdancewic, S.: Combining events and threads for scalable network services implementation. SIGPLAN Not. 42(6), 189–199 (2007)

[10] McNamara, B.: F# async on the server side (March 2010), http://tinyurl.com/fsasyncserver (retrieved 5/9/2010)

[11] Meijer, E., Beckman, B., Bierman, G.: LINQ: reconciling object, relations and XML in the.NET framework. In: SIGMOD 2006: Int. ACM Conf. on Mgmt. of Data. ACM, New York (2006)

[12] Odersky, M., Spoon, L., Venners, B.: Programming in Scala, Artima, USA (2008)

[13] Petricek, T., Skeet, J.: Real World Functional Programming: With Examples in F# and C#. Manning, USA (2009)

[14] Rompf, T., Maier, I., Odersky, M.: Implementing first-class polymorphic delimited continuations by a type-directed selective CPS-transform. In: ICFP 2009: Proc. of the 14th ACM SIGPLAN Int. Conf. on Func. Prog. (2009)

[15] Srinivasan, S.: Kilim: A Server Framework with Lightweight Actors, Isolation Types & Zero-copy Messaging. Ph.D. thesis, University of Cambridge (2010)

[16] Srinivasan, S., Mycroft, A.: Kilim: Isolation-typed actors for java. In: Ryan, M. (ed.) ECOOP 2008. LNCS, vol. 5142, pp. 104–128. Springer, Heidelberg (2008)

[17] Syme, D.: F# 2.0 Language Specification, http://tinyurl.com/fsspec

[18] Syme, D.: Simplicity and compositionality in asynchronous programming through first class events (March 2006), http://tinyurl.com/composingevents, (retrieved: January 2010)

[19] Syme, D., Granicz, A., Cisternino, A.: Expert F#. Apress (2007)

[20] Virding, R., et al.: Concurrent programming in ERLANG, 2nd edn. Prentice Hall, Englewood Cliffs (1996)

[21] Vouillon, J.: OCaml light weight threading library (2002), http://ocsigen.org/lwt/

[22] Wehrman, I., Kitchin, D., Cook, W.R., Misra, J.: A timed semantics of Orc. Theor. Comput. Sci. 402, 234–248 (2008)

Kanor

A Declarative Language for Explicit Communication

Eric Holk[1], William E. Byrd[1], Jeremiah Willcock[1], Torsten Hoefler[2], Arun Chauhan[1], and Andrew Lumsdaine[1]

[1] School of Informatics and Computing
Indiana University
Bloomington, IN 47405, U.S.A.
{eholk,webyrd,jewillco,achauhan,lums}@cs.indiana.edu
[2] Blue Waters Directorate
University of Illinois at Urbana-Champaign
Urbana, IL 61801, U.S.A.
htor@illinois.edu

Abstract. Programmers of high-performance applications face two major implementation options: to use a high-level language which manages communication implicitly or to use a low-level language while specifying communication explicitly. The high-level approach offers safety and convenience, but forces programmers to give up control, making it difficult to hand-tune communications or to estimate communication cost. The low-level approach retains this control, but forces programmers to express communication at a verbose, tedious, and error-prone level of detail.

We advocate a complementary third approach in which the programmer declaratively, but explicitly, specifies the essence of the communication pattern. The programmer lets the implementation handle the details when appropriate, but retains enough control to hand-encode communications when necessary. In this paper we present Kanor, a language for declaratively expressing explicit communication patterns, and demonstrate how Kanor safely, succinctly, and efficiently expresses both point-to-point and collective communications.

1 Introduction

Large parallel computers, and the software that runs on them, are important to many areas of science and engineering. The largest of these computers consist of many separate nodes, connected by a high-performance network. These computers implement a message passing model for parallelism: processes have separate address spaces and communicate through messages. Programming languages and libraries can abstract this model, exposing instead a model with a global address space and implicit communication of data. Thus, programmers face a choice between these two approaches.

The implicit approach to communication is exemplified by languages such as X10 [4], UPC [14], and Co-array Fortran [12]; the *de facto* standard for explicit communication is the Message Passing Interface (MPI) [11]. There is a tradeoff between the implicit and explicit approaches to message passing, however. Implicit approaches are easier to

R. Rocha and J. Launchbury (Eds.): PADL 2011, LNCS 6539, pp. 190–204, 2011.
© Springer-Verlag Berlin Heidelberg 2011

program, but have more opaque performance characteristics, and thus their performance is harder to predict or tune. Explicit approaches are more difficult to program, requiring communication to be specified at a very fine-grained level of detail and thus leading to more errors, but allow more knowledge and control over a program's behavior and thus its performance.

In this paper we advocate a third, complementary approach in which the programmer uses a high-level declarative language to explicitly specify communication within an otherwise imperative program. This approach allows both programmer control and ease of programming, while allowing programs to be incrementally converted from fully explicit approaches to our declarative language.

Many, if not most, MPI applications are written in a bulk synchronous parallel (BSP) style [15]: each process runs the same program—*Single-Program, Multiple Data* (SPMD)—and alternates between steps of purely local computation and communication. One compute/communicate phase is called a *superstep*; there is a global synchronization at the end of each superstep. Examples of programs that are conveniently expressed in BSP style include iterative solvers, sparse matrix-vector multiplication, and many *n*-body algorithms.

We have designed a high-level, declarative language, *Kanor*, for specifying collective communication in BSP-style programs. Kanor provides a balance between declarativeness and performance predictability and tunability. We have implemented a prototype compiler for Kanor which infers the types and sizes of the data being sent automatically and generates efficient code. As a result, the programmer can express communication safely, simply, and concisely, while paying little to no abstraction penalty, as shown by a performance evaluation. The declarative, high-level nature of Kanor, combined with its simple parallel assignment semantics, exposes opportunities for future optimizations.

Our paper makes the following contributions:

- A declarative language, Kanor, for explicitly expressing collective communication within BSP-style programs concisely and declaratively (Section 4). Kanor extends C++'s type enforcement to communication patterns, and avoids deadlocks, unintentional race conditions, non-deterministic behavior based on message size, and other semantic pitfalls of MPI.
- A categorization of common communication patterns based on the knowledge available to the communicating processes (Section 3). We then show how Kanor takes advantage of this classification to communicate efficiently (Sections 5 and 6).
- Evaluation rules for Kanor (Section 4.1). The details of these rules are important to the language's properties: even a small change to the evaluation rules can radically change the language's expressiveness.
- A set of core algorithms that can be used to implement Kanor's evaluation scheme efficiently (Section 5).
- A prototype implementation of Kanor, which compiles Kanor expressions into C++ and MPI code (Section 6).
- A performance evaluation of Kanor against MPI, demonstrating that the convenience of Kanor's abstractions imposes minimal abstraction penalty when compared to point-to-point MPI communication (Section 7).

2   Motivation

Despite MPI's utility and popularity, MPI has its shortcomings. Consider this BSP-style MPI communication, in which every processor sends a different value to every processor whose process identifier (or *rank*) is even.

```
r = 0;
if(rank % 2 == 0)
   for(j = 0; j < P; j++)
      MPI_Irecv(&A[j], 1, MPI_INT, j, tag, MPI_COMM_WORLD, &reqs[r++]);
for(i = 0; i < P; i++)
   if(i % 2 == 0)
      MPI_Isend(&B[i], 1, MPI_INT, i, tag, MPI_COMM_WORLD, &reqs[r++]);
MPI_Waitall(r, reqs, MPI_STATUSES_IGNORE);
```

The *MPI_Isend* and *MPI_Irecv* functions perform nonblocking sends and receives, respectively, while *MPI_Waitall* returns once all of the sends and receives have completed.

As this example shows, MPI requires programmers to write a considerable amount of code at an error-prone level of detail to express even very simple communication pattens. MPI does provide functions to concisely perform a fixed set of *collective* communications, such as broadcasts. Collective statements are desirable because they are concise, and can be optimized in system-specific ways to vastly outperform their point-of-point equivalents. Even the simple communication pattern above, however, is awkward to express using these collectives.

The programmer needs the ability to express collective communication succinctly and declaratively, allowing the compiler to infer details such as the type of data being sent. Ideally, the programmer would write the communication above as similarly to:

```
@communicate {
   A[j]@i <<= B[i]@j where i in world, j in world, i % 2 == 0
}
```

The semantics of this idealized language would be based on parallel assignment, relieving the programmer from worries about deadlock and race conditions.

In addition to its verbosity, another problem with MPI is that it defeats C++'s type enforcement. Consider this MPI snippet:

```
double b = 0.0;
float a = 1.0;

if(recv_rank == rank)
   MPI_Recv(&b, 1, MPI_DOUBLE, send_rank, 0, MPI_COMM_WORLD,
            MPI_STATUS_IGNORE);
if(send_rank == rank)
   MPI_Send(&a, 1, MPI_FLOAT, recv_rank, 0, MPI_COMM_WORLD);
```

This example compiles and runs, but the result is clearly unintended. In some MPI implementations, rank 0 may end with the value $5.26354e{-}315$ for b, rather than the desired value of 1.0. Not only is this result incorrect, this program's behavior is undefined according to the MPI specification, meaning the program may misbehave in subtle and mysterious ways on different implementations. It is easy to see how this error might occur in a large program—a programmer might initially write a program using *floats*, then change it to use *doubles*. If the programmer misses a *float*, the program will likely produce incorrect results.

Instead, the programmer should be able to write something like:

double b = 0;
float a = 1.0;

@communicate { *b@recv_rank <<= a@send_rank* }

and let the compiler and runtime ensure the *float* value is implicitly converted to *double*, preserving the intended behavior for compatible data types. When the data types are incompatible, the code should fail to compile, rather than behaving incorrectly at runtime.

Kanor has all the desirable properties described above—indeed, the *@communicate* blocks above are correct, running Kanor code.

3   Exploiting Communication Knowledge

For a declarative language for communication to be efficient, it is essential to exploit all available information about each communication pattern. Kanor's design is informed by a multi-level classification of communications, based on each process's knowledge of the global communication pattern. These patterns are a refinement of those our group identified previously [7].

Global Knowledge. Each process can determine the entire communication pattern. This global knowledge may enable tree-based communication with logarithmic rather than linear overhead. An advantage of Kanor is that it allows the compiler to generate tree-based communication as an optimization, without forcing the programmer to write special-case code for efficiency.

Corresponding Knowledge. Each process knows only a subset of the complete communication topology, but has complete knowledge of the communication in which it will be participating.

Sender Knowledge. Senders know only the destinations they will send to; receivers do not know which senders they will receive from. The sender knowledge case requires the receiver to perform a termination protocol. The Kanor runtime uses the Non-blocking Barrier eXchange (NBX) protocol [8], which allows receiver processes to receive an unknown amount of data with minimal overhead.

Receiver Knowledge. Receivers know only the senders they will receive from; senders do not know which receivers they will send to. This case requires the receiver to notify the sender processes from which it wishes to receive data. After this notification, communication then becomes equivalent to the corresponding knowledge case.

These categories do not cover all possible applications or communication patterns. For example, some communications might fit a third-party knowledge pattern. However, these categories cover the majority of today's parallel applications [15], and thus simplify and direct our language design. It is important to note that other types of communication patterns can be transformed into to one of the three categories that Kanor supports by performing additional communication steps.

Communication in Kanor is *sender-driven*. Each *@communicate* block corresponds to either the global knowledge, corresponding knowledge, or sender knowledge case; in all three cases, the sender knows the destination. The receiver knowledge case, which is not as common as the first three cases, and requires an additional communication step, can be expressed in Kanor as two independent *@communicate* blocks. In the current Kanor implementation, the programmer may annotate each *@communicate* block with an optional pragma indicating the global, corresponding, or sender knowledge case; if no pragma is supplied, the compiler assumes the sender knowledge case. A future version of the compiler should be able to infer this pragma in most cases. Incorrectly specifying the hint is erroneous, and can lead to unspecified program behavior.

4   The Kanor Language

Figure 1 contains the grammar for Kanor. The nonterminals *integer*, *variable*, and *expr* represent standard C++ integer literals, identifiers and expressions. The grammar extends C++ by allowing statements to also include the *collective_stmt*.

Kanor allows *set comprehensions*, similar to the comprehensions found in Python and Haskell. The comprehension contains *generator* clauses, which bind variables to values in a set, and *filter* clauses, which restrict messages to be sent only when the filters' Boolean expressions evaluate to true. As might be expected, data is sent from the sender's process to the storage location on the receiver process; the complete evaluation rules are given in Section 4.1.

Each top-level *@communicate* block encapsulates a logical communication, which comprises one or more logically independent reductions (described below). The *@communicate* form supports an optional compiler hint, which must be either *global*, *corresponding*, or *sender*. These hints correspond to the first three classes of communication knowledge described in Section 3; the compiler's use of these hints is essential for good performance (Section 6). It should be possible for the compiler to infer this hint in many cases; when in doubt, the compiler can use the default *sender* hint.

A remote reference, of the form $e_0@e_1$, can appear only within a reduction. The right-hand-side of a remote reference must evaluate to a processor rank; the left-hand-side must evaluate to a data item (on the sender) or a location for data to be stored (on

collective_stmt	::=	@communicate *hint comprehension*
hint	::=	ϵ | global | corresponding | sender
remote_ref	::=	*expr* @ *expr*
reduction	::=	*remote_ref* <<= *remote_ref*
		| *remote_ref* << *variable* << *remote_ref*
		| *reduction* , *reduction*
comprehension	::=	{ *reduction* where (*clause* ,)* *clause* }
		| { *reduction* }
set_expr	::=	*expr* | { *expr* ... *expr* }
clause	::=	*variable* in *set_expr* | *expr*

Fig. 1. Grammar for Kanor

the receiver). The rules for evaluating e_0 and e_1 are critical to the design of Kanor, and are described in detail in Section 4.1.

Our fundamental unit of communication is the generalized reduction construct, of the form:

$$e_0 @ e_1 << op << e_2 @ e_3 \text{ where } e_4$$

From left-to-right, the reduction comprises four major parts: receiver remote reference, reduction operator, sender remote reference, and qualifier. The variable op must evaluate to a reduction function (described below); e_4 is the *qualifier* of the set comprehension. Because the majority of communication statements simply move data, we allow *transfer* statements, which are merely syntactic sugar for reductions using a special operator that performs assignment. A transfer of the form:

$$e_0 @ e_1 <<= e_2 @ e_3 \text{ where } e_4$$

is equivalent to:

$$e_0 @ e_1 << \text{assign} << e_2 @ e_3 \text{ where } e_4$$

The qualifier portion of a reduction uses comprehension syntax, which expresses the "control structure" of a communication pattern more succinctly than conditionals or loops. Comprehensions allow declarative specification using concepts and notation many programmers are already familiar with. The body of the comprehension contains generator expressions and filter expressions. Generator expressions are of the form

$$x_0, \ldots, x_n \text{ in } e$$

where x_0 through x_n are variables to be bound, and e is an expression that must evaluate to a set S. When the comprehension is evaluated, the variables x_0 through x_n are independently assigned values from the set S, in effect forming a Cartesian product. A filter expression is an arbitrary Boolean expression, which may reference variables bound in any generators that appear before it. Each filter expression is evaluated once for each generator assignment of variables that are in scope. If every filter expression evaluates to true for a given set of variable assignments, the sender and receiver remote references are evaluated with those variable bindings and a message is sent; otherwise, the remote references are not evaluated for those bindings. Details of these evaluation rules are given in Section 4.1.

Once a message is received, the receiver updates the values within the storage location by means of a reduction operator op. The operator has the signature:

$$op(e_0 : \mathbf{ref}\ \tau_0,\ e_2 : \tau_1)$$

where e_0 represents the storage address to be updated, and e_2 represents the message's data. The reduction operator is called once per message received. As is explained in Section 4.1, the operator expression is evaluated, and the resulting operator applied, on the receiving process. Here is a simple reduction operator written in C++, which updates the storage location with the sum of the values received:

```
template<typename T>
void sum(T &left, T right) {
    left += right;
}
```

We assume user-defined reduction operators are both commutative and associative. The behavior of non-commutative or non-associative reduction operators is undefined.

The order of evaluation is unspecified between e_1, e_2, and e_3 on the sender and between e_0 and op on the receiver. The operator op is call-by-value, and is applied only after all of its arguments have been evaluated.

The dependency chain within a Kanor communication can only be of length one: no read can depend upon another read. Kanor also uses parallel assignment semantics: all reads occur before all writes. This allows us to perform analyses similar to those in static single assignment languages. Parallel assignment is an important part of Kanor's semantics, as it guarantees there are no dependencies within a communication block. Parallel assignment makes it much easier to write programs whose communication patterns contain cycles, such as circular shift. Values destined for the same location are accumulated using the reduction operator. However, it is erroneous to make multiple writes to the same location using Kanor's assignment operator (<<=); the semantics of overlapping assignments is undefined.

4.1 Evaluation Rules

Kanor is a language for *explicit* communication: the programmer specifies the sending and receiving processes, the data to be sent, and where the data should be stored upon receipt. To make specifying this information easy, Kanor's comprehension syntax allows programmers to build sets of variable bindings (that is, environments) using generators and filters. Consider this communication, similar to the first one presented in Section 2, annotated to show information explicitly provided by the programmer:

A[j] @ i <<= B[i] @ j where i in world, j in {0...i}, i % 2 == 0

storage location / receiver rank / reduction operator / data / sender rank / generator / generator / filter

It may seem that this information is sufficient to fully specify the communication, given that Kanor's parallel assignment semantics allows the order in which messages are sent to be left unspecified. However, this is not the case; it is also necessary to specify *where* and *in which environment* each of these sub-expressions should be evaluated.

An important note about terminology: when we say that an expression e is evaluated on process p in some environment env, we are referring to the semantics of Kanor, rather than its implementation. As an optimization, the Kanor implementation may use a completely different evaluation strategy, so long as the program behaves *as if* expression e were evaluated in env on process p. (On a related note, side-effecting expressions within a communication block should be avoided, as their behavior is unspecified.)

The programmer could be required to specify explicitly where expressions should be evaluated—for example, indicating whether the storage location expression should be evaluated on the sender or the receiver. Although this is the most general approach, the level of detail required would make even the simplest communication cumbersome to write. Instead, the rules for evaluating Kanor expressions are fixed and implicit:

A[j] @ i <<= B[i] @ j where i in world, j in {0...i}, i % 2 == 0

A:receiver, j:sender / sender / receiver / sender / all / all

The sender's rank, along with *where*-bound generators and filters, are evaluated by every process; this is necessary to determine which processes are senders. Furthermore, the *where*-bound clauses are evaluated from left to right—this ordering is necessary since clauses may reference variables introduced in previous clauses. The data expression and the receiver's rank are evaluated on the sender's process. Evaluation of the storage expression is more complicated: the expression is evaluated on the receiver's process, except for *where*-bound variables, which are evaluated on the sender's process and sent if necessary.

The evaluation rules presented above are subtle: the slightest change can radically change the expressiveness of the language. For example, it may seem that the receiver rank should be evaluated on every processor, rather than just on the sender:

$$A[j] @ \underbrace{i}_{all} <<= B[i] @ j \text{ where } i \text{ in world, } j \text{ in } \{0...i\}, i \% 2 == 0$$

The symmetry of this approach is intuitively appealing: the expressions for both sender and receiver ranks use the same evaluation rules. However, using this scheme the programmer cannot directly express the sender knowledge case, in which the ranks of receiver processes are known only to the senders.

Consider another example of changing the evaluation rules. If all subexpressions, other than *op*, are evaluated only on the sender, the evaluation model is equivalent to a remote memory *put* or *accumulate* operation. If all subexpressions are evaluated on the receiver, the model is equivalent to a remote memory *get*. Some collectives, such as *MPI_Alltoallv*, cannot be expressed using only one stage of communication using *put* or *get*, but can be expressed as a single stage in Kanor. (Kanor supports, but is not restricted to, *put*.) For this reason, some operations from other languages and interfaces that superficially resemble Kanor's transfer statement, such as MPI 2's one-sided operations, actually have very different properties because of the different locations at which the subexpressions are evaluated.

5   Core Algorithms

The evaluation semantics described in Section 4.1 can be implemented in a straightforward manner, using the algorithms presented below. We present algorithms for both the *corresponding* and *sender* communication cases. Communication blocks that are marked as *global* or *corresponding* use the Corresponding Communication Algorithm. Sender-knowledge communication blocks use the Sender Communication Algorithm.

The Corresponding Communication Algorithm is given in Figure 2. In the corresponding case, both parties are able to determine which messages will be sent and in what order. This allows the receiver to post nonblocking receives ahead of time and thereby avoid more complicated communication protocols. For each environment generated by the *where* clauses, each process p checks to see if it is sending, receiving, or both. The algorithm then evaluates and applies the reduction operator to the received messages.

Sender-knowledge communication blocks use the algorithm given in Figure 3. This is a slight modification of the NBX algorithm [8]. The algorithm first posts nonblocking

1 **Algorithm:** CORRESPONDING COMMUNICATION ALGORITHM

2 **Input:** Receiver rank expression: E_e
       Sender rank expression: E_s
       Data expression: E_d
       Storage location expression: E_l
       List of environments for where clauses: *EnvSet*
       Local environment: L
       My rank: m

3 *receives* $\leftarrow$ *empty list*
4 **foreach** *e* in *EnvSet* **do**
5 $\quad$ $e' \leftarrow$ *extend_env* (L, e)
6 $\quad$ *sender* $\leftarrow$ *eval* (E_s, e')
7 $\quad$ *receiver* $\leftarrow$ *eval* (E_r, e')
8 $\quad$ **if** *sender* $= m$ **then**
9 $\quad\quad$ *data* $\leftarrow$ *eval* (E_d, e')
10 $\quad\quad$ **start sending** *data* **to** *receiver*
11 $\quad$ **if** *receiver* $= m$ **then**
12 $\quad\quad$ **begin receiving** *data* **from** *sender*
13 $\quad\quad$ *loc* $\leftarrow$ *eval* (E_l, e')
14 $\quad\quad$ *operator* $\leftarrow$ *eval* (E_o, e')
15 $\quad\quad$ *receives* $\leftarrow$ *append(receives, ⟨loc, data, operator⟩)*
16 **wait for all sends and receives to complete**
17 **foreach** ⟨*loc, data, operator*⟩ in *receives* **do**
18 $\quad$ **apply** *operator* **to** ⟨*loc, data*⟩

Fig. 2. Algorithm for the corresponding knowledge case

sends as before, but the sends in this case require an acknowledgment from the receiver before completing the send. It then enters the NBX termination loop. This loop tests to see if an incoming message is pending, and if so receives the message and stores the result in the output list. It then checks if all pending sends have completed. If so, the algorithm begins a nonblocking barrier which will signal that all processes have finished communicating. Each process continues to receive messages until the barrier is completed.

In this case, receivers do not know how many messages they will receive, in which order the messages will arrive, or the environments used on the senders to generate the messages. For this reason, the sender must include the values of *where*-bound variables that are used by the receiver. As a message is received, the reduction operator is applied within the environment included in the message rather than the one available locally.

6   Implementation

Our prototype implementation consists of two parts: a compiler written in Scheme and a runtime library written in C++. The Scheme portion of the compiler converts Kanor expressions into C++. The resulting code relies heavily on the runtime library, which performs most of the work in the communication and reduction operations.

1 **Algorithm:** SENDER COMMUNICATION ALGORITHM

2 **Input**: Receiver rank expression: E_e
    Sender rank expression: E_s
    Data expression: E_d
    Storage location expression: E_l
    List of environments for `where` clauses: *EnvSet*
    Local environment: L
    My rank: m

3 **foreach** e *in EnvSet* **do**
4    $e' \leftarrow$ *extend_env* (L, e)
5   *sender* $\leftarrow$ *eval* (E_s, e')
6   **if** *sender* $= m$ **then**
7   *data* $\leftarrow$ *eval* (E_d, e')
8       $fv \leftarrow$ *vars*$(e) \cap$ *free_vars*(E_l)
9   *vals* $\leftarrow$ *lookup*(fv, e')
10   **send** $\langle data, vals \rangle$ **to** *eval* (E_r, e')

11 *done* $\leftarrow$ *false*
12 *barrier_active* $\leftarrow$ *false*
13 **while** *not done* **do**
14   *probe for message*
15   **if** *message waiting* **then**
16   **receive** $\langle data, e', sender \rangle$
17   **send acknowledgment to** *sender*
18       $e' \leftarrow$ *extend_env* (L, e')
19   *loc* $\leftarrow$ *eval* (E_l, e')
20   *operator* $\leftarrow$ *eval* (E_o, e')
21   **apply** *operator* **to** $\langle loc, data \rangle$

22   **if** *barrier_active* **then**
23   **if** *barrier is complete* **then**
24   *done* $\leftarrow$ *true*

25   **else**
26   **if** *all sends have been acknowledged* **then**
27   *start nonblocking barrier*
28   *barrier_active* $\leftarrow$ *true*

Fig. 3. Algorithm for the sender knowledge case

6.1 Compiler

There is a small wrapper script for the compiler that extracts Kanor *@communicate* blocks, converts them into S-expressions, and passes them to the main Kanor compiler, which compiles them into C++ using MPI. The resulting C++ code then replaces the *@communicate* block. The design of the Scheme portion of the compiler is modeled after the nanopass framework [13]. Structuring the compiler into many passes, each of which performs very little work, enables rapid experimentation with a variety of implementation approaches, which is crucial during this early prototype implementation phase.

At a high level, the compiler converts *where* clauses into C++ *for* loops or *if* statements as appropriate. The innermost body adds transfer expressions to a context implemented by the runtime. For example,

@communicate corresponding { *a@i <<= b@0* **where** *i* **in world**, *(i % 2) == 0* }

would compile into something like:

```
{
  corresponding_communicate ctx;
  for(int i = 0; i < world.size(); i++)
    if((i % 2) == 0) { ctx.add_transfer(a, i, b, 0); }
}
```

The other main function performed by the compiler is synthesis of message structures and associated reduction operators. This is necessary for sender-only knowledge *@communicate* blocks in order to handle environments correctly. For example, consider the statement:

@communicate sender {
  A[k]@i <<= B[k]@j
  where *i* **in world**, *j* **in world**, *k* **in** {*0 ... 10*}, *k % stride == 0*
}

Here, receivers cannot predict where to store values they receive, because the location depends on the value of *stride* on the sender processor. Thus, when a sender sends the value of *B[k]*, it must also send the associated value of *k* so the receiver can store it in the correct location. In order to do this, the compiler generates a structure such as:

struct *send_data* {
  int *k;*
  double *B_k;*
  *send_data(**int** k, **double** B_k) : k(k), B_k(B_k) {}*
};

The compiler also wraps the user-specified reduction operator (assignment in this case) with a new operator that unpacks the message structure, such as:

void *set_array(**double** *A, send_data msg) { A[msg.k] = msg.B_k; }*

Finally, the compiler also generates serialization code for messages, such as those using array slices, that might have variable lengths.

6.2   Runtime

The primary purpose of the runtime library is to implement the various communication protocols. This is facilitated by a context class, as mentioned previously. The context class provides an *add_transfer* method, which indicates that a certain data transfer will take place. The context class then executes the set of transfers. We provide contexts for both corresponding and sender communication protocols, and the compiler selects the correct context based on the user-supplied hint. The context is also responsible for managing any temporary buffer space needed to realize Kanor's semantics.

The corresponding context implements the algorithm in Figure 2. For corresponding communication, the receiver can always tell how many messages it will receive, and therefore can start a receive for each transfer in which it is the receiver. Likewise, the context initiates a send for each transfer where a given processor is sending.

The sender context is somewhat more complicated because the communication protocol is more complex. Since receivers cannot determine the amount of data to expect, we must use the algorithm given in Figure 3. This algorithm handles, with minimal overhead, the case where each processor may receive an unknown amount of data. For each transfer in which a given processor is sending, the sender context initiates a synchronous send—i.e., a send that will not complete unless the message is received and acknowledged. After all sends have been started, the context enters a receive and termination loop. If messages are waiting to be received, the context receives the message and applies the reduction operator. Once all of a process's sends have completed, it starts a nonblocking barrier [5]. The barrier completes only after all processes have received all the data that they will receive.

7 Performance

Programmers using a declarative language for communication can enjoy the benefits discussed in Section 2 while paying little or no *abstraction penalty*. That is, the resulting communication can be as efficient as the MPI equivalent. Furthermore, the declarative approach enables optimizations that can make some communications more efficient than their lower-level equivalents.

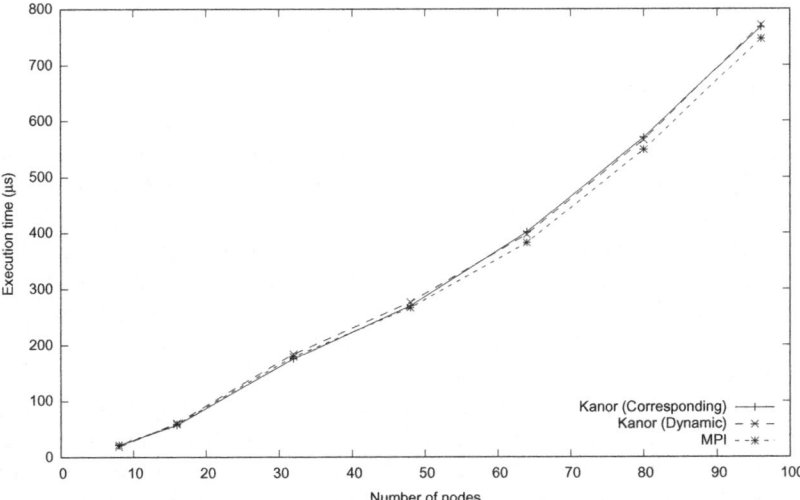

Fig. 4. Time required to execute the first example communication statement from Section 1 as the number of processes increases. This graph compares point-to-point MPI communication with Kanor versions using both the corresponding sender algorithms.

To show that our approach is feasible, we have conducted preliminary benchmarks for our unoptimized Kanor implementation. Evidence that Kanor is competitive with point-to-point MPI code can be seen in Figure 4, which shows the time in microseconds to execute the first example from Section 1 as the number of processors increases. The graph shows three communication variants: a Kanor version using the corresponding-knowledge algorithm, a Kanor version using the sender-knowledge algorithm (NBX), and a point-to-point MPI version. The reported time is the arithmetic mean of four runs, each of 15,000 collective operations. Measurements were performed on Odin, a 128-node InfiniBand cluster (Single Data Rate). Each node is equipped with two 2 GHz Dual Core Opteron 270 CPUs and 4 GiB RAM. In order to emphasize the communication cost, we limited the program to only one task per node. Figure 4 shows that there is minimal overhead as a result of using Kanor.

8   Related Work

Partitioned Global Address Space (PGAS) languages, such as UPC [14], Co-array Fortran [12], X10 [4], and Chapel [3], provide programmers with explicit control over data placement, but still use shared-memory-like semantics with implicit communication. They distinguish between references to local vs. remote memory, however; the earlier High-Performance Fortran (HPF) language was similar to PGAS, but without this explicit distinction [9]. These languages differ from Kanor in several ways: they provide a global address space, they do not allow (or expect) programmers to specify communication explicitly, they do not segregate communication from computation, and they do not provide collective semantics for general communications. Kanor, on the other hand, exposes a distributed address space without direct access to remote memory; communication operations must be specified explicitly, rather than implicitly through a memory consistency model. Kanor also has separate communication blocks, separated from an application's computation. These communication operations are collective, matching the BSP model often used in message-passing programs.

Kanor @*communicate* blocks are similar to *sparse collective operations* as proposed for the upcoming MPI-3 standard [6]. The main difference is that Kanor allows a simpler high-level specification of the patterns while retaining all optimization possibilities.

Erlang is a declarative programming language designed for developing highly scalable, reliable concurrent applications [1]. Erlang supports dynamic creation and destruction of processes. Although Erlang is a declarative, functional programming language, its message passing abstractions resemble those in imperative languages since programmers write individual sends and receives. Unlike Kanor, Erlang does not provide or encourage collective communication.

Eden [10] is a high-level declarative language for parallel programming. Their approach is to start with a more declarative language (Haskell) and add support for parallelism. In contrast, we are adding declarative features to C++. While performing on par with MPI is an explicit non-goal for Eden, there is nothing fundamental about the design of Kanor that prevents it from achieving performance similar to pure MPI programs. Eden has a much richer processor abstraction than is provided by Kanor.

Data Parallel Haskell (DPH) adds *parallel arrays* to Haskell along with operations on parallel arrays, e.g., fold. DPH lacks mechanisms to send messages explicitly, and lacks X10- or Chapel-like constructs to express locality. However, it supports nested parallelism, similar to NESL, which is a nested data-parallel language [2].

XcalableMP's [16] *gmove* construct specifies collective communications as pragmas using concepts similar to those in Kanor. However, a single *gmove* statement cannot perform data reductions and covers only the global knowledge case while other cases require a mix of multiple pragmas and serial code.

9   Conclusion and Future Work

We demonstrated it is both feasible and desirable to use a declarative domain-specific language to express communication patterns explicitly. Programs that use Kanor are shorter, simpler, and safer than their MPI equivalents.

Perhaps the greatest limitation of our approach is that some problems are not naturally expressed in BSP style. Another limitation is that receiver-only knowledge patterns can't be expressed within a single @*communicate* block. Receiver-only patterns are inherently inefficient, however, so this limitation is minor.

Our model is not restricted to message passing over distributed memory. We also hope to explore a shared memory version of Kanor. There are two obvious approaches to integrating shared memory into the Kanor model. The first is to allow multiple threads per Kanor process. The second is to allow multiple Kanor processes within a single address space, but allow them to communicate only through Kanor.

We also plan to add communication optimizations to the Kanor execution engine. Those optimizations are similar to optimizations for sparse collective operations [6].

We intend to continue exploring different evaluation rules, to better understand their effects on the expressiveness of Kanor. We plan to explore one-sided and non-blocking communication to exploit the communication/computation overlap inherent in BSP applications. An interesting problem is to infer the *global/corresponding/sender* annotations. We may also allow additional programmer annotations (for example, whether a reduction operator is commutative) to enable additional optimizations.

Acknowledgments. This research was supported in part by NSF grant CSR-0834722 and by a grant from the Lilly Foundation. The Odin cluster used for our benchmarks was purchased using NSF grant EIA-0202048.

We thank Pushkar Ratnalikar and Nilesh Mahajan for porting several MPI programs to Kanor, investigating several papers describing related work, and for their comments on the paper. Amr Sabry and Dan Friedman provided helpful comments on earlier drafts. We also thank Nick Edmonds, Josh Hursey, Joseph Cottam, and members of Indiana's Open Systems Lab and PL Wonks groups for many helpful suggestions. We appreciate the insightful comments provided by the anonymous referees.

References

1. Armstrong, J.: The development of Erlang. In: International Conference on Functional Programming, pp. 196–203. ACM, New York (1997)
2. Blelloch, G.: NESL: A nested data-parallel language (version 3.1). Tech. Rep. CMU-CS-95-170, CMU (January 1995)

3. Chamberlain, B., Callahan, D., Zima, H.: Parallel programmability and the Chapel language. Int'l. Journal of High Performance Computing Applications 21(3), 291–312 (2007)
4. Charles, P., Grothoff, C., Saraswat, V.A., Donawa, C., Kielstra, A., Ebcioglu, K., von Praun, C., Sarkar, V.: X10: an object-oriented approach to non-uniform cluster computing. In: Object-Oriented Programming, Systems, Languages, and Applications, pp. 519–538 (2005)
5. Hoefler, T., Lumsdaine, A., Rehm, W.: Implementation and performance analysis of non-blocking collective operations for MPI. In: Supercomputing. IEEE/ACM (November 2007)
6. Hoefler, T., Traeff, J.L.: Sparse collective operations for MPI. In: International Parallel & Distributed Processing Symposium, HIPS 2009 Workshop, Rome, Italy (May 2009)
7. Hoefler, T., Willcock, J., Chauhan, A., Lumsdaine, A.: The Case for Collective Pattern Specification. In: 1st ACM Workshop on Advances in Message Passing (AMP 2010) (June 2010)
8. Hoefler, T., Siebert, C., Lumsdaine, A.: Scalable communication protocols for dynamic sparse data exchange. In: Principles and Practice of Parallel Programming, pp. 159–168. ACM, New York (2010)
9. Kennedy, K., Koelbel, C., Zima, H.: The rise and fall of High Performance Fortran: An historical object lesson. In: History of Programming Languages III, p. 7-1–7-22. ACM, New York (2007)
10. Loogen, R., Ortega-Mallén, Y., Peña-Marí, R.: Parallel functional programming in Eden. Journal of Functional Programming (15), 431–475 (2005)
11. MPI Forum: MPI: A Message-Passing Interface Standard. Version 2.2 (September 4, 2009)
12. Numrich, R.W., Reid, J.: Co-array Fortran for parallel programming. SIGPLAN Fortran Forum 17(2), 1–31 (1998)
13. Sarkar, D., Waddell, O., Dybvig, R.K.: A nanopass infrastructure for compiler education. SIGPLAN Not. 39(9), 201–212 (2004)
14. UPC Consortium: UPC Language Specification, v1.2 (May 2005), http://upc.lbl.gov/docs/user/upc_spec_1.2.pdf
15. Valiant, L.G.: A bridging model for parallel computation. Communications of the ACM 33(8), 103–111 (1990)
16. XcalableMP Specification Working Group: Application Program Interface Version 1, Draft 0.7. Tech. rep. (November 2009)

Joinads: A Retargetable Control-Flow Construct for Reactive, Parallel and Concurrent Programming

Tomas Petricek[1] and Don Syme[2]

[1] Faculty of Mathematics and Physics, Charles University in Prague, Czech Republic
[2] Microsoft Research, Cambridge, United Kingdom
tomas@tomasp.net, dsyme@microsoft.com

Abstract. Modern challenges led to a design of a wide range of programming models for reactive, parallel and concurrent programming, but these are often difficult to encode in general purpose languages. We present an abstract type of computations called *joinads* together with a syntactic language extension that aims to make it easier to use joinads in modern functional languages.

Our extension generalizes pattern matching to work on abstract computations. It keeps a familiar syntax and semantics of pattern matching making it easy to reason about code, even in a non-standard programming model. We demonstrate our extension using three important programming models – a reactive model based on events; a concurrent model based on join calculus and a parallel model using futures. All three models are implemented as libraries that benefit from our syntactic extension. This makes them easier to use and also opens space for exploring new useful programming models.

1 Introduction

Today, we often write programs for environments that are in some way non-standard when contrasted to traditional expression-based computation. In parallel programming, multiple functions can execute at one time; in concurrent programming, we need to express synchronization of multiple processes; in reactive programming, we write code that waits for events from the GUI or completion of background tasks and acts in response. Academia offers many programming models for these domains, and more and more of them are being used by main-stream developers, though often awkwardly through object-model, library-based encodings.

This raises the question of providing language support for those models. Specialized languages become overly specific, while library-based solutions often result in unnatural encodings where the declarative intent of the program is lost. We believe that the best option lies in between. If we identify a repeating pattern, we can provide a syntactic extension that enables a large number of programming models. This approach is successfully utilized by Haskell's monads [2], computation expressions in F# [1] and LINQ queries in C# [25]. Language supported, pattern-based approaches are particularly appealing in the area of reactive, parallel and concurrent programming, where we need to choose between different programming models.

R. Rocha and J. Launchbury (Eds.): PADL 2011, LNCS 6539, pp. 205–219, 2011.
© Springer-Verlag Berlin Heidelberg 2011

In this paper, we identify a repeating pattern that we call *joinad*. It arises when we need to pattern match on abstract computations as opposed to pattern matching on concrete values. The key contributions of our work are the following:

Practically useful. Joinads naturally fit with many important programming models. Section 2 supports this claim by showing a reactive programming model (Section 2.1) inspired by imperative streams and FRP [17, 23]; a concurrent programming model (Section 2.2) based on join calculus [5] bearing similarities to JoCaml and Cω [6, 7]; and a parallel programming model (Section 2.3) based on futures, which can nicely express some aspects of Manticore [12].

Lightweight extension. We present a construct that allows pattern matching on abstract computations (e.g. event, channel or future). The construct is just a syntactic sugar and is translated into calls to two simple operations provided by a joinad. We describe the two operations as well as the translation procedure (Section 3).

Well-founded. As usual when describing abstract computation types, we identify a set of laws that needs to be followed by joinad operations. We chose laws such that our generalized pattern matching construct keeps the familiar semantics of ML-style pattern matching (Section 4) and we describe the relationship between joinads and other abstract computations (Section 5), most notably commutative monads.

This paper presents joinads as an extension to F# computation expressions. Thanks to their relations with monads, the presented ideas could be applied to any language with support for monads. We start by giving background on F# computation expressions.

1.1 Computation Expressions

Computation expressions [1, 3] are a syntactic mechanism in F# that provides convenient syntax for a range of computations. As with Haskell monadic syntax and LINQ queries, F# computation expressions are just a syntactic mechanism. In practice, they are usually used with established computation type (e.g. monoids, monads or additive monads [4; Ch. 2]) which satisfies specific laws.

We demonstrate computation expressions using a reactive programming model described in detail in [4]. As we'll see later, the work presented in this paper can be used (among other things) to encode complex interaction patterns in this reactive programming model. We work with values of type Event<'T>, which represents running computations that emit values of type 'T along the way. The type can be modeled as a sequence of time-value pairs. The following example shows a counter of button clicks that limits the rate of clicks to one per second:

```
1: let rec counter n = event {
2:   let! me = btn.Click
3:   let! _ = Event.sleep 1000
4:   return n + 1
5:   return! counter (n + 1) }
```

Let's look what the code does assuming appropriate definitions of event, Event.sleep and the Click property. The recursive function returns a computation Event<int>. Its body is wrapped in an event { ... } block, which provides the meaning of constructs such as `return`, `return!` and `let!` The computation starts by waiting for the `btn.Click` event (line 2). The meaning of the `let!` construct is that it waits for the first occurrence of the specified event and runs the rest of the code once afterwards. Next, we create an event that will occur after 1 second and wait for its occurrence (line 3).

The `return` construct is used to emit values from the event (line 4). We can call it multiple times because an event may be triggered repeatedly. The `return!` construct performs a tail-call to implement looping and wait for the next `Click`.

In computation expressions, the semantics of the control-flow in the syntactic fragment enclosed by event { .. } is determined by the operations on the `event` value. The expected types of operations and translation rules are defined in [3], and in this case the `event` value supports the following operations:

```
event.Bind        : M<'T> → ('T → M<'R>) → M<'R>
event.Combine     : M<'T> * M<'T> → M<'T>
event.Return      : 'T → M<'T>
event.ReturnFrom  : M<'T> → M<'T>
```

The type signatures bare similarity to the `MonadPlus` typeclass in Haskell, although the library for events described above does not satisfy the usual `MonadPlus` laws. The following snippet demonstrates how the translation looks for the above example.

```
let rec counter n =
  event.Bind (btn.Click, fun me ->
    event.Bind (Event.sleep 1000, fun _ ->
      event.Combine (
          event.Return n,
          event.ReturnFrom (counter (n + 1)))))
```

Uses of the `let!` construct are translated into calls to the `Bind` operation and the rest of the computation is transformed to a continuation. In this example, binding waits for the first occurrence of an event, and so the continuation will be called at most once, but other computations may run it multiple times (e.g. each time an event occurs).

The `return` construct is translated into calls to the `Return` operation, which has the same type signature as monadic *unit* and lifts a value `'T` into a computation `M<'T>`. The `return!` construct translates to the `ReturnFrom` operation, in this case implemented as an identity function. Finally, when we sequence multiple event generators, the computations are combined using the `Combine` construct.

2 Joinads by Example

In this section, we introduce our lightweight syntactic extension and we'll explore several practically useful programming models that can benefit from it. The translation to underlying operations will be discussed later in section 3.

2.1 Reactive Programming with Events

First we show a more complicated example of user interaction logic using the reactive programming model from the previous section. Let's say that we want to reset the counter by pressing the `Esc` key. In practice, this means that we need to wait for either

Click event or KeyDown event that carries the Esc key code as a value. Unfortunately, this cannot be written directly using existing constructs. Using let! we can wait for multiple events only sequentially, but not in parallel.

What do we do about this? One approach is to use a combinator library that allows us to filter and compose events. However, a combinator approach to waiting for multiple events makes the syntax more involved and forces the programmer to leave the computation expression syntax. A solution using this approach is available in Appendix A [27] for a comparison. The alternative approach described in this paper is to add a new syntactic control flow construct to computation expressions to express joining computations. What should this control flow operator look like? It should

- accept multiple computations as inputs,
- select a computation path based on the values produced by computations, and
- enable its use with different computation types (be retargetable).

In functional languages, the similarity to pattern matching is easy to note. In ML-like languages, the match construct accepts multiple values as inputs, and selects a computation path based on the inputs. In our proposal, the match! construct plays an analogous role for computations. Similarly, just as let! allows binding on computation values, match! allows pattern matching on computation values. The resettable counter can be written as follows:

```
1:  let rec counter n = event {
2:    match! btn.Click, win.KeyDown with
3:    | !_, _    -> let! _ = Event.sleep 1000
4:                  return n + 1
5:                  return! counter (n + 1)
6:    | _, !Esc -> return! counter 0 }
```

The match! construct takes one or more computations as arguments (line 2). In our example, we give it two values of type Event<'T>. The patterns (lines 3, 6) belong to a syntactic category that we call *computation patterns*. The form "!<*pat*>" means that we need to obtain a matching value from the computation (in case of events, we wait until the event emits a value matching the underlying ML-style pattern <*pat*>). We call this form a *binding pattern*. The second form (written as "_") is called *ignore pattern*. It specifies that we don't need to obtain any value from the computation. Note that there is a difference between "_" and "!_" (line 3). In the first case, we don't need the value at all, while in the second case, we need to obtain the value (i.e. wait for an event), but we ignore it afterwards.

The meaning of match! in the event-based reactive programming model is that it waits for the first combination of event occurrences that enables a particular clause (when waiting for multiple events, the values of last occurrences are remembered). In the previous example, each clause has only a single *binding pattern* meaning that each clause waits only for a single event. In the second clause (line 7), the value has to match the pattern Esc, so some occurrences of the KeyDown event will be ignored.

As we'll see in section 4, match! should generalize the let! construct. This is indeed the case for events – if we pattern match only on a single computation and specify an irrefutable pattern, the behavior is the same as when using let!

2.2 Concurrent Programming with Joins

Our second example is based on Join calculus [5], which provides a declarative way for expressing synchronization patterns. Joins have been used as a basis for language features [6, 7], but it is also possible to implement them as a library [8, 10].

Programming model based on Join calculus expresses synchronization using *channels* and *join patterns*. A channel can be viewed as a thread-safe container into which we can put values without blocking the caller. A join pattern is a rule saying that a certain combination of values in channels should trigger a specified reaction (and remove values from the channels). We can use match! to specify the combinations of values by pattern matching on multiple channels of type Channel<'T>. A simple unbounded buffer can be implemented as follows:

```
1: let put = new Channel<int>()
2: let get = new Channel<ReplyChannel<int>>()
3:
4: let buffer = join {
5:   match! put, get with
6:   | !num, !chnl -> chnl.Reply num }
```

We start by defining two channels (lines 1, 2). The first one is used for putting values into the buffer, and the second one for obtaining them. The type ReplyChannel<int> is essentially a continuation taking int. In our example, the continuation will be invoked by the buffer as soon as a value (provided by a call to put) is available.

The buffer is implemented using the match! construct provided by the join computation expression. Join patterns are encoded as clauses of match! In our example, we have a single clause (line 6) consisting of two bindings. This means that the body will be called when there is a value in the put channel and also a continuation in the get channel. When the join pattern fires, we pass the num value to the continuation.

The match! construct becomes essential when we have multiple join patterns, each of them binding on one or more channels. The next example shows a buffer that allows storing of two distinct types of values using two input channels. Values can be read using a get channel that returns them as strings. This logic can be encoded using two join patterns that bind on the get channel and one (putInt) or the other (putString) channel for storing values:

```
1: let putInt = new Channel<int>()
2: let putString = new Channel<string>()
3: let get = new Channel<ReplyChannel<string>>()
4: let buffer = join {
5:   match! get, putInt, putString with
6:   | !chnl, !n, _ -> chnl.Reply ("Number: " + (string n))
7:   | !chnl, _, !s -> chnl.Reply ("String:" + s) }
```

Each clause combines two channels (lines 6 and 7) and ignores the third one. If we get an integer value and a reply channel chnl in the first join pattern (line 6), we send a number converted to a string as the reply. The second clause is quite similar.

2.3 Parallel Programming with Futures

The next example shows how to multiply values in a binary tree. We use futures –
values of type Future<'T> that represent a computation that is (or may be) running in
the background and eventually produces a value of type 'T. A computation future
creates a future and can wait for the results of another future using let! The match!
extension allows us to wait for multiple features and pattern matches on the results:

```
1: let rec treeProd t = future {
2:    match t with
3:    | Node(lt, rt) ->
4:       match! treeProd lt, treeProd rt with
5:       | !0, _  -> return 0
6:       | _, !0  -> return 0
7:       | !a, !b -> return a * b
8:    | Leaf(n) -> return n }
```

The function creates a future. It starts by standard pattern matching on the tree (line
2), which is just a discriminated union. If the tree is a node, we recursively call the
treeProd function to create two futures to process both of the branches (line 4). Then
we need to wait for both of the futures to produce a value, which is done using pattern
matching on computations with two binding patterns (line 7). In case when one future
completes earlier and produces 0, we know the overall result immediately, and we can
return it (lines 5 and 6) and the computation automatically cancels remaining futures.

When using match! with futures, it waits for the first future to produce a value and
then checks whether it can run any of the clauses. If yes, it follows the selected clause
and cancels remaining futures. In the other case, it waits for more futures to complete.
This behavior is in many ways similar to the pcase construct in Manticore [12].

3 A Language Extension for Joinads

In this section, we present our language extension for F# in detail. Just like other
aspects of F# computation expressions, it is a retargetable control flow construct
implemented by a syntactic translation to function calls. We first show how the translation works on the examples from the previous section and then present formal translation rules. The joinad operations and laws are discussed in section 4.

3.1 Introducing Operations

The translation of match! requires three functions – the usual *map* operation and two
additional operations that we call *merge* and *choose*. In this section, we gradually
introduce how the translation works, starting with a case where we need only *map* and
a slightly simplified *choose* that doesn't allow refutable patterns in match! clauses.

Simplified choose. We start by looking at the example from section 2.1, but we ignore the fact that the second clause contains a pattern that may fail – we reset the
counter whenever KeyDown occurs. This way, we get an example with multiple clauses
where each clause contains a single binding with an irrefutable pattern.

In this case, we only need an operation that allows us to select one of the clauses. This is the purpose of the *choose* operation, which is explained in figure 1. The translation also needs the *map* operation, which allows us to transform values "inside the computation" and has the usual type ('T → 'R) → M<'T> → M<'R>.

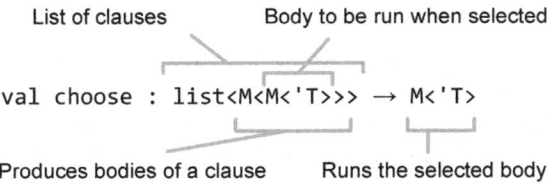

List of clauses   Body to be run when selected

val choose : list<M<M<'T>>> → M<'T>

Produces bodies of a clause   Runs the selected body

Fig. 1. The *choose* operation takes a list of computations. Each of the computations in the list carries (or produces) other computations. These wrapped computations represent the body of the clause that should be called when the clause is selected.

If you're familiar with the definition of monads in terms of *join*, *map* and *unit*, you probably noticed that our *choose* operation looks similar to *join*, except that it takes a list of M<M<'a> computations instead of just a single one. As we'll see in section 4, when a joinad is also a monad, *choose* should be a generalization of *join*. The following code shows desugared version of the example from section 2.1:

```
1: let rec counter n =
2:   choose [
3:     map (fun me -> event {
4:       let! _ = Event.sleep 1000
5:       return n + 1
6:       return! counter (n + 1) }) btn.Click;
7:     map (fun ke -> event {
8:       return! counter 0 }) win.KeyDown ]
```

The two clauses are translated into two elements of a list passed as the argument to *choose* (line 2). Each computation representing a clause is constructed by taking the source event and projecting values emitted by the event into event computations representing the body that should be executed when the clause is selected. This is done using the *map* operation (lines 3 and 7).

Merge. In the previous example each clause contained only a single binding pattern. This means that we didn't need to obtain values from a combination of computations. If we wanted to do that, we would need some way of merging two computations into a single one carrying tuples. To enable this, we need a *merge* operation with the following type signature:

val ⊕ : M<'T> → M<'U> → M<'T * 'U>

The merge operation takes two computations that may produce value of different types and constructs a single computation that produces a tuple of values. The meaning of the operation depends on the computation, but as we'll see in section 4, it should obey certain laws. We'll discuss how the operation relates to monads in section 5 and focus on the translation for now. The following example shows a translated version of the first join pattern example from section 2.2:

```
1: let buffer =
2:   choose [ map (fun (num, chnl) ->
3:     join { chnl.Reply num }) (put ⓜ get) ]
```

The example uses only a single clause, so the list passed to *choose* consists of a single element. However, the clause binds on multiple channels, so we need to obtain values from both of the channels simultaneously. This is achieved by merging the channels using the ⓜ operator (line 3) and then passing the merged channel as an argument to the *map* operation.

The implementation of the *merge* operation for join channels is perhaps the most complicated of the three examples presented in this paper. It creates a new channel, but when a clause is selected in *choose*, we need to remove values from the original channels (e.g. put and get). This can be done by creating an *alias channel* that keeps reference to the two merged channels.

Choose with failures. Earlier we wrote that *choose* takes a list of computations that contain computations to be used if the clause is selected. This simplification does not take failure into account. The outer computation consists of pattern matching that may fail or succeed. In the second case, it produces an inner computation that can be used to continue with. As a result, the actual type signature of *choose* is the following[1]:

```
val choose : list<M<Option<M<'T>>>> -> M<'T>
```

When compared with the signature shown earlier, the only change is that the inner computation of type M<'T> is now wrapped in the Option<'T> type. This allows us to represent pattern matching failure using the None case.

We show the handling of patterns by looking at the translation of an example from section 2.3, which used futures to multiply leaves of a tree. The next snippet shows the code generated for the last two clauses of the example (one that returns 0 when the second future yields 0 and the general case where we wait for both of the futures). The values f1 and f2 store the result of calling treeProd on lt and rt respectively:

```
1: choose [
2:   ...
3:   map (function
4:     | 0 -> Some(future { return 0 })
5:     | _ -> None) f2;
6:   map (function
7:     | a, b -> Some(future {
8:         return a * b })) (f1 ⓜ f2) ]
```

---

[1] In a strict language like F#, we also need to delay the inner M<'T> value to ensure that its side-effects are evaluated only when a clause is actually selected. We omit this detail for simplicity.

The first clause is translated into a computation that applies the map operation to the f2 value (lines 3-5). The function given as an argument to map will be called with a value produced by the future. If the value is 0, it returns Some with a future computation to run (line 4) otherwise it returns None (line 5). The second clause is similar, with the exception that it first combines two futures using the ⊕ operator. Also, the pattern matching always succeeds, so we can omit the None case.

The interesting case is when f2 produces a value. As a result, the first computation of the list we gave to choose also finishes. If it produces Some, the choose operation cancels all other futures in the list (which in turn cancels the f1 future) and runs the body provided in the Some discriminator. In case of non-zero result, it continues waiting until some other clause produces Some. If all clauses produce None, then the choose operation throws a match failure exception.

3.2 Syntax Extension

Let's now look at the syntax of the extension. In addition the standard constructs described in [3], we add a single new case to the *cexpr* category. The match! construct takes one or more expressions as arguments and has one or more computation clauses.

cpat	= _	Ignore pattern
	!*pat*	Binding pattern
ccl	= $cpat_1, \ldots, cpat_k \rightarrow cexpr$	Computation match clause
cexpr	= **match!** $expr_1, \ldots, expr_k$ **with**	Computation pattern matching
	$ccl_1 \mid \ldots ccl_p$	...consisting of several clauses

Clauses do not consist of standard patterns, but are formed by computation patterns.

As a result, we need to introduce a new syntactic category for clauses (*ccl*) and a new category for computation patterns (*cpat*). A computation clause looks like an ordinary clause with the exception that it consists of computation patterns (instead of usual patterns) and the body is computation expression (instead of standard expression). Finally, a computation pattern can be either an ignore pattern (written as "_") or a binding pattern, which is a standard F# pattern [3] prefixed with "!". In the next section, we describe a translation that transforms computation expressions that include match! into ordinary F# expressions.

3.3 Translation Semantics

We extend the translation defined in the F# specification [3] by adding a case for the match! construct. The translation is defined in terms of three functions. The first one translates an expression into an expression that does not contain computation expressions. The next two deal with the body of a computation expression and with a computation clause respectively:

$$[\![-]\!] \quad : \quad expr \rightarrow expr$$
$$\langle\!\langle - \rangle\!\rangle \quad : \quad cexpr \rightarrow ident \rightarrow expr$$
$$\langle - \rangle \quad : \quad ccl \rightarrow ident \times [\, ident\,] \rightarrow expr$$

In section 1.1, we saw that computation expressions are wrapped in blocks denoted by an expression. The result of this expression is a *computation builder*, which exposes operations defining the computation. In the translation, we pass the builder to functions as an identifier and we write $merge_m$ to denote the *merge* operation provided by the builder m. When translating a clause, we also need the parameters of match! These are stored in fresh values and passed to the function as a list of identifiers:

$$\llbracket \text{ } expr \text{ } \{ \text{ } cexpr \text{ } \} \text{ } \rrbracket \quad \equiv \quad \textbf{let } m = expr \textbf{ in } \langle\!\langle \text{ } cexpr \text{ } \rangle\!\rangle_m$$

$$\langle\!\langle \textbf{ match! } expr_1, ..., expr_k \textbf{ with } \quad ccl_1 \mid ... ccl_p \text{ } \rangle\!\rangle m \quad \equiv \tag{1}$$
$$\textbf{let } v_1 = expr_1 \textbf{ in } ... \textbf{ let } v_k = expr_k \textbf{ in}$$
$$choose_m [\text{ } \langle \text{ } ccl_1 \text{ } \rangle_{m, (v1, ..., vk)}; \text{ } ... ; \langle \text{ } ccl_p \text{ } \rangle_{m, (v1, ..., vk)} \text{ }]$$

$$\langle \text{ } cpat_1, ..., cpat_k \text{ -> } cexpr \text{ } \rangle_{m, (v1, ..., vk)} \quad \equiv \tag{2}$$
$$map_m \text{ } (\textbf{function } (pat_1, ...), pat_n \rightarrow \text{Some } \langle\!\langle \text{ } cexpr \text{ } \rangle\!\rangle_m$$
$$\mid \_ \rightarrow \text{None}) \text{ } cargs$$

$$\textbf{where} \quad \{ \text{ } (pat_1, v_1), ..., (pat_n, v_n) \text{ } \} = \text{ } \{ \text{ } (pat, v_i) \mid cpat_i = !pat; \text{ } 1 \leq i \leq k \} \tag{3}$$
$$cargs = v_1 \text{ } ⊕_m ... ⊕_m v_{n-1} ⊕_m v_n \quad \text{for} \quad n \geq 1 \tag{4}$$

When translating match! (1), we construct a fresh value for each of the arguments. This guarantees that any side-effects of an expression used as an argument will be executed only once. The rest of the rule translates all clauses of the pattern matching and creates an expression that chooses one clause using the $choose_m$ operation.

When translating a clause (2), we need to identify which of the arguments are matched against a *binding pattern*. This is done in (3) where we construct a list containing an ordinary pattern (extracted from the binding pattern) and a computation, to be matched against it. Next we combine all needed computations into a single value using the merge operator (4). The operator is left-associative, so when combining for example three values, the resulting value will be of type M<('a * 'b) * 'c>.

Finally, we pass the combined computation as an argument to a map_m operation. In the projection function, we match the actual value against the patterns extracted earlier. If the matching succeeds we return Some containing a delayed and translated body of the clause. The result of translating a computation clause will be of a type M<Option<M<'T>>>.

4 Reasoning About Joinads

So far we described the types of operations that a joinad defines and a translation of our lightweight language extension. Since joinad is an abstract type, we cannot specify the semantics of its operations in general. However, we can specify that they should follow certain algebraic laws. In this paper, we identify some of the laws that we would expect to hold about joinad operations. We do not claim a completeness result for these laws (c.f. Haskell Arrows [22, 26] where equations have been identified, but a completeness result is elusive).

When using standard pattern matching, we have an intuition about transformations that do not change the meaning of program. Since our match! construct bears a close resemblance to an ordinary match, we want to be able to perform similar syntactic transformations without affecting the semantics:

$$
\begin{array}{l}
\textbf{match!}\ m_{p(1)},\ \dots,\ m_{p(n)}\ \textbf{with} \\
\quad |\ cpat_{1,p(1)},\ \dots,\ cpat_{1,p(n)} \rightarrow cexpr_1\ |\ \dots \\
|\ cpat_{k,p(1)},\ \dots,\ cpat_{k,p(n)} \rightarrow cexpr_k
\end{array}
\qquad
\begin{array}{l}
\dots\text{are equivalent for} \\
\text{any permutation } p \text{ of } n \text{ numbers}
\end{array}
\tag{1}
$$

$$
\begin{array}{l}
\textbf{match!}\ m\ \textbf{with} \\
\quad |\ !var_1 \text{ -> } cexpr_1 \\
\quad |\ !var_2 \text{ -> } cexpr_2
\end{array}
\quad\equiv\quad
\begin{array}{l}
\textbf{match!}\ m\ \textbf{with} \\
\quad |\ !var_1 \text{ -> } cexpr_1
\end{array}
\tag{2}
$$

$$
\begin{array}{l}
\textbf{match!}\ m\ \textbf{with} \\
\quad |\ !var \rightarrow cexpr
\end{array}
\quad\equiv\quad
\begin{array}{l}
\textbf{let!}\ var = m \\
cexpr
\end{array}
\tag{3}
$$

$$
\begin{array}{l}
\textbf{match!}\quad m\ \{\textbf{return}\ e_1\}, \\
\qquad\qquad m\ \{\textbf{return}\ e_2\}\ \textbf{with} \\
|\ !var_1,\ !var_2 \rightarrow cexpr
\end{array}
\quad\equiv\quad
\begin{array}{l}
m\ \{\textbf{match}\ e_1,\ e_2\ \textbf{with} \\
\quad |\ var_1,\ var_2 \rightarrow cexpr\ \}
\end{array}
\tag{4}
$$

We first give a brief overview of the equations and then look at simpler laws about the underlying joinad operations that are imposed by these equations. Many joinads are also monads, so the equations (3) and (4) relate match! to operations that are provided by monad (namely *map* and *join* used by let! and *unit* that enables return).

1. *Reordering.* The equation specifies that we can arbitrarily reorder the arguments and patterns of the match! construct. By analyzing the translation, we can see that this only changes the order in which the *merge* operations are applied to computations, so this equation imposes laws about the merge operation.

2. *Match first.* In ML-style pattern matching, we can have overlapping patterns and the compiler can identify unreachable clauses. This equation provides similar guarantees for the match! construct. The equation matches on a single computation, so it talks only about the *choose* operation.

3. *Correspondence to binding.* When the computation provides the let! construct, the meaning of match! in the degenerated case should be the same as the meaning of let! This equation describes a relation between *choose* and monadic *join*.

4. *Matching on units.* If the computation is a monad and provides the *unit* operation, we can specify the meaning of matching on two unit computations. This equation specifies an important aspect of *merge* operation.

As already mentioned, joinad needs to provide the *map* operation. This is common to all functors and follows usual laws [9], so we only discuss laws specific to joinads.

4.1 Merge Operation Laws

The laws that should hold about the *merge* operation are shown below. The first two laws follow from the equation 1 (reordering of arguments). The last law should hold only when the computation is a monad. In that case, the third law is required by the equation 4 (matching on units).

$$
\begin{array}{ll}
u \oplus (v \oplus w) \equiv \text{map assoc } ((u \oplus v) \oplus w) & \text{(associativity)} \\
u \oplus v \equiv \text{map swap } (v \oplus u) & \text{(commutativity)} \\
\text{unit } (a, b) \equiv (\text{unit } a) \oplus (\text{unit } b) & \text{(unit merge)}
\end{array}
$$

$$
\begin{array}{ll}
\textbf{where} & \text{assoc } ((a, b), c) = (a, (b, c)) \\
& \text{swap } (a, b) = (b, a)
\end{array}
$$

The first two laws can be used to arbitrarily rearrange elements of a sequence of computations that is aggregated using the *merge* operation. Together with properties of the translation, this guarantees that the equation 1 will hold. The commutativity law reveals an interesting connection with commutative monads as discussed in section 5.

The third law (*unit merge*) specifies how the *merge* operation behaves with respect to monadic *unit*. In general, we cannot say anything about matching on multiple computations, so this law provides some cue in the case when the computation is a monad. We can apply the law to the equation 4 to get an equation that uses match! with only a single argument. The rest of the equation follows from the fact that *choose* is a generalization of the monadic *join* (as discussed in section 4.2). It may be of interest that this law is very similar to the *product law* of causal commutative arrows [24].

4.2 Choose Operation Laws

The equation 2 (match first) talks almost directly about the *choose* operation, but we can express it in simpler terms. The equation 3 (correspondence to binding) shows a property that must hold when a joinad computation also forms a monad. The laws about *choose* are less obvious due to the complexity of the operation:

$$
\begin{aligned}
&\text{choose } [\text{ map } (\lambda v \rightarrow \text{Some } expr_1) \ m; \\
&\qquad\qquad \text{map } (\lambda v \rightarrow \text{Some } expr_2) \ m \ ] \qquad \text{(ordering)} \\
&\equiv \text{choose } [\text{ map } (\lambda v \rightarrow \text{Some } expr_1) \ m \ ]
\end{aligned}
$$

$$
\text{join} \equiv \text{choose } [\text{ map } (\lambda v \rightarrow \text{Some } v) \ ] \qquad \text{(correspondence)}
$$

The ordering law is essentially the result of direct translation of the equation 3. It specifies that the order of elements in the list given as the argument to *choose* matters. In particular, when there are multiple clauses that always succeed, the body of the first clause will be used. Notably, this law doesn't hold for proposals based on the MonadPlus typeclass [11, 13]. However, we believe that this property of ML-style pattern matching is essential for pattern matching on computations as well.

The correspondence law is applicable only when the computation in question is also a monad meaning that it defines operations *join* and *unit* in addition to *map*, *choose* and *merge*. This is a very important special case that deserves our attention. As mentioned in section 3.1, the *choose* operation bears similarity with monadic *join*. The type of the argument of *choose* is list<M<Option<M<'T>>>>, while the type of *join* is just M<M<'T>>. The correspondence law essentially says that the natural restriction of *choose* to a compatible type is equivalent to *join*.

5   Related Notions of Computations

In this section, we discuss the relationship between joinads and monads. We also discuss an interesting special case when a computation is joinad and a commutative monad. Due to the space restrictions, we do not cover relationships with idioms (also called applicative functors), which use an operation similar to our *merge*, but with a different set of laws. The thesis [4; Ch. 5] contains more information on this topic.

5.1 Relation with Monads

When the computation is a monad, it needs to follow a set of monad laws that can be formulated in terms of *join*, *map* and *unit* (see for example [20]). As we saw earlier, if a joinad is also a monad, the *join* operation can be expressed in terms of *choose*. This means that a computation which is both joinad and monad can be defined just in terms of *choose*, *merge*, *map* and *unit*.

In that case, the computation needs to obey the laws of joinads (discussed in the previous section), but also the laws of monads [20]. We need to reformulate monad laws that involve *join* in terms of *choose*, but this can be easily done by replacing *join* with the definition from the correspondence law.

5.2 Commutative Monads

Judging just from the type signature, it appears that the *merge* operation could be implemented in terms of *bind* and *unit* in a monad. We would use *bind* to obtain values of both of the arguments in a sequence and then use *unit* to return a tuple. This definition has the right type, but if we look at the merge laws, we find a problem.

The commutativity law of joinads states that reordering the arguments of *merge* should not change the meaning of code. This is not, in general, true for the implementation described above. However, if the monad is commutative, we can change the order of bindings and as a result, the described implementation is correct. A more detailed discussion including a proof can be found in [4].

In a retrospective on Haskell, Peyton-Jones considered working with commutative monads as an interesting open problem [15]. Although they are not sequential, the do-notation in Haskell [18] allows only a sequential use. Our work makes it possible to write code that works with commutative monads using match! in a less sequential fashion. If we have four values of type Option<float> representing possibly missing values that specify a location of a rectangle, we can calculate the center as follows:

```
maybe { match! mleft, mtop, mwid, mhgt with
      | !l, !t, !w, !h -> return (l + w/2), (t + h/2) }
```

We cannot write the calculation directly because the values are not numeric types. We first need to extract their content. Using match! we can obtain values of all four computations at once. In commutative monads, the order doesn't matter, so the arguments to match! can be rearranged in any way. The syntax still requires rebinding of all symbols, but it offers an interesting alternative to the do-notation.

6 Related Work

We describe operations and laws of abstract computation type that makes it possible to pattern match on computations when composing computations. We discussed how our work relates to monads [2] and in particular commutative monads. Other related computation types include applicative functors [16] and arrows [22, 24]. We believe that it may be interesting to consider whether a generalized pattern matching could be provided for these computation types as well.

The existing work on pattern matching mainly focused on providing better abstraction when pattern matching on standard values [14, 21]. Extensible patterns in Scala [19] can be composed using custom operators. Some authors propose a generalization based on MonadPlus typeclass. This is an interesting alternative to our work, but it does not obey all equations that we intuitively expect (as discussed in section 4).

7 Conclusions

The key claim of this paper is that a range of important modern programming models can be encoded using a simple, retargetable and theoretically well founded extension. We describe an abstract computation *joinad* and present a lightweight syntax that makes it easy to write computations based on joinads. We use it for encoding declarative programming models for concurrent, reactive and parallel programming.

Our extension is based on pattern matching and we made a special effort to preserve the user's existing intuition about pattern matching. By requiring several laws about basic operations, we guarantee that usual reasoning about pattern matching applies in our generalized scenario. Finally, joinads are related to monads and in particular commutative monads which are considered as an interesting open problem. We show that our construct can be used for binding on multiple monadic values in a less sequential fashion than the one provided by the usual do-notation.

Acknowledgements. We thank to Simon Peyton Jones, Gregory Neverov, Dmitry Lomov and James Margetson as well as anonymous reviewers of this and earlier version of this paper for useful comments and suggestions. Tomas is grateful to Microsoft Research for an internship invitation, which made this work possible.

References

1. Syme, D., Granicz, A., Cisternino, A.: Expert F#, ch. 9. Apress (2007)
2. Wadler, P.: Monads for functional programming. In: Jeuring, J., Meijer, E. (eds.) AFP 1995. LNCS, vol. 925. Springer, Heidelberg (1995)
3. Syme, D.: F# Language Specification, http://tinyurl.com/fsspec
4. Petricek, T.: Reactive Programming with Events (Master thesis), Charles University (2010)
5. Fournet, C., Gonthier, G.: The reflexive CHAM and the join-calculus. In: POPL 1996 (1996)
6. Fournet, C., Le Fessant, F., Maranget, L., Schmitt, A.: JoCaml: A language for concurrent distributed and mobile programming. In: Jeuring, J., Jones, S.L.P. (eds.) AFP 2002. LNCS, vol. 2638, pp. 129–158. Springer, Heidelberg (2003)
7. Benton, N., Cardelli, L., Fournet, C.: Modern concurrency abstractions for C#. ACM Trans. Program. Lang. Syst 26(5), 769–804 (2004)
8. Russo, C.: The Joins concurrency library. In: Hanus, M. (ed.) PADL 2007. LNCS, vol. 4354, pp. 260–274. Springer, Heidelberg (2006)
9. Yorgey, B.: The Typeclassopedia. The Monad.Reader Issue 13, http://tinyurl.com/tycls
10. Haller, P., Van Cutsem, T.: Implementing Joins Using Extensible Pattern Matching. In: Wang, A.H., Tennenholtz, M. (eds.) COORDINATION 2008. LNCS, vol. 5052, pp. 135–152. Springer, Heidelberg (2008)

11. Tullsen, M.: First class patterns. In: Pontelli, E., Santos Costa, V. (eds.) PADL 2000. LNCS, vol. 1753, p. 1. Springer, Heidelberg (2000)
12. Fluet, M., Rainey, M., Reppy, J., Shaw, A.: Implicitly-threaded parallelism in Manticore. In: Proceedings of ICFP 2008 (2008)
13. Syme, D., Neverov, G., Margetson, J.: Extensible Pattern Matching via a Lightweight Language Extension. In: ICFP (2007)
14. Wadler, P: Views: A way for pattern matching to cohabit with data abstraction. In: POPL 1987 (1987)
15. Peyton Jones, S.: Wearing the hair shirt - A retrospective on Haskell. Invited talk POPL (2003), Slides available online at http://tinyurl.com/haskellretro
16. McBride, C., Paterson, R.: Applicative programming with effects. Journal of Func. Programming 18 (2008)
17. Scholz, E.: Imperative streams - a monadic combinator library for synchronous programming. In: Proc. ICFP (1998)
18. Peyton Jones, S. (ed.): Haskell 98 Language and Libraries—The Revised Report. Cambridge University Press, Cambridge (2003)
19. Emir, B., Odersky, M., Williams, J.: Matching Objects with Patterns. In: Bateni, M. (ed.) ECOOP 2007. LNCS, vol. 4609, pp. 273–298. Springer, Heidelberg (2007)
20. King, D., Wadler, P.: Combining Monads. In: Proceedings of Glasgow Workshop on Functional Programming (1992)
21. Okasaki, C.: Views for Standard ML. In: Proc. of Workshop on ML, pp. 14–23 (1998)
22. Hughes, J.: Generalising Monads to Arrows. Sci. of Comput. Prog. 37, 67–111 (2000)
23. Elliott, C.: Declarative event-oriented programming. In: Proceedings of PPDP 2000 (2000)
24. Liu, H., Cheng, E., Hudak, P.: Causal commutative arrows and their optimization. In: ICFP 2009 (2009)
25. Bierman, G.M., Meijer, E., Torgersen, M.: Lost In Translation: Formalizing Proposed Extensions to C#. In: Proc. of OOPSLA 2007 (2007)
26. Lindley, S., Wadler, P., Yallop, J.: The arrow calculus, Technical Report EDI-INF-RR-1258, School of Informatics, University of Edinburgh (2008)
27. Petricek, T., Syme, D.: Joinads (Extended version), http://tinyurl.com/joinads

Results on Out-of-Order Event Processing

Paul Fodor[1], Darko Anicic[2], and Sebastian Rudolph[3]

[1] State University of New York at Stony Brook, USA
[2] FZI Forschungszentrum Informatik, Haid-und-Neu-Straße 10-14, 76131 Karlsruhe, Germany
[3] Institut AIFB, Universität Karlsruhe, Karlsruhe, Germany

Abstract. Complex Event Processing (CEP) has the task of processing streams of events with the goal of detecting event patterns of interest. Today's CEP systems typically assume the *total order* of streaming events. In practice, real-time processing often faces delays caused by network latencies, sensor and machine failures etc. By handling *out-of-order* events a CEP processor needs to keep certain events longer than they are normally needed (in order to handle *late* events). Therefore, an effective removal of overdue events is needed. This work provides a framework for processing events, including also out-of-order events. The framework also implements a general low-level garbage collector. Our approach is based on *deductive rules* where detection of complex events amounts to an inference procedure. Therefore the framework features reasoning capabilities. We provide an open source implementation, and present experimental results of the proposed framework.

1 Introduction

In recent years there has been made a significant paradigm shift toward *real-time* computing. Traditionally, databases and data warehouses are used to analyze what happened in the past. On the other hand, Complex Event Processing (CEP) is about processing real-time events, i.e. CEP is about what has just happened or what is about to happen in the future. Moreover, the CEP systems may provide intelligence by means of automated deduction that happen in real time.

An *event* represents something that occurs, happens or changes the current state of affairs. For example, an event may signify a problem or an impending problem, a threshold, an opportunity, information becoming available, a deviation, etc. We distinguish between *atomic* (simple) and *complex* events. An atomic event is defined as an instantaneous occurrence of interest at a point in time. In order to describe more complex dynamic matters that involve several atomic events, formalisms have been created which allow for combining atomic into *complex events*, using event operators and temporal relationships. The field of Complex Event Processing has the task of processing streams of atomic events with the goal of detecting complex events according to meaningful event patterns.[1] However, in most cases it is typically assumed that events in an event stream are *totally ordered*: the order in which events are received by the system

---

[1] Apart from this task (also known as pattern matching), CEP further addresses other issues like event filtering, routing, transformation, etc.

R. Rocha and J. Launchbury (Eds.): PADL 2011, LNCS 6539, pp. 220–234, 2011.

is the same as their timestamp order. This assumption is called *total order assumption* [7]. In reality events may arrive *out-of-order* due to network latencies, different sources and even machine failures. Many event processing and experimental systems [1,6,3] cannot handle out-of-order events properly. They process events at the time when they come. Hence, a late event will have a larger timestamp than the events which have already arrived earlier. As a consequence, systems not considering out-of-order arrival will disregard the timestamp and may either detect incorrect complex events or fail to detect some valid patterns that occurred [7]. To solve this problem, other systems [7,4,5] propose to use *buffers* to keep event history for a certain time window. If out-of-order events occur, they will be *reordered* in the buffer so that the event stream afterwards can be threated (and processed) as an in-order stream. While this approach works in general, it causes a certain *delay* in event processing. The main requirement of CEP systems is to process data (events) at near *real-time*. This implies that keeping the whole or parts of unnecessary history of events is undesired or even unacceptable. Such approaches rather belongs to database processing, and do not comply with the CEP philosophy of efficient, real-time event detection.

In this paper we present a solution for out-of-order event processing which *does not delay* events. A complex event is split up into a set of *binary goals*, i.e. each goal represents a subpattern of two events. Goals are chained so that in order to fulfill a goal, previous goals in the chain need to be already fulfilled. A complex event is detected when the top goal is achieved. Our approach is based on *deductive rules*. Rules are triggered by relevant events, and they insert certain goals (showing the progress of a complex event detection). In this paper we show how this approach can effectively handle both, in-order and out-of-order CEP. Moreover, since it is grounded on deductive rules, our approach can evaluate background knowledge (while detecting complex events) in order to derive real time situations of interest.

1.1 Motivating Example

We present the following possible use-case to motivate and exemplify the rationale of this paper: A large hedge fund consists of multiple independent but closely cooperating agents and branches. Its main fund is trading stock instruments and is international in scope. Its investment strategy employs complex event processing and automated mathematical models to analyze and execute trades purely electronically. The hedge fund uses CEP based models to predict price changes in stocks. These models are based on analyzing event streams as they are gathered, then looking for movements to make predictions. One such program might monitor stocks of two companies (e.g., Google Inc. with symbol "G", and Microsoft Corporation, "M"). For instance, one rule detects complex event ce_1 when there is increase in Google stock price for more than 20%, see rule (1). Likewise, complex event ce_2 detects the increase in Microsoft stocks of the same percentage, see rule (2). Event ce_3 is represented by rule (3) and triggered when both, ce_1 and ce_2 occur.

To allow more expressive patterns which go beyond of the state-of-the-art [1,6,7,4,5], we integrate *temporal* knowledge (events) with *static* or *updatable* knowledge (for instance, background knowledge related to liquidity of the company). The latter knowledge may be represented as a set of *facts* and *rules*, and can be *reasoned* about when certain events occur. For example, rule (4) checks a special condition proving that company C is *transactional* and *not banned* from trading. Such a company can be determined by additional rules, defining what is a transactional and for trading company (which we omit for space reasons). We see that these rules are *domain specific* knowledge as they, for example, specifies stock trade *policies* specific for certain hedge fonds. We also see that we do not talk only about detection of complex events (e.g., an event a is followed by event b in last 10 seconds), but rather about detection of *real-time situations*, e.g., stocks of company A increased by 15% in the period when stocks of its competitor decreased for 20% and/or are banned from trading. What is a competitor to certain company, and when is a company banned from trading is specified as domain knowledge. Further, it is worth noting that the liquidity of the company may *change* in time. Therefore to detect this situation, rule (4) (as well as other policy rules) need to be evaluated every time when complex events (ce_1, ce_2 and ce_3) occur. Hence to detect real-time situations of interest we combine CEP with an on-line evaluation of the background knowledge. Detection of a real-time situation can be useful for triggering external actions, e.g., whenever complex event ce_3 is detected buy "G"stocks, see rule (5).

$$ce_1 \leftarrow \big(stock(Agent1,'G',Pr1,Vol1) \text{ SEQ } stock(Agent2,'G',Pr2,Vol2)\big) \\ \text{WHERE } (Pr1 < 1.20 * Pr2, verify\_company\_cat("G")). \tag{1}$$

$$ce_2 \leftarrow \big(stock(Agent1,'M',Pr1,Vol1) \text{ SEQ } stock(Agent2,'M',Pr2,Vol2)\big) \\ \text{WHERE } (Pr1 < 1.20 * Pr2, verify\_company\_cat("G")). \tag{2}$$

$$ce_3 \leftarrow ce_1 \text{ AND } ce_2. \tag{3}$$

$$verify\_company\_cat(C) : -category(C, transactional), not\ prohibited(C). \tag{4}$$

$$ce_3 : -trigger\_external\_action(buy\_stock("G", 100)). \tag{5}$$

One significant problem of the model is that stock events (multiplexed from all their traders, agents, sources and observers) may arrive in an *out-of-order* fashion. This happens due to latencies in the network connections form the different sources, or due to different system clocks under events have been generated. As a consequence, out-of-order events may cause a CEP system to detect *wrong* complex events, and hence produce wrong predictions of stock changes.

The out of order event processing problem has two obvious solutions: one is to implement a multiplexer with a delay period (i.e., delay propagation of events for a few seconds, while events are received and ordered in the proper order of their creation date); the other one is to change the event composition algorithm so to accept out-of-order events in the same way as in-order events. The first solutions has the main disadvantage that it has to *delay* processing (while the main requirement for CEP is efficiency in response time) and it needs to store events (which breaks another important requirement of CEP, i.e., to process events as they come and to store as little of the history data as possible). Event processing deals with huge amounts of events (e.g., tens of thousands per second and more), so a delaying mechanism is not optimal. While related work [7,4,5] so far has relayed on that line of research, in this paper we propose a solution founded on the second approach.

The problem of processing of out-of-order events is strongly connected to another important issue. Namely by handling out-of-order events a CEP processor needs to keep certain events longer than they are usually needed (in order to handle late events). Therefore, an effective *garbage collection* of overdue events (from the temporary history of events) is needed. This work also provides the design and implementation of a general low-level garbage collector for events, integrated with an out-of-order event processor.

2   Event Processing in ETALIS

Before we present the solution for out-of-order events, we introduce the reader with our open-source complex event processing system ETALIS[2]. The syntax of *ETALIS Language for Events* allows for the description of *event* patterns as event rules of the form: $complexEvent \leftarrow EventPattern$. Events occur over time intervals. Time instants as well as durations are modeled as nonnegative rational numbers $q \in \mathbb{Q}^+$. Events can be atomic or complex, while no distinction is made in their applicability to rules. An *atomic event* refers to an instantaneous occurrence, i.e., the time interval length is zero. Although not a requirement, atomic events are ground (i.e. predicates followed by arguments which are terms not containing variables). Intuitively, the arguments of a ground atom describing an atomic event denote information items (i.e. event data) that provide additional information about the event.

Events participate in composition rules to trigger complex events. When an *event stream* of atomic events is fed into the system, all patterns are considered and complex events are triggered. The event stream is formalized as a mapping $\epsilon : Ground \rightarrow 2^{\mathbb{Q}^+}$ from ground predicates into sets of nonnegative rational numbers. It thereby indicates at what time instants what simple events occur. As a side condition, it is required that ϵ is free of accumulation points, i.e. for every $q \in \mathbb{Q}^+$, the set $\{q' \in \mathbb{Q}^+ \mid q' < q$ and $q' \in \epsilon(g)$ for some $g \in Ground\}$ is finite.

Given an event stream ϵ, an interpretation $\mathcal{I}$ is called a *model* for a rule set $\mathcal{R}$ – written as $\mathcal{I} \models_\epsilon \mathcal{R}$ – if the following conditions are satisfied:

C1 $\langle q, q \rangle \in \mathcal{I}(g)$ for every $q \in \mathbb{Q}^+$ and $g \in Ground$ with $q \in \epsilon(g)$

C2 for every rule $atom \leftarrow pattern$ and every variable assignment μ , $\mathcal{I}_\mu(atom) \subseteq \mathcal{I}_\mu(pattern)$ where $\mathcal{I}_\mu$ is inductively defined as displayed in Figure 1.

It is worth noting that Figure 1 defines the pattern language which subsumes the set of all possible relations of Allen's Interval Algebra [2]. This set can be used for rich temporal reasoning. However, further analysis of the language is out of the scope of this paper. Instead, we focus how the language constructs from Figure 1 can be detected, not only in streams of "in-order" events but also with the existence out-of-order events. We continue first by briefly explaining how "in-order" events are processed in ETALIS (Subsection 2.1); then in Section 3 we develop an algorithm for dealing with out-of-order events.

2.1   In-Order Event Processing in ETALIS

Given a set of event patterns and a stream of input events, the ETALIS system can compute the final model of all events. To achieve this, ETALIS implements *event-driven*

---

pattern	$\mathcal{I}_\mu$ (pattern)
$\text{pr}(t_1, \ldots, t_n)$	$\mathcal{I}(\text{pr}(\mu^*(t_1), \ldots, \mu^*(t_n)))$
p WHERE t	$\mathcal{I}_\mu(p)$ if $\mu^*(t) = true$
	$\emptyset$ otherwise.
q	$\{\langle q, q \rangle\}$ for all $q \in \mathbb{Q}^+$
$(p).q$	$\mathcal{I}_\mu(p) \cap \{\langle q_1, q_2 \rangle \mid q_2 - q_1 = q\}$
p_1 SEQ p_2	$\{\langle q_1, q_4 \rangle \mid \langle q_1, q_2 \rangle \in \mathcal{I}_\mu(p_1) \text{ and } \langle q_3, q_4 \rangle \in \mathcal{I}_\mu(p_2) \text{ for some } q_2, q_3 \in \mathbb{Q}^+ \text{ with } q_2 < q_3\}$
p_1 AND p_2	$\{\langle \min(q_1, q_3), \max(q_2, q_4) \rangle \mid \langle q_1, q_2 \rangle \in \mathcal{I}_\mu(p_1) \text{ and } \langle q_3, q_4 \rangle \in \mathcal{I}_\mu(p_2) \text{ for some } q_2, q_3 \in \mathbb{Q}^+\}$
p_1 PAR p_2	$\{\langle \min(q_1, q_3), \max(q_2, q_4) \rangle \mid \langle q_1, q_2 \rangle \in \mathcal{I}_\mu(p_1) \text{ and } \langle q_3, q_4 \rangle \in \mathcal{I}_\mu(p_2)$
	$\text{for some } q_2, q_3 \in \mathbb{Q}^+ \text{ with } \max(q_1, q_3) < \min(q_2, q_4)\}$
p_1 OR p_2	$\mathcal{I}_\mu(p_1) \cup \mathcal{I}_\mu(p_2)$
p_1 EQUALS p_2	$\mathcal{I}_\mu(p_1) \cap \mathcal{I}_\mu(p_2)$
p_1 MEETS p_2	$\{\langle q_1, q_3 \rangle \mid \langle q_1, q_2 \rangle \in \mathcal{I}_\mu(p_1) \text{ and } \langle q_2, q_3 \rangle \in \mathcal{I}_\mu(p_2) \text{ for some } q_2 \in \mathbb{Q}^+\}$
p_1 DURING p_2	$\{\langle q_3, q_4 \rangle \mid \langle q_1, q_2 \rangle \in \mathcal{I}_\mu(p_1) \text{ and } \langle q_3, q_4 \rangle \in \mathcal{I}_\mu(p_2) \text{ for some } q_2, q_3 \in \mathbb{Q}^+ \text{ with } q_3 < q_1 < q_2 < q_4\}$
p_1 STARTS p_2	$\{\langle q_1, q_3 \rangle \mid \langle q_1, q_2 \rangle \in \mathcal{I}_\mu(p_1) \text{ and } \langle q_1, q_3 \rangle \in \mathcal{I}_\mu(p_2) \text{ for some } q_2 \in \mathbb{Q}^+ \text{ with } q_2 < q_3\}$
p_1 FINISHES p_2	$\{\langle q_1, q_3 \rangle \mid \langle q_2, q_3 \rangle \in \mathcal{I}_\mu(p_1) \text{ and } \langle q_1, q_3 \rangle \in \mathcal{I}_\mu(p_2) \text{ for some } q_2 \in \mathbb{Q}^+ \text{ with } q_1 < q_2\}$
NOT$(p_1).[p_2, p_3]$	$\mathcal{I}_\mu(p_2 \text{ SEQ } p_3) \setminus \mathcal{I}_\mu(p_2 \text{ SEQ } p_1 \text{ SEQ } p_3)$

Fig. 1. Definition of extensional interpretation of event patterns.

backward chaining rules (which will be explained below). These rules are executed in a *data-driven* fashion. That is, the inference system incrementally furthers the pattern completion as relevant events occur. As soon as the last event required for a pattern fulfillment is observed, the inference system triggers the complex event.

A user defines event patterns of the form given in the left column of Figure 1. When submitted, ETALIS automatically transforms these patterns into event-driven backward chaining rules. These are executable rules that enable detection of complex events at run time. The transformation is performed as follows.

First, an event pattern is binarized left associatively, i.e., operations are coupled to generate only binary formulas, introduce intermediate events for every binary formula and replace these formulas in the original program. This eases the process of automatic construction of *event-driven* rules and helps in implementation of various event operators defined by the language semantics (Figure 1). Apart from this, the consideration of events on "two by two" basis enhances the computation sharing in the pattern detection, and hence helps in achieving better run-time performance. For instance, a formula: $e \leftarrow p_1$ SEQ p_2 SEQ $p_3 \ldots$ SEQ p_n (e is detected when an event p_1 is followed by $p_2, \ldots$, followed by p_n) is binarized by introducing intermediate events (goals) as:

$$e \leftarrow temp_{n-1} \text{ SEQ } p_n$$
$$temp_{n-1} \leftarrow temp_{n-2} \text{ SEQ } p_{n-1}$$
$$\ldots \qquad\qquad\qquad\qquad\qquad\qquad (6)$$
$$temp_1 \leftarrow p_1 \text{ SEQ } p_2$$

Second, each binary formula is then compiled into a set of event-driven backward chaining rules. Each operator, defined by the language semantics, has a specific transformation which is provided by ETALIS system. Due to the space restriction, only the transformation for the sequential conjunction is sketched below. Implementation of other operators follow similar design patterns.

Transformation 2.1 accepts as input a binary sequence $e_i \leftarrow a$ SEQ b, and produces event-driven backward chaining rules[3]. These rules are represented by $r(a)_1$ and $r(b)_1$ in Transformation 2.1. They belong to two different classes of rules. We refer to the first class as to rules used to *generate goals*. The second class correspond to *checking rules*.

---

[3] Here we assume that the process of binarization (which is trivial) has already been completed so that Transformation 2.1 accepts as input only binary patterns.

$r(a)_1$ is a rule that generates goals of type $goal(b^{[-,-]}, a^{[T_1,T_2]}, e_i^{[-,-]})$ when an event a occurs (i.e., when the rule head $r(a)_1$ is satisfied) at some $[T_1, T_2]$. Its interpretation is that "an event a has occurred at $[T_1, T_2]^4$, and we are waiting for b to happen, in order to detect e_i". Obviously the goal does not carry information about times for b and e_i, as we don't know when they will occur. In general, the *second* event in a goal always denotes an event that has just occurred, whereas the role of the *first* event is to specify what we are waiting for, to detect an event that is on the *third* position. Now when an event b happens at some $[T_3, T_4]$, the rule $r(b)_1$ will execute. The rule checks whether $goal(b^{[-,-]}, a^{[T_1,T_2]}, e_i^{[-,-]})$ is true (meaning that an a occurred prior to the occurrence of b, if $T_2 < T_3$) in which case it triggers a (more) complex event $e_i^{[T_1,T_4]}$. Additionally the rule deletes $goal(b^{[-,-]}, a^{[T_1,T_2]}, e_i^{[-,-]})$ to free up the memory (this is an optional operation, and in certain applications it may be omitted).

Transformation 2.1. Sequential conjunction.

Input: event binary goal $e_i \leftarrow a$ SEQ b.

Output: event-driven backward chaining rules for SEQ operator.

For each event binary goal $e_i \leftarrow a$ SEQ b {

    whenever a occurs at some $[T_1, T_2]$, apply all rules $r(a)_i$:

    $r(a)_1$:- insert $goal(b^{[-,-]}, a^{[T_1,T_2]}, e_i^{[-,-]})$;

    whenever b occurs at some $[T_3, T_4]$, apply all rules $r(b)_j$:

    $r(b)_1$:- **if** $goal(b^{[-,-]}, a^{[T_1,T_2]}, e_i^{[-,-]})$ exist and $T_2 < T_3$ **then**

        delete that goal, and trigger event $e_i^{[T_1,T_4]}$ **end if**

}

We have implemented Transformation 2.1, as well as transformations for other operations from Figure 1. Each rule from Transformation 2.1 has been represented as a Prolog rule. In this sense ETALIS is a compiler of event pattern formulas into Prolog rules. ETALIS executes complied rules in a top-down execution mode finding all (complex) events that are triggered as consequences of an event stream.

Although it is out of scope of this paper, let us mention that in our approach event processing is considered under different *consumption policies* [6]. For example, we want to detect event a followed by event b, and the stream contains events: a, a, b. It is a question which event a will be taken for the pattern detection, the first or the second instance. In event processing, consumption policies (or event contexts) deal with an issue of selecting particular events occurrences when there are more than one event instance applicable and consuming events after they have been used in patterns. In ETALIS we have implemented *recent*, *chronological*, and *unrestricted* policy (see [6]); and for practical use with out-of-order events, recent and chronological policies are used.

3   Out-of-Order Events

Let us consider an example event stream from Figure 2. The figure shows four events[5] in the order they have arrived. The time scale shows that the first event occurred at a time

---

[4] Apart from the time stamp, an event may carry other data parameters that are omitted here in order to make rules more readable.

[5] Here each event has the same format as events from Subsection 1.1.

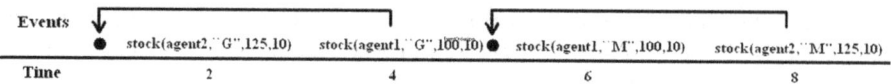

Fig. 2. Received vs. real order of events

point $t_1=2$, the second one at $t_2=4$ and so on. We see that $stock(agent1,"G",100,10)$ has arrived after $stock(agent2,"G",125,10)$, however the arrow over the event, indicates its correct position on the time scale. Therefore, this event is said to have arrived out-of-order. The dot in the figure shows the correct position of the event (i.e., if it was an "in-order" event). Similarly $stock(agent2,"M",125,10)$ is also an out-of-order event, and should have been reported before $stock(agent1,"M",100,10)$.

When the given event stream is used for detection of complex event patterns defined by the rules (1)-(3), the following two issues arise.

Missed complex event pattern due to an out-of-order stream. We see that a sequence $stock(agent1,"G",100,10)$, $stock(agent2,"G",125,10)$ should be detected as a valid pattern. However, with the execution model presented in Section 2 this will not be possible. The problem is that when $stock(agent2,"G",125,10)$ arrives, the system checks whether some $stock(agent1,"G",100,10)$ has previously happened. Since there was no goal inserted by any occurrence of $stock(agent1,"G",100,10)$ (at the time of the check), $stock(agent2,"G",125,10)$ will simply be discarded. At the moment when the event $stock(agent1,"G",100,10)$ is received, the event $stock(agent2,"G",125,10)$ is gone. Thus the sequence $stock(agent1,"G",100,10)$ SEQ $stock(agent2,"G",125,10)$ is missed.

False positives complex event pattern due to out-of-order stream. Evaluating rule (2) for the given stream of events, the pattern $stock(agent1,"M",100,10)$ SEQ $stock(agent2,"M",125,10)$ for ce_2 is detected. However these pattern represents an incorrect sequence. It should not have been detected if the out-of-order had been processed correctly.

3.1   Out-of-Order Event Processing in ETALIS

In this subsection we present a solution for handling out-of-order events. To explain our approach which deals with late events let us consider a simple event binary goal: $e_i \leftarrow a$ SEQ b (using the binarization, other more complicated examples can also be reduced to this case). The solution modifies the initial Transformation 2.1. by adding additional rules. A rule that generates a goal (i.e., $r(a)_1$) is accompanied by a checking rule (i.e., $r(a)_2$) and vise versa (the checking rule, $r(b)_1$, is now added a rule that generates a goal, $r(b)_2$, see also Section 2.1). Therefore we process the sequence in both directions: an in-order direction (as in Transformation 2.1); and an out-of-order direction (with newly added rules in Transformation 3.1.). Although, we show here just the transformation for the sequence operator, we have implemented transformations for all thirteen operators inspired from Allen's Interval Algebra and also our additional various operators dealing with negation, constraints on event rules and aggregates.

Transformation 3.1. Sequence with Out-of-Order Events.

Input: event binary goal $e_i \leftarrow a$ SEQ b.

Output: event-driven backward chaining rules for SEQ operator.

For each event binary goal $e_i \leftarrow a$ SEQ b {

  whenever $a^{[T_1,T_2]}$ occurs apply all rules $r(a)_i$:

  $r(a)_1$:- insert $goal(b^{[-,-]}, a^{[T_1,T_2]}, e_i^{[-,-]})$;

  $r(a)_2$:- **if** $goal\_out(a^{[-,-]}, b^{[T_3,T_4]}, e_i^{[-,-]})$ exist and $T_2 < T_3$ **then**

        delete that goal and trigger event $e_i^{[T_1,T_4]}$;

      end if

  whenever $b^{[T_3,T_4]}$ occurs apply all rules $r(b)_j$:

  $r(b)_1$:- **if** $goal(b^{[-,-]}, a^{[T_1,T_2]}, e_i^{[-,-]})$ exist and $T_2 < T_3$ **then**

        delete that goal and trigger event $e_i^{[T_1,T_4]}$;

      end if

  $r(b)_2$:- insert $goal\_out(a^{[-,-]}, b^{[T_3,T_4]}, e_i^{[-,-]})$;

}

Rules $r(a)_1$ and $r(a)_2$ will be evaluated when an event $a^{[T_1,T_2]}$ occurs (i.e., at $[T_1, T_2]$). Rule $r(a)_1$ will insert a goal $goal(b^{[-,-]}, a^{[T_1,T_2]}, e_i^{[-,-]})$ into the database. Additionally rule $r(a)_2$ will check whether the event a is an out-of-order event, in which case the system will also trigger an event e_i. The event a is an out-of-order event if a goal $goal\_out(a^{[-,-]}, b^{[T_3,T_4]}, e_i^{[-,-]})$ exists in the database, and $T_2 < T_3$. The latter condition says that although event $a^{[T_1,T_2]}$ just happened (at some $[T_1, T_2]$), there is an event $b^{[T_3,T_4]}$ that has already happened such that its timestamp is bigger that the a's timestamp. This suggests that event a is an out-of-order event, and an event $e_i^{[T_1,T_4]}$ should be indeed triggered.

Rules, that will fire when an event $b^{[T_3,T_4]}$ occurs (at some $[T_3, T_4]$), work similarly as those for $a^{[T_1,T_2]}$. Rule $r(b)_1$ will check whether an event $a^{[T_1,T_2]}$ has already happened (i.e., $goal(b^{[-,-]}, a^{[T_1,T_2]}, e_i^{[-,-]})$ exists in the database); and if yes, it will trigger an event $e_i^{[T_1,T_4]}$. That is an in-order case of processing events a and b. Additionally rule $r(b)_2$ will insert a goal $goal\_out(a^{[-,-]}, b^{[T_3,T_4]}, e_i^{[-,-]})$, which will be used by $r(a)_2$ if an out-of-order event a occurs.

Effectively, the price paid for handling out-of-order events is mainly reflected throughout insertion of out-of-order goals (e.g., $goal\_out(a^{[-,-]}, b^{[T_3,T_4]}, e_i^{[-,-]})$) and the fact that they need to be cleared up after certain time (to free up the memory). Therefore, in the next section we discuss a solution for the effective garbage collection of outdated out-of-order goals.

4   Windowing and Pruning the Outdated Events

To deal with out-of-order events safely, no data can ever be purged from memory [7] since event processing assumes processing of infinite streams of data. However, this requirement is an exaggeration in reality and is impracticable due to overuse of memory. Network latencies can be approximated, so it is clear that, at some point, data must be deleted from memory. In the transformation above, occurrences of each event are recorded by inserting a goal in memory. Some of these goals are removed at the time they are "consumed" to build more complex events, while the others can be pruned using a time window[6]. Due to the requirement in CEP that patterns are defined on time windows, we have developed time-based garbage collection strategies. The time-based garbage collection is the natural approach for CEP to release the memory necessary for the execution of events.

We have implemented the time guarantees for out-of-order event detection in different ways: pushed constraints; general garbage collection; and event-pattern garbage collection.

The common way to deal with garbage collection of overdue events is to define a time window for the event pattern and check this constraint during the composition of the complex event. For instance, an event binary goal: $ruleId([ooo\_window(10)])rule$: $e_i \leftarrow a$ SEQ b SEQ c specifies that the length of a time window for out-of-order events is 10 seconds (i.e., $ooo\_window(10)$). This means the system guarantees that out-of-order events will be processed correctly if their delay is shorter that the specified window.

4.1 Pushed Constraints

Our first implementation for out-of-order complex event detection in ETALIS modifies the binarization by pushing the constraints for time guarantees into binary events during binarization, and Transformation 3.1 with checking the constraints before triggering composed events. Pushing the constraints during binarization ensures that time guarantees are checked at each step, so unnecessary intermediary sub-complex events are not generated if the time guarantees are not satisfied. For predicative rules, we push variants for all the terms and variables used in the rule to ensure that all bindings are satisfied during execution (equivalent to a lifting from propositional to predicative logic).

One advantage of this approach is that any constraints can be verified, not only for out-of-order event detection. Such constraints are common in event processing, e.g., the event detection started after or before a certain time. Moreover, this approach is declarative, i.e., new constraints can be defined for any rule and the handling of the constraints is defined by writing a user defined $check\_constraint$ rule for that constraint type. However, the approach also has important disadvantages. First, ETALIS enables sharing of common formulas during binarization (i.e., shared intermediate complex events are computed only once and shared in multiple event formulas). Pushing the constraints and labels for each rule makes sharing not possible anymore. However, a bigger disadvantage is the fact that the time guarantee is checked for each detected event. An efficient solution would clear events when they are overdue, i.e., not every time an event is detected. For instance, if the system detects 100,000 events in two seconds and the time window is set to 2 seconds, then the system is expected to clean the overdue events only once (after two seconds), i.e., without performing 100,000 checks.

4.2 General and Pattern-Based Garbage Collection

We prune expired goals periodically using alarm predicates. The general approach for garbage collection (GC) is utilized to reduce an event path on which out-of-order events are processed. Essentially it enables an out-of-order event to be late for a fixed window

---

[6] When specified time elapses, goals from unfulfilled patterns can be deleted.

Transformation 4.1. Sequence with constraint checks.

Input: event binary goal $RuleLabelConditions e_i \leftarrow a$ SEQ b.

Output: event-driven backward chaining rules for SEQ operator.

For each event binary goal $RuleLabelConditions e_i \leftarrow a$ SEQ b {

whenever $a^{[T_1,T_2]}$ occurs apply all rules $r(a)_i$:

$r(a)_1$:- insert $goal(b^{[\cdot,\cdot]}, a^{[T_1,T_2]}, e_i^{[\cdot,\cdot]})$;

$r(a)_2$:- **if** $goal\_out(a^{[\cdot,\cdot]}, b^{[T_3,T_4]}, e_i^{[\cdot,\cdot]})$ exist and $T_2 < T_3$

    and $check\_constraints(RuleLabelConditions)$ **then**

      delete that goal and trigger event $e_i^{[T_1,T_4]}$;

    end if

whenever $b^{[T_3,T_4]}$ occurs apply all rules $r(b)_j$:

$r(b)_1$:- **if** $goal(b^{[\cdot,\cdot]}, a^{[T_1,T_2]}, e_i^{[\cdot,\cdot]})$ exist and $T_2 < T_3$

    and $check\_constraints(RuleLabelConditions)$ **then**

      delete that goal and trigger event $e_i^{[T_1,T_4]}$;

    end if

$r(b)_2$:- insert $goal\_out(a^{[\cdot,\cdot]}, b^{[T_3,T_4]}, e_i^{[\cdot,\cdot]})$;

}

of time with respect to system clock, denoted by $SystemClock$. The GC window W specifies the maximum time range between the first and last event for any pattern detection (i.e., infinitely long complex patterns are of no interest). Every event $e_i^{[T_1,T_2]}$ should be kept in memory at least the time defined by W, and all events are allowed to be purged if $SystemClock > [T_1 + W]$. GC is applied for all intermediate goals, not only for out-of-order event processing.

We use an alarm rule (7) to prune unnecessary goals. This, sort of, garbage collector is triggered by the system generated events (defined by the system time $SystemClock$ and the GC window W).

$$\begin{aligned}
&garbageCollector(SystemClock) \leftarrow \\
&\quad findAll(goal(\_, X([T_1, T_2], W), \_) \text{ SEQ } SystemClock > [T_1 + W], \\
&\quad goal(\_, X([T_1, T_2]), \_, L)), \\
&\quad\quad while\_do(member(goal(\_, X([T_1, T_2]), \_, L)))(\\
&\quad\quad del(goal(\_, X([T_1, T_2]), \_))) \\
&\quad and\ alarm(garbageCollector(SystemClock + W), W).
\end{aligned} \tag{7}$$

This means that for a time window of 10 seconds, the following sequence of events will not be detected by the rule (1): $stock(agent1,'' G'', 110, 10)$, that is triggered and received at time 2; and $stock(agent1,'' G'', 100, 10)$, that is triggered at time 1 and received at time 21. The general garbage collection works well when there is a single garbage collection window W for the whole system (e.g., the network delay is the same for all sources).

The window essentially specifies what is a guaranteed "minimum" time, ensured by the system, that out-of-order events will be processed correctly: if the GC via alarms is set to W time window, the presented procedure correctly handles out-of-order events within that window.

Let us consider now a case when different elements in the system have *different delays* and time guarantees, i.e., there exist different garbage collection times for different patterns. In this case, the garbage collection alarms are defined at the level of *each rule*.

The procedure starts GC alarms for each rule separately, looking for intermediate goals for those rules checking the condition $SystemClock > [T_1 + Window(e_i)]$.

Similarly to the pushed constraints case, rules are defined with properties, and the binarization pushes the rule properties to sub-components. However, alarm events for garbage collection are scheduled to happen in $Window(e_i)$ time. The scheduling of alarms is done right after the compilation of pattern rules in an event program. The approach is conservative: if one writes patterns without garbage collection window, no alarm is generated. However, we also permit dynamic properties by inserting/deleting properties on-the-fly $ins/del(property(RuleId, PropertyName, PropertyValue))$. In this case, the GC is started *automatically* during the execution (depending on the situation). This means that if the system currently has more available memory it can extend the window time W (which guarantees correct out-of-order event processing); and opposite, if system is currently short with memory (due to other tasks), it can temporarily shorten the window. In this respect, our approach offers possibility for both, the *time-based* as well as the *memory-based* GC and out-of-order processing.

5   Performance Evaluation

We have implemented techniques for dealing with out-of-order events (see Section 3 and Section 4) in ETALIS. It is a Prolog-based system that serves as a testbed for validating the proposed approach. ETALIS automatically compiles the user-defined complex event program into Prolog rules suitable for event-driven pattern detection (e.g., Transformation 3.1 for sequence).

The test cases presented here were carried out on a workstation with Pentium dual-core processor 2GHz CPU and 3GB memory running on Ubuntu Linux. The ETALIS was tested using Yap Prolog version 5.1.3[7]. To test out-of-order event processing in our system, we have developed an automatic event stream generator. We have created different sets of event streams where probability of occurrences of out-of-order events varies between $p=0$ and $p=0,33$, i.e., between 0% and 33% of events are out-of-order. We also show a test, conducted with real data set.

In the remaining part of this section we report the results obtained from the experiments. Results are produced by ETALIS system, which is an open source project. Unfortunately, since related approaches for dealing with out-of-order events [7,4,5] are not open source systems we could not compare performance of ETALIS with them.

Out-of-order experiments. As a test program in this experiment, we consider rules (1)-(2). The test program is executed in two modes: first with the in-order events, and second with streams that contain out-of-order events.

Figure 3 shows experimental results we obtained for *sequence* operator (i.e., rules (1)-(2)). In particular, Figure 3 shows the throughput comparison with in-order and out-of-order event streams achieved by ETALIS (the y-axis). The x-axis shows different percentages of out-of-order events, ranging between 0% (in-order events) until 33% (in average, every third event in the stream is an out-of-order event). We see that the performance loss when out-of-order events are handled is moderate even for high percentage

---

[7] Yap Prolog: http://www.dcc.fc.up.pt/~vsc/Yap/

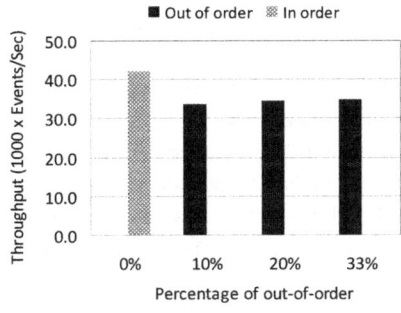

Fig. 3. Sequence: throughput comparison

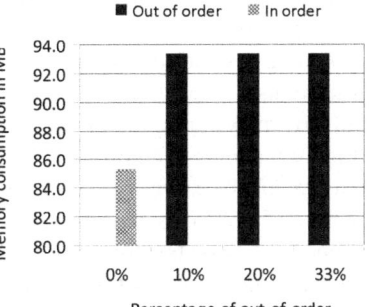

Fig. 4. Sequence: memory consumption

of out-of-order events. It happens mainly due to the fact that more events (goals) are kept in memory; hence more data needs to be indexed and processed. This is evident in Figure 4 which shows considerable bigger memory consumption with out-of-order events. However ETALIS was capable to keep memory consumption constant, even for frequent out-of order events.

For example, an approach presented in [7] completes a similar test with a 60,000 stream in 200 seconds, a 80,000 stream in 400 seconds, i.e., approximatively between 200 and 300 events/second (see Figure 9 in [7]). It is also evident that the presented throughput depends exponentially on number of events. The results were obtained on two Pentium4 3,0GHz machines, each with 512M RAM. Our tests on ETALIS were performed on an 100000 event streams, and we have achieved a linearly-dependent throughput ranging between 30000 and 40000 events per second (for different percentages of out-of-order events). Moreover our approach, when processing out-of-order events, does not introduces *delay* through buffering and reordering as it occurs in related work in [7,4,5] (see Section 1). Unfortunately the source code from [7] (as well as form [7,4,5]) is not open source, hence we could not access and compare that implementation with ETALIS on the same machine.

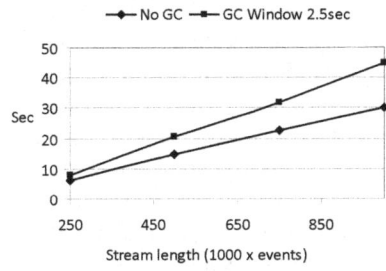

Fig. 5. The execution time for garbage collection

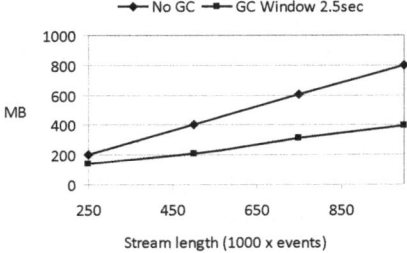

Fig. 6. The memory consumption for garbage collection

Garbage collection test. Figure 5 compares processing of out-of-order events for the previous test but with significantly larger event streams. We run the test with no GC, and with the GC set to pruning window of to 2.5 seconds. The data sets for the garbage collection tests are significantly larger (up to one million of events). From Figure 5 we see that the execution with the GC takes longer. It is due to the fact that garbage collection requires additional processing (i.e., kicks in and releases memory by processing alarm events). However, in may cases this processing overhead is necessary as for large event stream system quickly exceeds the available memory.

Figure 6 shows a memory consumption for the given test. We see that for a 500,000 event stream the memory consumption with no GC is as double as the memory consumption of a GC version with W=2.5 seconds. This test consists of simple non-recursive sequence patterns, but for complex programs and recursive event patterns an efficient resource management is necessary.

Knowledge-based CEP with out-of-order. CEP can be combined with evaluation of the *background knowledge* to detect real-time situations of interest. To demonstrate this functionality, let us consider the following example. Suppose we want to detect the stock price increase in a supply chain system of companies. The following pattern monitors two *stock price increases* in two companies (occurred within certain time window), and checks whether the companies are parts of the *supply chain system*.

```
trendIncrease() ← (stockIcr(CompanyA) SEQ stockIcr(CompanyB)).10
    AND inSupChain(CompanyA, CompanyB).
```

The supply chain system is represented as a set of explicit links between companies, e.g., with linked($CompanyA, CompanyB$) we represent two interconnected businesses involved in the ultimate provision of a product. We assume that such explicit relationships are continuously being updated via according *information events* (e.g., a data mining tool processes different information sources and generates these events). The following transitive closure pattern can then be used to span over semantic relationships between companies scenario where direct supply relationships are represented *explicitly*, and hence discover *implicit* relationships.

```
inSupChain(X, Y) ← linked(X, Y).
inSupChain(X, Z) ← linked(X, Y) AND inSupChain(Y, Z).
```

We tested this application scenario with presence of *out-of-order* events, and results are shown in Figure 7 and Figure 8. In particular, Figure 7 shows throughput obtained for *stockIcr* complex events. To detect *stockIcr* event, ETALIS needs to detect stock price increases of two companies and check the *supply-chain* connectivity (*inSupChain* relations) among them. To prove *inSupChain* relations the system needs to traverse up to 1000 links between companies' relations in real time (on-the-fly) when respective events occur. Percentage of out-of-order events was 20%. For this, rather hard test, we see that throughput declines as ETALIS needs to evaluate more background knowledge (and out-of-order events occur), though memory consumption is kept constant.

Test with real dataset and out-of-order events. All presented tests so far were carried out with probabilistic synthetic data streams. We could not find real out-of-order data sets available (as they are usually kept proprietarily). Still to present a more realistic scenario, we took a history stream of IBM stocks, recorded since 1962 up to now and pro-

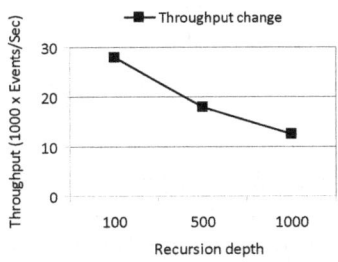

Fig. 7. Throughput change as the size of companies' relations varies from 100 to 1000

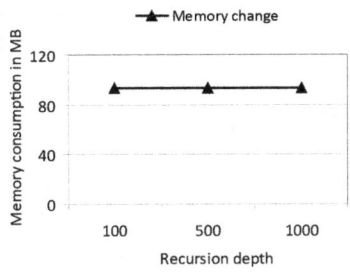

Fig. 8. Memory consumption in the knowledge-based CEP test

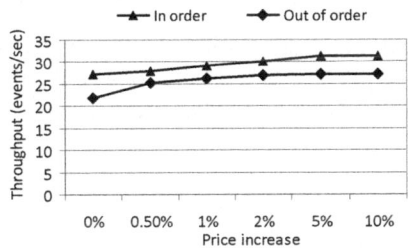

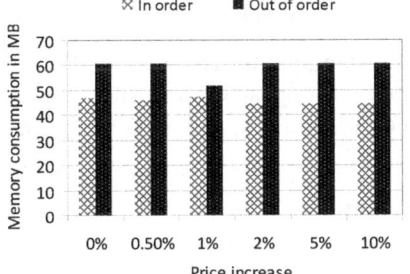

Fig. 9. Stock price change on a real data set

vided by Yahoo Finance[8]. We have modified timestamps of 20% of events so to appear as out-of-order. Format of events provided by Yahoo Finance is stock($ID, Date, Opn, High, Low, Cls, Vol, Adj$) where ID is a company ID; $Date$ is a current date; Opn, $High$, Low, Cls denote the opening, the highest, the lowest, and closing price, respectively; Adj is the closing price adjusted for dividends and splits. The event pattern is represented by rule (8). We monitored the price increase of two successive stock updates w.r.t Adj data. Additionally a filter for the price increase was specified by X, where X varied between 0% and 10%. Figure 9 compares results obtained for the original stream (in-order) and the one modified with out-of-order timestamps. The second graph in Figure 9 shows memory consumption for these two cases.

$$
\begin{aligned}
\text{stockIncr}(ID, Adj_1, Adj_2) \leftarrow \\
\text{stock}(ID, Date_1, Opn_1, High_1, Low_1, Cls_1, Vol_1, Adj_1) \\
\text{SEQ} \\
\text{stock}(ID, Date_2, Opn_2, High_2, Low_2, Cls_2, Vol_2, Adj_2) \\
\text{WHERE } (Adj_1 * X < Adj_2).
\end{aligned}
\tag{8}
$$

We see that the throughput with in-order and out-of-order events is different due to the price we pay for computation of delayed events. We can also observe that the throughput with and without out-of-order events slightly increases as the filter condition gets

---

[8] Yahoo Finance: http://finance.yahoo.com/

tighter. This result is understandable since in this case less complex events is being computed and the throughput (based on the input stream) raises up.

6   Conclusion

We have described an approach for event processing and inferencing over event streams that may also contain out-of-order events. Due to the fact that in real applications one can approximate the latency of the network and other causes for out-of-order events, it is possible to define certain time windows as limits for out-of-order events. We studied various ways to realize these time windows. We presented the design and implementation of out-of-order event processing, combined with general low-level garbage collectors in ETALIS system. We have conducted an experimental study which shows the effectiveness of our approach in minimizing the CPU cost and memory consumption.

Acknowledgments. The work of one of the authors, Darko Anicic, was partially supported by European Commission funded project SYNERGY (FP7-216089). We thank Ahmed Khalil Hafsi and Jia Ding for their help in testing the ETALIS prototype.

References

1. Agrawal, J., Diao, Y., Gyllstrom, D., Immerman, N.: Efficient pattern matching over event streams. In: SIGMOD (2008)
2. Allen, J.F.: Maintaining knowledge about temporal intervals. Communications of the ACM 26(11), 832–843 (1983)
3. Alves, A.: Extensions to logic programming inference engines to support cep. In: RuleML 2009 (2009)
4. Barga, R.S., Goldstein, J., Ali, M.H., Hong, M.: Consistent streaming through time: A vision for event stream processing. In: CIDR (2007)
5. Brito, A., Fetzer, C., Sturzrehm, H., Felber, P.: Speculative out-of-order event processing with software transaction memory. In: DEBS 2008. ACM, New York (2008)
6. Chakravarthy, S., Krishnaprasad, V., et al.: Composite events for active databases: Semantics, contexts and detection. In: VLDB. Stanford University, USA (1994)
7. Li, M., Liu, M., Ding, L., Rundensteiner, E.A., Mani, M.: Event stream processing with out-of-order data arrival. In: ICDCSW (2007)

Nettle: Taking the Sting
Out of Programming Network Routers

Andreas Voellmy and Paul Hudak

Yale University
andreas.voellmy@yale.edu, paul.hudak@yale.edu

Abstract. We describe a language-centric approach to solving the complex, low-level, and error-prone problem of *network control*. Specifically, we have designed a domain-specific language called *Nettle*, embedded in Haskell, that allows programming *OpenFlow* networks in an elegant, declarative style. Nettle is based on the principles of *functional reactive programming* (FRP), and as such has both continuous and discrete abstractions, each of which is leveraged in the design. We have implemented Nettle and tested it on real OpenFlow switches. We demonstrate our methodology by writing several non-trivial OpenFlow controllers.

1 Introduction

Networks continue to increase in importance and complexity, yet the means to configure them remain primitive and error prone. There is no precise language for describing what a network should do, nor how it should behave. At best, network operators document their complex requirements informally, but then are faced with the daunting and unreliable task of translating their specifications by hand into the low-level, device-specific, often arcane scripts used to control today's commercial switches and routers. This low-level programming model often results in devices and protocols interacting in unexpected ways [6], and gives little hope in validating high-level protocols and policies such as traffic engineering, business relationships, and security policies [14,3].

We believe that these problems can be overcome through the use of advanced high-level programming languages and tools that allow one to express overall network behavior as a single program expressed in a declarative style. Although this idea has been suggested by several researchers [3,11], the development of an actual solution has been elusive. There are two aspects of our approach that we believe will result in a successful outcome: First, we abandon conventional switches in favor of flexible, dynamically adaptable *programmable switches*. In particular, we have focused our efforts on *OpenFlow switches* [1], which present a flexible, dynamic, remotely programmable interface that allows them to be controlled from a logically centralized location.

Second, we use advanced programming language ideas to ensure that our programming model is expressive, natural, concise, and designed precisely for networking applications. Specifically, we borrow ideas from *functional reactive*

R. Rocha and J. Launchbury (Eds.): PADL 2011, LNCS 6539, pp. 235–249, 2011.

programming (FRP) and adopt the design methodology of *domain-specific language* (DSL) research.

Our overall approach, which we call *Nettle*, allows us to radically rethink the problem of network configuration. Indeed, we like the mantra, "Don't *configure* the network, *program it!*" [15]. In doing this at a high level, we enable the development of new, powerful, and natural network policies, protocols, and control algorithms.

2 Overall Approach

In this paper, we focus on the problem of configuring a network of OpenFlow switches, varying in size from a single router to several hundred. Such a network may belong to a commercial entity, an Internet service provider (ISP), a university, etc. Typically, certain border routers of such a network interface to the Internet, but our focus is on the internal interactions and coordination between local switches. Unlike most conventional networks, all of the OpenFlow switches communicate with a centralized *controller*. It is here that a Nettle program runs, thus implementing a global control policy for the entire local network. Although a centralized controller will ultimately present problems as the network is scaled upward in size, it is adequate to handle most moderately-sized networks.

Figure 1 illustrates our software architecture. At the bottom are OpenFlow switches themselves. One level up is Haskell, our host language. Above that is a library, Nettle/OpenFlow, that abstractly captures the OpenFlow protocol.

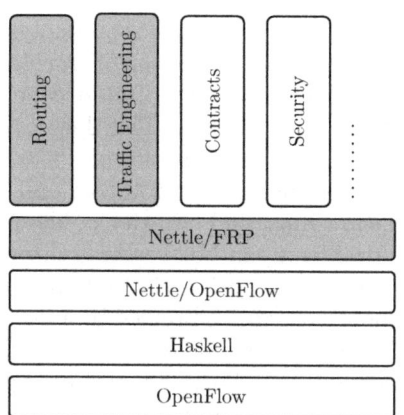

Fig. 1. Nettle layered system architecture

The next layer in our stack is an instantiation of the Functional Reactive Programming (FRP) paradigm. FRP is a family of languages that provide an expressive and mathematically sound approach to programming reactive systems in a declarative manner. FRP has been used successfully in computer animation, robotics, control systems, GUIs, interactive multimedia, and other areas in which there is a combination of both continuous and discrete entities [13,4].

Above the FRP layer, we plan to implement an extensible family of DSLs, each member capturing a different network abstraction. For example, we may have one DSL for access control, another for traffic engineering, and another for interdomain contracts. As a concrete example, in [15] we describe a DSL for expressing a class of dynamic security policies for campus networks and its implementation on Nettle's FRP layer.

In this paper we focus on the Nettle components that are shaded in Figure 1. Our contributions, as outlined in this paper, include:

1. A *core* Nettle/FRP language that supports the development of higher-level control languages by providing two key abstractions:
   (a) A discrete, event-based abstraction that declaratively captures communication patterns to and from OpenFlow switches.
   (b) A notion of continous, time-varying quantities that capture higher-level abstractions such as traffic volume on individual network links.
2. A simple, declarative approach to dynamic routing, based on Nettle/FRP's discrete communication abstraction.
3. A simple, declarative approach to traffic engineering, based on Nettle/FRP's abstraction of continuous quantities.
4. An implementation of Nettle/FRP in the context of the software architecture of Figure 1. We have tested our system on reference implementations of the OpenFlow switches, as well as on real OpenFlow switches.

3   Functional Reactive Programming

In this section we briefly introduce the key ideas and constructs of Nettle/FRP, whose design is strongly influenced by *Yampa* [8], an FRP-based DSL that we previously designed for robotics and animation.

The simplest way to understand Nettle/FRP is to think of it as a language for expressing electrical circuits. We refer to the wires in a typical circuit diagram as *signals*, and the boxes (that convert one signal into another) as *signal functions*. For example, this very simple circuit has two signals, x and y, and one signal function, *sigfun*:

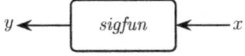

This is written as a code fragment in Nettle simply as: $y \leftarrow sigfun \prec x$, which uses Haskell's *arrow syntax* [9,12]. It is beyond the scope of this paper to describe arrows in detail, but note that signal functions such as *sigfun* will have a type of the form $SF\ T_1\ T_2$, for some types T_1 and T_2, in which case x will have type T_1, and y will have type T_2. Although signal functions act on signals, the arrow notation allows one to manipulate the instantaneous values of the signals, such as x and y.

Nettle/FRP has many built-in signal functions, including ones for integration and differentiation. Of course one can also define new signal functions. For example, here is a definition for *sigfun* that integrates a signal that is one greater than its input:

$$sigfun :: SF\ Double\ Double$$
$$sigfun = \mathbf{proc}\ x \rightarrow \mathbf{do}$$
$$\quad y \leftarrow integral \prec x + 1$$
$$\quad returnA \prec y$$

The first line is a type signature that declares *sigfun* to be a signal function that converts time-varying values of type *Double* into time-varying values of type *Double*. The notation **proc** $x \rightarrow$ **do**... introduces a signal function, giving the name x for the instantaneous values of the input. The third line adds one to this instantaneous value, and sends the resulting signal to the integrator. Finally, we specify the output of the signal function by feeding y into *returnA*, a special signal function that returns the final result.

We can also create and use signal functions that operate on tuples of signals. For example, a signal function $exp :: SF\ (Double, Double)\ Double$ that raises its first argument to the power of its second, at every point in time, could be used as follows:

$$z \leftarrow exp \prec (x, y)$$

In Section 7 we will see how continuous signals can be used to program controllers that alter traffic flow based on signals representing message volume on a link. However, we first wish to focus on a different use of signals, namely to represent *streams of control messages* flowing to and from OpenFlow switches. Nettle/FRP represents message streams as continuous signals that are only defined at discrete points in time. A discrete signal that periodically carries information of some type T has type *Event* T, whose values are either *NoEvent* or *Event* T (the word *Event* is overloaded). Therefore, for example, a signal function that converts a stream carrying messages of type M_1 into a stream carrying messages of type M_2 has type $SF\ (Event\ M_1)\ (Event\ M_2)$.

In a conventional language, an event-based system might be implemented by some kind of call-back mechanism and a loop that handles messages as they arise, one by one. But in Nettle, it is done much more declaratively, where we think of, and program with, message streams as a whole.

Nettle/FRP provides a powerful collection of signal functions and event operators, most of which we introduce as we encounter them in this paper. For reference, they are summarized in Figure 2.

4   FRP for OpenFlow Control

OpenFlow switches maintain a *flow table* containing *flow entries* consisting of a *match* condition, a list of *forwarding actions*, expiration settings, and flow statistics. The match condition can optionally match on most Ethernet, IP, or transport protocol header fields. The forwarding actions include forwarding to

$$
\begin{array}{ll}
never & :: SF\ a\ (Event\ b) \\
hold & :: a \rightarrow SF\ (Event\ a)\ a \\
accum & :: a \rightarrow SF\ (Event\ (a \rightarrow a))\ (Event\ a) \\
integral & :: SF\ Double\ Double \\
tag & :: Event\ a \rightarrow b \rightarrow Event\ b \\
liftE & :: (a \rightarrow b) \rightarrow Event\ a \rightarrow Event\ b \\
mapFilterE & :: (a \rightarrow Maybe\ b) \rightarrow Event\ a \rightarrow Event\ b \\
mergeEventsBy & :: (a \rightarrow a \rightarrow a) \rightarrow [Event\ a] \rightarrow Event\ a
\end{array}
$$

Fig. 2. Signal function and event combinators

specific ports on the switch, flooding the packet, dropping the packet and many other options. When a packet is received by a switch, it searches for a matching entry. If matches are found, the highest priority one is chosen, its forwarding actions are executed and its statistics are updated. If the list of actions is empty, the packet is dropped. If no match is found, the packet is encapsulated and sent to the controller in an OpenFlow message. Optional expiration settings cause a flow entry to expire after some prescribed time.

OpenFlow switches attempt to establish a TCP connection with a controller at a pre-configured IP address. This connection typically takes place over a control network that is separate from the main data network. The OpenFlow protocol defines a variety of messages, including messages to query a switch for information, to command a switch to send a packet and to modify the flow table of a switch. Other messages allow a switch to inform the controller of relevant events, such as the arrival of a packet not matching any flow rule.

We can think of a controller abstractly as a black box which transforms a stream of messages from switches into a stream of commands for switches. We therefore define a Nettle controller as any value having the type:

$$SF\ (Event\ (SwitchID, SwitchMessage))\ (Event\ SwitchCommand)$$

Here we model messages from switches with the *SwitchMessage* data type and commands to switches with the *SwitchCommand* data type. The *SwitchMessage* data type is a sum of several message types. Typically a user is interested in a particular kind of event, and we provide projection functions for each variant in the *SwitchMessage* sum type. For example, the function *switchJoinE* extracts just the messages that occur when a switch connects with the controller. This particular message carries information about the joining switch in the form of a *SwitchFeatures* record. Figure 3 lists the particular projections we will use in this paper. We will explain their meaning as we encounter them in the examples.

*SwitchCommand*s are commands that send packets, modify flow tables, and request information. Among the most important of these is *insertRule*, which can

$$
\begin{array}{ll}
switchJoinE & :: Event\ (SwitchID, SwitchMessage) \rightarrow Event\ (SwitchID, SwitchFeatures) \\
packetInE & :: Event\ (SwitchID, SwitchMessage) \rightarrow Event\ (SwitchID, PacketIn)
\end{array}
$$

Fig. 3. Nettle event projections used in this paper

be used to insert a *FlowRule* into a switch's flow table. We write a *FlowRule* as *predicate* $\Longrightarrow$ *actions*, where *predicate* has type *PacketPredicate* and *actions* has type *ForwardingAction*. For example, the following is a flow rule that forwards packets with source Ethernet address *addr* to port *port*:

$$ethSourceIs\ addr \Longrightarrow sendOnPort\ port$$

Commands can be combined to create compound commands with the command sequencing operator $\oplus$. Figure 4 summarizes the commands used in this paper. We will explain their meaning as we encounter them in the examples.

$$
\begin{array}{ll}
clearTable & :: SwitchID \rightarrow SwitchCommand \\
sendPacketIn & :: ForwardingAction \rightarrow (SwitchID, PacketIn) \rightarrow SwitchCommand \\
insertRule & :: FlowRule \rightarrow SwitchID \rightarrow SwitchCommand \\
deleteRules & :: PacketPredicate \rightarrow SwitchID \rightarrow SwitchCommand \\
(\oplus) & :: SwitchCommand \rightarrow SwitchCommand \rightarrow SwitchCommand \\
(\Longrightarrow) & :: PacketPredicate \rightarrow ForwardingAction \rightarrow FlowRule
\end{array}
$$

Fig. 4. Nettle commands used in this paper

4.1 Basic Event Handling and Switch Commands

The simplest possible controller is one that does nothing at all:

$$
\begin{aligned}
&controller_0 = \textbf{proc}\ msgE \rightarrow \textbf{do} \\
&\quad cmdE \leftarrow never \prec\!\!- msgE \\
&\quad returnA \prec\!\!- cmdE
\end{aligned}
$$

We use the *never* signal function which never outputs any events.

It is a good idea to clear the flow table of every switch as soon as it connects with the controller, so that our switches start in a known state. We can do this by executing a *clearTable* command whenever a *SwitchJoin* event occurs:

$$
\begin{aligned}
&clearOnJoin = \textbf{proc}\ msgE \rightarrow \textbf{do} \\
&\quad returnA \prec\!\!- liftE\ f\ (switchJoinE\ msgE) \\
&\quad \textbf{where}\ f\ (sid, \_) = clearTable\ sid
\end{aligned}
$$

Here we use *switchJoinE* to extract the switch join events from the input message stream. For each such event, we apply the function f to the event, which in turn applies *clearTable* to the *SwitchID* of the joining switch, giving a command that will delete all entries from the flow table of the joining switch. In order to apply a function to each event in an event stream, we use $liftE :: (a \rightarrow b) \rightarrow Event\ a \rightarrow Event\ b$.

Having cleared the table of all connected switches, the switches will send any incoming packets to the controller. In a network that doesn't contain any cycles among its switches, it is safe to simply flood packets, and we can accomplish this in Nettle by writing:

$$
\begin{aligned}
&floodPackets_1 = \textbf{proc}\ msgE \rightarrow \textbf{do} \\
&\quad returnA \prec\!\!- liftE\ f\ (packetInE\ msgE) \\
&\quad \textbf{where}\ f = sendPacketIn\ flood
\end{aligned}
$$

Here we use *packetInE* to extract only the *PacketIn* messages from the incoming message stream. For each such event, we apply *sendPacketIn flood*, instructing the switch to send the referenced packet using the action *flood* (of type *ForwardingAction*), which results in the switch forwarding the packet on every port except the incoming port (i.e. the port on which the packet was received).

We can now create a single controller that combines both the table clearing and packet flooding controllers, as follows:

$$controller_1 = \textbf{proc } msgE \rightarrow \textbf{do}$$
$$clearE \leftarrow clearOnJoin \; \prec msgE$$
$$floodE \leftarrow floodPackets_1 \; \prec msgE$$
$$returnA \prec mergeEventsBy \; (\oplus) \; [\, clearE, floodE \,]$$

In this signal function we feed the incoming message stream to *both* signal functions, naming events in the resulting message streams *clearE* and *floodE*. We then merge these two command streams, resolving the simultaneous occurrence of commands with $\oplus$, and output the merged command stream.

4.2 Programming the Flow Table

In the previous controller, the switches sent a *PacketIn* message to the controller for *every* incoming packet, and the controller responded with an explicit command for the switch to flood the packet. We can dramatically improve the performance of the network by installing a flow rule at the switch to flood every packet, thereby avoiding the need for the switch to communicate with the controller for every packet and taking advantage of specialized packet forwarding hardware at the switch. We install the flow rule, whenever a switch joins the network:

$$floodPackets_2 = \textbf{proc } msgE \rightarrow \textbf{do}$$
$$returnA \prec liftE \; f \; (switchJoinE \; msgE)$$
$$\textbf{where } f \; (sid, \_) = insertRule \; (anyPacket \Longrightarrow flood) \; sid$$

insertRule rule sid is a command that installs rule *rule* on switch *sid* and *anyPacket* is a packet predicate that matches every packet. Again, we can combine this in parallel with *clearOnJoin* to form a complete controller:

$$controller_2 = \textbf{proc } msgE \rightarrow \textbf{do}$$
$$clearE \qquad \leftarrow clearOnJoin \; \prec msgE$$
$$tableModE \leftarrow floodPackets_2 \; \prec msgE$$
$$returnA \prec mergeEventsBy \; (\oplus) \; [\, clearE, tableModE \,]$$

5 Learning Switch

In this section, we will program a so-called *learning switch*. Traditionally, a learning switch is an Ethernet switch which initially acts much like an Ethernet hub, flooding frames received on one port to all other ports. However, a learning switch also maintains a table of Ethernet addresses and ports, such that if (a, p) is in the table, then p is the port at which the switch most recently received a frame *from* the host with address a. Since the switch received a packet *from a* on port p, port p must be on the path *to a* (assuming our network is loop-free). Consequently, when a switch receives a frame addressed to a, it forwards the frame on port p if (a, p) is in its table at that time, or else floods it on all ports other than the incoming one. In addition, a learning switch typically expires entries in the flow table after some period of inactivity.

As a first step to building our learning switch controller, we will program a component which performs the "learning" part; that is, it builds the table described above for each switch, inferring the direction of each host from every switch in the network. We implement this table using the *Map* data type from Haskell's standard library, which implements maps from keys to values (dictionaries). We will use that data type's *insert* function to add or update the value associated with a key. We will build the table by transforming each packet-in event into a table update and accumulating these updates with *accum*:

$$nextHopsSF = \textbf{proc } msgE \rightarrow \textbf{do}$$
$$hostMapE \leftarrow accum\ empty \prec liftE\ updateMap\ (packetInE\ msgE)$$
$$returnA \prec hostMapE$$

accum empy takes as input an event stream carrying state-modifying functions. At each event in its input stream, it applies the state-modifying function carried by the event to the current state, updates the current state with that new value, and outputs an event carrying the updated value. As a result, the output signal will start out as the empty map, and will output an updated map whenever a packet in event occurs. The function *updateMap* is straightforward: it updates the table for key $(sid, addr)$ to be the port ID of the port on which the packet was received:

$$updateMap\ (sid, PacketIn\ \{\ receivedOnPort, enclosedFrame\ \}) =$$
$$insert\ (sid, sourceAddress\ enclosedFrame)\ receivedOnPort$$

We can now use *nextHopsSF* to program our controller. The controller will monitor the packet in events, and for each such event, if it has learned the direction the packet should travel, it will install appropriate flow rules at the switches to forward similar packets in the learned direction. If it has not learned the direction the packet should travel, it will simply flood the packet on all ports, without installing flow rules in any switches:

$$controller_3 = \textbf{proc } msgE \rightarrow \textbf{do}$$
$$nextHopsE \leftarrow nextHopsSF \prec msgE$$
$$nextHops \leftarrow hold\ empty \prec nextHopsE$$
$$\textbf{let } tableModE = mapFilterE\ (packetToCmd\ nextHops)\ (packetInE\ msgE)$$
$$clearE \leftarrow clearOnJoin \prec msgE$$
$$floodE \leftarrow floodPackets_1 \prec msgE$$
$$returnA \prec mergeEventsBy\ (\oplus)\ [\,clearE, tableModE, floodE\,]$$

Here we pass the output stream of *nextHopsSF* through *hold empty*, which turns the event stream into a signal defined at all times by starting off as *empty* and then holding the value of the last event in its input signal. We evaluate *packetToCmd nextHops* on every incoming packet, which results in a

Maybe SwitchCommand value. Applying *mapFilterE* (*packetToCmd nextHops*) filters out those packet events for which *packetToCmd nextHops* evaluates to *Nothing*, and evaluates to an event carrying x whenever *packetToCmd nextHops* evaluates to *Just x*. The function *packetToCmd* looks up the source and destination ports in the *nextHops* and if these are both present, returns a command, and otherwise returns nothing:

> *packetToCmd nextHops* (*sid, PacketIn* {*enclosedFrame*}) =
> **case** *lookup* (*sid, s*) *nextHops* **of**
>   *Just ps* → **case** *lookup* (*sid, r*) *nextHops* **of**
>   *Just pr* → *Just* (*makeCommand sid s ps r pr*)
>   *Nothing* → *Nothing*
>   *Nothing* → *Nothing*
> **where** (*s, r*) = (*sourceAddress enclosedFrame, destAddress enclosedFrame*)

In turn, the function *makeCommand* outputs a command consisting of three commands in sequence:

> *makeCommand sid s ps r pr* =
> *deleteRules* (*ethSourceDestAre s r* ∨ *ethSourceDestAre r s*) *sid* ⊕
> *insertRule* (*flowFromTo s ps r pr* 30) *sid* ⊕
> *insertRule* (*flowFromTo r pr s ps* 30) *sid*

The first deletes any existing rules matching packets from source s to destination r or vice versa. The second command inserts a rule that forwards any incoming traffic on port *ps* from s with destination r on outgoing port *pr*. The third rule is similar. Both inserted flows are set to expire after 30 seconds of inactivity. We omit the straightforward definition of *flowFromTo* here.

The inserted rules match on *both* the destination and the *source* address of a packet. Matching on the source is in fact crucial to the correctness of the controller. If we omit matching on the source address, then the switch will forward traffic from any sources — including sources whose location is unknown to the controller — toward the destination, bypassing the controller. This may result in the controller not learning the location of some hosts and consequently flooding packets unnecessarily.

6   Declarative Routing

The learning switch router in the previous section is arguably too low-level: the overall goal of the program is lost in the details of stream transformers. It would be preferrable to express our program by simply describing the forwarding table of each switch in our network at every moment in time. To do this, we will describe the forwarding tables in terms of quantities which themselves vary over time. We illustrate this idea by rewriting our learning switch in this fashion.

The essential feature of the learning switch controller is that it inserts flow rules in switches so that, at any time, the packets for any pair of hosts whose location is known at that time are forwarded directly between them with no flooding. Thus, the collection of rules present in a switch at any time depends on which host locations are known and where those hosts are at that time. If we name the current values of these quantities *knownHosts* and *nextHops*, we can express the desired collection of rules for switch *sid* as the following set:

$$\{ inPortIs \ sp \wedge ethSourceIs \ s \wedge ethDestIs \ d \implies sendOnPort \ dp$$
$$| \ s, d \in knownHosts, s \neq d, sp \in nextHops \ sid \ s, dp \in nextHops \ sid \ d \}$$

Motivated by this, we define a *SwitchProgram* to be a signal function that periodically outputs updated flow rules for each switch:

type *SwitchProgram* =
  SF (*Event* (*SwitchID*, *SwitchMessage*)) (*Event* (*SwitchID* → [*FlowRule*]))

A collection of switches governed by a *SwitchProgram* should forward traffic at any moment according to the flow rules of the most recent event of the output stream of the program. For example, we can implement the program for the learning switch as follows:

```
program₁ = proc msgE → do
    knownHosts ← knownHostsSF —≺ msgE
    nextHopsE  ← nextHopsSF    —≺ msgE
    nextHops   ← hold empty    —≺ nextHopsE
    let rules₁ sid =
        [inPortIs sp ∧ ethSourceIs s ∧ ethDestIs d ⟹ sendOnPort dp
        | s ← knownHosts, d ← knownHosts, s ≢ d,
          Just sp ← lookup (nextHops (sid, s)),
          Just dp ← lookup (nextHops (sid, d))
        ]
    returnA —≺ tag nextHopE rules₁
```

Here we use a Haskell *list comprehension* to simulate the set we wrote previously. Generators such as *s ← knownHosts* introduce a variable to range over a given list. The left hand sides of generators can be patterns, such as in the final generator in the example above. In this case, the results include only those elements for which the pattern match succeeds. Guards, such as $s \neq d$ filter elements from the resulting list.

We use *nextHopsSF* to output an event stream carrying updated next hop maps for the network. *knownHostsSF* outputs a list of hosts whose location is known, and is easily implementable in terms of *nextHopsSF*. Since both the *knownHosts* and *nextHops* values change precisely when the output stream of *nextHopSF* has an event, we output an updated list of flow rules at exactly that moment, using *tag* to output the value of *rules₁* at exactly the moments when *nextHopE* carries a value.[1]

This approach allows us to easily extend our program in various ways. For example, we can modify the previous controller to have switches simply flood all ARP (Address Resolution Protocol) Ethernet frames as follows: (unchanged parts are elided):

---

[1] In addition to the rules that a switch should follow, the user must also specify how the controller should process packets for which no rule applies. Specifying this is straightforward, and we omit the description here due to space constraints.

$program_2 = \mathbf{proc} \ msgE \rightarrow \mathbf{do}$

    ...

    $\mathbf{let} \ rules_1 \ sid = ...$

    $\mathbf{let} \ rules_2 \ sid = [\, arp \Longrightarrow flood \,]$

    $\mathbf{let} \ rules \ \ sid = rules_1 \ sid \ {+\!\!+} \ rules_2 \ sid$

    $returnA \prec tag \ nextHopE \ rules$

Although in this case no packet will match more than one rule, we adopt the convention that the first rule in the list matching a packet applies. This convention allows us to compose rule sets with one taking precedence over another.

There are many feasible ways to implement a *SwitchProgram*. Due to space constraints we omit discussion of our simple implementation. However, we note that our implementation converts a *SwitchProgram* into a signal function:

$runSP :: SwitchProgram \rightarrow$
$\qquad SF \ (Event \ (SwitchID, SwitchMessage)) \ (Event \ SwitchCommand)$

Thus, we are able to implement the run-time envionment for our higher-level abstraction within Nettle/FRP. In this way, Nettle/FRP provides a convenient and powerful tool for exploring and implementing high level networking languages and abstractions.

7 Time-Varying Quantities

In this section we show how we can use continuous values in programming a dynamic load-balancing controller. This is a feature that other controller frameworks do not provide, but which we expect to be very useful in programming dynamic network controllers.

Consider a load balancing problem in which a single switch S has three links l_1, l_2 and l_3, as shown in Fig. 5. We assume that there are many traffic sessions in the network so that we can approximately model the network traffic using *traffic flow rates*. We will name the flow rates for links l_2 and l_3 as f_2 and f_3, respectively. In this highly simplified scenario, we imagine that traffic enters the system on link l_1 and that the switch can reach all destinations of this traffic by forwarding on either l_2 or l_3. Let r_{ideal} be the desired ratio of traffic that should flow over link l_2, r_{actual} be the actual ratio, and e be the error. That is:

$$r_{actual} = \frac{f_2}{f_2 + f_3}$$
$$e \qquad = r_{ideal} - r_{actual}$$

We would like our controller to maintain a balance of traffic such that $e \approx 0$. Note that the sign of e indicates whether the flow on port 2 should be increased or decreased: when $e < 0$, the flow should be decreased, otherwise it should be increased.

We implement a simple "dial" to control our switch. We will have a "dial", named a, that ranges over IP addresses, viewed as 32 bit integers. At any moment in time, we will forward all traffic destined to addresses less than or equal to a via link 2 and any traffic destined toward address greater than a via link 3. This

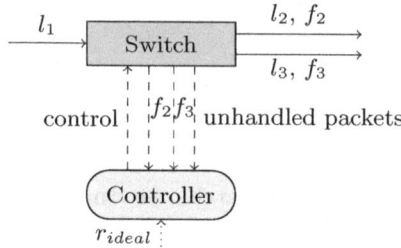

Fig. 5. Control system for Sec. 7. Solid lines correspond to physical links used by the network to send data traffic. Dashed lines indicate switch-controller communication.

dial is depicted in Fig. 6. Note that the ratio of addresses less than a to the total addresses does not indicate how much traffic will flow over links 2 and 3, since traffic could be unevenly distributed over the address space. Still, under a given traffic distribution, the dial's setting will determine how much traffic flows on each link: increasing a increases traffic on link 2 while decreasing it increases traffic on link 3, and it makes some sense to change the dial setting in proportion to the size of the current error. Furthermore, since traffic patterns change over time, there is no single right setting, and we will have to adjust it as our system evolves.

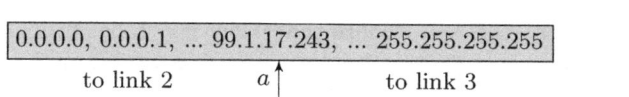

to link 2 a to link 3

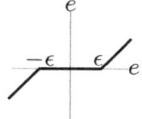

Fig. 6. The "dial" of Sec. 7   **Fig. 7.** Graph of the *dead zone* in $\hat{e}$

In order to use traditional control theory techniques, we first turn the problem into a continuous one. We define a new, real-valued version of our dial, u, ranging over $[0, 1]$. We can translate from u to a as follows:

$$a = \lfloor 2^{32} * u \rfloor \ .$$

As we argued above, we would like to change u in proportion to the error. We can write this as a simple differential equation:

$$\dot{u} = ke$$

Integrating, we find that:

$$u(t) = k \int_0^t e(\tau)\mathrm{d}\tau + u(0)$$

We have now arrived at a familiar integral control. However, due to the discrete nature of our system, our control will be unstable. At any time there are a finite number of flows, and it will not be possible to split these flows in two groups so that the error is zero. We can mitigate this problem by introducing a *dead zone* into the error signal. We define a new error signal $\hat{e}(t)$ as follows:

$$\hat{e}(t) = \begin{cases} e(t) - \epsilon & \text{if } e(t) > \epsilon \\ e(t) + \epsilon & \text{if } e(t) < -\epsilon \\ 0 & \text{otherwise} \end{cases}$$

Fig. 7 graphs the relationship between e and $\hat{e}$. Introducing the dead zone into the error term effectively turns the error signal off, once the controller is sufficiently close to reducing the error to 0. The size ϵ we need will depend on our assumptions about the minimum number and size of flows in our network.

We can now directly translate this mathematical model into Nettle code. The following defines a signal function implementing u, assuming the initial value u_0, gain k, dead zone size *eps*, and a suitable definition of *deaden* are defined elsewhere:

$uSF = \mathbf{proc}\ (f_2, f_3, r_{ideal}) \rightarrow \mathbf{do}$
  $\mathbf{let}\ r_{actual} = f_2\ /\ (f_2 + f_3)$
  $\mathbf{let}\ error\ \ = r_{ideal} - r_{actual}$
  $i \leftarrow integral \longrightarrow\!\!\!< deaden\ eps\ error$
  $returnA \longrightarrow\!\!\!< k * i + u_0$

We omit the overall controller, which includes signal functions providing the flow rates f_2, f_3 and the user determined r_{ideal}. Although the simplistic control algorithm presented here does not perform well in practice (because of a delay in observing port flow rates), it nevertheless illustrates how continuous quantities can be used to implement network control algorithms; a more sophisticated controller would have the same structure.

8   Discussion and Related Work

We have implemented all of the ideas in this paper (and more) using standard Haskell using the GHC Haskell compiler. We have tested our controllers using a reference implementation of OpenFlow version 1.0. We have also done preliminary tests of some of our controllers on real OpenFlow switches, which demonstrate that our controllers perform comparably with existing control frameworks, such as NOX [2]. All of our code is available on `hackage.haskell.org`

Future work includes refinements to Nettle/FRP and improvements to our dynamic continuous controller design. We also plan to develop more DSLs at the top-most layer of our software architecture, to capture more domain specific features, such as security and business relationships. We are also interested in studying the problem of protocol and policy verification techniques.

We previously used the name "Nettle" for an embedded DSL in Haskell for describing BGP router configurations [16]. At the risk of creating some confusion (since the languages are entirely distinct and have different purposes), we have reused that name for the language we present in this paper.

NOX [2] is an open-source library for writing controllers for OpenFlow switches in C++ and Python. Both NOX and Nettle provide a framework for writing controllers that hide low-level details from the user, allow fine-grained control over switch behavior, and provide an event-based programming model with extensible collections of events.

Nettle provides a more declarative approach to event-based programming by handling entire message streams, instead of individual messages. Nettle has a more expressive language for composing controllers – in parallel as in NOX, but also in sequence, and in many other combinations. The interactions between controllers is made explicit through lightweight input and output types of the components. In contrast, the interaction of NOX components requires investigating the internals of each component, since modules may interact imperatively by method invocation. Nettle also provides an elegant, declarative mechanism for describing time-sensitive and time-varying behaviors, whereas in NOX these must be simulated by delays and timers. Finally, Nettle has continuous quantities that reflect abstract properties of a network, such as the volume of messages on a network link. We are not aware of any other language that has this capability.

Flow-based Management Language (FML) [7] is a declarative policy language for configuring networks. An FML program is a Datalog-like set of rules that ultimately describe which forwarding actions should hold of flows. Although FML provides a higher-level abstraction than Nettle, many applications cannot be expressed in FML. In particular, FML has no way of expressing dynamic policies, where forwarding decisions change over time. Nettle provides a more concrete abstraction that exposes the message-passing interface to OpenFlow switches, but within a strongly typed language, Haskell, and within an expressive FRP layer. This allows Nettle users to extend Nettle and program in ways very similar to FML, as seen in Section 6.

Frenetic [5] is an FRP-based language for controlling OpenFlow networks, embedded in Python. Frenetic presents a "program like you see every packet" abstraction, thus providing a higher-level abstraction than Nettle. Nettle on the other hand, introduces FRP at the message stream level, while leveraging the embedding in Haskell to enable the development of higher level abstractions.

The Declarative Networking [10] approach uses a Datalog-like language to express routing protocols as recursive queries executing over a distributed collection of routers. Declarative Networking thus targets a different type of system than Nettle, since Nettle is aimed at OpenFlow-based systems in which switches have no query-processing capabailities.

Acknowledgements. This research was supported in part by STTR grant number ST061-002 from the Defense Advanced Research Projects Agency. We thank our STTR industrial partner, Galois, Inc. for its support, Ashish Agarwal for help with the Haskell/OpenFlow layer, and Nick Feamster and Sam Burnett with feedback and help testing Nettle on their OpenFlow network.

References

1. http://www.openflowswitch.org/
2. http://noxrepo.org/wp/
3. Caesar, M., Rexford, J.: BGP routing policies in ISP networks. IEEE Network 19(6), 5–11 (2005)
4. Elliott, C., Hudak, P.: Functional reactive animation. In: International Conference on Functional Programming, pp. 263–273 (June 1997)
5. Foster, N., Harrison, R., Meola, M.L., Freedman, M.J., Rexford, J., Walker, D.: Frenetic: A high-level langauge for openflow networks. In: ACM Workshop on Programmable Routers for Extensible Services of Tomorrow (PRESTO) (November 2010)
6. Griffin, T.G., Jaggard, A.D., Ramachandran, V.: Design principles of policy languages for path vector protocols. In: SIGCOMM 2003: Proceedings of the 2003 Conference on Applications, Technologies, Architectures, and Protocols for Computer Communications. pp. 61–72. ACM, New York(2003)
7. Hinrichs, T.L., Gude, N.S., Casado, M., Mitchell, J.C., Shenker, S.: Practical declarative network management. In: WREN 2009: Proceedings of the 1st ACM Workshop on Research on Enterprise Networking, pp. 1–10. ACM, New York (2009)
8. Hudak, P., Courtney, A., Nilsson, H., Peterson, J.: Robots, arrows, and functional reactive programming. In: Jeuring, J., Jones, S.L.P. (eds.) AFP 2002. LNCS, vol. 2638. Springer, Heidelberg (2003)
9. Hughes, J.: Generalising monads to arrows. Sci. Comput. Program. 37(1-3), 67–111 (2000)
10. Loo, B.T., Hellerstein, J.M., Stoica, I., Ramakrishnan, R.: Declarative routing: extensible routing with declarative queries. In: SIGCOMM 2005: Proceedings of the 2005 Conference on Applications, Technologies, Architectures, and Protocols for Computer Communications, pp. 289–300. ACM, New York (2005)
11. Mahajan, R., Wetherall, D., Anderson, T.: Understanding BGP misconfiguration. In: SIGCOMM, Pittsburgh, PA, pp. 3–17 (August 2002)
12. Paterson, R.: A new notation for arrows. In: ICFP 2001: Proceedings of the sixth ACM SIGPLAN International Conference on Functional Programming, pp. 229–240. ACM, New York (2001)
13. Peterson, J., Hager, G., Hudak, P.: A language for declarative robotic programming. In: International Conference on Robotics and Automation (1999)
14. Ramachandran, V.: Foundations of Inter-Domain Routing. Ph.D. thesis, Yale University (May 2005)
15. Voellmy, A., Agarwal, A., Hudak, P., Feamster, N., Burnett, S., Launchbury, J.: Don't configure the network, program it! domain-specific programming languages for network systems. Tech. Rep. YALEU/DCS/RR-1432, Yale University (July 2010)
16. Voellmy, A., Hudak, P.: Nettle: A language for configuring routing networks. In: Taha, W.M. (ed.) DSL 2009. LNCS, vol. 5658, pp. 211–235. Springer, Heidelberg (2009)

Determining Actual Response Time in P-FRP*

Chaitanya Belwal and Albert M.K. Cheng

Department of Computer Science,
University of Houston, TX, USA
{cbelwal,cheng}@cs.uh.edu

Abstract. A purely functional model of computation, called Priority-based Functional Reactive Programming (P-FRP), has been introduced as a new paradigm for building real-time software. Unlike the classical preemptive model[1] of real-time systems, preempted events in P-FRP are aborted and have to restart when higher priority events have completed, making the response time of events dependent on the execution pattern of higher priority events. Though methods to determine approximate values for the response time of P-FRP events have been presented, no convenient method has yet been established to determine actual response time. A common method for computing actual response time in the preemptive model does not give guaranteed results in P-FRP. A simulation based approach is computationally expensive and not feasible in most practical situations. We show that an exhaustive enumeration technique for idle periods is a more efficient technique, and can be easily adopted to determine actual response time in P-FRP.

Keywords: real-time systems, embedded systems, response time, schedulability analysis, functional programming.

1 Introduction

Functional Reactive Programming (FRP) [22] is a declarative programming language for modeling and implementing reactive systems. It has been used for a wide range of applications, notably, graphics [7], robotics [15], and vision [16]. FRP elegantly captures continuous and discrete aspects of a hybrid system using the notions of *behavior* and *event*, respectively. Because this language is developed as an embedded language in Haskell [9], it benefits from the wealth of abstractions provided in this language. Unfortunately, Haskell provides no real-time guarantees, and therefore, neither does FRP.

To address this limitation, resource-bounded variants of FRP were studied [13,20,21]. Recently, it was shown that a variant called priority-based FRP (P-FRP)

---

* This work is supported in part by U.S. National Science Foundation under Award no. 0720856.

[1] In this paper the classical preemptive model refers to a real-time system in which tasks can be preempted by higher priority tasks, and can resume execution from the point they were preempted.

R. Rocha and J. Launchbury (Eds.): PADL 2011, LNCS 6539, pp. 250–264, 2011.

[13], combines both the semantic properties for FRP, guarantees resource bounded-ness, and supports assigning different priorities to different events.

In P-FRP, higher priority events can preempt lower-priority ones. However, a re-quirement [19] in the functional programming model is that the state of the system cannot be changed, and no function can have side effects. Hence, to maintain this guarantee of stateless execution, the functional programming paradigm requires the execution of a function to be atomic in nature. To comply with this requirement, as well as allow preemption of lower priority events, P-FRP implements a transactional model of execution. Using only a copy of the state during event execution and atomi-cally committing these changes at the end of the event handler, P-FRP ensures that handling an event is an "all or nothing" proposition. This preserves the easily under-standable semantics of the FRP and provides a programming model where response times to different events can be tweaked by the programmer, without ever affecting the semantic soundness of the program. Thus, a clear separation between the seman-tics of the program and responsiveness of each handler is achieved.

This transactional execution model used in P-FRP is not new, and such models have been presented in the past. These are the transactional memory systems [11] and lock-free execution for critical sections [1]. The development of these systems was primarily motivated by the need to avoid concurrency or precedence constraint issues, which have been a problem in the classical preemptive model [18]. Studies on the temporal properties of the transactional model are being done by some research groups. However, the response time studies currently available [1,8] provide only basic schedulability analysis by modifying existing methods developed for the pre-emptive model. A study to find actual response time for this execution model has not been presented yet.

Previous work on P-FRP [13,17] provided basic results on schedulability and ap-proximate upper bounds on response times. Though approximate upper bounds pro-vide only a general idea on the schedulability of events, the methods to compute them are much faster [4,6,17]. In this paper we use the term 'actual' to differentiate from approximate or bounded response time. Actual response time is a more accurate indi-cator of the temporal properties of events in the system. Hence, actual response time is more useful when an accurate modeling of the system is required , such as in the design phase of a real-time system, or in developing exact schedulability tests.

An iterative method first presented by Audsley et al in [2] (termed Audsley's method in this paper), is a common approach for determining actual response time in the preemptive model. In this method, it is assumed that the amount of processor time taken by an event to execute, is constant and equal to its worst-case execution time (WCET). However, since a preempted event is aborted, the amount of processor time taken by a lower priority event in P-FRP to complete execution, can be larger than its WCET, and thus not known *a priori*. Due to this reason the method in [2] is not guar-anteed to work with P-FRP (see section 3 for example), and new methods for deter-mining actual response time in P-FRP are required.

1.1 Contributions

This paper presents an efficient algorithm that can be used in place of a simulation, to determine the actual response times of events in P-FRP. This is an essential step for making this technology practically usable since it is not feasible to work out these response times by hand or ad-hoc methods. To conform to terminology used in referenced real-time system papers, P-FRP events will be referred to as tasks in the rest of this paper.

After reviewing basic concepts and the P-FRP execution model (Section 2) we:

- Present Audsley's iterative method for computing actual response time in the preemptive model (Section 3)
- Present an enumeration technique for idle periods, which has been termed as the *gap-enumeration* method (Section 4)
- Present an algorithm that determines the actual response time of a task using the gap-enumeration method (Section 5)
- Provide performance analysis between the time accurate and gap-enumeration algorithms (Section 6)

And conclude by reviewing related work (Section 7) and a reflection on these results (Section 8).

2   Basic Concepts and Execution Model of P-FRP

In this section, we introduce the basic concepts and the notation used to denote these concepts in the rest of the paper. In addition, we review the P-FRP execution model and assumptions made in this study.

2.1   Basic Concepts

Essential concepts for P-FRP are tasks and their associated priority, their associated time period and the dual concept of arrival rate, and their processing time; the concept of a time interval and release offset therein. In our task model, all these assumed to be known *a priori*. The notation and formal definitions for these concepts as well as a few others used in the paper are as follows:

- Let **task set** $\Gamma_n = \{\tau_1, \tau_2, \ldots, \tau_n\}$ be a set of n periodic tasks
- The **priority** of $\tau_k \in \Gamma_n$ is the positive integer k, where a higher number implies higher priority
- T_k is the **arrival time period** between two successive jobs of τ_k
- C_k is the **worst-case execution time** for τ_k
- $t_{copy}(k)$ is the time taken to make a **copy** of the state before τ_k starts execution (see section 2.2.1)
- $t_{restore}(k)$ is the time taken to **restore** the state after τ_k has completed execution (see section 2.2.1)
- P_k is the **processing time** for τ_k. Processing of a task includes execution as well as copy and restore operations. Hence, $P_k = t_{copy}(k) + C_k + t_{restore}(k)$
- $R_{k,m}$ represents the **release time** of the mth job of τ_k
- Φ_k represents the **release offset** which is the release time of the first job of τ_k. Or, $\Phi_k = R_{k,1}$. Hence, $R_{k,m} = \Phi_k + (m-1) \cdot T_k$
- A **level-k idle point** is a point in time, t in which no task having a priority k or higher is awaiting execution and ready to execute strictly before t

- A finite contiguous interval of non-zero length $[t_1, t_2)$ is a **k-gap**, if every $t \in [t_1, t_2)$, is a level-$(k+1)$ idle point.
- The **threshold** of the k-gap $[t_1, t_2)$ is time t_1
- $T|_{t_1}^{t_2}$ represent the **time window** for analyzing gaps, such that: $\forall t \in T|_{t_1}^{t_2}$, $t_1 \leq t$ $< t_2 \wedge t_1 \neq t_2$. This new notation is used to differentiate from k-gap time intervals
- D_k is the **relative deadline** of τ_k. If some job of τ_k is released at time $R_{k,m}$ then τ_k should complete processing by time $R_{k,m} + D_k$, otherwise τ_k will have a **deadline miss.** In this paper, $D_k = T_k$
- A **gap set** $\sigma_k(T|_{t_1}^{t_2})$ contains all the unique k-gaps present in the time interval $T|_{t_1}^{t_2}$. The k-gaps present in $\sigma_k(T|_{t_1}^{t_2})$ are also disjoint:

  for any two gaps $[t_{x1}, t_{y1}), [t_{x2}, t_{y2}) \in \sigma_k(T|_{t_1}^{t_2})$, if $t \in [t_{x1}, t_{y1})$ then $t \notin [t_{x2}, t_{y2})$
- $|\sigma_k(T|_{t_1}^{t_2})|$ represents the number of k-gaps present in $\sigma_k(T|_{t_1}^{t_2})$
- The **gap-transformation function** $\lambda(\sigma_k(T|_{t_1}^{t_2}), \Gamma_n)$ takes as input the gap set σ_k, and task set Γ_n. The function returns the gap set of the next lower priority task:
  $$\sigma_{k-1}(T|_{t_1}^{t_2}) = \lambda(\sigma_k(T|_{t_1}^{t_2}))$$
- The **gap-search function** $\mu(\sigma_k(T|_{t_1}^{t_2}), P_k)$ takes as input, the gap set $\sigma_k(T|_{t_1}^{t_2})$ and P_k, and returns the earliest k-gap larger than or equal to P_k present in σ_k:
  $$[t_{x1}, t_{y1}) = \mu(\sigma_k(T|_{t_1}^{t_2}), P_k), \text{ such that:}$$

  $t_{y1} - t_{x1} \geq P_k \wedge \nexists [t_x, t_y) \in \sigma_k(T|_{t_1}^{t_2}) \wedge t_y - t_x > P_k \wedge t_x < t_{x1}$

  If the gap search function returns a k-gap with threshold less than 0, then a k-gap larger than P_k does not exist in $\sigma_k(T|_{t_1}^{t_2})$
- The **computational steps** of an algorithm is a numerical measurement of the number of times major iterations of the algorithm have been performed during execution. This value gives us a general idea of the performance of the algorithms considered in this paper
- The **response time** of a τ_k written as RT_k is the relative time after its release at which τ_k completes processing
- **Interference** on τ_k is the action where the processing of τ_k is interrupted by the release of a higher priority task. In P-FRP, an interference forces τ_k to abort and re-process later.

2.2 Execution Model and Assumptions

In this study all tasks are assumed to execute in a uniprocessor system with no precedence constraints. When a job of higher priority task τ_i is released, it can immediately preempt an executing lower priority task, and changes made by the lower priority task are rolled back. The lower priority task will be restarted when the higher priority task has completed processing. Due to P-FRP's transactional nature of execution, all tasks are assumed to run without concurrency constraints. In the algorithms to derive the actual response time of task τ_j, we have considered the release offset of τ_j to be 0.

When some task is released, it enters a processing queue Q which is arranged by priority order, such that all arriving higher priority tasks are moved to the head of the queue. The length of the queue is bounded, and no two instances of the same task can be present in the queue at the same time. This requires a task to complete processing before the release of its next job. To maintain this requirement we assume a *hard* real-time system with task deadline equal to the time period between jobs. Hence, $\forall \tau_k \in \Gamma_n$, $D_k = T_k$. A task set is schedulable in some time interval, only if no task in the set has a deadline miss.

Once τ_i enters Q two situations are possible. If a task of lower priority than i is being processed, it will be immediately preempted and τ_i will start processing. If a task of higher priority than τ_i is being processed, then τ_i will wait in the Q and start processing only after the higher priority task has completed. An exception to the immediate preemption is made during *copy* and *restore* operations which is explained in the following paragraph.

2.2.1   Copy and Restore Operations

In P-FRP, when a task starts processing it creates a 'scratch' state, which is a *copy* of the current state of the system. Changes made during the processing of this task are maintained inside such a state. When the task has completed, the 'scratch' state is *restored* into the final state in an atomic operation. Therefore, during the restoration and copy operations, the task being processed cannot be preempted by higher priority tasks. If the task is preempted after copy but before the restore operation, the scratch state is simply discarded. The context-switch between tasks only involves a state copy operation for the task that will be commencing processing. The time taken for copy ($t_{copy}(k)$) and restore ($t_{restore}(k)$) operations of τ_k is part of the processing time of the task, P_k.

Our current methods do not yet account for situations where higher priority tasks cannot preempt lower priority tasks. Hence, for the methods presented in this paper, the values of $t_{copy}(k)$ and $t_{restore}(k)$ for all tasks are kept same and equal to a single discrete time unit. Hence, $\forall k \in \Gamma_n$, $t_{copy}(k) = t_{restore}(k) = 1$.

Such small values of $t_{copy}(k)$ and $t_{restore}(k)$ are reasonable as copy and restore operations are only a fraction of the worst-case execution time of the task. However, for greater precision of results, in ongoing work we are developing methods where the values of $t_{restore}(k)$ and $t_{copy}(k)$ could be variable.

2.2.2   Critical Instant in P-FRP

In response time analysis for fixed-priority scheduling, a *critical-instant* of release is assumed. Critical instant is the time, at which task releases lead to the worst-case response time (WCRT) [14] of the task being analyzed. In their seminal work, Liu and Layland [14] showed that in fixed-priority scheduling for the preemptive model, the critical-instant for a lower priority task τ_i occurs when it is released at the same time as all higher priority tasks. Or, the release offset of task τ_j and higher priority tasks is the same. This is also termed as a *synchronous* release of tasks. As shown in [3], for P-FRP, a *synchronous* release of τ_j and higher priority tasks is not guaranteed to result in the WCRT of τ_j.

The methods presented in this paper, determine the response time of a task only for a user specified release offset of higher priority tasks. Hence, the release offsets required by the methods presented in this paper, are assumed to be known *a priori*. These release offsets, may or may not lead to the WCRT for the task being analyzed. To determine the WCRT for a given P-FRP task, all possible combinations of release offsets of higher priority tasks have to be generated. Then the time-accurate or gap-enumeration algorithms, presented in this paper, have to be used to compute the actual release time under each of the possible release offset combinations. Finally, the highest value of the response time computed under each release offset combination will be the WCRT for the task.

3 Computing Actual Response Time in the Preemptive Model

In an important paper, Audsley et al [2] demonstrated that if tasks are synchronously released, the response time of τ_i (RT_i) can be determined using the following equation:

$$RT_i = P_i + B_i + \sum_{\forall j > i} \left\lceil \frac{RT_i}{T_j} \right\rceil \cdot P_j \qquad (3.1)$$

B_i is the blocking time due to concurrency control protocols, which is not applicable in our case. Since RT_i appears on both sides of the equation, an iterative approach using initial approximate values of RT_i can be used. If RT_i^n represents the nth approximate value of RT_i, and ignoring the blocking time, equation 3.1 can be written as:

$$RT_i^{n+1} = P_i + \sum_{\forall j > i} \left\lceil \frac{RT_i^n}{T_j} \right\rceil \cdot P_j \qquad (3.2)$$

The iteration starts with $RT_i^0 = 0$ and terminates when $RT_i^{n+1} = RT_i^n$. Since, in the preemptive model a synchronous release leads to the WCRT, equation 3.1 also computes the WCRT for a task. As shown in [2], equation 3.1 can also be modified to determine response time when tasks have non-zero offsets (tasks are released *asynchronously*) or encounter *release jitter*.

Let's take a simple application of this equation, using the following P-FRP task set:

Task	P	T
τ_1	20	100
τ_2	20	70
τ_3	10	40

We have to compute the response time of τ_1 using equation 3.1, assuming a synchronous release of tasks. The iterations of the computation are given below:

#1, $n=0$: $RT_1^1 = 20 + (\left\lceil \frac{0}{40} \right\rceil \cdot 10 + \left\lceil \frac{0}{70} \right\rceil \cdot 20) = 20$ #3, $n=2$: $RT_1^3 = 20 + (\left\lceil \frac{50}{40} \right\rceil \cdot 10 + \left\lceil \frac{50}{70} \right\rceil \cdot 20) = 60$

#2, $n=1$: $RT_1^2 = 20 + (\left\lceil \frac{20}{40} \right\rceil \cdot 10 + \left\lceil \frac{20}{70} \right\rceil \cdot 20) = 50$ #4, $n=3$: $RT_1^4 = 20 + (\left\lceil \frac{60}{40} \right\rceil \cdot 10 + \left\lceil \frac{60}{70} \right\rceil \cdot 20) = 60$

Since, $RT_1^3 = RT_1^4$, the iteration will terminate giving us the response time for τ_1 as 60. In *Figure 1* we show how P-FRP processes the tasks in the time window $T\mid_0^{100}$, resulting in the response time of τ_1 as 70. *Figure 1* also illustrates the fact that, even though the processing time of τ_1 if 20 and is known *a priori*, it takes a total processor time of 30 to complete processing due to an abort at time 40.

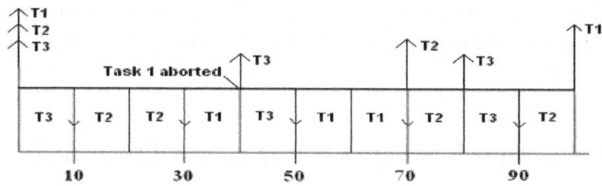

Fig. 1. Task execution graph showing τ_1 completing processing at time 70. T1, T2 and T3 represent tasks τ_1, τ_2 and τ_3 respectively.

3.1.1 Ras and Cheng's Modification for P-FRP

An attempt to apply Audsley's method in P-FRP was made by Ras and Cheng in [17]. An abort cost to the original equation has been added. The modified equation is given as:

$$WCRT_i = P_i + B_i + \sum_{\forall j \in hp_i} \left\lceil \frac{WCRT_i}{T_j} \right\rceil \cdot P_j + \sum_{\forall j \in hp_i} \left\lceil \frac{WCRT_i}{T_j} \right\rceil \cdot \max_{k=i}^{j-1} P_k \qquad (3.3)$$

hp_i represents the set of tasks having a higher priority than τ_i. The initial value for $WCRT_i$ is set to P_i. This equation computes the response time under a synchronous release. However, it could converge for only a few cases. Also, the authors' assertion that eq. 3.3 can compute the WCRT, is not quite correct. This is because in P-FRP a synchronous release is not guaranteed to lead to WCRT. Applying equation 3.3 to our example, and setting $wcrt_1^0 = 20$:

$$1: \ wcrt_1^1 = 20 + (\left\lceil \frac{20}{40} \right\rceil \cdot 10 + \left\lceil \frac{20}{70} \right\rceil \cdot 20) + \left\lceil \frac{20}{40} \right\rceil \cdot 20 + \left\lceil \frac{20}{70} \right\rceil \cdot 20 = 90$$

$$2: \ wcrt_1^2 = 20 + (\left\lceil \frac{90}{40} \right\rceil \cdot 10 + \left\lceil \frac{90}{70} \right\rceil \cdot 20) + \left\lceil \frac{90}{40} \right\rceil \cdot 20 + \left\lceil \frac{90}{70} \right\rceil \cdot 20 = 190$$

$$3: \ wcrt_1^3 = 20 + (\left\lceil \frac{190}{40} \right\rceil \cdot 10 + \left\lceil \frac{190}{70} \right\rceil \cdot 20) + \left\lceil \frac{190}{40} \right\rceil \cdot 20 + \left\lceil \frac{190}{70} \right\rceil \cdot 20 = 290$$

This computation will go on indefinitely and will never converge.

Clearly, Audsley's method, and its modified version are not guaranteed to compute the actual response time in P-FRP, and a different approach is required.

A straightforward way for computing the response time in P-FRP, is to use a time-accurate simulation that progresses through every time tick, and runs tasks based on the P-FRP execution model. Due to limited space, the pseudo-code for such an algorithm is given in [3]. The computational complexity of this algorithm is bounded by $O((T_j - P_j) \cdot (n-j)^2 \cdot T_k^2)$, derivation of which is also provided in [3].

4 Gap-Enumeration Method

The time-accurate simulation method iterates through every time step till the response time of the task being analyzed is found. This approach is computationally intensive, since several iterations have to be performed. We present a different method using enumeration of k-gaps, based on the following characteristics of the P-FRP execution model. Due to limited space, we have not given proofs and detailed pseudo-code of some of our methods. These are available in [3].

Lemma 4.1 [3, 5.1]. *A task τ_j can be processed only in elements of the set $\sigma_j(T \mid_{t_1}^{t_2})$.*

Lemma 4.2 [3, 5.2]. *For task τ_j to be schedulable, one j-gap of at least length P_j will exist between any two successive jobs of τ_j.*

Lemma 4.3 [3, 5.3]. *In the gap set $\sigma_j(T \mid_{t}^{t+T_j})$ one element will be more than P_j for τ_j to be schedulable.*

The mechanism of the gap-enumeration method works as follows: Let, task set $\Gamma_n = \{\tau_1, \tau_2,...,\tau_n\}$. We have to determine the response time of the first job of τ_j (RT_j) $(j < n)$. Without loss of generality, assume all tasks are released at the same time as τ_j (time 0). From lemma 4.1, we know that τ_j can only be processed inside the elements of the set $\sigma_j(T \mid_{0}^{T_j})$. These elements are all the j-gaps available after the processing of tasks τ_n to τ_{j+1}. From lemma 4.2, we know that one of the j-gaps in the time interval $T \mid_{0}^{T_j}$, has to be larger than P_j for τ_j to be schedulable. We will first find the set $\sigma_j(T \mid_{0}^{T_j})$, and then search through this set for the first j-gap which is larger than P_j. τ_j will be processed in this j-gap making the response time of τ_j equal to $t_1 + P_j$, where t_1 is the threshold of this j-gap.

To find $\sigma_j(T \mid_{0}^{T_j})$ we progressively analyze gap sets of all higher priority tasks. The n-gap that is available for τ_n to run, is the entire length of the time interval $T \mid_{0}^{T_j}$. Hence, $\sigma_n(T \mid_{0}^{T_j}) = \{[0, T_j)\}$. The first job of τ_n will be released at time 0, and the second at time T_n. The mth job of τ_n will be released at $(m-1) \cdot T_n$. The $(n-1)$-gap left between the 1st and 2nd job is $[P_n, T_n)$. Similarly the $(n-1)$-gap left between the 2nd and 3rd job is $[T_n+P_n, 2 \cdot T_n)$. Therefore, $\sigma_{n-1}(T \mid_{0}^{T_j}) = \{[P_n, T_n), [T_n+P_n, 2 \cdot T_n)... ,[(m-2) \cdot T_n , (m-1) \cdot T_n) \}: (m-1) \cdot T_n \leq T_j$.

We see that the gap set $\sigma_{n-1}(T \mid_{0}^{T_j})$ is created after accounting for the processing of all jobs of τ_n, in the gap set $\sigma_n(T \mid_{0}^{T_j})$. Hence, the gap set $\sigma_n(T \mid_{0}^{T_j})$ has been transformed by the processing of all jobs of τ_n to result in $\sigma_{n-1}(T \mid_{0}^{T_j})$. We use the gap transformation function to account for the processing of the current task, and get the gap set for the next lower priority task. Or,

$$\sigma_{n-1}(T \mid_{0}^{T_j}) = \lambda\, (\sigma_n(T \mid_{0}^{T_j}),\Gamma_n).$$

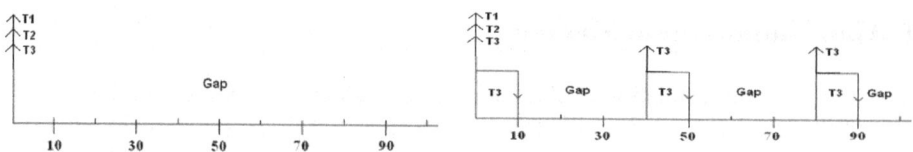

Fig. 2(a). 3-gap available for processing of τ_3, $\sigma_3(\text{T}\,|_0^{100}) = \{[0,100)\}$

Fig. 2(b). 2-gaps available for processing of τ_2, $\sigma_2(\text{T}\,|_0^{100}) = \{[10,40), [50,80), [90,100)\}$

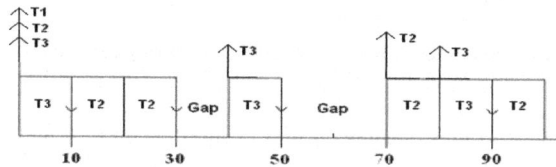

Fig. 2(c). 1-gaps available for processing of τ_1, $\sigma_1(\text{T}\,|_0^{100}) = \{[30,40), [50,70)\}$

From lemma 4.1, we know that τ_{n-1} can only be processed in the gaps present in $\sigma_{n-1}(\text{T}\,|_0^{T_j})$. When we process all jobs of τ_{n-1} in $\text{T}\,|_0^{T_j}$, some of the $(n-1)$ gaps present in $\sigma_{n-1}(\text{T}\,|_0^{T_j})$ will be used or reduce in size, leading to the formation of $(n-2)$-gaps. Hence, after accounting for the processing of all jobs of τ_{n-1} in $\text{T}\,|_0^{T_j}$, the gap set $\sigma_{n-2}(\text{T}\,|_0^{T_j})$ is created. The gap-transformation function can also be used to get the set $\sigma_{n-2}(\text{T}\,|_0^{T_j})$. Hence,

$$\sigma_{n-2}(\text{T}\,|_0^{T_j}) = \lambda\,(\sigma_{n-1}(\text{T}\,|_0^{T_j}),\Gamma_n)$$

Similarly,

$$\sigma_{n-3}(\text{T}\,|_0^{T_j}) = \lambda\,(\sigma_{n-2}(\text{T}\,|_0^{T_j}),\Gamma_n)$$

$$\dots$$

$$\sigma_j(\text{T}\,|_0^{T_j}) = \lambda\,(\sigma_{j+1}(\text{T}\,|_0^{T_j}),\Gamma_n)$$

Once $\sigma_j(\text{T}\,|_0^{T_j})$ is available we use the gap search function to give us the first j-gap in which τ_j can complete processing. Hence,

$$[t_1, t_2) = \mu(\sigma_j(\text{T}), P_j).$$

Therefore,

$$RT_j = t_1 + P_j$$

Let us illustrate this method by a simple case. Consider the example given in Section 3. Here, $\Gamma_3 = \{\tau_1, \tau_2, \tau_3\}$ and T_1, T_2, T_3 are 100,70,40 respectively. The processing times P_1, P_2, P_3 are 20,20,10 respectively and all tasks are released at time 0. We have to determine the actual response time for τ_1.

In the time interval $T\vert_0^{100}$, the 3-gap available to process τ_3 is the entire length of the time interval period. Therefore, $\sigma_3(T\vert_0^{100}) = \{[0,100)\}$ *(Figure 2(a))*. τ_3 will be processed at times 0,40 and 80 leaving 2-gaps in between each job. Therefore, $\sigma_2(T\vert_0^{100}) = \{[10,40), [50,80), [90,100)\}$ *(Figure 2(b))*. The first job of τ_2 is processed in the 2-gap [10,30), and the second job starts processing at time 70, but is aborted by second job of τ_3 at time 80. τ_2 will restart processing in the 2-gap [90,100). Hence, $\sigma_1(T\vert_0^{100}) = \{[30,40), [50,70)\}$ *(Figure 2(c))*. Since the length of the 1-gap [50,70) is more or equal to P_1, τ_1 will complete processing in this gap. Therefore,

$$RT_1 = 50 + 20 = 70.$$

5 Algorithm to Determine Actual Response Time

We now present an algorithm that can determine the actual response time of τ_j, using the gap-enumeration method. The pseudo-code of the algorithm is given below. The algorithm takes Γ_n and τ_j as input and returns the actual response time of τ_j. In line 3, we assign an initial value to $\sigma_n(T\vert_0^{T_j})$. Between lines 4 to 7, we successively compute the gap sets $\sigma_{n-1}(T\vert_0^{T_j})$ to $\sigma_j(T\vert_0^{T_j})$. Once the gap set for τ_j is known, we retrieve the earliest j-gap larger than P_j, using the gap search function $\mu(T\vert_0^{T_j}, P_j)$ (line 8), and then compute the response time of τ_j (line 10).

If k-gaps to process lower priority tasks are not present, then the task set is not schedulable. In line 6, we check if gaps to process the lower priority task are present. If an i-gap to process a task τ_i is not present, -1 is returned, signifying that the task set is not schedulable. A similar check in line 9 returns -1, if no j-gap is found to run τ_j.

Algorithm 5.1

```
1.  input: Γₙ, τⱼ
2.  output: RTⱼ or -1

3.  σₙ( T|₀^Tⱼ ) ← {[0,Tⱼ]}
4.  loop i ← n to j+1

5.         σᵢ₋₁( T|₀^Tⱼ ) ← λ (σᵢ( T|₀^Tⱼ ), Γₙ)

6.            if(|σᵢ₋₁( T|₀^Tⱼ )| = 0) return -1
7.  end loop

8.  [t₁, t₂) ← μ(σⱼ( T|₀^Tⱼ ), Pⱼ)
9.  if(t₁ < 0) return -1
10. RTⱼ = t₁ + Pⱼ
11. return RTⱼ
```

5.1 Gap-Enumeration with Dynamic Window Size

Algorithm 5.1 enumerates all the gaps present in the time window $T\,|_0^{T_j}$. In certain cases, the time window $T\,|_0^{T_j}$ could be large and much higher number of gaps than required, could be enumerated. If $T\,|_0^{T_j}$ is divided into smaller slices, the gap-enumeration algorithm can be made more efficient. We can divide the time window $T\,|_0^{T_j}$ into m windows ($1 \le m \le T_j$), of size $\left\lceil \dfrac{T_j}{m} \right\rceil$ and enumerate the gaps starting from window $T\,|_0^{\left\lceil \frac{T_j}{m} \right\rceil}$. If no j-gap to run τ_j is found, then the length of the window is progressively incremented by $\left\lceil \dfrac{T_j}{m} \right\rceil$. A modified form of algorithm 5.1, which uses dynamic size windows is given in [3]. The time complexity of this algorithm is bounded by $O(T_j \cdot (n-j) \cdot |\sigma_i(T\,|_0^{T_j +1})| \cdot jobs_i \cdot \log(!2 \cdot 2 \cdot |\sigma_i(T\,|_0^{T_j +1})|))$, derivation of which is available in [3].

5.2 Gap-Transformation Function

The gap transformation function $\lambda(\sigma_i(T\,|_0^L), \Gamma_n)$, for a task τ_i, is an important component in determining the response time of tasks in P-FRP. It analyzes the gap-set $\sigma_i(T\,|_0^L)$ for gaps in which τ_i could be processed, changes those gaps and returns the transformed gap-set. The pseudo-code for the implementation of this function is available in [3].

5.3 Gap-Search Function

The gap search function $\mu(\sigma_k(T\,|_0^L), P_k)$ does a simple search on $\sigma_k(T\,|_0^L)$ and retrieves the first k-gap whose size is larger than P_k. The algorithm for the search depends on the type of data structure used to store the gaps. Due to its guaranteed bounds for search and insertion time, we use a red-black tree (RB-tree) [5] to store the gap. A red-black tree, is a self balancing binary tree where each node has a color attribute of red or black. Other properties of a RB-tree are:

- The root node is black
- All leave nodes are black
- Children of every red node are black
- Path from leaf to root contain same number of black nodes

The gaps are stored in a RB-tree with threshold as the index. *Figure 3* shows the RB-tree for a sample gap set: $\sigma_k(T)=\{[10,40), [50,80), [90,100), [120,140), [170,190), [230,260), [300,320)\}$. The search function $\mu(\sigma_k(T), P_k)$ is reduced to transversing the RB-tree from the left most leaf node (earliest gap), to the right most leaf node. The search order for the sample set based on node index is 10, 50, 90, 120, 170, 230, 300.

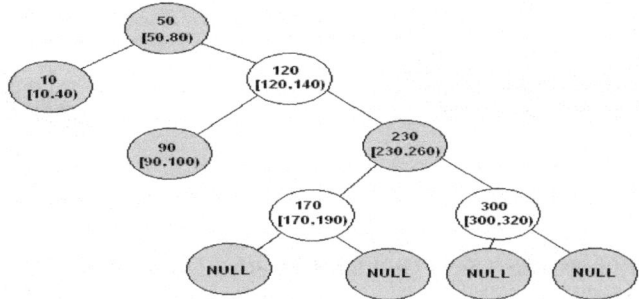

Fig. 3. RB-tree for sample gap set. The shaded nodes denote a black node while the non-shaded are red nodes. The null nodes do not contain any data.

6 Analysis

Since the Time-accurate simulation (TAS) method is the only other known method for computing actual response time in P-FRP, we present an experimental analysis of the performance of the Gap-enumeration (GE) algorithm, relative to TAS. For every addition and deletion operation in the RB-tree, the computational step is incremented by $\log(m)$, where m is the dynamically changing size of the RB-tree. Using computational steps for performance measurement is sufficient for this analysis, as it gives us a distinct idea of time that each algorithm will take to give the desired results.

We randomly generated 3 groups (groups A, B and C) of 500 schedulable task sets. Task sets in group A have 3 tasks, group B, 5 tasks and group C, 7 tasks. Each of the task sets in each group is unique in the sense, that at least 1 task is different between any two task sets. The arrival period for each of the tasks in all the 3 groups were selected from the range [40,60], while the processing times were selected from [4,10]. All tasks were assumed to be released simultaneously and the response time of the lowest priority task (τ_1) in each group was determined using the TAS and GE algorithms. In the GE algorithm, m was set to 1 for this analysis.

The difference in computational steps between the TAS and GE algorithms for task set of sized 3,5 and 7 are shown in *figures 4(a),5(a) and 6(a)*. The Δ in the *y*-axis is given as:

$$\Delta = \text{Computational Steps in TAS - Computational steps in GE}$$

It can be seen clearly that GE takes less number of computation steps as compared to the TAS algorithm. The delta values tend to increase as the number of tasks present in the set increase. This could be attributed to a generally larger response time when the number of tasks are high. In *figures 4(b), 5(b) and 6(b)* we show the relation between response time and Δ. It is clear, that as the response time increases, the delta values increase showing that the GE algorithm becomes much more efficient relative to TAS. Additional results of out analysis are available in [3].

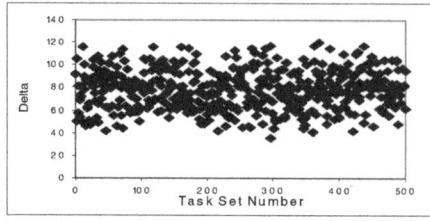

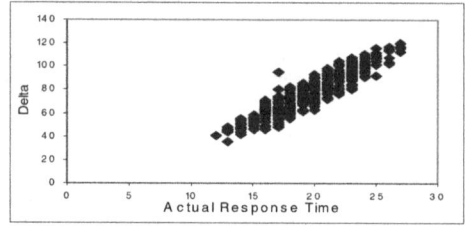

Fig. 4(a). *Delta* (Steps TAS – Steps GE) for tasks sets with 3 tasks

Fig. 4(b). *Delta* (Steps TAS – Steps GE) vs. response time for tasks sets with 3 tasks

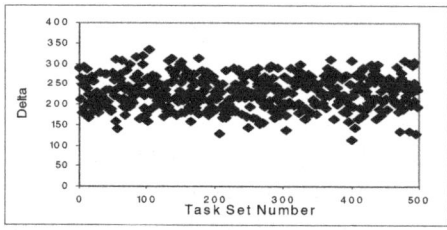

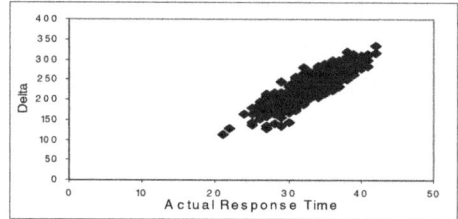

Fig. 5(a). *Delta* (Steps TAS – Steps GE) for tasks sets with 5 tasks

Fig. 5(b). *Delta* (Steps TAS – Steps GE) vs. response time for tasks sets with 5 tasks

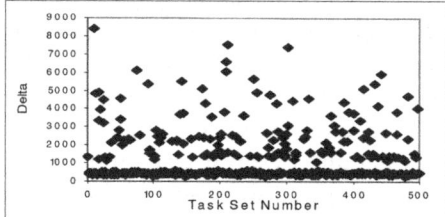

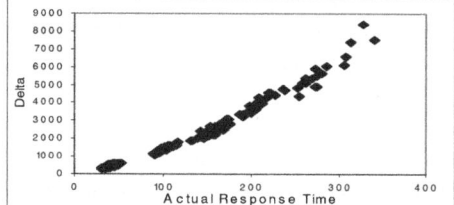

Fig. 6(a). *Delta* (Steps TAS – Steps GE) for tasks sets with 7 tasks

Fig. 6(b). *Delta* (Steps TAS – Steps GE) vs. response time for tasks sets with 7 tasks

7   Related Work

Response time analysis was first studied by Joseph and Pandya [12] and fixed priority scheduling was independently studied by Audsley et al [2]. In [2], an iterative method to compute actual response time in the preemptive model is given. Kaibachev et al [13] present a basic response time analysis for P-FRP by placing restrictions on execution times of higher priority tasks. The authors have derived the response time bound of a task, as equal to its arrival period. Ras and Cheng [17] have presented response time analysis and have compared the performance of P-FRP execution with priority inversion strategies. The authors present a method to derive upper bound on response time by extending the iterative method developed by Audsley et al [2]. However, as shown in this paper, this method is unusable for most task sets. The flaw is that the authors make explicit assumptions on the abort cost from higher priority tasks. The abort cost is different for individual task sets and cannot be generally applied. Both [13, 17] do not define any method to compute actual response times for P-FRP.

Transactional memory systems have been described by Herlihy and Moss [11]. Response time analysis for transaction memory using dynamic scheduling for multiprocessor systems has been done by Fahmy et al [8]. Davis and Burns [6] derive upper bounds on response time for fixed priority scheduling building upon the work done by Bini and Baruah [4]. Anderson et al [1] do response time analysis of the lock-free mechanism. Lock-free is a mechanism to avoid priority inversion [18] the implementation of which is via an unconditional loop that terminates when the necessary updates to the shared resource are complete. The schedulability conditions given for fixed-priority scheduling in [1] assume a constant 'extra computation time' in case of a failed update. If we consider this equivalent to an abort cost in P-FRP it cannot be a constant as the abort cost varies for every task. Comparisons between transaction memory based systems and lock-free processing and benefits of the former have been shown in Herlihy and Moss [11].

8   Conclusions and Future Work

A common method for determining actual response time in the preemptive model cannot be applied to the execution model of P-FRP, due to the abort of preempted tasks. A straightforward approach is to run a time accurate simulation of the P-FRP execution model. However the time complexity of this approach is high and, therefore it is not feasible in most practical situations.

The gap-enumeration method is a different approach for computing actual response time in the P-FRP execution model. Comparisons with the time-accurate method show that the gap-enumeration method is much more efficient than the former. For P-FRP systems with numerically higher response times, the gap-enumeration method offers engineers a fast alternative for the computation of actual response times. The performance of this method is directly proportional to the number of k-gaps present in the system. The number of k-gaps has no impact on the time accurate simulation method, whose computational complexity is primarily governed by the number of time steps that have to be covered.

While the gap-enumeration algorithm is faster than the time-accurate simulation, it is clearly not as efficient as Audsley's method [2]. However, we feel that due to the abort nature of tasks, computing response time using fixed iterations on a mathematical expression, as developed by Audsley et al, might not be feasible for P-FRP. Hence, algorithm based approaches, such as the gap-enumeration method, are perhaps, the only way to compute actual response time in P-FRP.

We have presented the gap-enumeration algorithm in its simple form. Several changes could be made to improve the efficiency of this method. The main computational cost incurred by the gap-enumeration method is during insertion, deletion and search of the data structure used to store k-gaps. A hash table could be used in conjunction with the RB-tree to index the locations of k-gaps thereby making the search, insertion and deletion operation more efficient. In ongoing work, we are also exploring a method where a 2-dimensional array is used to keep track of gaps created for each task.

References

1. Anderson, J.H., Ramamurthy, S., Jeffay, K.: Real-time computing with Lock-free Shared Objects. ACM Transactions on Comp. Sys. 5(6), 388–395 (1997)
2. Audsley, N., Burns, A., Richardson, M., Tindell, K., Wellings, A.: Applying new scheduling theory to static priority preemptive scheduling. Software Engineering Journal 8(5), 284–292 (1993)
3. Belwal, C., Cheng, A.M.K.: Determining Actual Response Time in P-FRP. Technical Report: UH-CS-10-05, Dept. Of Computer Science, University of Houston (2010)
4. Bini, E., Baruah, S.K.: Efficient Computation of Response Time Bounds under Fixed-priority Scheduling. In: Proc. of the 15th Conference on Real-Time and Network Systems, pp. 95–104 (2007)
5. Cormen, T.H., Leiserson, C.E., Rivest, R.L., Stein, C.: Red-Black Trees. In: Introduction to Algorithms, 2nd edn., ch. 13, pp. 273–301. MIT Press/McGraw-Hill (2001)
6. Davis, R.I., Burns, A.: Response Time Upper Bounds for Fixed Priority Real-Time Systems. In: RTSS 2008, pp. 407–418 (2008)
7. Elliott, C., Hudak, P.: Functional reactive animation. In: ICFP 1997, pp. 263–273 (1997)
8. Fahmy, S.F., Ravindran, B., Jensen, E.D.: Response time analysis of software transactional memory-based distributed real-time systems. ACM SAC Operating Systems (2009)
9. Hammond, K.: Chapter 1 – Is it Time for Real-Time Functional Programming. In: Gilmore, S. (ed.) Trends in Functional Programming, vol. 4. Intellect Ltd. (2005)
10. Haskell, http://www.haskell.org
11. Herlihy, M., Moss, J.E.B.: Transactional memory: architectural support for lock-free data structures. ACM SIGARCH Computer Architecture New 21(2), 289–300 (1993)
12. Joseph, M., Pandya, P.: Finding Response Times in a Real-Time System. BCS Computer Journal 29(5), 390–395 (1986)
13. Kaiabachev, R., Taha, W., Zhu, A.: E-FRP with Priorities. In: EMSOFT 2007, pp. 221–230 (2007)
14. Liu, C.L., Layland, L.W.: Scheduling Algorithms for Multiprogramming in a Hard-Real-Time Environment. Journal of the ACM 20(1), 46–61 (1973)
15. Peterson, J., Hager, G.D., Hudak, P.: A Language for Declarative Robotic Programming. In: ICRA 1999. IEEE, Los Alamitos (1999)
16. Peterson, J., Hudak, P., Reid, A., Hager, G.D.: FVision: A Declarative Language for Visual Tracking. In: Ramakrishnan, I.V. (ed.) PADL 2001. LNCS, vol. 1990, p. 304. Springer, Heidelberg (2001)
17. Ras, J., Cheng, A.: Response Time Analysis for the Abort-and-Restart Task Handlers of the Priority-Based Functional Reactive Programming (P-FRP) Paradigm. In: RTCSA 2009 (2009)
18. Sha, L., Rajkumar, R., Lehoczky, J.P.: Priority Inheritance Protocols: An approach to Real Time Synchronization. Transactions on Computers 39(9), 1175–1185 (1990)
19. Swaine, M.: It's Time to Get Good at Functional Programming. Dr. Dobbs Journal (December 2008), http://www.drdobbs.com
20. Wan, Z., Taha, W., Hudak, P.: Real - time FRP. In: ICFP 2001, pp. 146–156. ACM Press, New York (2001)
21. Wan, Z., Taha, W., Hudak, P.: Task Driven FRP. In: Adsul, B., Ramakrishnan, C.R. (eds.) PADL 2002. LNCS, vol. 2257, p. 155. Springer, Heidelberg (2002)
22. Wan, Z., Hudak, P.: Functional reactive programming from first principles. In: ACM SIGPLAN Conference on Programming Language Design and Implementation, pp. 242–252 (2000)

Author Index